# UNITY IN ADVERSITY

The EU is at a crossroads of constitution and conscience. *Unity in Adversity* argues that EU market citizenship is incompatible with a pursuit of social justice, because it contributes to the social exclusion of women and children, promotes a class-based conception of rights, and tolerates in-work poverty. The limitations of EU citizenship are clearest when EU nationals engage with national welfare systems, but this experience has been neglected in EU legal research.

*Unity in Adversity* draws upon the groundbreaking EU Rights Project, working first hand with EU nationals in the UK, providing advice and advocacy, and giving ethnographic insight into the process of navigating EU and UK welfare law. Its study of EU law in action is a radical new approach, and the case studies illustrate the political, legal and administrative obstacles to justice faced by EU nationals. Taken together, the strands demonstrate that 'equal treatment' for EU nationals is an illusion. The UK's welfare reforms directed at EU nationals are analysed as a programme of declaratory discrimination, and in light of the subsequent referendum, should be treated as a cautionary tale—both to the EU, to take social justice seriously, and to other Member States, to steer away from xenophobic law-making.

**Volume 80 in the Series Modern Studies in European Law**

**Modern Studies in European Law**

**Recent titles in this series:**

The Pluralist Character of the European Economic Constitution
*Clemens Kaupa*

Exceptions from EU Free Movement Law
*Edited by Panos Koutrakos, Niamh Nic Shuibhne and Phil Syrpis*

Reconceptualising European Equality Law: A Comparative Institutional Analysis
*Johanna Croon-Gestefeld*

Marketing and Advertising Law in a Process of Harmonization
*Edited by Ulf Bernitz and Caroline Heide-Jörgensen*

The Fundamental Right to Data Protection:
Normative Value in the Context of Counter-Terrorism Surveillance
*Maria Tzanou*

Republican Europe
*Anna Kocharov*

Family Reunification in the EU
*Chiara Berneri*

EU Liability and International Economic Law
*Armin Steinbach*

The EU and Nanotechnologies: A Critical Analysis
*Tanja Ehnert*

Human Rights Between Law and Politics:
The Margin of Appreciation in Post-National Contexts
*Edited by Petr Agha*

The European Union and Social Security Law
*Jaan Paju*

The Rule of Law in the European Union: The Internal Dimension
*Theodore Konstadinides*

The Division of Competences between the EU and the Member States:
Reflections on the Past, the Present and the Future
*Edited by Sacha Garben and Inge Govaere*

**For the complete list of titles in this series, see
'Modern Studies in European Law' link at
www.bloomsburyprofessional.com/uk/series/modern-studies-in-european-law**

# Unity in Adversity

## EU Citizenship, Social Justice and the Cautionary Tale of the UK

Charlotte O'Brien

·HART·
PUBLISHING
OXFORD AND PORTLAND, OREGON
2017

Hart Publishing
An imprint of Bloomsbury Publishing Plc

Hart Publishing Ltd
Kemp House
Chawley Park
Cumnor Hill
Oxford OX2 9PH
UK

Bloomsbury Publishing Plc
50 Bedford Square
London
WC1B 3DP
UK

www.hartpub.co.uk
www.bloomsbury.com

Published in North America (US and Canada) by
Hart Publishing
c/o International Specialized Book Services
920 NE 58th Avenue, Suite 300
Portland, OR 97213-3786
USA

www.isbs.com

HART PUBLISHING, the Hart/Stag logo, BLOOMSBURY and the
Diana logo are trademarks of Bloomsbury Publishing Plc

First published 2017

British Library Cataloguing-in-Publication Data
A catalogue record for this book is available from the British Library.

ISBN:  HB:     978-1-84946-719-3
       ePDF:  978-1-50991-853-9
       ePub:  978-1-50991-852-2

Library of Congress Cataloging-in-Publication Data

Names: O'Brien, Charlotte, author.

Title: Unity in adversity : EU citizenship, social justice and the cautionary tale of the UK / Charlotte O'Brien.

Description: Oxford ; Portland, Oregon : Hart Publishing, an imprint of Bloomsbury Publishing Plc, 2017.  |
Series: Modern studies in European law ; volume 80  |  Includes bibliographical references and index.

Identifiers: LCCN 2017032008 (print)  |  LCCN 2017035618 (ebook)  |
ISBN 9781509918522 (Epub)  |  ISBN 9781849467193 (hardback : alk. paper)

Subjects: LCSH: Europeans—Legal status, laws, etc.—Great Britain.  |  Citizenship—Great Britain.  |
Citizenship—European Union countries.  |  Social legislation—Great Britain.  |
Social legislation—European Union countries.

Classification: LCC KD4144 (ebook)  |  LCC KD4144 .O37 2017 (print)  |  DDC 342.2408/30941—dc23

LC record available at https://lccn.loc.gov/2017032008

Typeset by Compuscript Ltd, Shannon
Printed and bound in Great Britain by CPI Group (UK) Ltd, Croydon, CR0 4YY

To find out more about our authors and books visit www.hartpublishing.co.uk. Here you will find extracts,
author information, details of forthcoming events and the option to sign up for our newsletters.

# Acknowledgements

There are so many people to thank it is hard to know where to begin. The empirical research was made possible thanks to an ESRC Future Research Leaders grant. The casework could not have happened without the Citizens Advice offices and their staff who worked with me and referred clients. Special mention must go to Linda Marsden, who backed the collaboration and basic setting up of the framework of the project from the very start.

The trouble with anonymity, essential as it is, is that I cannot thank the direct contributors or collaborators to the research itself without sounding cryptically vague—but here goes. Thanks to all the Citizens Advice offices who referred clients for first and second-tier advice, submitted evidence and who supported the project through requesting knowledge exchange events. And thanks to the wide range of other advice organisations across England and Wales who got involved and sought second-tier advice or submitted evidence. Similarly, thanks to the focus group participants and specialist interviewees. Of course, the anonymous clients themselves were at the heart of the empirical study—I am grateful to them for working with me and contributing crucial data to the research. They were keen that their cases be used to highlight problems in the hope that we would start discussing how to make things better.

This book owes a huge debt to an incredibly supportive group of colleagues who have offered constructive feedback and criticism on relevant work in recent years. Those who have commented upon and so (whether they realise it or not) have contributed to work represented here include: Michael Dougan, Helen Stalford, Niamh Nic Shuibhne, Eleanor Spaventa, Samantha Currie, Dimitry Kochenov, Gareth Davies, Adam Tucker, Tamara Hervey, Herwig Verschueren, Dagmar Schiek, Stefano Guibboni, Peter Dwyer and Roy Sainsbury. I've had tremendous support from York Law School, particularly Stuart Bell, Caroline Hunter, Jenny Steele and Simon Halliday. I've also had helpful input, including detailed dissections of legal arguments, from the Child Poverty Action Group and the AIRE Centre.

I would not have got through the analytical or dissemination stages of the project without the superb, scrupulous help of Jed Meers, on whose research assistance, impeccable organisational skills and expertise in all things technical I have been utterly dependent. And thanks to the always excellent Keleigh Coldron for her help in preparing the manuscript, to Richard Hart for his kind encouragement and enthusiasm, and to all at Hart Publishing, especially Emily Braggins and Emma Platt.

Thanks are due to the friends who have kept me going, especially my much-missed, late friend Claire. Somewhat inevitably, I have to end by thanking my family, who have borne the brunt of my being book-centric in recent months.

Thanks to my husband, Tom, for his staunch support and to my daughters, Lucy and Hannah, for their amiable tolerance, though I have no doubt that the finished product does not conform to their (current) idea of a decent book, afflicted as it is by a dearth of pictures. At least it contains stories.

*Charlotte O'Brien*
May 2017

# Contents

# Table of Cases

## Domestic Cases

## European Cases

# Table of Legislation

## UK

**Primary Legislation**

**Secondary Legislation**

## European Legislation

### International Legislation

# 1

# Introduction

WHERE DO WE go from here? The European Union's long-running identity crisis has become ever more shrill in recent years and has reached something of a peak with the UK's vote to leave. Prior to the referendum on UK membership, efforts to keep the British people on side included an unedifying scramble on the part of the European Council, the Commission and the Court of Justice to roll back progress on a social Europe and relinquish interests in social justice.

But it did not work out. The UK voted to leave anyway, and now it is essential to take stock and learn from the UK's cautionary tale. This book argues that Union citizenship has staunchly remained a market economy form of citizenship, deeply stratified according to socio-economic class, and inadequate to deliver principles of social justice. It is not just the 'economically inactive' who are ill-served, but workers in low-paid, low-status and low-security jobs, and those whose work histories are punctuated by, for example, periods of child care or adult care.

## I. AN EXCLUSIONARY MARKET CITIZENSHIP

This study argues that market citizenship endorses a system of law-as-lists, rather than law-as-justice, in which EU nationals must conform to anachronistic and patriarchal economic categories on a list. It entrenches existing power dynamics and reinforces enduring exclusionary market structures. Those who do not sufficiently serve that market on its own terms (children, lone parents, carers, disabled people and poorly paid and exploited workers, for example), fall through the gaps.

The EU's own species of welfare law is an offshoot of the single market: it is relatively indifferent to social justice principles. Both social security coordination and the concept of equal treatment on the grounds of nationality are conceived of as means to reduce obstacles to economic movement. Even in the heyday of the European Court of Justice's citizenship case law, it did not mean a great deal on the ground for EU nationals seeking to assert equal treatment rights within host state's welfare regimes. Since the case of *Brey*,[1] the ECJ has beaten a hasty and inelegant retreat, affirming the primacy of the list of economic categories in

---

[1] Case C-140/12 *Pensionsversicherungsanstalt v Peter Brey* EU:C:2013:565.

Directive 2004/38,[2] and absolving Member States from having to engage in questions of social justice when dealing with EU nationals.

Women, children and disabled people face disproportionate disadvantages in this market citizenship regime. But the Union's conceptions of equal treatment on the grounds of sex and disability similarly stem from the market, and a desire to increase EU citizens' market activity (while children's rights barely register on the market radar). The principles of activation flow through the free movement framework, fuelling the commodification of EU national workers, and their alienation from the fruits of their labours. This commodification process is not a neutral, 'rational' one, but reflects entrenched, discriminatory power imbalances.

An EU market citizenship that is indifferent to social justice permits Member States, and in particular the UK, to take activation to its logical conclusion with each others' nationals, and to find that once someone ceases to fit onto the economic list, they cease to be entitled to social protection. The UK has in recent years rolled out an activation-plus regime for EU nationals, introducing reforms that more quickly and more comprehensively disentitle those who fall between the gaps in the list provided by Directive 2004/38.

## II. A PROGRAMME OF DECLARATORY DISCRIMINATION

The UK government introduced a highly publicised raft of reforms throughout 2014 specifically targeting EU nationals. The then Prime Minister, David Cameron, penned articles in the national press, announcing that free movement needed to be 'less free'[3] and that we had to do something about the 'magnetic pull' of the UK welfare system.[4] This book argues that these reforms, along with the publicity, government documents and decision-maker guidance that accompanied them, form a programme of declaratory discrimination on the grounds of nationality.

Employers' discriminatory declarations can themselves be acts of discrimination.[5] The state ought to be held to at least as high standards of equal treatment, since its actions are capable of conditioning access to the labour market wholesale, not just to particular jobs. The pejorative and stigmatising language adopted when announcing its measures, along with stated intentions to reduce free movement, are discriminatory and are capable of forming declaratory obstacles to movement. The ECJ has prohibited discriminatory positive advertising

---

[2] Directive 2004/38/EC of the European Parliament and of the Council of 29 April 2004 on the right of citizens of the Union and their family members to move and reside freely within the territory of the Member States [2004] OJ L158/77.

[3] D Cameron, 'Free Movement within Europe Needs to be Less Free', *The Financial Times* 26 November 2013.

[4] D Cameron, 'We're Building an Immigration System that Puts Britain First', *The Telegraph*, 28 July 2014.

[5] Case C-54/07 *Centrum voor gelijkheid van kansen en voor racismebestrijding v Firma Feryn NV* EU:C:2008:397.

of national produce;[6] it does not seem much of a stretch to suggest that discriminatory *negative* advertising with regard to other states' nationals could be equally obstructive. The stated intentions to prevent people from exercising free movement rights could dissuade people from moving. Indeed, the government's *Before You Go* campaign warns of the 'dangers' of moving to the UK without an imminent job or adequate resources, explicitly aiming to dissuade EU nationals from moving in order to seek work.[7]

These declaratory obstacles found expression not just in official statements and publicity, but in the ensuing laws and non-legal guidance which emphasised the legal differentiation between own nationals and EU nationals, and codified a rejection of social justice principles for the latter. The lists have proliferated: lists of conditions, lists of circumstances in which a right to reside is lost, and lists of exclusions applied to EU national jobseekers.[8] Law-as-justice has receded further as UK courts have all but extinguished requirements to apply EU law proportionately, and so condoned a disregard of factors like social integration, past economic activity, absence of links with other states, vulnerability, need, and so on. Together, the UK and the ECJ have kicked over the dying embers of Union social citizenship.

### III. EU LAW IN ACTION AND ADMINISTRATIVE OBSTACLES TO SOCIAL JUSTICE

In order to appreciate the exclusions created by market citizenship, it is necessary to test EU law, and EU citizenship, in action. This study draws upon the findings of the *EU Rights Project*, a legal action research project funded by the Economic and Social Research Council (ESRC), in which I conducted an advice-led ethnography. This involved working directly with EU nationals, supporting them through first-tier advice and advocacy, and offering second-tier support (such as drafting) to advisers. I conducted a parallel ethnography, drawing up case studies accompanied with field notes and documentary excerpts. I supplemented the case studies with expert interviews, and preparatory and reflective focus groups with advisers.

It was only by attempting to use EU law that I could properly analyse its limits in practice. It is a novel and radical approach to studying EU law, which traditionally has tended to be dominated by doctrinalism or studies of implementation,

---

[6] Case 249/81 *Commission of the European Communities v Ireland* EU:C:1982:402.
[7] Department for Work and Pensions (DWP), *Response to the Report by the Social Security Advisory Committee—The Housing Benefit (Habitual Residence) Amendment Regulations 2014*, SI 2014/539 (November 2014), 4. Available at: www.gov.uk/government/uploads/system/uploads/attachment_data/file/376103/PRINT-HB-Habitual-Residence-Amendment-Regs-2014-SSAC-report.pdf.
[8] See DWP, *Decision-Maker Guidance Part 3—Habitual Residence and Right to Reside: IS/JSA/SPC/ESA (June 2015)* 073031 and 073080. The new jobseeker exclusions can be found in a list of legislation: The Jobseeker's Allowance (Habitual Residence) Amendment Regulations 2013 SI 2013/3196; The Housing Benefit (Habitual Residence) Amendment Regulations SI 2014/539; The Immigration (European Economic Area) (Amendment) (No 2) Regulations 2013/3032; and The Immigration (European Economic Area) (Amendment) (No 3) Regulations 2014 SI 2014/2761.

and as a method it committed me to being an active part of the field of study. The relevant law is so complex and opaque, and existing advice and support so scarce, that working with EU nationals was the only realistic way to get inside the claims and appeals processes, otherwise those processes would in many cases never have happened. The case studies highlight the problematic and discriminatory effects of the UK's legal reforms and, in particular, the interaction of legal and *administrative* obstacles to justice for EU nationals in the UK.

These case studies demonstrate that equal treatment on the grounds of nationality is an illusion. Clients faced severe welfare rights cliff-edges, and UK and EU law tolerated the enforced destitution of EU national children. The class contingent nature of market citizenship meant that many of the exclusions targeting the economically inactive actually affected EU national *workers* because of their fluid work statuses, or because of the detrimental effects of living under the threat of exclusion, or because of the heightened administrative burdens imposed on all EU nationals. Equal treatment 'just' for the economically inactive proved to be equal treatment for no one.

An exclusionary and punitive legal environment contributed to a default of administrative complexity, obstruction and suspicion. The administrative obstacles spoke to a minimalist approach to societal responsibility to give effect to equal treatment rights, and a low commitment to cross-border social justice. Particular administrative obstacles—such as poor decision-maker understanding, problematic decision-maker guidance, and a 'refuse-first, ask questions later' approach—all seemed to be exacerbated by the ongoing legal reforms.

## IV. OUTLINE OF THE BOOK

The premise of this book is that welfare, social justice and citizenship are inextricably interlinked. Chapter two explores this relationship in the context of EU welfare law, highlighting its mechanistic origins and purpose, and arguing that equal treatment on the grounds of nationality has been constructed as subsidiary to the higher objectives of the market. It also sets out the need to test EU citizenship through legal action research and explains the methods (and methodological background) of the *EU Rights Project* and its analytical framework.

EU citizenship was always extremely limited in terms of the social protections it offered EU migrants. Chapter three explores these limitations and, in particular, highlights the thorny issue of tolerated direct discrimination on the grounds of nationality in domestic welfare regimes. I suggest a narrative in which recent case law continues, and strengthens, the trajectory of market citizenship by dismantling the social trappings of earlier citizenship case law. A key lever for EU citizenship-based rights in those earlier cases was the concept of proportionality: that is, that equal treatment on the grounds of nationality was a primary law right attaching to EU nationals in their capacity as citizens, which could be subject to conditions and limitations, but those conditions and limitations must in their turn be subject to a proportionality review. But proportionality is crumbling, and the conditions and limitations are becoming constitutive of the rights in themselves, displacing primary law. Chapter four explores some of the key consequences of the demise of proportionality and highlights those groups—children and lone parent families— placed at a greater disadvantage. It makes the case for giving children's rights substantially more weight (or even just any weight) in EU free movement law.

The ideological presumptions bound up with market citizenship are explored in chapter five with a focus on the concepts of responsibility and fairness as defined in the activation agenda. Activation denies societal responsibility for disadvantage and poverty, promoting individualism and an associated political agenda. It infuses concepts of equal treatment on the grounds of sex and disability, so that discrimination is only relevant insofar as it interferes with the functioning of the existing market systems. As such it provides its own justification for the discriminatory exclusions market citizenship creates along lines of sex and disability. Notions of economic virtue endow that agenda with a moral claim, giving it more of a rhetorical pull and masking its political origins and effects. EU and UK law interact to make EU migrants an apotheosis of activation.

Chapter six analyses the activation-plus regime imposed on EU nationals in the UK and presents the case that the series of reforms amounts to a programme of declaratory discrimination and creates declaratory obstacles to movement. I look at the rules that have made the cliff-edge steeper, so that those who are classified as jobseekers are quickly disentitled from social protections, and also the rules that make the cliff-top narrower. A narrowing definition of the migrant worker makes it more likely that low-paid and part-time workers are shunted over the welfare cliff-edge. Various restrictions overlap and interact, so that many EU nationals at various points fall through the gaps in the list of Directive 2004/38. In particular, I look at the ways in which the lawful residence clock is re-set, so that long-term residents, with substantial work histories, can be denied permanent residence and, as a result, be later found to have no right to reside. One group of EU migrants especially disadvantaged by the law-as-lists approach is that of victims of domestic abuse.

While chapter six considered equal treatment claims, chapter seven looks at the problems attending attempts to invoke the social security regulation legislation. This draws primarily upon case studies to highlight the shortcomings of the coordinating instruments, which require claimants to access and use complicated— and, in many cases, unclear—points of law. The principles of exportation and aggregation do not work smoothly. Member State resistance of competence belies a rather minimalist approach to social solidarity and market citizenship's law-as-lists approach enables them to limit their responsibilities. The states themselves have little incentive to be good coordinators or to avoid claimants being caught between two systems and protected by neither.

Failures of coordination are only one type of administrative obstacle. Chapter eight explores some of the myriad administrative hurdles encountered during the *EU Rights Project*. These include 'getting it wrong' through, for example, poor decision-making and poor information-gathering. The chapter then explores procedural deficiencies that reveal a lack of will to 'get it right' (such as normalising delay, and refusing first and asking questions later). Some of the more frustrating obstacles were those that stopped us putting things right: obstacles to our communication with the relevant decision-makers, obstacles to decision-makers communicating amongst themselves, and bureaucratic hurdles placed in the way of communication. These obstacles were amplified because the claimants were EU nationals. All had direct consequences for social justice, and reflected a considerably dehumanised process, congruent with a market citizenship and law-as-lists framework.

Having argued that market citizenship is inadequate for the realisation of social justice, chapter nine then indeed does argue that European social justice is possible. In accepting market norms and values, we not only neglect questions of social justice in individual cases, but we neglect questions about the kind of society we want 'social Europe' to promote. We need to challenge the language of responsibility-centric, competition-based fairness, and to resurrect concepts of need, social responsibility and egalitarianism. Chapter nine suggests we resuscitate the idea of fairness as a rights-giving principle of administrative justice, and that we can make decision-making fairer if we resurrect, and reinforce, the requirement of a proportionality review of restrictions on EU nationals' rights. But simply saying 'proportionality' is not enough: we need to establish which principles are to have weight, and here I suggest that we explicitly adopt some European principles of social justice—starting with protecting child welfare and the promotion of gender equality.

## V. SOME NOTES ON TERMINOLOGY AND TEXT

Throughout, both EU and EEA are used, depending on the context and the literature/law in question. The emphasis in this book is upon the reach and effects of Union citizenship, and so 'EU nationals' are the focus.

In my case studies I have, naturally, changed the names of clients. However, I wanted to make sure that the cases were as anonymous as possible. I have therefore worked out a simple scheme for switching each EU Member State for another, so the nationalities and states referred to are, where possible, changed from those in the original cases. The exception is John who, by the nature of the case as a UK national returning to the UK, could not easily be switched. Where dates are given I have altered these as well, while making sure that the duration of periods of time in question are the same, and that events are still documented as happening in the relevant legal period (for example, before the end of transition measures, or before the 2014 reforms, and so on).

The fieldwork all took place before the introduction of the Immigration (European Economic Area) Regulations 2016. These largely replicate the regulations which were in force at the time of the advice work: the Immigration (European

Economic Area) Regulations 2006. While tidying up that instrument's multiple amendments, they have introduced some more stringent or punitive provisions. Much of the work completed here was based on the 2006 Regulations, and I have given references to the 2016 Regulations where there are relevant differences.

## VI. THE UK AS A CAUTIONARY TALE

The cacophony of negative messages coming from UK authorities, and to some extent from EU institutions, has created a toxic politics of free movement which could not help but percolate into administrative culture. This book argues that the administration of welfare cannot be disaggregated from the government's own messages and guidance to decision-makers. Nor can the government's programme of scapegoating EU nationals be dissociated from the UK public's vote to leave the EU in the EU membership referendum.

That referendum result should not be a basis for retreating from the project of social Europe, or for abandoning the attempt to establish European social justice principles, on the grounds of popular prejudice towards, and distaste for, each other's nationals. Nor is it grounds for promoting more commodification and alienation and rendering free movement even more of a prerogative for the privileged. Rather, it repeats a lesson from history: that we do not make populations more tolerant by adopting discriminatory laws and by using the law as a tool of stigma.

Substantial legal reforms have accentuated administrative obstacles and contributed to the construction of EU national benefit claims as 'problems', feeding into messages about how decision-makers should (or more accurately, should not) use their discretion. This has significant ramifications for EU nationals during the course of the UK's exit from the EU, which will involve a more dramatic legal upheaval, and for other states going through periods of reform and welfare retrenchment. The EU needs to think about whether and how it wishes to guard the efficacy of EU law, and whether its citizens merit social protection, should the risks of administrative friction become more acute in times of legal transition.

Our apparent desensitisation to market citizenship means that it has become even more influential. If unquestioned, it shapes our ideas of fairness, personhood and fundamental rights and lays claim to our construction of morality itself. If we accept this, we not only neglect questions of social justice in individual cases, but we neglect questions about the kind of society we want Europe to be.

# 2

# Welfare, Citizenship and Social Justice in Action

## I. INTRODUCTION

WELFARE, CITIZENSHIP AND social justice are deeply interlinked: social protection is an expression of social justice and a precondition for social inclusion.[1] The very concept of a welfare state implies a citizen–state relationship and, by extension, is linked to nationality and citizenship. The idea of social justice is bound up with that of solidarity, suggesting a network of relationships and the notion of membership.[2] Citizenship has come to define to whom we owe the greatest duty of social justice,[3] and welfare the most important mechanism by which it is met.

Borders still matter, in no small part because they delineate the in-group—the people entitled to membership from a national effort at collective solidarity. The salience of the boundaries of the nation state is bound up with the continued existence of a bounded, national welfare state. Whether EU citizenship can really present a post-national citizenship depends on how well it adapts those boundaries and allows EU citizens to be accommodated within other Member States' solidarity networks.[4] The development of EU citizenship scholarship has largely

---

[1] AM Magnussen and E Nilssen, 'Juridification and the Construction of Social Citizenship' (2013) 40 *Journal of Law and Society* 2, 228, 238.

[2] On linking membership to social justice: B Jordan, *The New Politics of Welfare* (London, Sage, 1998); on linking solidarity to membership: M Ross, 'Solidarity: A New Constitutional Paradigm for the EU?' in M Ross and Y Borgmann-Prebil (eds), *Promoting Solidarity in the European Union* (Oxford, OUP, 2010); C Jacqueson, 'For Better or For Worse? Transnational Solidarity in the Light of Social Europe' in N Countouris and M Freedland (eds) *Resocialising Europe in a Time of Crisis* (Cambridge, CUP, 2013).

[3] These categories are not fixed but are defined through, and as a result of, dispute and the outcome of power struggles: J Clarke, K Coll, E Dagnino and C Neveu, *Disputing Citizenship* (Policy Press, Bristol, 2014).

[4] Verschueren argues that restrictions on free movement are a mechanism for delineating welfare systems (see H Verschueren, 'European (Internal) Migration Law as an Instrument for Defining the Boundaries of National Solidarity Systems' (2007) 9 *European Journal of Migration and Law*, 307). Kostakopoulou argues that the hierarchy of national over European citizenships is unhelpful, and that we should aim for a multi-layered, multicultural conception of citizenship (see: D Kostakopoulou, 'European Union Citizenship: Writing the Future' (2007) 13 *European Law Journal*, 623; and D Kostakopoulou, 'Thick, Thin and Thinner Patriotisms: Is This All There Is?' (2006) 26 *Oxford Journal of Legal Studies* 1, 73).

become a study of equal treatment, and a study of EU citizens' welfare rights in other states as citizens, rather than workers, so including (at least some of) the 'economically inactive'.[5]

But there has never been equal treatment between own-state citizens and EU citizens, and EU citizenship has never been a social citizenship. It has continued to be a market citizenship, indifferent to child poverty and destitution.[6] In theory we have a default of equal treatment, which is then modified by conditions,[7] but this is not the case. This book argues that equal treatment on the grounds of nationality is an illusion: nationality is still determinative of social rights, and market citizenship has facilitated the rise in the UK of declaratory discrimination on the grounds of nationality by the state. Economic conditions have been constitutive of welfare rights. This chapter covers the key EU and UK welfare laws that have shaped EU citizenship rights and modified our understandings of equal treatment on the grounds of nationality. It then presents the case for studying EU law in action, outlining the basis for legal action research into the rights of EU citizens, and explaining the methodology for the *EU Rights Project*, the source of many findings presented in this book.

## II.  EU WELFARE RIGHTS: REDUCING OBSTACLES TO MOVEMENT

Freeing up movement has meant the dismantling of obstacles to movement, and EU welfare law has operated explicitly as an obstacle-reducer. Since the creation of the free movement regime, Community/Union law has provided for some cross-border welfare rights, in the form of social security coordination.[8] In conceiving of EU welfare measures as mechanisms, I use Niamh Nic Shuibhne's work drawing together the horizontal themes across different branches of free movement law. Nic Shuibhne described 'the interconnected nature of EU objectives' as being

---

[5] The treatment of the economically inactive has been considered a litmus test for EU citizenship, see: HUJ d'Oliveira, 'Union Citizenship: Pie in the Sky?' in A Rosas and E Antola (eds), *A Citizen's Europe: In Search of a New Order* (London, Sage Publications, 1995); H Verschueren, 'Free Movement of EU Citizens: Including for the Poor?' (2015) 22 *Maastricht Journal of European and Comparative Law* 1, 10; D Thym, 'The Elusive Limits of Solidarity: Residence Rights of and Social Benefits for Economically Inactive Union Citizens', (2015) 52 *CML Rev* 1, 17; AP Van der Mei, *Free Movement of Persons within the European Community: Cross Border Access to Public Benefits* (Oxford, Hart, 2003).

[6] Hervey noted in 1995 that reference to the market was a mechanism by which to maintain structural inequality and thereby protect dominant interests. See T Hervey, 'Migrant Workers and their Families in the European Union: The Pervasive Market Ideology of Community Law' in J Shaw and G More (eds) *New Legal Dynamics of European Union* (Oxford, OUP, 1995).

[7] According to the CJEU in Case C-85/96 *María Martínez Sala v Freistaat Bayern* EU:C:1998:217, which appeared to establish a default of equal treatment, the logic of which meant that Member States could only avoid equal treatment duties through expulsion (E Spaventa, 'Seeing the Wood Despite the Trees? On the Scope of Union Citizenship and its Constitutional Effects' (2008) 45 *CML Rev* 13, 29), or 'keep[ing] them out in the first place': M Dougan, 'Fees, Grants, Loans and Dole Cheques: Who Covers the Cost of Migrant Education Within the EU?' (2005) 42 *CML Rev* 943, 971.

[8] Council Regulation No 3 concerning social security for migrant workers [1958] OJ L30/561.

'in Russian doll format [in which] the creation of an internal market is a central objective of the Union; free movement is a central objective of the internal market; and non-discrimination is a central objective of free movement'.[9] The rationale for coordination has been that workers should not suffer a loss of the value of their social security contributions on moving between Member States, since that would be a significant obstacle to movement. 'Free' movement for workers required more than mere permission to reside and work. Establishing 'as complete a freedom of movement for workers as possible'[10] requires 'the elimination of legislative obstacles' which could disadvantage migrant workers,[11] which the Court of Justice found (in *Nonnenmacher*) was the aim of Articles 48–51 of the Treaty of Rome, upon which the first coordinating regulation was based. The Court added: 'in case of doubt the abovementioned articles and the measures taken in implementation of them must therefore be construed so as to avoid placing migrant workers in an unfavourable legal position, particularly with regard to social security'.[12]

Whereas EU welfare law is about coordinating/permitting integration into national welfare regimes to promote free movement, those national welfare regimes are deeply intertwined with social justice objectives. Jordan suggests that a main principle of social justice is meeting 'need',[13] and argues that a simplistic something-for-something principle—that you only get out what you have paid in—is 'totally inappropriate for a liberal democratic polity ... it reverts to pre-modern forms of serfdom, or the barbarity of the workhouse'.[14] Social justice, as interpreted for the purposes of this study, requires not merely protecting those able to pay their way, but also those disadvantaged by society through disabling environments, difficult job markets, poorly paid work, work that is poorly adapted to female social security 'risks' (exacerbated by high childcare costs), the state of actually being a child, and so on. It presents an alternative focus, and stands in contrast to, the objectives of neoliberalism and law and policy measures that punish the poor.[15] Advancing neoliberalism has coincided with rising inequality in income and power[16] and the market economy demotes the social objective

---

[9] N Nic Shuibhne, *The Coherence of EU Free Movement Law: Constitutional Responsibility and the Court of Justice* (Oxford, OUP, 2013) 108–09.

[10] Case 75/63 *Mrs MKH Hoekstra (née Unger) v Bestuur der Bedrijfsvereniging voor Detailhandel en Ambachten* EU:C:1964:19, 1.

[11] Case 92/63 *M Th Nonnenmacher, widow of H E Moebs v Bestuur der Sociale Verzekeringsbank* EU:C:1964:40, 1.

[12] ibid, 1.

[13] Above, n 2, 99. Jordan notes that the politically popular idea of identifying 'genuine need' is problematic since it stigmatises those perceived as not in 'genuine' need. Jordan appears to endorse the position of Doyal and Gough that a commitment to social justice requires recognising universal and objective needs (as argued in L Doyal and I Gough, *A Theory of Human Need* (Basingstoke, Macmillan, 1991)).

[14] ibid, 67.

[15] L Wacquant, *Punishing the Poor: The Neoliberal Government of Social Insecurity* (London, Duke University Press, 2009).

[16] C Crouch, 'Entrenching Neo-Liberalism: The Current Agenda of European Social Policy' in N Countouris and M Freedland, above n 2.

of meeting the needs of others to 'the level of by product'.[17] This study adopts Wacquant's interpretation of neoliberalism as 'not an economic regime but a political project of state-crafting that puts … the trope of individual responsibility at the service of commodification', where the highest form of individual responsibility is (a particular kind of) economic activity. The sacralisation of economic activity results in a system that rewards the privileged. It 'practises liberalism at the top of the class structure and punitive paternalism at the bottom'.[18] A market economy, created by and reinforcing neoliberal currents, is often misleadingly aligned with the rhetoric of choice.[19] But this is an illusion. The ability to choose requires social freedom.[20] Social freedom requires resources: the means to make choices freely, not under the duress of destitution.[21]

It is not necessary for the purposes of this study to identify the appropriate content of social justice measures. Member States have already provided their own implicit social justice definitions in the schemes of their welfare states.[22] The question here is to what extent EU law permits EU migrants access to social justice provided at national level (that is, offers EU migrants protection in circumstances that Member States have already recognised as requiring socially just interventions). As Thym notes, citizenship 'has always been a projection sphere for different visions of social justice',[23] and so we must ask why EU citizenship has not so far commanded any such vision. The EU's failure to offer such a guarantee is symptomatic of a mechanistic system concerned with promoting the higher-order objectives of the internal market[24] and of a citizenship that is more concerned with procedural

---

[17] A Somek, 'Alienation, Despair and Social Freedom' in L Azoulai, S Barbou des Places and E Pataut (eds) *Constructing the Person in EU Law: Rights, Roles, Identities* (Oxford, Hart Publishing, 2016) 36.

[18] L Wacqaunt, 'Three Steps to a Historical Anthropology of Actually Existing Neoliberalism' (2012) 20 *Social Anthropology/Anthropologie Sociale* 1, 66, 66.

[19] 'The language of the internal market directives encompass a rhetoric of choice … the European citizen … is concerned not with entitlements but with provisions' (M Everson 'The Legacy of the Market Citizen' in J Shaw and G More (eds) *New Legal Dynamics of European Union* (Oxford, Clarendon Press, 1995) 87.

[20] Somek, above, n 17, 43: 'it remains an open question, however whether structures of social freedom are part of the ethos of the European Union and of its law'.

[21] Magnussen and Nilssen argue that 'generally for many people, access to social rights … is an important premise for individual freedom and social inclusion. Problems such as poverty, homelessness, illness and illiteracy often lead to reduced self-determination, subservience, and social exclusion'. See above, n 1, 238.

[22] Though note many commentators who suggest that national welfare states have lost sight of social justice as an aim (see K Veitch, 'Law, Social Policy and the Constitution of Markets and Profit Making' (2013) 40 *Journal of Law and Society*, 1, 137).

[23] D Thym, 'Towards "Real" Citizenship? The Judicial Construction of Union Citizenship and its Limits', in M Adams et al (eds), *Judging Europe's Judges: The Legitimacy of the Case Law of the European Court of Justice* (Oxford, Hart, 2013) 162.

[24] Or the bigger 'Russian doll', to use Nic Shuibhne's metaphor, above n 9. Note also the plea that 'if the notion of European citizenship is to have substance rather than being part of a 'legitimation theatre for the Internal market Programme … new versions of social citizenship' are required (M Castle-Kanerova and B Jordan, 'The Social Citizen?' in R Bellamy and A Warleigh (eds), *Citizenship and Governance in the European Union* (London, Continuum, 2001) 137).

probity than with social justice per se.[25] Chalmers has argued that the EU already engages in a certain amount of redistribution, but does so with a 'diminished sense of public law',[26] while Kochenov has noted that a powerful vision of social justice within the EU judiciary is not only painfully absent,[27] but has been fairly explicitly rejected: contemporary EU law, Kochenov writes, 'preaches that injustice, apparently, is a necessary addition to the system of multilevel constitutionalism', and is an inevitable side-effect of the existing legal order. Some commentators warn against attempts to construct ideas of cross-border social justice, because of the risk of diluting commitments to solidarity at a national level,[28] or of delegitimising the EU project.[29] But the idea that solidarity cannot be 'stretched' is redolent of a Hayekian argument. Hayek argued that the moral feelings which lead to considerations of social justice derived from attitudes only possible in small groups and they could not be extrapolated to a national scale without an 'attenuation' of the rights of those in the smaller groups.[30] This argument is essentially cycled upwards when we contend that the parameters of nationality are essential for the meaningful pursuit of social justice. Instead, we should turn the question on its head. A failure to recognise or engage with the increasingly cross-border nature of welfare law[31] and the cross-border creation of social *injustice* risks diluting and delegitimising national projects for social justice. Dominant theories of redistributive justice are not easily applied to transnational scenarios since they tend to treat social and political units as self-evidently national creations.[32] One aim of this book is to show that while politicians argue that exclusion of non-nationals is necessary in order to prevent national social justice measures being undermined,[33]

---

[25] On the ECJ's consideration of 'real links' as setting procedural rather than substantive requirements, see C O'Brien, 'Real Links, Abstract Rights and False Alarms: The Relationship Between the ECJ's "Real Link" Case Law and National Solidarity' (2008) 33 *EL Rev* 5, 643.

[26] D Chalmers, 'The European Redistributive State and a European Law of Struggle' (2012) 18 *European Law Journal* 5, 667.

[27] D Kochenov, 'Citizenship Without Respect: The EU's Troubled Equality Ideal' (2010) *Jean Monnet Working Paper* 08/10, 3.

[28] A Somek, 'Solidarity Decomposed: Being and Time in European Citizenship' (2007) 6 *EL Rev* 787.

[29] K Hailbronner, 'Union Citizenship and Access to Social Benefits' (2005) 42 *CML Rev* 5, 1245. Dougan notes concerns that the Union lacks the 'moral force required to justify the redistribution of wealth' (see M Dougan, 'The Spatial Restructuring of National Welfare States within the European Union: The Contribution of Union Citizenship and the Relevance of the Treaty of Lisbon' in U Neergaard, R Nielsen and L Roseberry (eds), *Integrating Welfare Functions into EU Law* (Copenhagen, DJØF, 2009) 155).

[30] F Hayek, *The Mirage of Social Justice* (Chicago, University of Chicago Press, 1978).

[31] Questions of welfare solidarity now have a necessarily European dimension: 'nationality and territoriality can no longer claim an absolute monopoly in defining membership of and exclusion from the domestic solidaristic communities' (Dougan, above n 29, 155).

[32] Jordan, above n 2, 18.

[33] Joint letter from J Mikl-Leitner (Minister of the Interior, Austria), HP Friedrich (Minister of the Interior, Germany), F Teeven (Minister for Immigration, Netherlands) and T May (Home Secretary, UK) to the President of the European Council for Justice and Home Affairs and to Commissioners Reding, Malmström and Andor, (April 2013). Available at: docs.dpaq.de/3604-130415_letter_to_presidency_final_1_2.pdf.

the current tolerance of injustice as a necessary and automatic component of EU citizenship actually undermines Member States' own claims to social justice instead. This reflects poorly on domestic as well as EU level commitments to social justice. But this can change, and European social justice is indeed possible.

## A. The Mechanistic Objectives of Social Security Coordination

From early on, EU welfare law has been conceived of mechanistically, to dismantle obstacles to the exercise of an economic right of movement. The *SARL Manpower* case[34] predated Regulation 1408/71,[35] and addressed the purpose of the first social security coordinating instrument, Regulation 3.[36] In making the posting state the competent state for social security, the Court found that Article 13 of the legislation was aimed at 'overcoming the obstacles likely to impede freedom of movement of workers and at encouraging economic interpenetration whilst avoiding administrative complications for workers, undertakings and social security organizations'.[37] This agenda was reaffirmed in *Farrauto*,[38] a few years later, dealing with Regulation 4 (which implemented and supplemented Regulation 3).[39] The rules on social security for migrant workers were, according to the Court, 'contained in measures aimed at ensuring freedom of movement for workers' and were 'concerned with removing certain obstacles of a material and administrative nature which could prevent workers from moving between the Member States'.[40]

The twin principles of coordination under the ensuing coordinating Regulation 1408/71, and its replacement Regulation 883/2004,[41] are of aggregation and exportation. Aggregation means not losing accrued rights: so having contributions, or periods of residence, or insurance, in other Member States considered by the paying state (though note that there are special rules on pensions, to allow for several Member States to contribute to a pension, rather than requiring the host state to foot the whole bill).[42] Exportation means that in some circumstances, people can take their benefits with them: for example, frontier workers who work in one state but live just over the border, may be entitled to 'export' that benefit (that is, continue to receive it from the competent state, even though it is paid

---

[34]    C-35/70 *SARL Manpower v Caisse primaire d'assurance maladie de Strasbourg* EU:C:1970:120.
[35]    Regulation (EEC) No 1408/71 of the Council of 14 June 1971 on the application of social security schemes to employed persons and their families moving within the Community, OJ [1971] L 149/02.
[36]    Regulation No 3 of the Council of the EEC of 25 September 1958 concerning social security for migrant workers, as amended by Regulation No 24/64 of 10 March 1964.
[37]    *SARL Manpower*, above n34, 10.
[38]    Case 66–74 *Alfonso Farrauto v Bau-Berufsgenossenschaft* EU:C:1975:18.
[39]    Regulation No 4 of the Council of 3 December 1958 (OJ of 16.12.1958, 597) implementing and supplementing Regulation No 3 on social security for migrant workers.
[40]    *Farrauto*, above n 38, 4.
[41]    Regulation (EC) No 883/2004 of the European Parliament and of the Council of 29 April 2004 on the coordination of social security systems OJ [2004] L 200/1.
[42]    Arts 50–52 of Regulation 883/2004.

in another state).[43] In coordinating, rather than harmonising, the system allows Member States to continue to operate different welfare states, with different benefits and different conditions, but aims to make the transition between systems smoother, to avoid workers having their contribution slates wiped clean each time they move between states. In *Engelbrecht*,[44] the Court applied the same rationale as in *Farrauto* to Regulation 1408/71, that EU legislation on the area of social security coordination is about obstacle removal:

> The exercise of the right to free movement within the Community is impeded if a social advantage is lost or reduced … Such a result might well discourage Community workers from exercising their right to free movement and would therefore constitute a barrier to that freedom enshrined in Article 48 of the Treaty.[45]

An opposition to obstacles to economic movement does not amount to a manifesto for harmonising welfare systems: the emphasis on coordination keeps the control of the content and conditions of domestic welfare rules. EU nationals could not be guaranteed the same entitlements when moving between Member States, because of differences between benefit regimes, but where states set conditions as to residence, insurance and contributions, coordination means not losing that contribution record. The first task in a coordination regime is to establish the 'competent' state. Regulation 883/2004 provides an order of priorities[46] for establishing competence which essentially falls to the state with whom the claimant has the strongest economic link (that is, where she is or recently was a worker) or, failing that, the state from which a claimant receives unemployment benefits or, failing that, the state of residence becomes competent.

That EU social security coordination is about removing obstacles to economic movement was further underlined in *Hendrix*,[47] where the Court found that permitted exceptions in Regulation 1408/71 had to be adapted. That Regulation, following a lengthy back-and-forth conversation[48] between judiciary and legislature, allowed Member States to exclude special non-contributory benefits from exportation,[49] so long as they met the criteria and were listed in the appropriate annex. *Hendrix* featured a reverse frontier worker (someone who moved his state of residence, while continuing to work in his home state). He was a disabled worker, his employer was exempted from paying him more than 70 per cent of the minimum wage, and Mr Hendrix was then entitled to a supplementary benefit

---

[43] Art 7 of Regulation 883/2004 on 'waiving of residence rules'.

[44] Case C-262/97 *Rijksdienst voor Pensioenen v Robert Engelbrecht* EU:C:2000:492.

[45] ibid, 41–42.

[46] Art 11(3), Regulation 883/2004.

[47] Case C-287/05 *D P W Hendrix v Raad van Bestuur van het Uitvoeringsinstituut Werknemersverzekeringen* EU:C:2007:494.

[48] See M Dougan, 'The Bubble That Burst: Exploring the Legitimacy of the Case Law on the Free Movement of Union Citizens' in M Adams, H de Waele, J Meeusen and G Straetmans (eds), *Judging Europe's Judges: The Legitimacy of the Case Law of the European Court of Justice* (Oxford, Hart, 2013).

[49] Art 70 Regulation 883/2004.

(the *wajong*) which had been confirmed as a genuine special non-contributory benefit,[50] duly listed, and so excluded from the provisions on exportation. As such, Mr Hendrix lost entitlement when he moved his state of residence. This made his employment, which continued to be subject to the minimum pay exemption, untenable. However, the Court found that the provisions of Regulation 1408/71 must be interpreted in light of the objective of Article 42 EC, to 'contribute to the establishment of the greatest possible freedom of movement for migrant workers'.[51] This objective was so overriding that the exception to exportation provided for in the legislation had to be adjustable. Here, the Court noted that the national legislation allowed for the waiving of the residence rule where there was an 'unacceptable degree of fairness'. The national court was exhorted to conduct a fairness assessment of the residence rule (and application of Article 10a of Regulation 1408/71) taking into account 'the fact that Mr Hendrix has exercised his right of freedom of movement as a worker and that he has maintained economic and social links to the Netherlands'. The ultimate priority is the removal of obstacles to economic movement, and even permitted restrictions, in the form of residence rules for benefits, must be susceptible to review and adjustment in individual cases where they appeared excessively obstructive.

### III. EQUAL TREATMENT AS A COMPONENT OF COORDINATION

The concept of aggregation is bound up with the concept of equal treatment: an EU migrant's contributions in another Member State must be treated the *same* as contributions made in the competent Member State. This was echoed in the preamble to the coordinating Regulation 1408/71 (the successor to Regulation No 3), which stated that benefits should be awarded with 'such aggregation of periods of residence completed in any other Member State as is necessary and without discrimination on grounds of nationality'. The Regulation contained an equal treatment provision requiring EU nationals to be 'subject to the same obligations and enjoy the same benefits' as nationals. The idea of aggregation as equal treatment is more pronounced in the newer coordinating regulation, Regulation 883/2004. Article 5 states:

> (b)   where, under the legislation of the competent Member State, legal effects are attributed to the occurrence of certain facts or events, that Member State shall take account of like facts or events occurring in any Member State as though they had taken place in its own territory.

Rather than being separate concepts, we see here the idea that coordination requires some equal treatment, because discrimination is an obstacle to movement. In *Masgio*[52] this relationship was further spelled out. That case involved national rules for calculating a social security benefit which treated pensions

---

[50]   Case C-154/05 *Kersbergen-Lap and Dams-Schipper* EU:C:2006:449.
[51]   *Hendrix*, above n 47, 52.
[52]   Case C-10/90 *Maria Masgio v Bundesknappschaft* EU:C:1991:107.

from other Member States differently to German pensions. The Court found that legislation 'which places Community workers who have exercised their right to freedom of movement in a worse position than those who have not done so … [was] liable to constitute an obstacle to freedom of movement for workers'.[53] The equal treatment regulation, Regulation 1612/68, was the 'specific expression' of the Treaty-based right to equal treatment for migrant workers,[54] and it is grounded entirely in removing obstacles to free movement:

> Whereas *freedom of movement for workers should be secured* within the Community … whereas *the attainment of this objective entails the abolition of any discrimination* based on nationality between workers of the Member States as regards employment, remuneration and other conditions of work and employment.[55]

The preamble drew a connection between equal treatment (as regards social entitlements and family reunification) and the elimination of obstacles for movement, on the basis that promoting integration promotes movement. It stated that '*obstacles to the mobility* of workers shall be eliminated, in particular as regards the worker's right to be joined by his family and the *conditions for the integration* of that family into the host country'. These points have been reproduced in the regulation's replacement, Regulation 492/2011.[56] Equal treatment in fact and law is required, according to the preamble, so that free movement may be exercised 'in freedom and dignity':[57] if it could not be so exercised, then that would be an obstacle to it being exercised at all. Regulation 1612/68 contained an early key equal treatment provision in the context of welfare benefits, requiring EU national workers to 'enjoy the same social and tax advantages as national workers'.[58] The concept of social advantages has been interpreted broadly to include: rights to study finance;[59] family railway discounts;[60] an entitlement to request a change of language for criminal proceedings;[61] the rights of residence of unmarried partners;[62] and certain forms of social assistance.[63] In *Even*,[64]

---

[53] ibid, 23.

[54] Case C-371/04 *Commission of the European Communities v Italian Republic* EU:C:2006:668.

[55] Regulation 1612/68, preamble.

[56] Recitals (2) and (6), Regulation (EU) No 492/2011 of the European Parliament and of the Council of 5 April 2011 on freedom of movement for workers within the Union (codification) OJ [2011] L 141/1.

[57] ibid, recital (6).

[58] Art 7(2); reproduced as Art 7(2) in Regulation 492/2011.

[59] Case C-337/97 *CPM Meeusen v Hoofddirectie van de Informatie Beheer Groep* EU:C:1999:284.

[60] Case 32–75 *Anita Cristini v Société nationale des chemins de fer français* EU:C:1975:120.

[61] Case 137/84 *Criminal proceedings against Robert Heinrich Maria Mutsch* EU:C:1985:335.

[62] Case 59/85 *State of the Netherlands v Ann Florence Reed* EU:C:1986:157.

[63] AG Cosmas has conflated social assistance and social advantages, suggesting all benefits are 'either … social security benefits within the meaning of Article 51 of the Treaty and Regulation No 1408/71 … [or] alternatively … a social advantage, within the meaning of Article 7 of Council Regulation 1612/68/EEC of 15 October 1968 on freedom of movement for workers within the Community [1968] OJ L257/2, and are part of the social assistance system'. (See Case C-160/96 *Manfred Molenaar and Barbara Fath-Molenaar v Allgemeine Ortskrankenkasse Baden-Württemberg* EU:C:1998:84; AG Opinion, 23.)

[64] Case 207/78 *Criminal proceedings against Gilbert Even and Office national des pensions pour travailleurs salariés (ONPTS)* EU:C:1979:144.

Article 7(2) was found to comprise all advantages 'which, whether or not linked to a contract of employment, are generally granted to national workers primarily because of their objective status as workers or by virtue of the mere fact of their residence on the national territory'.[65]

The Court conceives of access to social rights as necessary to promote integration and the promotion of integration as necessary to promote free movement. Discrimination has been represented as an obstacle to movement and equal treatment as a means to remove that obstacle. Indeed, the Court has given fundamental rights more generally a rather instrumental role, serving the principle of free movement.[66] In *Wardyn*, the Court noted that 'the importance of ensuring the protection of the family life of citizens of the Union *in order to eliminate obstacles* to the exercise of the fundamental freedoms guaranteed by the Treaty has been recognised under European Union law',[67] so the fundamental human right to family life served a subsidiary obstacle-removing, movement-promoting role.

## A. Discrimination as an Obstacle to Movement

The treatment of discrimination as an obstacle to movement is a recurrent theme. In *Commission v French Republic*, the Court found that the 'general character', and the objective, of the prohibition of discrimination meant that 'discrimination is prohibited even if it constitutes only an obstacle of secondary importance as regards the equality of access to employment'.[68] So it need not be a primary obstacle, the important thing is combating discrimination that could amount to any form of obstacle: in *Morson*, the Court asserted that the very 'purpose' of the equal treatment provisions in the EEC Treaty was 'to assist in the abolition of all obstacles to the establishment of a common market in which the nationals of the Member States may move freely ... in order to pursue their economic activities'.[69] The Court reiterated the *Morson* finding in *Paolo Iorio*[70] and made clear that, by extension, the purpose of eliminating obstacles should also be read into the equal treatment regulation, Regulation 1612/68. When later making quite strident moves in developing Union citizenship in *Baumbast*,[71] a case that required the limitations placed on free movement to be applied proportionately,[72] the Court

---

[65] ibid, 22.

[66] S Reynolds, 'Explaining the Constitutional Drivers Behind a Perceived Judicial Preference for Free Movement Rights' (2016) 53 *CML Rev* 643.

[67] Case C-391/09 *Malgožata Runevič-Vardyn and Łukasz Paweł Wardyn v Vilniaus miesto savivaldybės administracija and Others* EU:C:2011:291, 90.

[68] Case 167–73 *Commission of the European Communities v French Republic* EU:C:1974:35, 46.

[69] Joined Cases 35 and 36/82 *Elestina Esselina Christina Morson v State of the Netherlands and Head of the Plaatselijke Politie within the meaning of the Vreemdelingenwet; Sweradjie Jhanjan v State of the Netherlands* EU:C:1982:368, 15.

[70] Case 298/84 *Paolo Iorio v Azienda autonoma delle ferrovie dello Stato* EU:C:1986:33, 13.

[71] Case C-413/99 *Baumbast and R v Secretary of State for the Home Department* EU:C:2002:493.

[72] See M Dougan, 'The Constitutional Dimension to the Case Law on Union Citizenship' (2006) 31 *EL Rev* 613.

also vested the citizenship-based right to a proportionality review in the need to remove obstacles to movement. There, the Court found that that the child of an EU national worker should retain a right to reside to continue their education after their parent had ceased working in the UK, because preventing him/her continuing his/her education, by refusing a right to reside, 'might dissuade' their parents 'from exercising the rights to freedom of movement laid down in Article 39 EC and would therefore create an obstacle to the effective exercise of the freedom thus guaranteed by the EC Treaty'.[73] The idea that measures making free movement less attractive create an obstacle, lies behind the concerns about creating 'disadvantages' for free movers. Discrimination has been described as creating such a disadvantage: in *Collins*,[74] the Court referred to measures that created 'a difference in treatment' between own nationals and EU nationals, and so which placed 'at a disadvantage Member State nationals who have exercised their right of movement'.[75] The language of disadvantage, or a movement penalty, invokes the idea of an obstacle to movement, and in *Prete*, Advocate General Cruz Villalón described the nationality requirement in *Collins* as 'an obstacle to the freedom of movement for workers'.[76] The Court again reiterated that discriminatory practices could create barriers to movement in *Raccanelli*,[77] citing *Walrave and Koch*[78] and *Bosman*.[79]

The EU's conception of equal treatment as a means to reduce obstacles to movement is particularly clear in the 2014 Enforcement Directive,[80] which elides the concepts, requiring Member States to do more in the fight 'against unjustified restrictions and obstacles to the right to free movement, and discrimination on grounds of nationality', bundling the concepts together interchangeably in eight places, and also referring to discrimination as a type of obstacle to movement.[81] It exhorts Member States to enforce the Equal Treatment Directive (492/2011) because 'the free movement of workers is … still a major challenge' and Union workers 'may still suffer from unjustified restrictions or obstacles to the exercise of their right to free movement, such as … discrimination on grounds of nationality'.[82] The preamble to the Directive concludes that there is 'a gap

---

[73] ibid, 52.

[74] Case C-138/02 *Brian Francis Collins v Secretary of State for Work and Pensions* EU:C:2004:172.

[75] ibid, 65.

[76] Case C-367/11 *Déborah Prete v Office national de l'emploi* EU:C:2012:668, 38.

[77] Case C-94/07 *Andrea Raccanelli v Max-Planck-Gesellschaft zur Förderung der Wissenschaften eV* EU:C:2008:425.

[78] Case 36–74 *BNO Walrave and LJN Koch v Association Union cycliste internationale, Koninklijke Nederlandsche* EU:C:1974:140.

[79] Case C-415/93 *Jean-Marc Bosman and others and Union des associations européennes de football (UEFA) v Jean-Marc Bosman* EU:C:1995:463.

[80] Directive 2014/54/EU of the European Parliament and of the Council of 16 April 2014 on measures facilitating the exercise of rights conferred on workers in the context of freedom of movement for workers OJ [2014] L128/8.

[81] ibid; 'Union workers may still suffer from unjustified restrictions or obstacles to the exercise of their right to free movement, *such as* non-recognition of qualifications, discrimination on grounds of nationality and exploitation', recital 5.

[82] ibid.

between the law and its application in practice that needs to be addressed'.[83] Discrimination from this perspective is a problem primarily because of its interference with free movement, affirmed in the Directive as a fundamental principle and a pillar of the internal market.[84]

Equal treatment on the grounds of nationality is a function of co-ordination, allowing the transition into different welfare regimes. The Regulation 1612/68 principle of equal treatment with regard to social advantages is echoed in Directive 2004/38.[85] Article 24(1) states that, subject to conditions provided for in primary and secondary law, 'all Union citizens residing on the basis of this Directive in the territory of the host Member State shall enjoy equal treatment with the nationals of that Member State within the scope of the Treaty'. That this includes social assistance is made clear by the derogation in Article 24(2), which provides for the exceptions in which Member States are not obliged to confer social assistance (in the first three months of residence, or to those with jobseeker status). To reside 'on the basis of this Directive', an EU national must fall into one of the categories of people with a right of residence for more than three months,[86] as listed in Article 7. If that is established, then the EU national is entitled to equal treatment as a matter of free movement law because discrimination would be an obstacle to such movement. In theory, secondary legislation does not provide an exhaustive list of those entitled to equal treatment, because such a right is based on an expansive primary law provision. Article 18 of The Treaty on the Functioning of the European Union (TFEU)[87] states that within 'the scope of application of the Treaties, and without prejudice to any special provisions contained therein, any discrimination on grounds of nationality shall be prohibited' and applies to citizens of the Union. The right to move and reside between Member States is also given broad construction in the TFEU: Union citizens 'shall ... have, inter alia: (a) the right to move and reside freely within the territory of the Member States'.[88] However, this right is subject to 'the conditions and limits defined by the Treaties and by the measures adopted thereunder'. Here we have the crucial intersection with domestic law. The relevant UK legislation focuses very much on implementing EU secondary, not primary, law. The governing regulations in force during the fieldwork part of this study were the Immigration (European Economic Area) Regulations 2006.[89] These were repeatedly updated: the replacement Immigration (European Economic

---

[83]    ibid.

[84]    ibid, recital (1).

[85]    Directive 2004/38/EC of the European Parliament and of the Council of 29 April 2004 on the right of citizens of the Union and their family members to move and reside freely within the territory of the Member States [2004] OJ L158/77.

[86]    Residence during the first three months does not attract social assistance entitlement under Art 24(2) Directive 2004/38, for EU migrants other than workers, the self-employed, persons who retain that status or their family members (see recital (21)).

[87]    The Treaty on the Functioning of the European Union (Consolidated version 2016) OJ [2016] C 202/47.

[88]    Art 21 TFEU.

[89]    SI 2006/1003.

Area) Regulations 2016[90] are intended to tidy up the regulations and neatly incorporate the multiple amendments while making some significant changes.[91] For the purposes of this study, though, the 2016 Regulations are broadly the same as the amended 2006 ones. These regulations implement the categories covered by Article 7 of Directive 2004/38, and establish the concept of a 'right to reside', a term of legal art that introduces and disguises nationality discrimination. UK nationals automatically have a right to reside, but EU nationals must demonstrate that they meet the conditions of Directive 2004/38. Other pieces of legislation then make the right to reside a prerequisite for access to specific welfare benefits. Some provisions also mention a Treaty-based right of residence, but in order to explicitly *exclude* it from triggering equal treatment with regard to benefit access.[92] EU nationals are required to demonstrate that they have a right to reside, as defined in the 2006/2016 Regulations, so falling within the ambit of Article 7 Directive 2004/38, in order to be eligible for a range of benefits including child benefit, child tax credit, housing benefit, council tax reduction, pension credit, income-based jobseeker's allowance, income support, income-based employment and support allowance,[93] and sure start maternity grants.[94] Not having a right to reside creates an automatic exclusion from the benefits in question: there is no provision for recourse to primary Treaty rights. The right to reside condition is constitutive of the right to benefits: there is no presumption of equal treatment to be modified in a subsequent stage. The condition comes first.

## B. Key UK Welfare Rights

The UK welfare system is convoluted and complex.[95] It can be broadly divided into three types of benefit: (1) contributory; (2) means-tested; and

---

[90] SI 2016/1052.

[91] Such as creating a right to remove people where the Secretary of State believes them to have 'misused' the free movement provisions (see Regulation 23(6)(c)).

[92] For example, The Child Benefit (General) Regulations, SI 2006/223 require a person to be treated as being in Great Britain to be eligible, and add that anyone without a 'right to reside' will not be treated as present. They further provide that a 'person shall be treated as not being in Great Britain … where he … has a right to reside in the United Kingdom by virtue of … Article 20 of the Treaty on the Functioning of the European Union (in a case where the right to reside arises because a British citizen would otherwise be deprived of the genuine enjoyment of the substance of their rights as a European Union citizen)' (see Regulation 23(4)(b)(ii)). This is aimed at those invoking Case C-34/09 *Gerardo Ruiz Zambrano v Office National de L'Emploi (ONEm)* EU:C:2011:124; for further, see ch 4.

[93] Social Security (Persons from Abroad) Amendment Regulations 2006, SI 2006/1026, reg 6(3)—income support; reg 7(3)—jobseekers allowance; reg 9(2)—pension credit; and The Employment and Support Allowance Regulations 2008, SI 2008/794, reg 70.

[94] ibid, regs 4(3) and 5(3)—housing benefit; reg 8(2)(b)—social fund maternity and funeral expenses.

[95] For a guide to the structure and conditions, see Child Poverty Action Group (CPAG), *Welfare Benefits and Tax Credits Handbook* (London, CPAG, 2017). For a critical analysis of recent reforms to the whole UK welfare system, see S Royston, *Broken Benefits: What's Gone Wrong with Welfare Reform* (London, Policy Press, 2017).

(3) specific-circumstance related. The system places less emphasis on contributory principles[96] than some others in the EU.[97] Means-tested benefits are intended to supplement low incomes as well as help those out of work, and many claimants of means-tested benefits are in work.[98] The primary focus of this study is on the last two categories: that is, access to means-tested benefits, and problems arising from the coordination regime with regard to special circumstance benefits. Means-tested benefits include means-tested versions of out-of-work benefits—due to unemployment (jobseeker's allowance) or illness (employment and support allowance (ESA))—for those who do not have sufficient contributions for the contributory versions. ESA is divided into two groups: (1) the 'work related activity group', for those able to perform some work-related activity; and (2) the support group, for those unable to conduct such activity.

The main means-tested benefit for those who cannot work due to having pre-school children is income support. The main in-work means-tested benefit to supplement low incomes is working tax credit, which includes a childcare element, if applicable. Other key means-tested benefits, which may be awarded to claimants in or out of work, are housing benefit (to help meet housing costs), council tax support and child tax credit. Child benefit used to be a universal family benefit, but in 2013 became subject to upper-end means-testing.[99]

The key 'special situation' benefits relate to disability and care. Disability living allowance has been (mostly) replaced for adults with personal independence payment[100] but is still the main disability-related benefit for children. Both contain 'care' and 'mobility' components, and claimants may qualify for one or both parts. Attendance allowance is the equivalent for people aged 65 and over, but it does not include a 'mobility' component.[101] The carers of people entitled to any of those benefits may be eligible for carers allowance, which depends on having limited capacity for work due to care. These special situation benefits are 'special non-contributory benefits' under the EU social security coordination regime.[102]

---

[96] The contributory benefits are income-replacement benefits for people out of work due to unemployment (jobseeker's allowance), illness (ESA) or retirement (state retirement pension). Though there are exceptions for 'permitted work'. Contributory ESA in the work-related activity group is time-limited to one year's maximum claim.

[97] Such as the Netherlands; see F Pennings, 'The Response of Residence-Based Schemes in the Netherlands to Cross-Border Movement' (2016) 18 *European Journal of Social Security* 2, 106.

[98] Working tax credit is a means-tested benefit only available to people in work.

[99] Provided for in s 8 and Sch 1 to the Finance Act 2012, which introduced c 8 into Pt 10 (ss 681B–681HI, on the 'high income child benefit charge') of the Income Tax (Earnings and Pensions) Act 2003.

[100] People born on or before 8 April 1948 can still continue to receive the mobility component of disability living allowance.

[101] Those who were previously on disability living allowance/personal independence payment and receiving a mobility component can before turning 65 continue to receive it.

[102] Case C-299/05 *Commission of the European Communities v European Parliament and Council of the European Union* EU:C:2007:608; Case C-537/09 *Ralph James Bartlett and Others v Secretary of State for Work and Pensions* EU:C:2011:278.

The UK has seen a vast amount of recent and continuing welfare reform generally, mostly aimed at deficit reduction.[103] The biggest such change is aimed at simplification: the replacement of a series of means-tested benefits—income support, income-based jobseeker's allowance, income-related employment and support allowance, child tax credit, working tax credit and housing benefit—with a new combined benefit, universal credit. This huge undertaking, an upheaval of a vast tranche of the benefits system, has proved incredibly complicated and logistically difficult, and the move is taking longer than planned.[104] At the time of writing, a number of areas in the UK are at the pilot stage, where only the simplest claims (single people of working age who would be new claimants of jobseeker's allowance) are being transitioned to universal credit, and claimants who have complicated circumstances (which includes EU nationals) are on the 'old' benefit regime. But there are some areas in the UK where universal credit is at 'full service', which means that it is no longer possible to claim the old benefits. Even so, there are a number of issues with regard to EU national claimants that have yet to be resolved. The government has announced that it classifies universal credit as 'social assistance', so as to invoke the exclusion in Article 24(2) of Directive 2004/38 to exclude EU national jobseekers from universal credit in their entirety (a position analysed in more detail in chapter five). This makes the distinction between 'worker' and 'jobseeker' all the more crucial yet, at the time of writing, the Department of Work and Pensions (DWP) has yet to issue any guidance on this matter.[105]

The general welfare reform programme has included a raft of changes directed specifically at EU nationals, the nature and effects of which are explored in more detail in chapter five. However, while the UK has been one of the more vocal and high-profile rights-restricting states, the tendency towards limiting EU nationals' rights, the imposition of right to reside tests, and the deployment of narrow interpretations of case law and EU legislation, is not a solely UK phenomenon. There have been echoes of free movement scepticism and benefit tourism fears elsewhere in the EU. Blauberger and Heindlmaier have studied the social assistance rules in Germany and Austria. The two systems are legally different, with Austria implementing restrictive residence rules, and Germany implementing liberal residence rules but restrictive rules on rights to benefits. But Blauberger and Heindlmaier argue that because controlling access to benefits is administratively easier and less costly than controlling presence and initiating expulsions, the two systems

---

[103] Hence the plan to 'save £12 billion a year on welfare bills by 2019–2020', announced in a document that makes 11 references to 'lower welfare' or a 'lower welfare society' (HM Treasury, *Spending Review and Autumn Statement 2015 Update*, 27 November 2015, available at: www.gov.uk/government/publications/spending-review-and-autumn-statement-2015-documents/spending-review-and-autumn-statement-2015.

[104] *The Guardian* reported on the 'seventh announced delay since 2013' which meant the scheme was five years behind the original timetable (P Butler and P Walker, 'Universal Credit Falls Five Years Behind Schedule', *The Guardian*, 20 July 2016. Available at: www.theguardian.com/society/2016/jul/20/universal-credit-five-year-delay-2022-damian-green.)

[105] Correspondence with DWP has not yielded any.

produce de facto similar results: EU migrants are tolerated residents who 'enter at their own risk'.[106] In the Netherlands, Pennings argues that policy is focused more on activation than dealing with non-nationals, but notes an increase in measures that restrict the rights of free movers.[107] In Denmark, Catherine Jacqueson points to the exclusion of homeless EU nationals from any state support, and notes that Danish authorities are more restrictive than the ECJ when it comes to defining migrant workers entitled to equal treatment under Article 45 TFEU.[108] She suggests that there is a 'cold wind towards immigrants and their access to welfare benefits ... currently blowing in Denmark'.[109]

Equal treatment on the grounds of nationality has been conceived of at EU level as a tool of the internal market. Member States treat it as a procedural hoop, rather than anything that commands substantive power, and so enact legislation specifically to create and normalise unequal treatment. The UK experience should therefore be a useful, instructive one and, I would argue, presents something of a cautionary tale for Member States following the same line of xenosceptic law-making. EU citizenship may offer the means to push EU law away from the single market paradigm,[110] and so bring us to think of equal treatment in more fundamental terms, rather than the shallow, malleable form it has assumed as a facilitator of economic movement. But it has not done so yet. In order to evaluate the nature and power of EU citizenship, it is necessary to gauge its traction within domestic law, and in particular whether and how citizenship rights are manifest at first instance. The vast majority of EU nationals are not party to cases that get litigated in the higher courts or referred to the Court of Justice of the European Union (CJEU), but instead are faced with administrative decision-making or, at most, a First-tier Tribunal. The next section explains the rationale for ground-up research into EU law and particularly legal action research.

## IV.  THE NEED TO STUDY EU CITIZENSHIP 'IN ACTION': THE *EU RIGHTS PROJECT*

In order to fully test the content of EU citizenship in a welfare benefit context, the *EU Rights Project* aimed to get inside the process of asserting and appealing

---

[106]  M Blauberger and A Heindlmaier, 'Enter at Your Own Risk: Free Movement of EU Citizens in Practice' (2017) 40, *West European Politics*, published online 13 March 2017.

[107]  Such as the use of a pro-rata principle in the Old-Age Pension Act resulting in 'persons who make use of free movement not receiving the full benefits of the Dutch system'. See above n 97, 127–28.

[108]  C Jacqueson, 'From Negligence to Resistance: Danish Welfare in the Light of Free Movement Law' (2016) 18 *European Journal of Social Security* 2, 183.

[109]  ibid, 197–98.

[110]  A process discussed in F Wollenschläger, 'A New Fundamental Freedom Beyond Market Integration: Union Citizenship and its Dynamics for Shifting the Economic Paradigm of European Integration' (2011) 17 *European Law Journal* 1, 1; note Kochenov refers to the 'omnipresent market paradigm', in D Kochenov, 'The Essence of EU Citizenship Emerging From the Last Ten Years of Academic Debate: Beyond the Cherry Blossoms and the Moon' (2013) 62 *International and Comparative Law Quarterly* 1, 97, 121.

claims. The project provided an advice and advocacy service through a Citizens Advice office.[111] This experience brought me into direct contact with the decision-making and administrative hurdles faced by clients. This first-hand, action-based approach to the research was necessary, because my prior experience of advice work made it clear that it would not be possible to get much insight into the claims and appeals process just through an observational study. An observational study would have required the availability of specialist advice for EU nationals, to enable them to negotiate the claims and appeals processes under study. But there are few, and decreasing, sources of information and advice available in the UK for EU nationals seeking support in a complex area of law. The UK overall has something of an 'advice deficit'[112] and the University of Warwick's comparative analysis on cuts to legal aid pointed to 'serious concerns about a loss of local expertise, and the emergence of advice deserts'.[113] The Civil Justice Council has criticised the reduction in legal support available for social welfare claimants since 'welfare benefits and tax credits are complex areas and many people need independent advice in order to understand their rights and obligations',[114] and also given the disproportionate impact of cuts in support upon women, ethnic minorities and people with disabilities. That complexity is significantly compounded for EU nationals, whose situations are governed by EU legislation and UK implementing legislation, and possibly the laws of other Member States, all interacting with the already labyrinthine domestic welfare system. Generalist advisers frequently reported themselves overwhelmed, or instantly worried, when they know they are dealing with EU law. As one participant in the preparatory focus group stated:

> You just feel when you get a case, you just think, somebody comes to you and they say, European, migrant, benefits. You just know it's going to be complex, a bit of a minefield, that things are going to go wrong.

In order to capture the legal landscape of experiences and problems encountered by EU nationals in the UK, to test whether the law-in-practice matches the law-in-theory, and to fully explore the limits on access to justice created by administrative obstacles, it was therefore necessary to offer EU nationals support for their claims and disputes to be aired in the first place. By setting up an advice and advocacy service, the *EU Rights Project* was able to access and produce data that would not otherwise have come to light, by pursuing cases and arguments that

---

[111] The service was based in Craven and Harrogate Districts Citizens Advice.

[112] Low Commission, *Tackling the Advice Deficit* (London, Legal Action Group, 2014).

[113] Warwick Law School, 'Access to Justice: A Comparative Analysis of Cuts to Legal Aid', *Report of an Expert Workshop Organised by the University of Warwick in Conjunction with Monash University* (2014). Available at: www2.warwick.ac.uk/fac/soc/law/research/centres/cjc/researchstreams/comparative/monash_access_to_justice_-_legal_aid_report_jan_2015.pdf.

[114] Civil Justice Council, 'Access to Justice for Litigants in Person (or Self-Represented Litigants)', *A Report and Series of Recommendations to the Lord Chancellor and to the Lord Chief Justice* (2011). Available at: www.judiciary.gov.uk/wp-content/uploads/2014/05/report-on-access-to-justice-forlitigants-in-person-nov2011.pdf.

would otherwise not have been pursued and, in so doing, increased access to justice in a small way for clients involved.[115]

## A. Advice-Led Ethnography

The *EU Rights Project* has thus developed a radical new methodology: advice-led ethnography, hopefully leading the way for EU legal action research in the UK. The Economic and Social Research Council (ESRC)-funded project is a collaboration between the University of York and Citizens Advice (Craven and Harrogate Districts). It received queries directly from clients, took on referrals from other Citizens Advice offices in the Yorkshire area, and gave second-tier advice to advisors from non-government organisations (NGOs) around the country, giving advice and offering drafting and advocacy services to EU nationals. Each referral went through a process of informed consent so that I could draw from the cases a separate, parallel research ethnography, comprising of field notes, anonymised case studies (including documentary extracts), and a research biography, all documenting the obstacles that we encountered. The aim was to gather rich, compelling data that provided an important snapshot of law in practice[116] through a relatively small-scale project on a few long-term cases, drawing out the problems they encountered within the welfare system to produce fine-grained data for the ethnographic study.[117] With each interaction with clients, or advisers contacting me for second-tier advice on behalf of their clients, I compiled field notes. As the aim was to be able to cover cases that required ongoing work, and multiple interactions, the objective was to collect a few, fine grained studies: over the course of 16 months of fieldwork, the plan was for 30 legal action research studies. However, the demand for input was so great that the project took on as many cases as possible, which amounted to 41 in total, featuring clients from 15 Member States. I also received evidence submissions: that is, pre-prepared case studies that did not require my input for a further six cases. I aimed to document, in particular, aspects of various interactions—letters, phone calls, form filling, appeal drafting, tribunal hearings, for example—that created hurdles in the claims and appeals processes. Bruno Latour argued, in an ethnography of the

---

[115] Ulster University has reported on the potential for university law clinics to help promote access to justice, noting 'good evidence of the public visibility and utility of law clinics as legal service providers and of their connections to other sources of help and support' (O Drummond and G McKeever, 'Access to Justice Through University Law Clinics', *Ulster University Report* (2015). Available at: www.ulster.ac.uk/lawclinic/files/2014/06/Access-to-Justicethrough-Uni-Law-Clinics-November-2015.pdf).

[116] C O'Brien, 'The EU Rights Project' (2015) 167 *Adviser* 8.

[117] D Forsythe, '"It's Just a Matter of Common Sense": Ethnography as Invisible Work' (1999) 8 *Computer Supported Cooperative Work*, 127; K Berry, 'The Ethnographic Choice: Why Ethnographers Do Ethnography' (2011) 11 *Cultural Studies* 2, 165; and L White, 'Subordination, Rhetorical Survival Skills, and Sunday Shoes: Notes on the Hearing of Mrs G' (1990) 38 *Buffalo Law Review* 1, 1.

French Conseil d'Etat, that the 'essence of law' is not to be found in 'a definition but in a practice, a situated material practice that ties a whole range of hetero-geneous phenomena in a certain specific *way*'.[118] I would suggest that where law 'happens' for EU migrants is at the collision site of practices from EU, domestic, local legal and administrative levels.[119] While Latour engaged in a context-free ethnographic description, the advice-led nature of this ethnography makes it deeply contextualised, and from the conscious perspective of an active contribu-tor to the exchanges under study, with the aim of testing the effects and content of EU citizenship.

Giving advice and doing research on the processes and outcomes of cases at the same time is necessarily challenging and requires ethical consideration. However, this project opened up the possibility to pursue ethically robust, practice-based research in a discipline that has sometimes dabbled in less systematic, methodi-cal practice-led approaches. Many legal realists engage in practice-based research, increasingly using real cases and personal narratives in their writing.[120] However, they tend not to apply a coherent overarching research design from the outset, which can result in an anecdotal and ad hoc approach. Without clear acknowl-edgement of research objectives from the start, it is possible that they are effec-tively covertly pursued as far as clients are concerned, and possibly inadvertently influence the advice they give. There is the risk of bypassing consent and avoiding the use of any systematic data gathering approach from the outset.

The *EU Rights Project* aimed to import the methodological awareness applied in other disciplines, specifically drawing upon practitioner ethnography, a method that has typically been conducted in education[121] or medical settings.[122] Practi-tioner ethnography helps to 'bridge the gap' between scholarship and practice.[123] It is therefore an appropriate platform for research into the gap between the theory

---

[118] B Latour, *The Making of Law: An Ethnography of the Conseil d'Etat* (Cambridge, Polity Press, 2013) x.

[119] Drawing upon J Shaw and N Miller, 'When Legal Worlds Collide: An Exploration of What Hap-pens When EU Free Movement Law Meets UK Immigration Law' (2013) 38 *EL Rev* 2, 137, Kotiswaran suggests it is especially important to do ethnography where different laws interact (see P Kotiswaran, 'Do Feminists Need an Economic Sociology of Law?' (2013) 40 *Journal of Law and Society* 1, 115).

[120] B Miller, 'Telling Stories About Cases and Clients: The Ethics of Narrative' (2000) 14 *Georgetown Journal of Legal Ethics* 1.

[121] J Carmichael and K Miller, 'The Challenges of Practitioner Research: Some Insights into Collaboration Between Higher and Further Education in the LiFE Project', in J Caldwell, et al (eds) *What a Difference a Pedagogy Makes: Researching Lifelong Learning and Teaching—Proceedings of 3rd International CRLL Conference* (Glasgow, Centre for Research in Lifelong Learning, 2006) 700.

[122] See T Barton, 'Understanding Practitioner Ethnography' (2008) 15 *Nurse Researcher* 2, 7.

[123] L Harvey and M Myers, 'Scholarship and Practice: The Contribution of Ethnographic Research Methods to Bridging the Gap' (1995) 8 *Information Technology and People* 3, 13. See also: M Fox, P Martin, and G Green, *Doing Practitioner Research* (London, Sage, 2007) 88; D Farrer, 'The Perils and Pitfalls of Performance Ethnography' (2007) 6 *International Sociological Association E-Bulletin* 17; and M Davies, 'Ethics and Methodology in Legal Theory A (Personal) Research Anti-Manifesto' (2002) 6 *Law Text Culture* 7.

and practice of EU citizenship. Gaps between law in the books and law in reality may not be cause for alarm,[124] but we can only know this if we know the gaps are there and study them. The premise of this project is that ignorance as to how EU citizenship works/does not work at the coalface is alarming. EU legal scholarship tends to be dominated by doctrinalism: my aim is to change how EU citizenship is discussed. My findings, combined with a dramatically shifting legal landscape, have led to the normative recommendations of the book, about the consequences of disregarding the dictates of social justice, the misappropriation of the language of equal treatment, and tolerating state-sanctioned declaratory discrimination.

Advice-led ethnography departs slightly from practitioner research, since practitioner ethnography usually focuses upon the impact of one's own practices, (for example, an academic wishes to study how lawyers work, so conducts an ethnography as a lawyer), whereas this study has been concerned with procedure and the practices of *others*: the administrators encountered during the course of the cases. In this, it echoes community-based participatory research or action research.[125] But I did not trial a particular change or action,[126] or require research subjects to set the research agenda;[127] instead, I worked with clients and advisors to identify whether administrative and/or strategy changes were required. Advice-based ethnography is thus a development on several existing collaborative methodologies.[128] The vast bulk of my data is from the case studies, which I triangulated with focus group work and expert interviews: I conducted two focus groups with advice workers from around England and Wales and five interviews with welfare specialists working in national NGOs. The first focus group, and first two interviews, were preparatory (that is, they were conducted before the ethnographic fieldwork started) and were helpful forums for identifying key issues,[129]

---

[124] E Edwardsson and H Wockelberg, 'European Legal Method in Denmark and Sweden: Using Social Science Theory and Methodology to Describe the Implementation of EU Law' (2013) 19 *European Law Journal* 3, 364, 366; D Nelken, 'The "Gap Problem" in the Sociology of Law: A Theoretical Review', (1981) 1 *Windsor Yearbook of Access to Justice* 35, 41.

[125] S Flicker, R Travers, A Guta, S McDonald and A Meagher, 'Ethical Dilemmas in Community-Based Participatory Research: Recommendations for Institutional Review Boards' (2007) 84 *Journal of Urban Health: Bulletin of the New York Academy of Medicine* 4, 478; E Houh and K Kalsem 'Theorizing Legal Participatory Action Research: Critical Race/Feminism and Participatory Action Research' (2015) 21 *Qualitative Inquiry* 3, 262.

[126] Agency for Healthcare Research and Quality, US Department of Health and Human Services, 'Community-Based Participatory Research: Assessing the Evidence' (2004) *Evidence Report/Technology Assessment* 99, 13; S Ashencaen Crabtree et al 'Community Participatory Approaches to Dengue Prevention in Sarawak, Malaysia' (2001) 60 *Human Organization* 3, 281.

[127] E Houh and K Kalsem, 'It's Critical: Legal Participatory Action Research' (2014) 19 *Michigan Journal of Race and Law* 2, 287; C Berg Powers and E Allaman, *How Participatory Action Research Can Promote Social Change and Help Youth Development* (2012). Available at: //cyber.harvard.edu/sites/cyber.harvard.edu/files/KBWParticipatoryActionResearch2012.pdf.

[128] M Minkler, P Fadem, M Perry, K Blum, L Moore and J Rogers, 'Ethical Dilemmas in Participatory Action Research: A Case Study from the Disability Community' (2002) 29 *Health, Education and Behaviour* 1, 14.

[129] As suggested in EF Fern, *Advanced Focus Group Research* (London, Sage, 2001).

while the later group and interviews were reflective (as in useful testing grounds of the advice-based data to see which perceptions and experiences were shared and/or struck a chord),[130] and the transcriptions showed how common problems generated a lot of enthusiastic inter-group discussion.[131]

The dual roles of adviser and researcher posed clear risks of one role unduly influencing the other.[132] But it should be remembered that in empirical work, dual roles are inevitable, and Ball argues that 'the researcher never can be the invisible fly on the wall, as sometimes is claimed, but is always and inevitably a part of the scene'.[133] There was arguably a benefit in being acutely aware of my active role in influencing the events under study. The project had several built-in safeguards: I reported to the Citizens Advice office manager, and requested case-checking from other advice supervisors, who although not experts in the area of law, made sure that the clients' best interests were being protected and all options explored. The research questions were shaped so as to harvest findings of interest whatever the outcome, to avoid creating an incentive to push a client to make any particular choices. I came to the project with over 11 years of experience of advice work, casework and case supervision in different Citizens Advice offices, so was familiar with the policies in place to protect client interests. Ultimately, while legal action research requires strong ethical awareness, it had the potential to be more ethical than alternatives. Had I pursued an observation-only project, there is a strong chance that I would have been silently watching people being given the wrong advice or receiving no help. As Laurie, studying the UK Upper Tribunal, notes: 'social security law in particular has consistently been recognised as being all but impenetrable to the non-expert'.[134] The complexity is compounded when dealing with EU social security law as well. The project was not intended to be an exploration of the weaknesses of the free legal advice sector, but of the strength of EU citizenship and the progress of welfare claims, even when clients had the necessary support to make and pursue those claims.

---

[130] J Kitzinger, 'The Methodology of Focus Groups: The Importance of Interaction Between Research Participants' (1994) 16 *Sociology of Health & Illness* 1, 103.

[131] An important factor according to Gill et al (see P Gill, K Stewart, E Treasure and B Chadwick, 'Methods of Data Collection in Qualitative Research: Interviews and Focus Groups' (2008) 204 *British Dental Journal* 6, 291).

[132] 'Practitioner research presents many ethical dilemmas to be resolved before and during the study. Communicating intent and potential hazards enables study participants to make informed judgements about whether they wish to continue' (Fox, Martin and Green, above n 123).

[133] SJ Ball, 'Self-Doubt and Soft Data: Social and Technical Trajectories in Ethnographic Fieldwork' in M Hammersley (ed), *Educational Research: Current Issues* (London, Paul Chapman, 1990) 34, cited in G Tricoglus 'Living the Theoretical Principles of Critical Ethnography in Educational Research' (2001) 9 *Educational Action Research* 1, 135.

[134] E Laurie, 'Assessing the Upper Tribunal's Potential to Deliver Administrative Justice' (2012) *Public Law* 288. Laurie also quotes Terry Rooney MP: 'anyone who claims to be an expert in social security legislation is either a liar, or they lead a very sad life'.

## B.  A Power-Sensitive Analysis

This was a study largely working with a disempowered demographic: a legally differentiated group excluded from rights, who were also politically disenfranchised within the host state, and whose claims and appeals were against powerful opponents (agents of the state). As such, it was important to be aware of the power dynamics at play, which themselves revealed a 'gap' between the theory and practice of equal treatment. In a US-based study of legal procedure and processes of subordination, White noted in 1990 that the norm of citizens' equal participation was at odds with the 'deeply stratified social reality [that] reveals itself when subordinated speakers attempt to use the procedures that the system affords them'.[135] This project involved subordinated speakers attempting to use procedures that might otherwise have been simply unknown to them, and so allows us to examine the 'deeply stratified social reality' of EU citizenship. It permits us to look at social injustices that might otherwise have remained hidden from the light of day, and to identify different mechanisms of disempowerment, paying attention to the language used by first-instance decision-makers to construct, or reconstruct, client cases. Lens and colleagues conducted a fascinating observational study on the 'choreographing' of justice and highlighted the importance of the language administrative judges employed to frame the people and situations upon which they were passing judgment. They noted that the 'spectre of power—the appellant's lack of it and the institution's abundance of it—is present in virtually every institutional exchange, from the front lines to the hearing room'.[136] The *EU Rights Project* divided the documentation and notes into different stages of a case, then using an inductive content analysis approach, coding and interpreting key messages from decision-makers, and their responses to our interventions. The analysis was sensitive to the issue of power, looking not merely at which words were being used, but what processes were being created, what was being required of clients, and why. This is especially important in the context of EU nationals who for a myriad of reasons (language, unfamiliarity with the system, lack of support networks, risk of total exclusion from the benefits system), risk being at even greater disadvantage than the average UK citizen in interactions with decision-makers.

It was during the course of the study that the UK government announced and rolled out a programme of welfare reforms targeting EU nationals,[137] and so the study turned to focus on how clients and decision-makers were navigating these reforms, and the effects upon clients' ability to access EU law-based rights. Even where, on paper, the changes might not make much legal difference to their rights, they were announced through mechanisms that made discriminatory intentions

---

[135]  White, above n 117, 4.

[136]  V Lens, A Ausberger, A Hughes and T Wu, 'Choreographing Justice: Administrative Law Judges and the Management of Welfare Disputes' (2013) 40 *Journal of Law and Society* 2, 199, 203.

[137]  Summarised by S Kennedy, 'Measures to Limit Migrants' Access to Benefits', *House of Commons Briefing Paper No 06889*, 17 June 2015 (London, House of Commons Library, 2015).

clear, and those acts of announcement, it is contended, amount to discrimina-tory acts and obstacles to movement. Meanwhile, the Court of Justice was busily dismantling the EU citizenship construct through a 'reactionary' period[138] of case law. In a sense, this actually reduced the gap between theory and practice, since the law 'in the books' appeared to be changing shape to reflect the restrictive approach that was being adopted in practice. But this has not reduced the need for evaluat-ing access to justice for EU nationals: indeed it has amplified it, since understand-ings and interpretations of the law are swiftly changing and highly contested.

## V. SUMMARY

EU welfare law has largely been constructed around the desire to reduce obstacles to movement for workers. The driving force behind social security coordination has been obstacle reduction, in the interests of promoting the single market. Even equal treatment for workers in the context of social advantages has been conceived of as a means to reduce obstacles to the functioning of the market. EU welfare law is an unusual brand of welfare law: it is not driven by concerns for social justice, and has little interest in the content of welfare provision.[139] National rules of eli-gibility for welfare benefits speak to concerns for social justice and these concerns are poorly served by EU market citizenship.

In order to best test the social content of EU citizenship, I conducted an advice-led ethnography in the *EU Rights Project*, working directly with EU nationals and advice workers, helping to advance arguments and make representations and doc-umenting our experiences. This kind of legal action research is a new way to study EU law in action, and was necessary simply because of the complexity of the inter-actions between EU and UK welfare law, and the scarcity of on-the-ground spe-cialists working with EU nationals at first instance. As an active participant, I have been particularly painfully aware of administrative obstacles and injustices, which have revealed how difficult it is realise equal treatment rights for EU nationals in the UK. The disjuncture between theory and practice of equal treatment reflects the tensions at the heart of EU market citizenship. The next chapter explores the weaknesses of EU citizenship when it comes to offering social protection, showing that as a form of market citizenship, it is inadequate and ill-suited to the task of promoting social justice.

---

[138] E Spaventa, 'Earned Citizenship: Understanding Union Citizenship Through Its Scope' in D Kochenov (ed), *EU Citizenship and Federalism: The Role of Rights* (Cambridge, CUP, 2017) 206.

[139] Though the EU does take strong views about the structure of welfare provision with regard to activation strategies; see ch 5.

# 3

# The Rise of Market Citizenship
# and The Illusion of Equal Treatment

## I. INTRODUCTION

THE EU'S DEVELOPMENT has been marked by what Scharpf termed 'constitutional asymmetry',[1] that is, a predisposition towards the economic at the expense of the social. Its roots are that of an economic community, based upon economic freedoms, leaving social rights somewhat behind. While attention to social and fundamental rights has increased, they have remained subordinated to a particular vision of the economic. EU discrimination law on grounds such as sex, race and disability has been based on perceived economic efficiencies to be gained from equal access to the workplace. When fundamental rights are weighed against economic freedoms, they have been typically 'on the back foot', with the priorities of the freedoms taking primacy[2] and fundamental rights assessed as to whether they constitute legitimate limitations. As a consequence, Union citizenship has emerged as a form of market citizenship; in spite of claims by different Advocate Generals that the migrant worker is 'not a mere source of labour, but a human being'[3] and that 'labour is not, in Community law, to be regarded as a commodity',[4] the construct of the Union citizen remains anchored in the *homo economicus*.[5]

The creation of EU citizenship in 1992 did not mark a significant departure from the European Community's economic orientation. Initially introduced to bolster popular support and, according to the Commission in 1995, with the eventual purpose of deepening European citizens' 'sense of belonging' to the EU',[6]

---

[1] F Scharpf, 'The European Social Model: Coping with the Challenges of Diversity', (2002) 40 *Journal of Common Market Studies* 645.

[2] C Barnard, 'Social Dumping or Dumping Socialism?' (2008) 67 *Cambridge Law Journal* 2, 262, 264; S Reynolds, 'Explaining the Constitutional Drivers Behind a Perceived Judicial Preference for Free Movement Rights' (2016) 53 *CML Rev* 643, 643.

[3] Opinion of AG Trabucchi in Case 7/75 *Mr and Mrs F v Belgian State* EU:C:1975:75, 5. Quoted by AG Mancini in Case 131/85 *Emir Gül v Regierungspräsident Düsseldorf* EU:C:1986:82, 4.

[4] Opinion of AG Jacobs in Case 344/87 *I Bettray v Staatssecretaris van Justitie* EU:C:1989:113, 29.

[5] M Everson, 'The Legacy of the Market Citizen' in J Shaw and G More, *New Legal Dynamics of European Union* (Oxford, Clarendon Press, 1995).

[6] European Commission, *Report on the Operation of the Treaty on the European Union* SEC (95) 731 10.5.1995 (Brussels, EU Commission, 1995) A18.

it nevertheless appeared as an anodyne, toothless[7] concept, 'too little, too late',[8] as 'an empty promise',[9] and a political concession made in an otherwise economic treaty. Weiler famously described the Maastricht model of citizenship as 'an embarrassment', resembling a carnet of tickets to free attractions, which are free precisely because they are unattractive.[10]

This chapter will explore the rising importance of EU citizenship in EU case law and highlight the limitations written into it from the start. In particular, it will demonstrate how the concept of a 'real link' was used as a get-around to allow Member States to still treat nationality as a legally relevant factor, notwithstanding the theoretical prohibition of nationality discrimination, and the requirement that any discrimination must be justified by legitimate objectives not based on nationality. This market citizenship model reveals a particular vision of economic rationality: namely a patriarchal, able-bodied one, in which social concerns are characterised as costs, and promoted only insofar as they serve the predetermined economic agenda which itself excludes reproductive labour and treats non-nationals as means of economic production.

## II. A DISGUISED TOLERANCE OF DIRECT NATIONALITY DISCRIMINATION

EU citizenship experienced an underwhelming first few years, in which the model of market citizenship was prominent.[11] D'Oliveira, writing in 1995, suggested that the limitations and conditions on free movement were in effect a declaration 'that not every citizen has the right to move and reside freely' and that the freedom of movement 'for all nationals of Member States, whether economically active as workers and self-employed or not' was as yet an 'Arcadian objective'.[12] If anything, it is receding ever further into the distance.

According to the prevailing narrative, EU citizenship's watershed moment came with *Martinez Sala*,[13] when the European Court of Justice (ECJ) found that EU nationals were entitled to invoke the primary law protection against nationality discrimination in their capacity as citizens: 'Article 8(2) of the Treaty attaches to the status of citizen of the Union ... the right ... not to suffer discrimination

---

[7] C Jacqueson, 'Union Citizenship and the Court of Justice: Something New Under the Sun? Towards Social Citizenship' (2002) 27 EL Rev 260, 263.

[8] A Follesdal, 'Union Citizenship: Unpacking the Beast of Burden' (2001) 20 *Law and Philosophy* 313, 314.

[9] S Besson and A Utzinger, 'Introduction: Future Challenges of European Citizenship—Facing a Wide-Open Pandora's Box' (2007) 13 *European Law Journal* 573, 574. See also D Tambini, 'Post-National Citizenship' (2001) 24 *Ethnic and Racial Studies* 195, 201.

[10] JHH Weiler, 'European Citizenship: Identity and Differentity' in M la Torre (ed), *European Citizenship: An Institutional Challenge* (Alphen an den Rijn, Kluwer Law International, 1998) 10.

[11] Everson, above n 5; S O'Leary, 'The Social Dimension of Community Citizenship' in A Rosas and E Antola (eds) *A Citizens' Europe: In Search of a New Order* (London, Sage, 1995) 162.

[12] HUJ d'Oliveira, 'Union Citizenship: Pie in the Sky?' in A Rosas and E Antola (eds), ibid, 70.

[13] Case C-85/96 *María Martínez Sala v Freistaat Bayern* EU:C:1998:217.

on grounds of nationality within the scope of application *ratione materiae* of the Treaty'.[14] This generated much excitement,[15] and criticism,[16] from commentators and launched a generation of citizenship case law (and citizenship academics). But even then, the ECJ hinted at the limitations of its finding. The Court stated that it did not need to enter into the question of whether the primary law right to reside for citizens, which might have been considered conditional upon secondary law provisions, conferred the status of lawful resident upon the claimant, because she had 'already been authorised to reside there' under national law. The question was left open as to how Member States might ascertain whether an EU national was 'lawfully residing' in their territory before affording them equal treatment. The Court's conclusion referred to a citizen 'such as the appellant in the main proceedings' and the facts of those proceedings were compelling—a Spanish national who had lived in Germany since she was 12—for 25 years at the point of her claim for child-raising allowance).

The ensuing patchwork of citizenship case law (for it would endow this area with an undue sense of coherence to call it a 'line') has served to emphasise the right of Member States to require EU nationals to have established a 'real link' with the host state before claiming equal access to its welfare benefits. And this duty will typically, or at least most convincingly, be discharged through economic activity: in *Commission v Netherlands* the fact of participating in the employment market was found to establish 'a sufficient link of integration' to be entitled to equal treatment because 'through the taxes he pays ... The migrant worker also contributes to the financing of the social policies of that state'.[17] The real link concept has also formed the grounds for maintaining that states of origin maintain responsibility for their mobile nationals, providing rights of benefit exportation, or the right to equal treatment as compared to non-movers on their return. In sum, it permits Member States to smuggle the variable of nationality in through the back door of their decision-making.

The continued relevance of nationality, in spite of its purported irrelevance, was made clear in cases in which Member States failed to assume welfare responsibility for their own nationals who had exercised free movement and returned.

[14] ibid, 62.

[15] Such as 'a tantalising prospect of Union citizenship as the source of wide-ranging social rights which are not directly related to economic/market activity' (T Downes, 'Market Citizenship: Functionalism and Fig Leaves' in R Bellamy and A Warleigh (eds), *Citizenship and Governance in the European Union* (London, Continuum, 2001) 101).

[16] C Tomuschat, 'Casenote: Case C85/96, *Maria Martinez Sala v Freistaat Bayern* [1998] ECR I2691' (2000) 37 *CML Rev* 449; Hailbronner noted 'the absence of a convincing methodology and the tendency to interpret secondary Community law against its wording and purpose' (K Hailbronner, 'Union Citizenship and Access to Social Benefits' (2005) 42 *CML Rev* 1245, 1251;); and Spaventa arguing that 'the link with the material scope of the Treaty ... is so artificial and flimsy to seem rather meaningless' (E Spaventa, 'Seeing the Wood Despite the Trees? On the Scope of Union Citizenship and its Constitutional Effects' (2008) *CML Rev* 13, 33).

[17] Case C-542/09 *Commission v Netherlands* EU:C:2012:346, 65–66; affirmed in Case C-20/12 *Elodie Giersch and Others v État du Grand-Duché de Luxembourg* EU:C:2013:411, 63.

In *D'Hoop*, the ECJ criticised the failure of a condition for the Belgian tide-over benefit (completing secondary education in Belgium) to accurately reflect a Belgian claimant's real links with her state of nationality. It found that the 'single condition' of the place of secondary education 'unduly favours an element which is not necessarily representative of the real and effective degree of connection between the applicant for the tide-over allowance and the geographic employment market, to the exclusion of all other representative elements'.[18] While this finding raised some concerns about the degree of judicial intrusion into national welfare arrangements,[19] the cumulative case law suggests that the real link test is not all that intrusive and amounts to two key principles: (1) that there must be substantial and good reasons to discount the connection of nationality, and those reasons must not amount to unjustified discrimination on the grounds of mobility (the obstacle to movement principle); and (2) that there should be some slight degree of flexibility in any real link test rather than the use of a 'single' condition that creates a blanket ban.[20]

## A.   The Continued Salience of Nationality: Real Links

The language of real links is used to legitimise continued differences in treatment based on nationality which represents, according to the Court, a 'special relationship of solidarity and good faith'.[21] Reliance on the establishment of a real link places nationals at an automatic advantage.[22] The fear that Member States might not give sufficient weight to the link of nationality, and so effectively penalise own nationals for having exercised their free movement rights, thus creating an obstacle to movement, has been a recurrent theme (surfacing in *Pusa*,[23] *Morgan and Bucher*,[24] and *Prinz and Seeberger*, for instance).[25]

With regard to the requirement for a degree of flexibility, the cases suggest that this is not a terribly onerous obligation for Member States: the main principle is that states should not rely exclusively on a single criterion. In *Geven*,[26] a rule

---

[18] Case C-224/98 *Marie*-Nathalie *D'Hoop v Office National de L'Emploi* EU:C:2002:432 39.

[19] A Somek, 'Solidarity Decomposed: Being and Time in European Citizenship' (2007) 32 *EL Rev* 787, 804–05.

[20] C O'Brien, 'Real Links, Abstract Rights and False Alarms: The Relationship Between the ECJ's "Real Link" Case Law and National Solidarity' (2008) 33 *EL Rev* 5, 643.

[21] Case C-135/08 *Janko Rottman v Freistaat Bayern* [2010] ECR I-01449, 51.

[22] 'Obviously, nationality can constitute prima facie evidence of integration' (K Lenaerts and T Heremans, 'Contours of a European Social Union in the Case-Law of the European Court of Justice' (2006) 2 *European Constitutional Law Review* 101, 107).

[23] Case C-224/02 *Heikki Antero Pusa v Osuuspankkien Keskinäinen Vakuutusyhtiö* EU:C:2004:273, 19.

[24] Joined Cases C-11/06 and C-12/06 *Rhiannon Morgan v Bezirksregierung Köln and Iris Bucher v Landrat des Kreises Düren* EU:C:2007:626, 26.

[25] Joined Cases C-523/11 and C-585/11 *Laurence Prinz v Region Hannover and Philipp Seeberger v Studentenwerk Heidelberg* EU:C:2013:90, 28.

[26] Case C-213/05 *Wendy Geven v Land Nordrhein-Westfalen* EU:C:2006:616.

excluding non-national part-time workers from the German child-raising allowance was considered legitimate because it offered two alternative ways to establish the requisite link (full-time work or residence). Residence was not regarded as the only connecting link so, according to the Court, more than one type of link was enough, even though this disadvantaged part-time frontier workers.[27]

Although some have suggested that the citizenship case law, at least up until *Förster*,[28] was a series of fundamental rulings speaking to the 'powerful expansion' of the scope of free movement,[29] the citizenship based rights that emerge in cases such as *Trojani*,[30] *Grzelczyk*[31] and *Bidar*,[32] viewed through the real link prism, did not amount to a direct entitlement for non-nationals to equal treatment, but to a much more muted right to have restrictions on benefit eligibility applied proportionately. While the EU has a social policy dimension,[33] what we have is at best a very dilute, instrumental form of social policy. That the 'real link' approach provides a get-around for treating nationality as relevant, when in theory it should not be, was evident in *Förster*, which to some represents a turning point, cooling the Court's fervour for equal treatment.[34] There, national rules in the Netherlands required EU nationals to have completed an uninterrupted period of five years of residence before becoming eligible for student maintenance grants. This represented quite a considerable yardstick, the same period of time as required for eligibility for permanent residence. However, the Court considered it an appropriate and proportionate condition for ensuring the requisite degree of integration into

---

[27] C O'Brien, 'Case Comment: Case C-212/05, *Gertraud Hartmann v Freistaat Bayern*, Judgment of the Grand Chamber of 18 July 2007, nyr; Case C-213/05 *Wendy Geven v Land Nordrhein-Westfalen*, Judgment of the Grand Chamber of 18 July 2007, nyr; Case C-287/05 *DPW Hendrix v Raad van Bestuur van het Uitvoeringsinstituut Werknemersverzekeringen*, Judgment of the Grand Chamber of 11 September 2007, nyr' (2008) 45 *CML Rev* 2, 499, 510.

[28] Case C-158/07 *Jacqueline Förster v Hoofddirectie van de Informatie Beheer Groep* EU:C:2008:630.

[29] V Trstenjak and E Beysen, 'The Growing Overlap of Fundamental Freedoms and Fundamental Rights in the Case-Law of the CJEU' (2013) 38 *EL Rev* 3, 295, 295.

[30] Case C-456/02 *Michel Trojani v Centre public d'aide sociale de Bruxelles (CPAS)* EU:C:2004:488.

[31] Case C-184/99 *Rudy Grzelczyk v Centre public d'aide sociale d'Ottignies-Louvain-la-Neuve* EU:C:2001:458.

[32] Case C-209/03 *The Queen, on the application of Dany Bidar v London Borough of Ealing and Secretary of State for Education and Skills* EU:C:2005:169.

[33] J Caporaso and S Tarrow, 'Polanyi in Brussels: Supranational Institutions and the Transnational Embedding of Markets' (2009) 63 *International Organization* 593, 614; D Damjanovic, 'The EU Market Rules as Social Market Rules: Why the EU Can be a Social Market Economy' (2013) 50 *CML Rev* 6, 1685, 1713.

[34] O Golynker, 'Case Comment: Case C-158/07, *Jacqueline Förster v Hoofddirectie van de Informatie Beheer Groep*, Judgment of the Court (Grand Chamber) of 18 November 2008, not yet reported' (2009) 46 *CML Rev* 6, 2021. Dougan notes an apparent back-tracking, but suggests that the 'judicial will' behind it is unclear (M Dougan, 'The Bubble That Burst: Exploring the Legitimacy of the Case Law on the Free Movement of Union Citizens' in M Adams, H de Waele, J Meeusen and G Straetmans (eds), *Judging Europe's Judges: The Legitimacy of the Case Law of the European Court of Justice* (Oxford, Hart, 2013); also Thym describes the Court in *Förster* as yielding to the red lines of the legislator (D Thym, 'Towards "Real" Citizenship? The Judicial Construction of Union Citizenship and its Limits' in M Adams, et al, ibid; Lenaerts considers the case instead an 'important exception' to the case law, (K Lenaerts, 'Union Citizenship, National Welfare Systems and Social Solidarity' (2011) 18 *Jurisprudence* 2, 397, 418.

the host society in light of the restriction in Article 24(2) excluding those not able to rely on a connection to economic activity from maintenance aid for studies (an exclusion that Member States would only be obliged to lift after an EU national had accrued a right to permanent residence). The Court found the rule provided 'a significant level of legal certainty and transparency'.[35]

At first glance it may seem as though this was a blanket rule, but a closer examination of the judgment reveals that there is a second route to entitlement: simply being a Dutch national. It is striking that this separate scheme for own-nationals is only mentioned in passing,[36] and disappointing that the question of *direct* discrimination goes unexamined. The judgment is framed as a question of whether the means of requiring a degree of integration is appropriate and proportionate. But this is the framework for examining whether indirect discrimination is justified (although the judgment does not acknowledge that it is dealing with discrimination at all). This rule was explicitly directly discriminatory. Centring the discussion on integration or real links disguises that fact and dodges the awkward issue of the contradictory position on EU law with regard to direct discrimination which should theoretically be harder to justify than indirect discrimination.

## B. Is Direct Discrimination Justifiable?

Direct discrimination in the context of Article 45 TFEU—against workers—can only be justified on grounds expressly provided by EU law: in the Treaty these are public policy, public security and public health, or the public service exception (Article 45(3) and (4)). Article 18, the general equal treatment provision applicable to all EU citizens, including the economically inactive, does not have such specific exceptions but states that the prohibition on discrimination shall apply 'without prejudice to any special provisions' within the scope of the Treaties. If we are to assume that this means that secondary legislation can suspend expectations of equal treatment, this still leaves us with the question of whether there is a difference between direct and indirect discrimination on the grounds of nationality *outside* of the scope of Article 45 TFEU. Other areas of EU equal treatment law recognise a material difference between direct and indirect discrimination,[37]

---

[35]   *Förster*, above n 28, 57.
[36]   ibid, 45.
[37]   Directive 2010/41/EU of the European Parliament and of the Council of 7 July 2010 on the application of the principle of equal treatment between men and women engaged in an activity in a self-employed capacity and repealing Council Directive 86/613/EEC, OJ [2010] L 180/1, Art 3(b); Directive 2006/54/EC of the European Parliament and of the Council of 5 July 2006 on the implementation of the principle of equal opportunities and equal treatment of men and women in matters of employment and occupation (recast) OJ [2006] L 204/23, Art 2(1)(a) and (b); Council Directive 2004/113/EC of 13 December 2004 implementing the principle of equal treatment between men and women in the access to and supply of goods and services OJ [2004] L 373/37, Art 2(a) and (b); Council Directive 2000/43/EC of 29 June 2000 implementing the principle of equal treatment between persons

including discrimination on the grounds of nationality *within* the scope of Article 45 TFEU.[38] Directive 79/7 on matters of social security states that it prohibits measures that discriminate 'directly or indirectly', without mentioning justification, but the case law on that provision relies upon the same distinction discussed here: that direct discrimination can only be justified on grounds prescribed by Union law,[39] and that indirect discrimination is capable of justification by a legitimate objective where the means are appropriate and do not go beyond what is necessary[40] (and where the aim is pursued in a consistent and systematic manner).[41]

But as far as nationality is concerned, there has been little judicial discussion on the appropriate framework for analysing *direct* discrimination against non-workers. Advocate General Sharpston noted in *Bressol*[42] that throughout Union law, the 'distinction between direct and indirect discrimination lacks precision'[43] and made a considered and persuasive attempt to offer a distinction: direct discrimination occurs 'when the category of those receiving a certain advantage and the category of those suffering a correlative disadvantage coincide exactly with the respective categories of persons distinguished only by applying a prohibited classification'.[44] In that case, the French community of Belgium had set a quota for non-resident students, defining residents as those who have their residence in Belgium, and have a right of permanent residence in Belgium. The Advocate General found that the second condition, having a right of permanent residence in Belgium, was directly discriminatory because those of Belgian nationality automatically had a right of permanent residence in Belgium. Thus the category of those with an advantage (an automatic permanent residence right) coincided exactly with a category of persons defined by a prohibited classification (nationality), and the category of persons with a disadvantage (not automatically having permanent

---

irrespective of racial or ethnic origin, OJ [2000] L 180/22, Art 2(2)(a) and (b); Council Directive 2000/78/EC of 27 November 2000 establishing a general framework for equal treatment in employment and occupation, OJ [2000] L 303/16, Art 2(2)(a) and (b).

[38] *Indirect* discrimination against migrant workers can be justified by a 'legitimate objective': *Giersch*, above n 17, whereas direct discrimination can only be justified by specific Treaty exceptions which must be interpreted narrowly (Case C-171/01 *Gemeinsam Zajedno/Birlikte Alternative und Grüne GewerkschafterInnen/UG and Others* EU:C:2003:260, 92–93; Case C-465/01 *Commission of the European Communities v Republic of Austria* EU:C:2004:530, 39–40).

[39] Case C-147/95 *Dimossia Epicheirissi Ilektrismou (DEI) v Efthimios Evrenopoulos* EU:C:1997:201, 27–28. See also Case C-187/98 *Commission of the European Communities v Hellenic Republic* EU:C:1999:535, 45.

[40] Case C-8/94 *CB Laperre v Bestuurscommissie beroepszaken in de provincie Zuid-Holland* EU:C:1996:36, 14; Case C-123/10 *Waltraud Brachner v Pensionsversicherungsanstalt* EU:C:2011:675, 70; Case C-343/92 *MA De Weerd, née Roks, and others v Bestuur van de Bedrijfsvereniging voor de Gezondheid, Geestelijke en Maatschappelijke Belangen and others* EU:C:1994:71, 33.

[41] Case C-123/10 *Waltraud Brachner v Pensionsversicherungsanstalt* EU:C:2011:675, 71.

[42] Case C-73/08 *Nicolas Bressol and Others and Céline Chaverot and Others v Gouvernement de la Communauté française* EU:C:2010:181.

[43] *Bressol*, Opinion of AG Sharpston EU:C:2009:396, 46.

[44] ibid, 53.

residence) also coincided with a category defined by nationality. The difference in treatment was 'clearly based on a criterion (the right to remain permanently in Belgium) which is necessarily linked to a characteristic indissociable from nationality', which meant that it was directly discriminatory.[45]

On identifying direct discrimination, the Advocate General turned to the question of justification, finding that 'the Court has never held that a measure that discriminates directly on grounds of nationality, contrary to Article 12 EC [now Article 18 TFEU], may be justified'.[46] There was no Treaty derogation from the general prohibition of discrimination and so any departure from the principle must be on the 'basis of explicit Treaty derogations'.[47] The Court in the same case simply ducked the issue raised by the Advocate General and treated the whole thing as a 'residence condition' which was 'more easily satisfied by Belgian nationals, who more often than not reside in Belgium, than by nationals of other Member States, whose residence is generally in a Member State other than Belgium',[48] so a matter of indirect discrimination. This is disingenuous: the first condition was a residence condition, but the other was a condition of a legal status, which was not 'more easily satisfied' by Belgian nationals, it was always and automatically satisfied by Belgian nationals. Consequently, the Court set in train a legal fiction that the award of rights automatically to nationals and only conditionally to non-nationals is indirectly discriminatory. It failed to address the continuing question of justification: is direct discrimination against non-workers on the grounds of nationality only capable of justification through explicit Treaty derogations, or can it be justified in the same way as indirect discrimination, and so is the prohibition considerably more dilute than that of direct discrimination elsewhere in the scope of the Treaty? The Court's earlier approach in *Grzelczyk*[49] would suggest the standard approach to direct discrimination applies. That case had dealt with a rule with a similar effect to that in *Bressol*: that is, that non-national EU claimants of the Belgian benefit had to demonstrate that they were workers within the scope of Regulation 1612/68. This condition for the benefit was not applied to own-nationals. The Court found that the 'fact that Mr Grzelczyk *is not of Belgian nationality is the only bar* to its being granted to him. It is not therefore in dispute that the case is one of *discrimination solely on the ground of nationality*'.[50] The Court then did not discuss justification, only the limitations prescribed by law: in that case, in Article 1 of Directive 93/96,[51] the Student Residence Directive that preceded Directive 2004/38, which required students to make 'a declaration ... that he has sufficient resources to avoid becoming a burden on the social assistance system

---

[45] ibid, 66–67.
[46] ibid, 128.
[47] ibid, 129.
[48] *Bressol* judgment, above n 42, 45.
[49] *Grzelczyk*, above n 31.
[50] ibid, 29; emphasis added.
[51] Council Directive 93/96/EEC of the Council of 29 October 1993 on the right of residence for students OJ [1993] L 317/59.

of the host Member State during their period of residence'.[52] Stating that the underpinning right is one of non-discrimination stemming from the Treaty, and in light of Union citizenship, the Court then took a narrow interpretation approach to this limitation, noting that it was 'merely requiring such a declaration', not requiring actual specific resources, and that as circumstances change, what was required was a declaration that was truthful at the time that it was made.[53] While a Member State may decide that a student no longer fulfilled the requirements of a Community law-based right to reside, it could not do so automatically as a consequence of recourse to social assistance. This was because the preamble to the Directive stated that students should not become unreasonable burdens, which necessarily implied that some degree of burden would be reasonable, hence the finding that the legislature had accepted 'a certain degree of financial solidarity between nationals of a host Member State and nationals of other Member States, particularly if the difficulties which a beneficiary of the right of residence encounters are temporary'.[54]

In a different context—cases involving the rules of legal procedure for disputes over payments for goods—the Court has expressed the prohibition on direct discrimination on grounds of nationality in emphatic terms. Swedish rules required foreign nationals not resident in Sweden wishing to bring action in a Swedish court against a Swedish legal person to furnish security to guarantee payment of judicial costs (if requested to do so by the defendant). In *Data Delecta*,[55] the Court identified direct discrimination and described Article 6 of the EC Treaty (an antecedent of Article 18 TFEU, which stated that 'within the scope of application of this Treaty, and without prejudice to any special provisions contained therein, any discrimination on grounds of nationality shall be prohibited') as requiring 'perfect equality of treatment in Member States of persons in a situation governed by Community law and nationals of the Member State in question'.[56] The Court examined similar requirements in *Hayes* and *Saldanha v Hiross*. In *Hayes*, the Court found that Article 6 required 'persons in a situation governed by Community law and nationals of the Member State concerned to be treated absolutely equally'.[57] In *Saldanha v Hiross*, the measure imposed on foreign nationals by the Austrian authorities was identified as direct discrimination. There, the respondent claimed that the discrimination could be justified on objective grounds: that is, increasing a defendant's chances of recovering costs, and noting the difficulty of enforcement against non-residents. The Court did not explicitly state that direct discrimination could not be objectively justified, but implied it, suggesting that the objective might have been relevant had the provision not been directly

---

[52] ibid, Art 1.
[53] *Grzelczyk*, above n 31, 40.
[54] ibid, 44.
[55] Case C-43/95 *Data Delecta Aktiebolag and Ronny Forsberg v MSL Dynamics Ltd* EU:C:1996:357.
[56] ibid, 16.
[57] Case C-323/95 *David Charles Hayes and Jeannette Karen Hayes v Kronenberger GmbH* EU:C:1997:169, 16.

discriminatory.[58] This suggests that, in some circumstances, the Court recognises a strong prohibition of direct discrimination on the grounds of nationality, requiring specific derogations within EU law.

### III. DEALING WITH LEGISLATIVE LIMITATIONS ON EQUAL TREATMENT

Directive 2004/38, the Residence Directive, provides at Article 24(1) for equal treatment between all Union citizens residing in a host state on the basis of the Directive 'subject to such specific provisions ... expressly provided for in the Treaty and secondary law'. This is immediately followed by one such specific provision, in the form of a derogation in Article 24(2), which absolves host Member States from the obligation to confer entitlement to social assistance during the first three months of residence (or longer, if a workseeker),[59] or to grant 'maintenance aid for studies, including vocational training, consisting in student grants or student loans' to people who have not yet accrued permanent residence unless they are in work or self-employment, or the family member of someone who is.

The Court has described the equal treatment provision of Article 24(1) as 'merely a specific expression' of the 'principle of equal treatment provided for in Article 18 TFEU',[60] so reinforcing the priority given to primary law. Article 24(2) is thus a derogation from Article 18 TFEU itself and so 'must be interpreted narrowly'.[61] The Court has seemed to suggest that the same approach should be adopted whether or not we are dealing with workers. In *Bressol*, it stated that the fact that claimants did not exercise economic activity was 'irrelevant' to the applicability of the Directive, 'since Directive 2004/38 applies to all citizens of the Union irrespective of whether they exercise an economic activity as an employee or as a self-employed person in the territory of another Member State or whether they do not exercise any economic activity there'[62] and Article 24(1) 'applies to every citizen who resides in the territory of the host Member State in accordance with that directive'.[63]

### A. Appealing to a Primary Law-Based Right of Equal Treatment

That primary law cannot be solely interpreted with reference to secondary law is underlined in *Baumbast*.[64] In that case, the Court invoked the primacy of

---

[58] Case C-122/96 *Stephen Austin Saldanha and MTS Securities Corporation v Hiross Holding AG* EU:C:1997:458, 29.

[59] According to recital (21) of the preamble, this exclusion only applies to 'Union citizens other than those who are workers or self-employed persons or who retain that status or their family members'.

[60] Case C-46/12 *LN v Styrelsen for Videregående Uddannelser og Uddannelsesstøtte* EU:C:2013:97.

[61] Case C-233/14 *European Commission v Kingdom of the Netherlands* EU:C:2016:396, 86.

[62] *Bressol*, judgment, above n 42, 36.

[63] ibid, 34.

[64] Case C-413/99 *Baumbast and R v Secretary of State for the Home Department* EU:C:2002:493.

Article 18 EC, which provided that 'Every citizen of the Union shall have the right to move and reside freely within the territory of the Member States, subject to the limitations and conditions laid down in this Treaty and by the measures adopted to give it effect'. In terms of Union citizens' (not workers') rights to free movement, the UK and German governments, and the European Commission, all argued in *Baumbast* that the wording of Article 18 EC—making it subject to limitations and conditions—meant that it was not a freestanding right. The Commission further argued that it was a right conditioned by secondary law, and must be linked to an economic activity or sufficient resources, and that Article 18 EC would be no use without pointing to another 'Community law foundation'[65] for a right to reside. The Court disagreed profoundly, stating that 'Union citizenship has been introduced into the EC Treaty and Article 18(1) EC has conferred a right, for every citizen, to move and reside freely within the territory of the Member States',[66] and that the right to reside under Article 18 EC 'is conferred directly on every citizen of the Union by a clear and precise provision of the EC Treaty'.[67] This meant that Mr Baumbast was able to rely upon Article 18 EC 'purely as a national of a Member State, and consequently a citizen of the Union'.[68]

The limitations and conditions could not be said to be constitutive of the right: rather those limitations must 'be applied in compliance with the limits imposed by Community law and in accordance with the general principles of that law, in particular the principle of proportionality'.[69] In that case, it was suggested that while Mr Baumbast did not fit the requirements set down in secondary law, a refusal of a right of residence would have been disproportionate, in light of the circumstances (for example, that he had sufficient resources, that he had worked and lived in the host state, that his family were living there, that the family had not been a burden on the public purse, and that they had comprehensive sickness insurance elsewhere). The Article 18 TFEU right to equal treatment would seem to require a similar approach: it sets out a fundamental principle so that limitations and conditions must be applied in compliance with the principle of proportionality. This echoes the approach in *Grzelczyk*, that Article 6 EC (now Article 18 TFEU) creates an underpinning right of equal treatment, which may then be subject to specific limitations and conditions, which should be narrowly construed and could not create automatic exclusions wherever the legislature envisaged the possibility of Union citizens posing some degree of 'burden', since some such burdens would be 'reasonable'.

*Grzelczyk*, with its concept of 'reasonable burden', and *Baumbast*, with its requirement for limitations to abide by the principle of proportionality, between them seemed full of promise.[70] Through an admittedly small crevice (a stipulation

---

[65] ibid, 79.
[66] ibid, 81.
[67] ibid, 84.
[68] ibid.
[69] ibid, 91.
[70] As described in M Everson, 'European Citizenship and the Disillusion of the Common Man' in R Nickel (ed), *Conflict of Laws and Laws of Conflict in Europe and Beyond: Patterns of Supranational*

that departures from equal treatment could be lawful, so long as they were not disproportionate), a sliver of solidarity peeped through in what appears to be a requirement for humane treatment. But proportionality never did fulfil its potential. In the UK, first instance decision-makers were not required to have regard to anything other than the prescribed right to reside categories, which were treated as exhaustive. A proportionality review of unequal treatment arose only, at best, in cases that reached the First-tier Tribunal. The ECJ has backed away from requiring Member States to have regard to anything other than the limitations in Directive 2004/38, revealing its conception of proportionality to have been substantively hollow in the first place.[71]

The treatment of the Directive's limitations, and the role/standard of proportionality review, is of particular importance when it comes to dealing with 'right to reside' tests applied only to non-nationals. In cases from *Brey* onwards, the Court has appeared to condone an approach in which limitations and conditions are constitutive of the right to equal treatment. But there is little ground for treating secondary law as irrefutably conditioning primary law rights and so subjugating Article 18 TFEU to Article 7 of Directive 2004/38. The Directive may provide a 'specific expression' of the principle of equal treatment but it does not, and cannot, provide the *only* possible expression of it. The Court's increased tolerance for an approach that assumes a default of direct discrimination is explored next.

## IV. FROM *BREY* ONWARDS: DISMANTLING EU SOCIAL CITIZENSHIP AND LEGITIMATING DIRECTLY DISCRIMINATORY 'RIGHT TO RESIDE' CONDITIONS

In *Brey*,[72] Directive 2004/38 began its transformation from an instrument to promote free movement and equal treatment into a means of restricting equal treatment and guarding against benefit tourism. Mr Brey, a German national pensioner resident in Austria, had claimed an Austrian compensatory supplement.

---

*and Transnational Juridification* (Antwerp, Intersentia, 2010); see S O'Leary, *The Evolving Concept of Community Citizenship: From the Free Movement of Persons to Union Citizenship* (The Hague, Kluwer Law International, 1997); M Ferrera, 'Towards an Open Social Citizenship: The New Boundaries of Welfare in the European Union' in G De Burca (ed), *EU Law and the Welfare State* (London, OUP, 2005); F Wollenschläger, 'A New Fundamental Freedom Beyond Market Integration: Union Citizenship and its Dynamics for Shifting the Economic Paradigm of European Integration' (2011) 17 *European Law Journal* 1, 1; D Kostakopoulou, 'Ideas, Norms and European Citizenship: Explaining Institutional Change'(2005) 68 *MLR* 233; O Golynker, 'Jobseekers' Rights in the European Union: Challenges of Changing the Paradigm of Social Solidarity' (2005) 30 *EL Rev* 111; and K Lenaerts and T Heremans, 'Contours of a European Social Union in the Case-Law of the European Court of Justice' (2006) 2 *European Constitutional Law Review* 101.

[71] Davies contends that the ECJ's solidaristic intentions in the early citizenship cases have been exaggerated and that the later cases present a logical refinement of preceding case law (see G Davies, 'Migrant Union Citizens and Social Assistance: Trying to Be Reasonable About Self-Sufficiency' (2016) 2 *Research Papers in Law*.

[72] Case C-140/12 *Pensionsversicherungsanstalt v Peter Brey* EU:C:2013:565.

This supplement had previously been characterised as a special non-contributory benefit, so a form of social security, covered by Regulation 883/2004.[73] If it fell within that regulation, then it was argued that it was subject to the regulation's equal treatment provision in Article 4, which states:

> Unless otherwise provided for by this Regulation, persons to whom this Regulation applies shall enjoy the same benefits and be subject to the same obligations under the legislation of any Member State as the nationals thereof.

Since it was not social assistance for the purposes of Regulation 883/2004, it was argued that it should not be considered social assistance for the purposes of Directive 2004/38, so would not affect Mr Brey's claim to have a right to reside based on sufficient resources. Indeed, some commentators had previously argued that full equal entitlement to special non-contributory benefits was the flip-side of the deal Member States struck when wishing to insist upon territorial restrictions. In excluding those benefits from the exportation provisions, the theory went, states were entitled to exclude *non*-residents, but had to include *all* residents.[74] Consequently, it was suggested that eligibility for special non-contributory benefits should count towards a claimant's assets, enabling them to point to sufficient resources.[75] The Court in *Brey* disagreed, making clear that such claimants could be excluded from equal rights to such benefits *ex ante*, meaning those benefits would not be awarded and would not count towards their resources.

## A. 'Nothing to Prevent' Direct Discrimination

The Court agreed that the benefit did fall within the scope of Regulation 883/2004 and specifically engaged Article 70(4) which states that special non-contributory benefits can be subject to a condition of residence in the paying state's territory. However, the Court then stated that this was a conflict rule to prevent overlapping, and was 'not intended to lay down the conditions creating the right to special non-contributory cash benefits'.[76] Noting that Regulation 883/2004 does not set up a common scheme of social security, the Court concluded—in a paragraph that in itself has come to justify the dispensing with equal treatment—that there was:

> nothing to prevent, in principle, the granting of social benefits[77] to Union citizens who are not economically active being made conditional upon those citizens meeting the

---

[73] Case C-160/02 *Friedrich Skalka v Sozialversicherungsanstalt der gewerblichen Wirtschaft* EU:C:2004:269.

[74] F Pennings, 'Inclusion and Exclusion of Persons and Benefits in the New Coordination Regulation' in M Dougan and E Spaventa (eds), *Social Welfare and EU Law* (Oxford, Hart, 2005) 252.

[75] H Verschueren, 'European (Internal) Migration Law as an Instrument for Defining the Boundaries of National Solidarity Systems' (2007) 9 *European Journal of Migration and Law* 307, 326.

[76] *Brey* judgment, above n 72, 41.

[77] The English translation uses the phrase 'social security benefits', but this appears to be a mistranslation, since the closest translation of the original is 'social benefits'.

necessary requirements for obtaining a legal right of residence in the host Member State.[78]

This is problematic since there is something that might 'in principle' prevent such a difference in treatment: Article 4 of Regulation 883/2004. That provision prohibits directly discriminatory conditions for eligibility for social security. Although the Regulation does not set up a common scheme of social security, it does set common conditions, and non-discrimination is one of those conditions. But the Court did not engage at all with Article 4. Instead it found that the benefit, while social security for the purposes of the Regulation, was nevertheless social assistance for the purposes of the Directive. The Court felt able to depart from the wording of the Regulation, by divining a general principle of restriction from Directive 2004/38. While finding that the aim of that Directive was to facilitate and strengthen free movement rights, the Court added that it was 'also intended … to set out the conditions governing the exercise of that right'.[79] The provision for a right to reside for those with sufficient resources, upon which Mr Brey sought to rely, was described as a condition 'intended … to prevent such persons becoming an unreasonable burden on the social assistance system of the host Member State'.[80] This condition was 'based on the idea that the exercise of the right of residence for citizens of the Union can be subordinated to the legitimate interests of the Member States—in the present case, the protection of their public finances'.[81] The Court offered a reductionist summary of the legislation, suggesting that the purpose of the coordinating regulation was to allow EU migrants to keep certain entitlements from their state of origin, while the Directive allowed 'the host Member State to impose legitimate restrictions in connection with the grant of such benefits to Union citizens who do not or no longer have worker status'.[82] But Regulation 883/2004 is not just about retaining rights in the state of origin: it provides for the potential competence of Member States of work and/or residence, and sets out common principles that bind whichever state is competent (principles of aggregation and of non-discrimination). Nor is Directive 2004/38, at first sight, just about legitimate restrictions—it is about legitimate entitlements. But the way we are supposed to read it has been transformed: like a gestalt image, the main object has retreated in perception, and the focus has shifted to the background.

The conjuring from Directive 2004/38 of a general licence to discriminate (or to 'subordinate' rights of equal treatment) on grounds of public finance feels rather vague, and contrasts sharply with the very specific derogations from equal treatment in Article 24(2). The Court argued that that provision is 'in a similar vein' to its argument about protecting public finances and says that with regard to Union

---

[78]  ibid, 44.
[79]  ibid, 53.
[80]  ibid, 57.
[81]  ibid, 55.
[82]  ibid, 57.

citizens (other than workers, the self-employed, and their family member(s)), the provision permits host states 'not to confer entitlement to social assistance, in particular for the first three months of residence'.[83] This is misleading. Article 24(2) does not exclude the economically inactive from social assistance '*in particular*' for the first three months. It is specific: it excludes social assistance entitlement only for the first three months, or longer for those who have entered as jobseekers and not yet found work.[84] But reading into it a general exclusion of the 'economically inactive' contributes to the Court's position that Directive 2004/38 is a scheme for protecting public finances, a position that may have been influenced by the fact that a significant number of Member States submitted observations in the case[85] and all argued that special non-contributory benefits should be subject to right to reside conditions applied to non-nationals.[86]

## B. The Consolation Prize of *Brey*: A Proportionality Assessment

In agreeing with the national governments, the Court proposed an expansive interpretation of social assistance covering all national, regional or local assistance that can be claimed by someone who might 'become a burden on the public finances of the host Member State ... which could have consequences for the overall level of assistance which may be granted by that state'.[87] An application for such assistance could be an indication that an individual lacked sufficient resources. But, the Court added, the authorities could not automatically assume that a claim for social assistance meant that the claimant could not have a right to reside by way of sufficient resources and, before reaching such a conclusion, must conduct an overall assessment of the 'specific burden which granting that benefit would place on the national social assistance system as a whole, by reference to the personal circumstances characterising the individual situation of the person concerned'.[88]

To support the requirement for a thorough proportionality assessment, the Court stated that 'several provisions' of the Directive 'specifically state that those nationals may receive such benefits'[89] and listed the indicators that some equal treatment is to be expected. These included that the derogation in Article 24(2) 'only' applies to the first three months and that Article 14(3) precludes expulsion as an automatic consequence of recourse to the social assistance system. The Court further noted that Member States are not permitted to set non-rebuttable

---

[83] ibid, 56.
[84] It also excludes persons other than workers, the self-employed and their family members from maintenance aid for studies unless and until the claimant has permanent residence.
[85] Austria, Germany, Ireland, Greece, the Netherlands, Sweden and the UK.
[86] *Brey* judgment, above n 72, 48.
[87] ibid, 61.
[88] ibid, 64.
[89] ibid, 66.

levels of sufficient resources and 'must take into account the personal situation of the person concerned'.[90] It also points to the suggestions in recital 16 of factors to be taken into account when deciding whether a claimant poses an unreasonable burden.

In short, the judgment is incoherent and leaves us little the wiser when it comes to an appropriate framework for assessing and possibly justifying direct discrimination on the grounds of nationality outside of Article 45 TFEU. The Court made no reference to Article 18 TFEU (and only one reference to Article 21 TFEU) so, other than reference to the Directive's objective being to strengthen the primary free movement right, seems little concerned with primary law. Nor did the Court engage with the concept of equal treatment—the only mention of 'discrimination' in the judgment appears in outlining the Commission's argument and equal treatment on the grounds of nationality is mentioned only twice (both in references to 'derogations' from the principle).[91] In any case, the primacy of equal treatment had been straightforwardly rejected in the first half of the judgment, which accords primacy instead to the legitimate interests of Member States and the protection of public finances, reading into Directive 2004/38 a constitutional principle of the legitimacy of discrimination that overrides apparently conflicting provisions in Regulation 883/2004.

In keeping with the earlier 'real link' case law, we see a very minimal concept of Union citizenship emerging, only now without engaging with the primary principle of equal treatment. What is reinforced is the idea of citizenship as a right to a proportionality assessment—the consolation prize of *Brey*.[92] One of the many curious features of *Brey* is that it dilutes entitlement but appears to increase Member State obligations: the requirement for proportionality in previous cases could be discharged by showing some element of flexibility, but did not pose particularly onerous duties, with the Court probably mindful of administrative practicality. In *Brey*, the Court suggests that authorities should take account of 'the amount and the regularity of the income which he receives; the fact that those factors have led those authorities to issue him with a certificate of residence; and the period during which the benefit applied for is likely to be granted to him',[93] and so suggest a detailed individualised assessment in pretty much all cases of economic inactivity. The Court also appeared to suggest a 'systemic' proportionality assessment alongside this individual one, looking at 'the proportion of the beneficiaries of that benefit who are Union citizens in receipt of a retirement pension in another Member State'.[94] This dual proportionality model is confusing,

---

[90] ibid, 67.

[91] *Brey* judgment, above n 72, 37.

[92] Although 'Union citizenship' appears among the keywords in the headnote, the judgment makes no mention of citizenship and gives only a brief nod to one of the Treaty citizenship provisions. It does, however, make clear that it is dealing with the rights of 'Union citizens'.

[93] Above n 72, 78.

[94] ibid.

and commentators have pointed out how the two tests conflict and how unworkable they are in requiring such a degree of detail.[95]

## C. Proportionality Crumbles

It seems that in overloading the concept of proportionality in *Brey*, the Court destroyed it. Turning it into an unworkable concept rendered it redundant, with little purchase in national systems. The fact that the Court did so in the context of a judgment that simultaneously affirms and denies any *ex-ante* right to equal treatment, while asserting the primacy of public finance concerns and condoning nationality-based exclusions from means-tested benefits, lends greater legitimacy to Member States' choice to ignore a too-cumbersome concept. This new reality is accepted, and effectively endorsed, in the cases leading on from *Brey*. In *Dano*,[96] the Court engaged in more detail with some of the threads left hanging by *Brey*, such as the specific and limited derogation from equal treatment in Article 24(2), the consequent reach of Article 24(1) in the case of economically inactive claimants, acknowledging the applicability of the non-discrimination principle in Article 4 Regulation 883/2004,[97] and the general applicability of the non-discrimination principle in Article 18 TFEU. But it made no mention of proportionality or of any requirement for an assessment of personal circumstances.

*Dano* sees the Court using a sledgehammer to crack an already cracked nut.[98] Its conclusions are essentially about benefit tourism and the need to allow Member States to refuse benefits 'to economically inactive Union citizens who exercise their right to freedom of movement solely in order to obtain another Member State's social assistance'.[99] But it was already widely accepted that EU law does not provide a mechanism for benefit tourism, or a right to reside 'solely' for the purposes of claiming another state's social assistance. That much could be discerned from the permission given to Member States to refuse a right to reside to those posing an unreasonable burden on public finances: someone moving *just* to claim benefits could be shown without much difficulty to be an unreasonable burden. Insofar as that is how the Court framed the issue, it would not have been a controversial conclusion, and certainly would be one in keeping with

---

[95] H Verschueren, 'Free Movement or Benefit Tourism: The Unreasonable Burden of Brey' (2014) 16 *European Journal of Migration and Law* 147; D Thym, 'The Elusive Limits of Solidarity: Residence Rights of and Social Benefits for Economically Inactive Union Citizens' (2015) 52 *CML Rev* 1, 17.

[96] Case C-333/13 *Elisabeta Dano and Florin Dano v Jobcenter Leipzig* EU:C:2014:2358.

[97] Regulation (EC) No 883/2004 of the European Parliament and of the Council of 29 April 2004 on the coordination of social security systems OJ [2004] L 200/1.

[98] Note Verschueren's concerns about the 'risk that under the pressure of public opinion, popular press and Eurosceptics, some Member States will interpret and apply the possibilities offered by the wording of the judgment in *Dano* as broadly as possible' (H Verschueren, 'EU Migrants and Destitution: The Ambiguous EU Objectives' in F Pennings and G Vonk (eds), *Research Handbook on European Social Security Law* (Cheltenham, Edward Elgar Publishing, 2015) 436.

[99] *Dano* judgment, above n 96, 78.

citizenship-enhancing cases such as *Trojani*, to find that benefit tourism in itself presented an unreasonable burden. But the Court went further than that. Having stated that Article 18 TFEU protected 'every Union citizen' from discrimination on the grounds of nationality, it added that this principle was given 'more specific expression in Article 24 of Directive 2004/38'. Noting that the claimant was not covered by the derogation in Article 24(2), having resided for over three months, the Court turned to Article 24(1), and also Article 4 of Regulation 883/2004, because the benefit claimed was a special non-contributory benefit, so social security within the meaning of that regulation. Since Article 24(1) applied to Union citizens residing *on the basis of the Directive*, the Court concluded that 'so far as concerns access to social benefits ... a Union citizen can claim equal treatment with nationals of the host Member State *only* if his residence in the territory of the host Member State complies with the conditions of Directive 2004/38'.[100] So Article 24(1) is treated as an exhaustive expression of the principle of equal treatment (as applied to social benefits) in Article 18 TFEU. A claimant would only be entitled to equal treatment if she fitted within the categories of Article 7 of Directive 2004/38 and complied with the relevant conditions. The Court thus found that in order to claim protection from Article 24(1), the claimant had to show she had sufficient resources. Without giving any detail as to what this means, or how this should be ascertained (or, indeed, how it should *not* be ascertained, for example, by reference to a specific threshold, or through an assumption based on the mere fact of having claimed a benefit),[101] the Court noted that the referring court considered the claimants not to have sufficient resources. As a result, 'they cannot invoke the principle of non-discrimination in Article 24(1) of the Directive', apparently closing down the discussion of equal treatment, with no mention of a possible primary law right or whether there was a need to ensure compliance with the principle of proportionality.

The Court's brief engagement with Article 4 of Regulation 883/2004 is odd: simply finding that because the regulation[102] allows special non-contributory benefits to be claimed in the state of residence 'in accordance with its legislation', there was nothing to prevent the grant of such benefits being made subject to a right to reside condition (invoking that paragraph from *Brey*). In other words, Member States are free to set discriminatory eligibility criteria, and this freedom prevents Article 4 from biting. But this is disingenuous, as in *Brey*, Article 4 *might* in principle prevent the application of a right to reside test to non-nationals, if it were weighed up properly against the competing principles and objectives. Instead, Article 4 becomes meaningless, apparently providing for a prohibition on discrimination except for when Member States wish to discriminate.

As the claimant was considered to fall outside of the protection of Article 24(1) of the Directive, and that of Article 4 of the Regulation, the Court simply

---

[100]  ibid, 69, emphasis added.
[101]  As was stated in *Brey*, judgment, above n 72, 64.
[102]  Art 70(4), Reg 883/2004.

concluded that the exclusion of such claimants from social assistance benefits was not unlawful. Moreover, it does so without having regard to the assessment of 'sufficient resources', or requiring the principle of proportionality to be applied at any stage. In wielding the sledgehammer to prohibit already prohibited benefit tourism (the already cracked nut), the Court began to deconstruct the limited precepts of Union citizenship in a case in which it was quite unnecessary. It continued that project in *Alimanovic*[103] and *Garcia Nieto*.[104] The contested national legislation in *Dano* had also excluded those whose right of residence arose 'solely out of the search for employment', but the facts of the case meant that the Court was not required to address the exclusion of jobseekers until faced with *Alimanovic*. There, the Court was asked again about the reach of the non-discrimination principles of Article 24 of Directive 2004/38 and Article 4 of Regulation 883/2004, again in the context of a special non-contributory benefit, and this time in the context of people with jobseeker status.

Again, the primary law right to equal treatment received little attention (other than in the referring court's last 'in the alternative' question). On the issue of non-discrimination, the Court went straight to Article 24 and reiterated that equal treatment could 'only' be claimed by those complying with the conditions of the Directive.[105] It then noted that jobseekers could only claim a directive-based residence right by relying on either Article 7 on retained worker status, or on Article 14(4)(b), which provides that Union citizens who entered the territory in order to seek employment 'may not be expelled for as long as the Union citizens can provide evidence that they are continuing to seek employment and that they have a genuine chance of being engaged'.

On the possibility of retaining worker status, the relevant provision for those who have worked for less than one year states that they shall retain worker status for 'no less than six months'.[106] It seems that the German rules have established this minimum as a maximum, providing for retention for no longer than six months. Research suggests that this approach is widely adopted across the EU, with many states turning the 'floor' into the 'ceiling'.[107] The Court seemed to approve this approach in *Alimanovic* when it noted simply that the claimant had been able to retain worker status for 'at least six months' and so they 'no longer enjoy that status'.[108] The claimants were therefore treated as falling under Article 14(4)(b). The Court treated that as automatically triggering the derogation from equal

---

[103] Case C-67/14 *Jobcenter Berlin Neukölln v Nazifa Alimanovic and Others* EU:C:2015:597.

[104] Case C-299/14 *Vestische Arbeit Jobcenter Kreis Recklinghausen v Jovanna García-Nieto and Others* EU:C:2016:114.

[105] *Alimanovic* judgment, above n 103, 49.

[106] Directive 2004/38, Art 7(3) OJ [2004] L 158/94.

[107] C O'Brien, E Spaventa and J De Coninck, *Comparative Report: The Concept of Worker Under Article 45 TFEU and Certain Non-Standard Forms of Employment* (Brussels, European Commission, 2016) 70.

[108] *Alimanovic* judgment above n 103, 55.

treatment in Article 24(2), so that there was no pre-existing right to equal treatment to be assessed and no discrimination to be justified.

This finding relies on two problematic assumptions as to the personal and material scope of the claim: (1) it is not clear either that the claimants should be treated as falling within Article 14(4)(b); or (2) that the benefits should be treated as social assistance falling within Article 24(2). Article 14(4)(b) applies to Union citizens who enter the state in search of employment and are continuing to seek employment. It does not obviously include former workers who no longer have worker status and are now seeking re-employment.[109] There are a number of reasons why a former worker may not have retained worker status, so we may be dealing with very recently unemployed former workers. There are conditions for retaining worker status, such as registering with an unemployment office. The *EU Rights Project* found a number of former workers who conducted their own job searches under their own steam, thinking they were avoiding creating financial or administrative burdens for the state, often successfully gaining work within months, but later finding out that they had left themselves with a 'status gap' because they would not be recognised to have retained worker status during their unregistered job-searching. UK case law requires such registration to be performed without 'undue delay'[110] and suggests that a delay of more than a few weeks could be undue delay. In the UK Upper Tribunal case of *VP*, Judge Ward made clear that this applies even to zero hours contract workers who are unaware that they have been made unemployed and are 'reasonably in my view, hanging on in the hope of further work from [his employer]' and that this would still result in undue delay.[111] Such workers would thus not retain worker status and be treated as jobseekers notwithstanding their recent work, even though they might have felt dissuaded from signing on at the job centre because they wanted to find work under their own steam and to avoid claiming benefits. In a submission to the Social Security Advisory Committee's consultation on the withdrawal of housing benefit from EU jobseekers who have not retained worker status, Wavertree Citizens Advice stated:

> It is our experience that unless the worker has immediately claimed jobseeker's allowance after losing their job, local authorities have refused housing benefit on the grounds that the gap between working and claiming jobseeker's allowance has caused the claimant to lose their worker status.[112]

If Article 14(4)(b) does not appropriately cover former-worker workseekers, then we are left with the difficult situation in which the Directive appears to have a gap,

---

[109] The two situations were found to be different in Case C-138/02 *Brian Francis Collins*, EU:C:2004:172, 30, which drew upon Case 39/86 *Lair* EU:C:1988:322.

[110] *Secretary of State for Work and Pensions v MK* CIS/2423/2009, 69.

[111] *VP v Secretary for Work and Pensions (JSA)* [2014] UKUT 32 (AAC), 62.

[112] DWP and the Social Security Advisory Committee, *The Housing Benefit (Habitual Residence) Amendment Regulations 2014 (SI 2014 No 539): SSAC Report* (London, Social Security Advisory Committee, 2012). Available at: www.gov.uk/government/uploads/system/uploads/attachment_data/file/376103/PRINT-HB-Habitual-Residence-Amendment-Regs-2014-SSAC-report.pdf 15.

not obviously making provision for former-worker workseekers who no longer retain worker status. This would prevent them from relying on Article 24(1), since they would not be residing in accordance with the Directive, but they might invoke Article 18 TFEU, rejecting the contention that 'only' those covered by Article 24(1) are entitled to equal treatment. But the Court avoided dealing with primary law by finding them subject to the same provision as newly arrived jobseekers who have never worked in the host state.

## D.  Targeting Means-Tested Benefits

The benefit in *Alimanovic* was termed an unemployment benefit. The Court acknowledged that if it was a benefit to facilitate access to the labour market, then it could not be social assistance from which EU jobseekers were excluded. However, the Court found that 'even if they form part of a scheme which also provides for benefits to facilitate the search for employment',[113] the 'predominant function of the benefits at issue in the main proceedings is in fact to cover the minimum subsistence costs necessary to lead a life in keeping with human dignity',[114] and so should be treated as social assistance. The *Vatsouras*[115] finding, that benefits to facilitate access to the labour market should not be categorised as social assistance, was, somewhat misleadingly, flipped to suggest that social assistance benefits could not be categorised as benefits to facilitate access to the labour market.[116] The second proposition does not follow from the first. Indeed, *Vatsouras* could be construed as suggesting that a benefit might have characteristics of social assistance, but if it facilitates access to the labour market it cannot be so categorised. *Alimanovic* switches the order of priority: facilitating access to the labour market is irrelevant if there is a hint of social assistance. Such a hint can be derived simply from the benefit being means-tested, since it is possible to claim that any means-tested benefit has at heart the purpose of enabling the recipient to lead a life in keeping with human dignity. Further, if you target means-tested benefits, you target those without means, and restrict the rights of benefit claims to those with resources (ie those who are less in need of them). This is almost a reverse human rights caveat. Domestic and EU laws tend to be subject to a human rights caveat: that the laws will take effect but must be interpreted and applied in such a way as to respect human rights,[117] by way of appearing to make the overall measure human rights compliant. The *Alimanovic* approach does the opposite, suggesting that jobseekers may be entitled to benefits unless that entitlement stems from need (ie unless their human right to dignity is at stake).

---

[113] *Alimanovic* judgment, above n 103, 43.

[114] ibid, 45.

[115] Joined Cases C-22/08 and C-23/08 *Vatsouras and Koupatantze* EU:C:2009:344, 45.

[116] *Alimanovic* judgment, above n 103, 46.

[117] In the UK, this requirement is imposed in s 3 of the Human Rights Act 1998; in the EU, it is imposed by the Charter of Fundamental Rights of the European Union [2000] OJ C-364/01.

The *Alimanovic* finding leads to the question as to whether there is such a thing as a means-tested benefit open to EU national jobseekers as a means of facilitating access to the labour market.[118] While quoting *Vatsouras*, the Court comes to the opposite conclusion about benefits awarded under the same scheme,[119] which in *Vatsouras* were found to be benefits to facilitate access to the labour market. It would have been helpful had the Court in *Alimanovic* engaged with its earlier reasoning and spelled out the distinctions between the cases: it may be that the benefit was considered substantially different because it was a 'long-term' benefit. If the only cash benefits that EU national jobseekers can apply for are contributory benefits, then *Collins* and *Vatsouras* become redundant. A claimant who has paid contributions and claims a return on them does not need to rely on notions of links with the labour market to claim some limited degree of worker-like equal treatment with regard to claims upon the public purse, as envisaged in *Collins* (which dealt with a means-tested benefit). They are entitled to the same reciprocity as own-nationals under Article 4 Regulation 883/2004, and are entitled to have contributions in different countries aggregated if need be.

The Court continued the trend set in *Dano* for dismissing proportionality. It explicitly referred to its finding in *Brey* that a decision that a claimant posed an unreasonable burden could only be made when taking into account the individual situation of the person concerned, and then departed from it, stating that no such individual assessment was necessary here. The reasoning given was that the Directive itself provided sufficient proportionality by 'establishing a gradual system as regards the retention of the status of "worker"' which 'takes into consideration various factors characterising the individual situation of each applicant for social assistance and, in particular, the duration of the exercise of any economic activity'.[120] This passage exaggerates the degree to which the provisions on retention of worker status do in fact establish a 'gradual' system. They set a minimum period of retention (so permit a limit) for those who have worked for less than 12 months, and do not mention a minimum period for those who have worked for more than 12 months. For the purposes of gradation, they do not take account of the duration of economic activity 'in particular'. Rather, they *exclusively* take account of duration of economic activity, and no other factors.

The reasoning that secondary law is inherently proportionate eviscerates the concept of proportionality. That concept was based on the idea that when primary law rights are at stake, and then modified or limited by conditions in secondary law, those conditions must be interpreted proportionately. The Court here simply treats the limiting conditions as the proportionality review itself. The conditions it refers to on retaining the status of worker are not terribly 'gradual'.

---

[118] In *Collins*, above n 109, a means-tested benefit was found to be an unemployment benefit.

[119] The German basic benefits for jobseekers falling under para 7 of the German Social Code, Book II.

[120] *Alimanovic* judgment, above n 103, 60.

They give slightly different provisions on retaining worker status for those who have worked for more than 12 months, effectively creating an extra condition of having to work for more than 12 months, to not automatically lose a right to equal treatment after six months of unemployment. As such, it is a restriction placed upon the right to equal treatment and so should be subject to the principle of pro-portionality. In just pointing to Article 7(3)(c), the Court diverts attention from the fact that that is not the only provision at issue. Having considered the claim-ant to fall within Article 14(4)(b) and so subject to the limitation in Article 24(2), the Court could have examined whether the application of that provision was proportionate.[121] The problem that the Court adverts to, with an emphasis on legal certainty and avoiding ambiguity,[122] is the administrative nightmare that it conjured up in *Brey*. Rather than addressing or modifying that construction, the Court endorses it while suggesting that cases will either require a full *Brey* propor-tionality test, or none at all and, here, have allocated entire swathes of cases to the 'none at all' category. Admittedly, a right to have restrictions on rights assessed for proportionality is a rather minimalistic way to give effect to the underlying pri-mary law right combined with Union citizenship. But at least it gives that status some meaning, and offers a hint that there is something human in the process.

The Court could have drawn upon the Advocate General's opinion. Advocate General Wathelet had emphasised the need to avoid blanket rules that create auto-matic exclusions, as did the rule at issue excluding EU national jobseekers from the unemployment benefit. He drew upon the body of citizenship case law 'that per-mits the entitlement of economically inactive citizens of the Union to certain ben-efits to be made subject to a requirement of integration in the host Member State' to argue that 'the demonstration of a *real link* with that state ought to prevent automatic exclusion from those benefits'.[123] He stated that it would be contrary to the primary law right of equal treatment, as 'affirmed in Article 18 TFEU and clari-fied in Article 4 of Regulation 883/2004 and Article 24 of Directive 883/2004'[124] to automatically exclude someone in the applicant's position from benefits without having regard to, inter alia, 'family circumstances, like the existence of close ties of a personal nature' which might suggest 'a lasting connection between the person concerned and the new host Member State'.[125] He added further that 'the fact that the person concerned has, for a reasonable period, in fact genuinely sought work is a factor capable of demonstrating the existence of that link with the host Member State' as was having worked in the past or 'even the fact of having found a new job after applying for the grant of social assistance'.[126]

---

[121] The Court has elsewhere recognised that Art 24(2) is a limitation upon a primary law right and should be interpreted narrowly.

[122] *Alimanovic* judgment, above n 103, 61.

[123] Case C-67/14 *Jobcenter Berlin Neukölln v Nazifa Alimanovic and Others*, Opinion of AG Wathelet EU:C:2015:210, 107. The AG referred to the idea of a 'real link' three times.

[124] ibid, 110.

[125] ibid, 109.

[126] ibid, 11.

The Court did not engage with any of these arguments, or try to reconcile its condoning of a blanket rule with prior case law. Nor did it engage with the submissions made as to the existence of real links between the applicants and the host state. The summary of the request for a preliminary ruling highlights the potentially strong links that might have been found in this case, while noting that the national rules in question excluded any consideration of these factors:

> [The test] does not allow a case-by-case examination of the link to the domestic labour market or of any other genuine link to the host Member State...The facts giving rise to the proceedings in the present case illustrate this. The applicants had previously been economically active in the Federal Republic of Germany, had a longstanding link to Germany and began a professional activity directly following the period at issue. It may therefore be presumed that, despite their residence status as employment-seeking European Union citizens, they at all times maintained a genuine link with the German labour market.[127]

None of this was discussed in the judgment.


## V.  SUMMARY

EU free movement and equal treatment law is riddled with incoherence and obfuscation. The apparently clear framework of legal reasoning that is to be adopted when dealing with discrimination does not sit well with an apparent desire to permit direct discrimination on the grounds of nationality. Nationality remains salient when it comes to welfare entitlement, but in theory, *direct* discrimination on the grounds of nationality is not open to objective justification. We have seen the creation of a legal fiction that right to reside tests are indirectly discriminatory, to get around the inconvenient legal framework.

The role of the primary law right to equal treatment is unclear. In theory, the primary law right comes first, and secondary laws are merely specific expressions of that right. As such, they should be interpreted proportionately, with conditions and limitations viewed as derogations from a primary law right. This was perhaps the key promise of EU citizenship. But this promise dwindled in the case law that has emerged since *Brey*. In *Brey*, the ECJ endorsed the application of right to reside tests to those who do not fit into Article 7 of Directive 2004/38, though it did hold out the hope of a proportionality review of such decisions. In doing so, however, it proposed an unworkable, onerous approach to proportionality. Rather than revising its pronouncements, the Court's subsequent approach has been to find that swathes of welfare decision-making do not require any proportionality review at all. In removing proportionality requirements from the exclusion of EU nationals from means-tested benefits for jobseekers (on the grounds that those benefits

---

[127] Case C-67/14 *Alimanovic*, Summary of the request for a preliminary ruling pursuant to Art 98(1) of the Rules of Procedure of the Court of Justice, para 21. I am grateful to Jason Coppel QC for sharing this with me.

serve to protect their dignity), we can see a strong socio-economic class dynamic at work.

To exclude proportionality, and the possibility of considering real links or integration, from benefit decision-making, is to deny the direct effect of the primary law right to equal treatment (contrary to *Baumbast*), and to strip the status of Union citizen of legal effect. The next chapter will explore the importance of proportionality, highlighting the problems that arise if we treat the conditions in secondary law as constitutive of routes to equal treatment. Such an approach can lead to painful manifestations of social injustice, negating important factors like integration through substantial periods of residence, absence of links with other countries, family ties, children who have been born in a host state and never lived anywhere else, considerable past economic activity, or continued economic activity that falls below the Member State's definition of work.[128] Disregarding these factors creates disadvantages and exacerbates destitution along the lines of class and gender, and penalising those who have, or are, children.

---

[128] See ch 6.

# 4

# *Discounting Proportionality and Exacerbating Disadvantage*

## I. INTRODUCTION

THE INADEQUACY OF market citizenship to deliver social justice might be mitigated by proportionality. A requirement that limitations on equal treatment be applied proportionately confirms, albeit in a rather minimal way, the underlying primacy of the equal treatment principle. Such a requirement was never very onerous, or particularly well respected, within first-tier decision-making in the UK. But it did offer an avenue to pursue in appeals, effectively arguing that claimants might be disproportionately disadvantaged by lacunae in the Residence Directive. The shift away from proportionality within the ECJ and UK judiciary is closing off lacuna-claims, and blocking considerations of circumstances, in which a strict application of the Directive would result in a disproportionate blow to social justice. The shift elevates the conditions of the Directive into the position of constitute elements of the basic right to equal treatment, so that those not meeting those conditions are simply ineligible for non-discrimination protections.

Those people most acutely affected by this conception of rights are those who most frequently fall within the ambit of social justice concerns: children, lone parents, victims of abuse, carers and people on low pay/in low security jobs. This chapter considers the precarious position of unmarried partners within the free movement framework, drawing upon *Garcia Nieto*[1] and *EU Rights Project* findings. It then highlights the disappearance of proportionality from the ECJ's case law, focusing on the many problems with the ECJ's approval of the UK's right to reside test, applied to family benefits in *Commission v UK*,[2] in particular noting the invisibility of children in the law upon children's rights as EU citizens. This invisibility has consequences upon the coherence of the law, as shown in a study of the 'patchy' status that emerges from *Teixeira*[3] and *Zambrano*,[4] and it has

---

[1] Case C-299/14 *Vestische Arbeit Jobcenter Kreis Recklinghausen v Jovanna García-Nieto and Others* EU:C:2016:114.

[2] Case C-308/14 *Commission v United Kingdom* EU:C:2016:436.

[3] Case C-480/08 *Maria Teixeira v London Borough of Lambeth and Secretary of State for the Home Department* EU:C:2009:642.

[4] Case C-34/09 *Gerardo Ruiz Zambrano v Office National de L'Emploi (ONEm)* EU:C:2011:124.

consequences for the moral basis of the law. A disregard for vulnerable subjects, combined with a diminished commitment to proportionality, severely undermines the capacity of market citizenship to uphold basic principles of social justice.

## II. THE RISKS FOR UNMARRIED PARTNERS

Unmarried partners suffer a particular disadvantage if proportionality is disregarded. Several *EU Rights Project* case studies show that EU national lone parents have been placed at greater risk of destitution, following shifts in EU and domestic law in the UK. If a lone parent is married to the estranged parent, the lone parent and her children may continue to derive a right to reside from the continuing marriage to a migrant worker, notwithstanding the separation, following *Diatta*.[5] But where the couple have not been married or obtained a civil partnership, the lone parent family is placed in immediate jeopardy on separation. This means that while they are part of the migrant worker's household, they are living in a precarious situation, placing worrying pressure upon victims of domestic abuse. Such automatic exclusion from a right to reside on separation is all the more concerning since it can have a serious, deleterious impact upon the children of unmarried partners, who may also be the children of the workers concerned. They will suffer significantly different treatment based on whether their parents were married/civil partnered, a factor over which they have little control, and which does not adequately or logically explain the difference in treatment.[6] One very brief case summary submitted to the project captures in three notes the trap this creates in situations of domestic violence: 'Client worked for four years. Domestic violence situation, including broken ribs. No benefits apart from jobseeker's allowance for three months, then nothing'.[7]

Even while living together, it seems that EU law might treat unmarried partners as less deserving than married/civil partnered ones. In the case of *Garcia Nieto*, the Court reviewed a claim for unemployment benefits from Mr Peña Cuevas and his son, within the first three months of his arrival in the host state (Germany). The Court basically applied its reasoning in *Alimanovic*,[8] that jobseekers were not entitled to social assistance, and suggested that this should apply to the claimant in the instant case, because he fell squarely within the derogation of Article 24(2) of Directive 2004/38. Again, the need for the derogation to be applied proportionately, and the possibility of requiring an individual assessment of circumstances, were dismissed, citing the *Alimanovic* finding that the Directive already does the work of dealing with proportionality and suggesting that this must apply a fortiori to this case.[9]

---

[5] Case 267/83 *Aissatou Diatta v Land Berlin* EU:C:1985:67.
[6] They will only get protection from *Teixeira* (above fn3) if they are in school, see below.
[7] Evidence submitted, not referred for first or second-tier advice.
[8] Case C-67/14 *Jobcenter Berlin Neukölln v Nazifa Alimanovic and Others* EU:C:2015:597.
[9] *Garcia Nieto*, above n 1, 48.

The reasoning serves to highlight the flawed logic of *Alimanovic*. The motivation of the Court appears to be, at least in part, to find that EU nationals who have worked must be in some way more deserving than those who have not. Thus, if we do not need a proportionality assessment for the former, then that finding should apply a fortiori to the latter. But the Court did not say in *Alimanovic* that all of the conditions of the Directive should be immune to proportionality review. It made a deeply problematic, but specific claim: that the restrictions on retention of worker status were automatically proportionate because they established a gradual system of entitlement. As noted in chapter two, this exaggerates the degree to which the provisions on retention of worker status do in fact establish a 'gradual' system, and the degree to which various factors are taken into account. But this is somewhat irrelevant, because the claimants in *Garcia Nieto* did not fall within the retention provisions (Article 7(3)). They were deemed to fall within Article 24(2). It is not credible to extrapolate from *Alimanovic* that, because some provisions which provide a (highly limited) degree of gradated entitlement escape proportionality review, so should other restrictions in the Directive that provide no kind of gradation at all. This seems to be adjudication-by-hunch about the deservingness of claimants, and a perception that because Article 7(3) deals with those who have worked, those who fall outside of it because of not having worked should be *less* entitled to a proportionality review. Article 24(2) provides a non-gradated derogation from a primary law based right to equal treatment. As such, it is necessary to ensure that it is interpreted narrowly[10] and applied proportionately, or at least not applied so as to exclude a proportionality review reliant upon primary law (as suggested by the Advocate General, who argued that even if Article 24(2) did not preclude the German rules at issue, automatic exclusion did conflict with Article 45 TFEU).[11] Advocate General Wathelet, in keeping with the Opinion he delivered in *Alimanovic*, maintained that in light of a substantial and consistent body of case law, proportionality should not be disregarded, and that the Directive did not permit automatic exclusions from equal treatment without some regard to personal circumstances. In particular, he invoked the citizenship-based real-link case law, stating that determining eligibility according to a single condition not necessarily representative of the claimant's real links with the state was disproportionate because it 'goes beyond what is necessary in order to attain the aim pursued'.[12] National authorities should, he claimed, take account of:

> Matters that can be inferred from family circumstances (such as the children's education or close ties, in particular of a personal nature, created by the claimant with the host Member State) or the fact that the person concerned has, for a reasonable period, in fact genuinely sought work are factors capable of demonstrating the existence of such a link with the host Member State.[13]

---

[10] Case C-75/11 *European Commission v Republic of Austria* EU:C:2012:605, 54.
[11] Case C-299/14 *Vestische Arbeit Jobcenter Kreis Recklinghausen v Jovanna García-Nieto and Others*, Opinion of AG Wathelet, EU:C:2015:366, 88.
[12] ibid, 85.
[13] ibid, 89.

Such a review need not be too onerous, and it may well be straightforward for the domestic court to find the proposed exclusion proportionate in most cases dealing with the first three months of residence. But allowing for the mere possibility of a proportionality plea at appeal stage is important for those cases that demand a degree of financial solidarity.

The Court nevertheless excused the provisions of Directive 2004/38 from a proportionality review without regard to the worker status of the claimant's partner. The Court accepted that Mrs Garcia Nieto was in work, earning a net wage of €600 per month, and paying social security contributions.[14] As a worker, she had a Directive 2004/38-based right to reside, under Article 7(1)(a), and would have been able to confer an equivalent right upon her family members under Article 7(1)(d). A family member is defined as a spouse, registered partner, direct descendant under 21 (or 'dependant'), and dependent direct relative, including that of the spouse or registered partner.[15] Family members residing on the basis of the Directive are not then subject to the exclusion in Article 24(2), according to recital (21), which states that the derogation from equal treatment for the first three months applies 'to Union citizens other than those who are workers or self-employed persons or who retain that status or their family members'.[16]

Mr Peña Cuevas was an unmarried partner, and the Court did not consider the possible 'family member' avenue at all. But Article 3 requires Member States to 'facilitate entry and residence for' other family members, including 'the partner with whom the Union citizen has a durable relationship, duly attested'. Some exploration of what this duty entails would have been welcome. It may not mean an automatic residence right, but we need to know what it does mean: it might indicate the possibility of a discretionary residence right. At the least, it would suggest that automatic exclusions based on Article 24(2) should not be waved through, but made subject to a proportionality assessment. Any consideration of the interaction between Article 3 and Article 24(2), and in light of Article 45 TFEU as well as Article 18 TFEU (since we are dealing with the freedoms of Mrs Garcia Nieto, the worker), would suggest that exclusions should not be automatic. We should be asking whether the interference with equal treatment of workers on the grounds of nationality is potentially disproportionate since it is based solely on the marital status of the worker and her partner.

*Garcia Nieto* highlights the fact that unmarried partners living with migrant workers have fewer rights than spouses. The *EU Rights Project* cases showed very significant relative disadvantage for unmarried partners on separation. While cohabiting, an unmarried partner has a right to reside in UK law as an 'extended

---

[14]  *Garcia Nieto*, judgment, above n 1, 28.

[15]  Art 2(2), Directive 2004/38/EC of the European Parliament and of the Council of 29 April 2004 on the right of citizens of the Union and their family members to move and reside freely within the territory of the Member States [2004] OJ L158/77.

[16]  Recital (21), Directive 2004/38, [2004] OJ L158/84.

family member'.[17] But on separation, they cannot derive any support from *Diatta*, which dealt with separating married partners, and so face a risk of destitution, as demonstrated by Elena in this first case study:

---

**Case Study: Elena—The Difference Marriage Makes**

Elena had lived in the UK for over eight years, and was working, with brief periods of unemployment, for seven. She was the primary carer of a young child under two. She had separated from an abusive husband and was trying to find accommodation. We went through a protracted process of claiming income support,[18] which eventually resulted in an initial refusal, on the grounds of not having a right to reside. It turned out that her marital status had been recorded as 'separated', without noting that she was in fact still married to a migrant worker. Once this point was made, the second-tier decision-maker (the Department for Work and Pensions' EU team) accepted that, assuming she could adduce proof of the marriage and of her husband's work, she would automatically still have a right to reside, and so would her child.

---

Aside from the administrative hurdles encountered, Elena's situation, legally speaking, was dramatically transformed as a result of this factor. Other clients in materially similar situations faced a much greater struggle to establish a right to reside where they had not been married to the fathers of their children, and the children were not yet in school. While it may be considered legitimate to not require the automatic equal treatment of unmarried partners, it is difficult to justify their automatic *unequal* treatment, without the possibility of a proportionality review. Such an approach impacts generally upon unmarried couples, but also has a disproportionate impact upon people in same-sex unions who are not afforded the opportunity to marry or register a partnership in a number of EU countries. Registered/civil partnerships do not exist in Bulgaria, Latvia, Lithuania, Poland, Romania and Slovakia,[19] and Italy has only very recently recognised same-sex partnerships.[20]

It might have been possible to confine the *Alimanovic/Garcia Nieto* dismissal of proportionality to those dealing with benefits defined as social assistance for the purposes of the Directive. But the Court has instead followed a more sweeping course, jettisoning proportionality and, with it, the precepts of Union citizenship in *Commission v UK*.

---

[17] reg 8(5) of the Immigration (European Economic Area) Regulations 2016, combined with reg 7(3).

[18] See ch 8 for more on the vicissitudes of the claim.

[19] See European Parliament, 'The Rights of LGBTI People in the European Union', *Briefing*, May 2015. Available at: www.europarl.europa.eu/EPRS/EPRS-Briefing-557011-Rights-LGBTI-people-EU-FINAL.pdf.

[20] Regulation of civil unions between same-sex and discipline of cohabitation (16G00082) (Gazzetta Ufficiale General Series 118 of 21 May 2016) Law 20 May 2016, n 76. Available at: www.gazzettaufficiale.it/eli/id/2016/05/21/16G00082/sg.

### III. THE UK RIGHT TO RESIDE TEST: DIRECT DISCRIMINATION
### AND LAW-AS-LISTS OVER LAW-AS-JUSTICE

The UK right to reside test is a condition of eligibility for several benefits. It is not a residence condition (that is, it is *not* a condition that an applicant be resident or have been resident), though it is a condition as to legal status. UK nationals automatically have a right to reside, whilst EU nationals have to demonstrate that they are exercising a right to reside conferred by Directive 2004/38.[21] This means being a worker or self-employed person, or retaining that status, or being the family member of someone with that status, or being a student, or being self-sufficient. Typically, this means being a worker or self-employed person, or their family member. The benefit eligibility of students in general, and EU national students in particular, is limited and EU national students must in any case declare sufficient resources (and have private health insurance). The approach to self-sufficiency in the UK means that it is never a route to eligibility for benefits. While the Court in *Brey*[22] stated that it was not open to national authorities to automatically conclude that a claimant was not self-sufficient because of their having made a claim for social assistance, and that they should look at individual circumstances, the UK has persisted in taking a different approach whereby a claim for social assistance is deemed to disprove self-sufficiency and so disentitle a potential claimant from benefits. According to Judge Ward in the Upper Tribunal case of *VP*,[23] this is because the finding in *Brey* was based on a system in which a right to reside based on self-sufficiency had to be established at the outset to get a residence card. It was only in such systems, the judge suggested, that a subsequent decision that someone did not have sufficient resources had to be proportionate. Since the UK did not have a residence card system, the first opportunity that the authorities might have to ascertain sufficient resources might be at the point someone claimed a benefit, and so it was open to them to deem that the claim alone meant that the resources were not sufficient.[24] That is the approach I encountered in the *EU Rights Project*.

---

**Case Study: Irina**[25]

Irina was refused income support after six-and-a-half years of working, punctuated by two short breaks in which she should have retained worker status. The Secretary of State for Work and Pensions submitted a response to her appeal that listed a number of possible rights to reside and gave reasons why he considered Irina ineligible for each. These included: '[Irina] has made a claim to benefit and therefore cannot be considered to be self-sufficient'.[26]

---

[21] P Larkin, 'Migrants, Social Security, and the "Right to Reside": A Licence to Discriminate?' (2007) 14 *Journal of Social Security Law* 2, 61.
[22] Case C-140/12 *Pensionsversicherungsanstalt v Peter Brey* EU:C:2013:565.
[23] *VP v Secretary for Work and Pensions (JSA)* [2014] UKUT 32 (AAC), 62.
[24] ibid, 79.
[25] More details of the case in ch 6.
[26] SSWP Response to appeal, quoted in field notes.

In short, decision-makers treat *Brey* as not applying to the UK. Judge Ward has since stressed that in the rare situations in which a claimant can be in a *Brey*-like situation in the UK (having effectively had their resources assessed and approved at a prior point) then the *Brey* proportionality duty does apply. In *AMS v SSWP*,[27] the Secretary of State for Work and Pensions had conceded that the claimant had in the past had sufficient resources and comprehensive sickness insurance. That concession, according to the judge, put her in the position of *Brey*, and 'obviate[d] any need to explore various other difficult questions about what sufficiency of resources actually entails'.[28] He noted that the restrictive post-*Brey* ECJ case law ('even *Dano*'),[29] did not explicitly overrule *Brey* or suggest no individual examination of circumstances was required. But he stood by the thrust of *VP*, so that most UK cases will still fall outside the *Brey* remit, unless in receipt of an unusual concession on the part of the Secretary of State. The *AMS* finding is nevertheless a generous interpretation of ECJ case law, given that the ECJ has proceeded to outline a host of situations in which the *Brey* duty of proportionality does *not* apply, which contributes to status gaps, and makes permanent residence all the more elusive.

One route to a right to reside is to become a permanent resident, but the problem for many long-term residents is that, unless they are in permanent, full-time work continuously for over five years, the chances are that the 'lawful residence' clock will keep getting re-started. We are often dealing with people who have been resident for considerably longer than five years, but whose work history has been punctuated with unemployment not duly registered, with periods of childcare, with periods of part-time work that are now more likely to be determined not to be work at all, and each event restarts the clock. The current law-as-lists approach, rather than law-as-justice, means that these people simply do not fit into one of the listed categories and so are automatically disentitled. They may have lived most or all of their lives in the host state, perhaps having been born there, but who, as children, could not themselves clock up the requisite years of work. State-recognised permanent residence seems out of reach for many long-term residents, and without factoring proportionality into decision-making, a large aggregate amount of work, long periods of social integration, and strong connections with the host state may all count for little, if anything, as decision-makers rely upon the strict, exclusionary and exhaustive list of types of right to reside that any EU national must be exercising at any one time. This can lead to manifestly absurd results:

**Case Study: Mariella—Over 55 Years in the UK**

Mariella, an EU national from Belgium, was in her late eighties. Her case was referred to me for second-tier advice. She had been living in the UK for over 55 years. She had

---

[27] *AMS v SSWP (PC)* [2017] UKUT 48 (AAC).
[28] ibid, 59.
[29] ibid, 38.

become ill and had applied for housing benefit, but this was turned down; the adviser understood that the local authority had deemed her not to have a right to reside. Her adviser was concerned about her not being able to fit into any category, since she did not have private health insurance to show self-sufficiency; she did not have any EU national family members in the UK; and the work she had done for decades had been reimbursed mostly in the form of food, shelter, a holiday allowance and other small amounts of money. We put together a request for a reconsideration based on: (a) a claim to permanent residence through her decades of work; (b) in the alternative, permanent residence based on her de facto self-sufficiency, and the need to interpret the sickness insurance criterion proportionately; and (c) the need to interpret the permanent residence provisions in a way commensurate with her Article 8 ECHR and Article 7 CFREU rights to a private life.

It felt quite absurd trying to fit Mariella into specific categories to show that she should have a right to reside. It seemed that her extremely lengthy history of lawful, law-abiding residence in the UK should count for something in itself. In several cases, the process of fitting clients into the given right to reside categories felt strange and artificial, because what we really wanted was for the compelling social justice components of their case to hold sway:

**Case Study: Elsa—14 Years in UK**

Elsa had been resident in the UK for over 14 years, mostly working. She had a long and complicated work history, punctuated by short periods of work-seeking and childcare. She had two school-aged children, both born in the UK, one of whom was a British citizen. Her homelessness application was refused, in a decision that featured several errors of law. The decision-maker did not understand the key cases applicable and failed to apply the basic domestic regulations.

At heart, the appeal I helped with was a correction of the original decision, and reassertion of Elsa's *Teixeira*[30] claim. But the most compelling factors seemed to be those that did not count for anything: her long history of lawful residence, the social integration of her children, and her substantial amounts of work done over the years. Adhering to a specific list of rights to reside without incorporating proportionality into the decision-making process means that a great many factors—including work and residence history—do not get taken into account. The necessary ingredients for reaching socially just decisions are omitted. While some of these decisions may be reversed through appeal, putting off the consideration of fairness to the appeal stage creates a significant obstacle to social justice, since many cases will not be appealed.

---

[30] *Teixeira* judgment, above n 3.

Another group of clients who fell through the gaps in the Directive were EU nationals who came to the UK as workers, and then married and became the spouses of workers, but of *British* workers rather than of workers from elsewhere in the EU. In some cases, they scaled down or stopped work, as in the case of Victoria below, and so in the event of the death of, or separation from, the British partner, were left without a right to reside, in spite of possibly long periods of residence:

---

**Case Study: Victoria**

Victoria, an EU national, had been resident in the UK for over 25 years. She had some work history a long time ago, but got married a few years after coming to the UK and had then been a housewife, to her British husband, and had done some unpaid supporting work for his business and provided elder family care. Her husband had recently died, and she needed financial support, but was worried that she would not be entitled to anything. She was too young for a bereavement allowance (for which you have to be between 45 and state pension age), so was looking at 'standard' means tested benefits, for which she needed to demonstrate a right to reside as a basis of claim.

---

Directive 2004/38 provides for a continuing right to reside for the spouse of a deceased migrant worker but, of course, Victoria's husband had not been a migrant worker. She would also have accrued permanent residence rights as the family member of a migrant worker had her husband been an EU national. In essence, we are left with a requirement for EU nationals to be (or to be family members of EU nationals who are) in work or self-employment. This is a requirement only placed upon EU nationals, not upon UK nationals. In this, it echoes the condition in *Grzelczyk*[31] placed upon EU nationals to fit within the scope of Regulation 1612/68 (that is, to be a worker) but which was not placed upon Belgian nationals. That condition was deemed to give rise to discrimination on the 'sole' grounds of nationality. The Commission received several complaints about the right to reside test and initiated infringement proceedings. Following the ECJ's findings in *Brey* onwards, that special non-contributory benefits could lawfully be subject to right to reside tests, the Commission altered its focus to litigate solely on the matter of child benefit and child tax credit (family benefits under Regulation 883/2004)[32] so considered social security, not special non-contributory benefits, and so not construed as social assistance for the purposes of Directive 2004/38.

---

[31] Case C-184/99 *Rudy Grzelczyk v Centre public d'aide sociale d'Ottignies-Louvain-la-Neuve* EU:C:2001:458.

[32] Regulation (EC) No 883/2004 of the European Parliament and of the Council of 29 April 2004 on the coordination of social security systems OJ [2004] L 200/1.

## A.   Putting the UK's Right to Reside Test to the Test: *Commission v UK*

*Commission v UK* was the Court's chance to grapple with the tricky question of the relationship between right to reside tests and the prohibition of direct discrimination on the grounds of nationality, as well as the thorny question of justifying direct discrimination. Indeed, the Commission explicitly complained of *direct* discrimination.[33] But the Court ducked the question, stating that 'a host Member State which, for the purpose of granting social benefits, such as the social benefits at issue, requires a national of another Member State to be residing in its territory lawfully commits indirect discrimination'.[34] This is a non-sequitur. The right to reside test is not a requirement 'to be residing in' the UK's territory. It is a condition that EU nationals have a specific legal status. Nevertheless, the Court ploughs on from that starting point to find that the condition is indirectly discriminatory because '*such a residence condition* is more easily satisfied by United Kingdom nationals, who more often than not are habitually resident in the United Kingdom, than by nationals of other Member States, whose residence, by contrast, is generally in a Member State other than the United Kingdom'.[35] It is worth spelling this out again: it is not a residence condition. It is nothing to do with where a claimant is resident (that is part of the habitual residence test). It is entirely about two questions: (1) is the claimant a UK national?; and, if not, (2) are they a worker/self-employed person?

It is not a condition that is 'more easily satisfied' or 'more often than not' satisfied by UK nationals: it is always and automatically satisfied by UK nationals, and so they are excused from meeting the economic activity condition. Treating the test as a residence condition is inaccurate and leads to an inadequate characterisation as indirect discrimination. A brief thought experiment shows why this is nonsense.[36] If a Member State announced that all EU national women were subject to a condition of economic activity for entitlement to benefits, but that EU national men would automatically have a right to reside, we could not characterise that as 'indirect' sex discrimination by arguing that it was a 'residence condition', or because men were 'more likely' to have a right to reside. Now, it may be argued that nationality is a different kind of category than sex, and that greater differences should be permitted, but as a matter of construction, the analogy shows that we are dealing with *direct* discrimination. The question of whether that should be lawful, or capable of justification, is secondary to identifying the type of discrimination at issue. It is discrimination on the sole grounds of nationality, and the category of people automatically receiving a right to reside, and the category of people excluded from an automatic right to reside, coincide exactly with the

---

[33] *Commission v UK* judgment, above n 2, 33. See C O'Brien, 'The ECJ Sacrifices EU Citizenship in Vain: *Commission v United Kingdom*' (2017) 54 *CML Rev* 1, 209.

[34] ibid, 76.

[35] ibid, 78.

[36] As suggested in O'Brien (2017) above n 33, 227.

national/non-national distinction, to adopt Advocate General Sharpston's defi-nition of direct discrimination in *Bressol*.[37] Yet the Court assumed an indirect discrimination framework, and did so without responding to the Commission's direct discrimination complaint.[38]

Having acknowledged that the condition is discriminatory, albeit claiming it to be indirectly discriminatory, the Court turned to the question of justifica-tion. Here, the Court could not simply follow the approach of invoking a spe-cific equal treatment derogation within Directive 2004/38. Here, the benefit did not fall within the ambit of the Directive's exceptions. Even so, the Court sought to import the general objective of restriction from the Directive into Regulation 883/2004. The Court recognised that indirect discrimination must be 'appropriate for securing the attainment of a legitimate objective and cannot go beyond what is necessary to attain that objective'.[39] Given that the narrative was shunted into the realm of indirect discrimination, the question of whether direct discrimina-tion can be justified—especially in the absence of a specific derogation—remains unanswered.

At this point, the Court conducted a rather astonishing judicial sleight of hand, even more striking than switching the 'right to reside' for a residence condition. Here, having identified that the right to reside condition was indirectly discrimina-tory, it then looked not at whether the condition was justified, but at whether the *checks* conducted to verify the condition were met and were justified, pointing out the requirement in Article 14(2) of Directive 2004/38 that checks on compliance with the Directive should not be systematic,[40] so implying that if the checks were not systematic, the condition would be justified. But that is a different question. Examining the procedural question of how checks are administered presupposes the legitimacy of the substantive condition that is being checked. Let us return to our thought experiment, and the imaginary Member State whose right to reside condition states that EU national women should be economically active, while EU national men automatically have a right to reside. Following the Court's logic in *Commission v UK*, the offending state would have to justify the procedures by which it checked whether claimants were women. It may be found that allowing self-declaration would be proportionate (as was the process of 'providing a set of data',[41] in *Commission v UK*), but that requiring a birth certificate or medical evi-dence in each case would be disproportionate, since the key principle was to avoid systematic verification. But this would still leave a patently discriminatory condi-tion intact: it is the condition, not the manner of checks for compliance with the condition, that is the main problem, and it is the condition that must be justified.

---

[37] Case C-73/08 *Nicolas Bressol and Others and Céline Chaverot and Others v Gouvernement de la Communauté française* Opinion of AG Sharpston EU:C:2009:396.
[38] The UK had argued that the Commission's complaint was inadmissible, but the Court did not even respond to that, see above n 2, 40.
[39] Above n 2, 79.
[40] ibid, 82.
[41] ibid, 83.

In skipping over the question of justification for the right to reside condition, the Court presumes that condition's lawfulness, and so it escapes proportionality scrutiny. The Commission had complained that the right to reside test created blanket exclusions regardless of circumstances, pointing out that it was an 'automatic mechanism that systematically and ineluctably bars claimants who do not satisfy it from being paid benefits, regardless of their personal situation and of the extent to which they have paid tax and social security contributions in the United Kingdom'.[42] The Court simply did not address this, and ignored the issue of automatic exclusion altogether, finding instead, that in light of the desire to protect public finances, it was incumbent on the Commission to demonstrate that the Court decided that the checks were disproportionate, were not appropriate, or went beyond what was necessary. This is a problematic reversal of the burden of proof—not least since (as Judge Ward noted in *AMS*)[43] the House of Lords had acknowledged in the UK in *Kerr v Department for Social Development*, the government is best placed to access information about the collective impacts of making awards, so to provide evidence going towards disproportionality.[44]

This denies Union citizens the right to a proportionality review when it comes to restrictions upon equal treatment, even in cases dealing with social security rather than social assistance. This reinforces the approach that only those fitting exactly within the categories provided for, and meeting the conditions of, Directive 2004/38 are entitled to equal treatment—even as regards matters that fall outside of that Directive's limitations. The idea of a primary law right of Union citizens to equal treatment seems to have dissolved, along with the one substantive equality right attaching to EU citizenship, a right to a proportionality assessment.

Evading a proportionality assessment had particular implications for the citizens whose rights were most at stake in *Commission v UK*—children. Children are themselves not expected to be economic actors, and so automatically fall outside any category of Directive 2004/38, other than that of family member. Their rights of residence are thus dependent upon those of their parents, which if lost means that children, if not yet of school age,[45] will by default fall through the gaps of EU law protection. But they have no control over their parents' migratory, employment, and relationship choices or misfortunes. Their right to reside is not something for which children can be held personally culpable. In some ways, children are a test of the true credentials of EU citizenship as a form of 'citizenship' rather than as a glorified economic contingency. The indications so far are not promising: children are barely considered in decisions directly about their welfare, and their exclusion and potential destitution are apparently collateral damage in pursuit of behaviour-driven, activation-focused policies directed at their parents and endorsed by the Court.

---

[42]  ibid, 47.
[43]  *AMS* judgment, above n 27.
[44]  *Kerr v Department for Social Development* [2004] UKHL 23, [2004] 1 WLR 1372.
[45]  If they are in school, they might be able to rely on *Teixeira*, above n 3.

## IV. CHILDREN AND PROPORTIONALITY

I'd always assumed that people who were brought here as children might be a strong case, but those haven't so far seemed to succeed.[46]

Eroding the proportionality principle renders the EU citizenship of children meaningless. A citizenship whose core right is access to a free movement framework grounded in economic activity, and which does not afford children personal independent rights, always had limited claims to being a 'citizenship' at all. But a residual, negative right not to be deprived of equal treatment rights where it would be disproportionate, might afford children some basic protection as EU citizens. A couple of UK cases show how easily this weak layer of citizenship has been peeled off and cast aside, under the influence of the ECJ.

### A. Dismissing Proportionality, Rewriting *Baumbast* and Disregarding Children's EU Citizenship: UK Courts

In the joined cases *Mirga and Samin*,[47] the UK Supreme Court drew explicitly upon *Dano*[48] and *Alimanovic* to find that 'a Union citizen can claim equal treatment with nationals of a country, at least in relation to social assistance, only if he or she can satisfy the conditions for lawful residence in that country'.[49] Ms Mirga's parents brought her to the UK from Poland at the age of 10. Four years later they were refused asylum and returned to Poland. Two years after that, in 2004, they returned, following the accession of Poland to the EU. Her mother died four months after their arrival and, some months after that, her father gave up work due to depression. When she finished her education she embarked on registered work, within the meaning of the UK transitional rules, but this finished after eight months. She later did some further months of unregistered work, then claimed income support on the grounds of pregnancy. She was found not to have a right to reside. The Supreme Court upheld this decision. In doing so, the Court adopted a narrow view of *Baumbast*,[50] in that proportionality only helps those who fall short of the stipulated legal requirements 'in one very small respect'.[51] Lord Neuberger, who delivered the judgment with which the other Supreme Court judges agreed, stated that 'Mr Baumbast's case was predicated on the fact that he did not need any assistance from the state'.[52] This is startling, because the ECJ was vehement in disputing that very same assertion from UK authorities in *Teixeira*: 'it cannot be

---

[46] From expert interview 1.
[47] *Mirga and Samin v Secretary of State for Work and Pensions and Anor* [2016] UKSC 1.
[48] Case C-333/13 *Elisabeta Dano and Florin Dano v Jobcenter Leipzig* EU:C:2014:2358.
[49] Above n 47, 54.
[50] Case C-413/99 *Baumbast and R v Secretary of State for the Home Department* EU:C:2002:493.
[51] Above n 47, 62.
[52] ibid.

argued on the basis of that judgment [*Baumbast*] that the granting of the right of residence at issue is conditional on self-sufficiency, *as the Court did not base its reasoning even implicitly on such a condition*'.[53] Counsel for Ms Mirga invoked the *Brey* requirement for a proportionality assessment. Lord Neuberger found that *Dano* and *Alimanovic* had extinguished this requirement. The *Alimanovic* statement that 'no such individual assessment is necessary in circumstances such as those in issue in this case', which might possibly have been limited to jobseekers, or even just to long-term jobseekers, or those seeking to retain worker status, has been found to mean, broadly and simply, that no such individual assessment is necessary where someone does not fit into the categories of Directive 2004/38. Lord Neuberger noted the *Alimanovic* finding that Article 7 discharged the requirement of proportionality and added: 'in my view, this makes good sense: it seems unrealistic to require "an individual examination of each particular case"'.[54]

He made clear that he considered that proportionality could not help those who fell outside of the given categories in Directive 2004/38, and that a proportionality assessment would be an undue burden in respect of such claimants. Requiring such an assessment would 'severely undermine the whole thrust and purpose of the 2004 Directive … save perhaps in extreme circumstances'. A requirement of proportionality review in every equal treatment case would 'place a substantial burden on a host member state'.[55] Lord Neuberger further made clear his doubt about whether proportionality could help even in wholly exceptional circumstances, stating '*even if* there is a category of exceptional cases where proportionality could come into play, I do not consider that either Ms Mirga or Mr Samin could possibly satisfy it',[56] with the phrase 'even if' implying that it might never be used at all, and if so, only in the rarest of cases. This approach has serious ramifications for EU citizenship since Directive 2004/38 is being treated as an exhaustive list of possible rights to reside. It has particularly swingeing effects upon children, who have no personal rights to reside within Directive 2004/38.

A UK Upper Tribunal judgment reveals how strict adherence to the Directive, combined with an economised, market citizenship, has the effect of negating a lifetime's worth of social integration. In *Sequeira-Batalha*,[57] a child who was born in the UK, and brought up in the UK, lived all of her life in the UK and never left for any significant period of time, and who was abandoned by her mother at the age of 16 and applied for income support at the age of 17, was refused the benefit and found not to have a right to reside. The First-tier Tribunal accepted that she did not fit within the categories of a right to reside in Directive 2004/38, but found that her situation revealed a gap in the Directive, where proportionality should step in and allow a right to reside. Judge Jacobs in the Upper Tribunal overturned

---

[53]    *Teixeira* judgment, above n 3, 67.
[54]    Above n 47, 68.
[55]    Ibid, 69.
[56]    Ibid, 70.
[57]    *Secretary of State for Work and Pensions v Sequeira-Batalha* [2016] UKUT 511 (AAC).

this decision and remade it upholding the decision-maker's refusal. In a striking passage, he argued that the claimant's case was 'not as strong as Ms Mirga's'. This is because Ms Mirga had previously done some work (eight months of registered work and approximately three months of unregistered work), whereas the claimant in *Sequeira-Batalha* had never worked. Thus her claim was seen as weaker, because it conformed even less than that in *Mirga* to the prescribed categories in Directive 2004/38. But on a wider view of proportionality, her claim is compelling. She had not worked because she was a child, and she had lived all of 17 years in the UK, having been born in the UK, while Ms Mirga had at the point of claim lived the majority of her life in Poland. The Department for Work and Pensions (DWP) takes the position that the best option for those EEA migrants who do not have a right to reside, and 'who lack savings or support networks and who are at real risk of ending up destitute *is to return home*'.[58] But it would be nonsensical to suggest that Ms Sequeira-Batalha had a home outside of the UK to go back to—you cannot 'go back' to somewhere you have never lived. She was still legally a child at the point of claim, and her parents were resident outside of the EU (in Angola). All of her lived experience, all of her social integration, had taken place in the UK. Yet while the First-tier Tribunal viewed this as a gap in the Directive, the Upper Tribunal judge asserted that it was a deliberate gap, through which the claimant should fall: 'the absence of a category allowing more easy access to a right to reside is not an omission that the courts should fill. Rather the absence is an indication of the scope of the policy'.[59]

On this view, the Court's role is simply to implement the policy-maker's intention, rather than assess the legitimacy of that policy. But it is difficult to justify a policy that systematically excludes children from relying upon EU citizenship: it would be ludicrous to describe children as 'benefit tourists' on the grounds that they do not work. The claimant in this case had no control over where she had been born or brought up, or over her state of need arising from parental abandonment. She could not have been expected in her childhood years to clock up five years of work. And she had no control over her parent's migratory, employment or relationship choices, which may have conferred some derived status. Curiously, the Upper Tribunal judgment does not engage even briefly with the status-history of her parents, so does not consider whether she might yet have some derived status, or even have acquired permanent residence through them. But regardless, a system that makes the rights of someone in this position entirely contingent upon the status-accidents of their parents, that views a lifetime's worth of residence as less compelling than 11 months of work, and that sticks rigidly to specific legal categories, so that EU citizenship adds nothing to the rights or status of children

---

[58] DWP, *Response to the Report by the Social Security Advisory Committee: he Housing Benefit (Habitual Residence) Amendment Regulations 2014 (SI 2014 No 539)* (2014), 4, para 7. Available at: www.gov.uk/government/uploads/system/uploads/attachment_data/file/376103/PRINT-HB-Habitual-Residence-Amendment-Regs-2014-SSAC-report.pdf, emphasis added.

[59] ibid, 12.

who do not have parents in any EU state, and who do not have a 'home' in a state other than that of residence, is anything but proportionate or humane. Indeed, it reveals the social justice chasm at the heart of EU free movement law.

## B. The Case for Recognising Children's Rights in EU Law

There is a sound legal case for treating children as more relevant beings in Union law.[60] Insofar as we can view Union citizenship as having a social dimension, and some concern with social integration (at least suggested by the old 'real link' and 'financial solidarity' case law, and in the recitals and provisions on expulsion in Directive 2004/38), there are many ways in which children may show stronger signs of integration than their parents. They may have been born in the host state, never have left, and have few, if any, links with their state of nationality. Here we might call upon Advocate General Wathelet's discussion of the 'construction' of citizenship in *NA*, in which case the German national children had no connection with Germany 'in whose territory they have never lived and whose language they do not speak. Having been born and gone to school in the United Kingdom, it is in that Member State that they have *constructed* their citizenship'.[61] In that case, the Court did not assess rights attaching to the children's citizenship: they could either attain rights dependent upon their EU national parents' work, through Regulation 1612/68, following *Teixeira* (providing conditions, for example, of being school age were met), or they might have an entitlement to reside in their own right (if they had sufficient resources). The Court noted the primary law right to move and reside in Article 21 TFEU and noted that the limitations and conditions referred to therein 'are those laid down in Article 7(1) of Directive 2004/38'. Article 21 TFEU was thus interpreted exclusively through the Directive and the children would have to show that they satisfied the conditions of Article 7(1) 'either themselves or through their mother'[62] to claim their own right to reside.

As with employment and migration status, children themselves are unlikely to command private resources (nor is the sufficiency of those resources something that they can control), and when we consider the extra condition, unmentioned in that case, that to have sufficient resources a citizen must have comprehensive sickness insurance cover in the host state,[63] the child's right to reside becomes a matter even further out of the child's own hands. Not only is there the exclusionary issue of the cost of such insurance, the simple matter of having secured it is again likely to be down to the decisions and actions of the parents. In neither *NA* nor

---

[60] The UNCRC could play a stronger role here, see H Stalford and E Drywood, 'Coming of Age? Children's Rights in the European Union' (2009) 46 *CML Rev* 1, 143.

[61] Case C-115/15 *Secretary of State for the Home Department v NA* Opinion of AG Wathelet EU:C:2016:259, 115, emphasis in original.

[62] Case C-115/15 *Secretary of State for the Home Department v NA* EU:C:2016:487, 78.

[63] Art 7(1)(b) Directive 2004/38.

*Commission v UK*, was there any discussion of a residual Article 21 TFEU claim outside of the confines of the Directive, nor any suggestion that the conditions therein be applied proportionately. Further, there was no thought given to the question of whether EU national children are entitled to a measure of equal treatment, as a matter of fundamental primary law, when compared to own-state nationals: Article 18 TFEU was completely absent from view in both cases.

Within this approach, there is no scope to consider social integration or how someone has constructed their citizenship, or the relationship of citizenship to a *direct* right to reside and to equal treatment, which may then be modified by conditions so long as they are proportionately applied. But the benefits in question in *Commission v UK* were benefits intended to provide for child welfare—child benefit and child tax credit. Framing these in terms of parental entitlement goes against not only the purpose of the benefits but also the approach taken in *Teixeira* and *Ibrahim*,[64] in which the Court recognised that the family's entitlement to benefits stemmed from the child's right to remain in the Member State after their parent had ceased to be a migrant worker, to pursue their education under 'the best possible conditions'.[65] The carer's right was not subject to a sufficient resources requirement, in the context of social assistance and housing, because that would have had a damaging impact upon the child's ability to exercise their right. Child benefit and child tax credit arguably have an even more direct relationship with the child's welfare. In *R (SG and Ors) v Secretary of State for Work and Pensions*,[66] the Supreme Court accepted that child tax credit is a benefit 'designed to meet the needs of children considered as individuals' because, as stated in *Humphreys v HM Revenue and Customs*, the aim of the benefit 'is to provide support for children. The principal policy objective is to target that support so as to reduce child poverty. *The benefit attaches to the child rather than the parent*'.[67]

The UN Committee on the Rights of the Child has investigated the effects of the UK's generalised child tax credit cuts, and reported that it was 'seriously concerned' about cuts that were imposed 'regardless of the needs of the households' involved and which jeopardised child welfare.[68] Such needs-blind reductions mean that the UK is possibly infringing its obligations under the United Nations Convention on the Rights of the Child (UNCRC). But in *Commission v UK*, the Court is condoning for EU nationals not just a reduction, but a wholesale exclusion from the benefits in question—an exclusion that, thanks to the all-encompassing treatment of the restrictions in Directive 2004/38 and the lack of a proportionality requirement,

---

[64] Case C-310/08 *London Borough of Harrow v Nimco Hassan Ibrahim and Secretary of State for the Home Department* EU:C:2009:641.

[65] From Art 12, Council Reg 1612/68/EEC of 15 October 1968 on freedom of movement for workers within the Community [1968] OJ L257/2, 478.

[66] *R (SG and Ors) v Secretary of State for Work and Pensions* [2015] UKSC 16, [2015] WLR 1449.

[67] *Humphreys v HM Revenue and Customs* [2012] UKSC 18, [2012] 1 WLR 1545, emphasis added.

[68] United Nations Committee on the Rights of the Child, *Concluding Observations on the Fifth Periodic Report of the United Kingdom of Great Britain and Northern Ireland* (3 June 2016), para 61. Available at: tbinternet.ohchr.org/Treaties/CRC/Shared%20Documents/GBR/CRC_C_GBR_CO_5_24195_E.docx.

is also imposed regardless of the needs of the households concerned. In approving the exclusions, the Court granted a measure that endangers the welfare of children, creates a greater risk of child poverty, and potentially infringes the UNCRC. The EU is not a party to the UNCRC, but that does not mean it falls entirely outside of the Court's concerns: far from it—there are multiple sources, including primary law, suggesting that the objectives of the UNCRC are central to the Union's objectives. The Treaty of Lisbon introduced the 'protection of the rights of the child' as a Union objective in Article 3 TEU.[69] The Charter of Fundamental Rights of the European Union, which also has primary law status, states that 'children shall have the right to such protection and care as is necessary for their well-being',[70] and adds that 'in all actions relating to children, whether taken by public authorities or private institutions, the child's best interests must be a primary consideration'.[71]

There has also been institutional support for stronger protection of children's rights within the EU. The Commission announced in 2011 that the 'standards and principles of the UNCRC must continue to guide EU policies and actions that have an impact on the rights of the child'.[72] Decisions by the Court are EU actions that are capable of having such an impact. A report by the European Parliament in 2012 argued that the rights of the child 'now constitute an integral part of fundamental rights which the EU and Member States are bound to respect by virtue of European and international law'.[73] The Court of Justice itself has recognised that the UNCRC has a role to play in its jurisprudence. In *Parliament v Council*, the Court found that the UNCRC was 'one of the international instruments for the protection of human rights of which it takes account in applying the general principles of Community law',[74] and noted the 'importance' of the relevant Charter provisions, even though at that point in time, the Charter was not legally binding.[75]

If they are genuinely an integral part of human rights protection in EU law, the rights of the child received startlingly little attention in *Commission v UK*. At the least, they provide a countervailing factor to be weighed against the 'need

---

[69] Treaty on European Union (consolidated version 2016) OJ [2016] C 202/13.

[70] Art 24(1) Charter of Fundamental Rights of the European Union [2000] OJ C-364/01.

[71] ibid, Art 24(2), taken from Art 3 of the United Nations Convention on the Rights of the Child Adopted and opened for signature, ratification and accession by General Assembly Resolution 44/25 of 20 Nov 1989, entry into force 2 Sep 1990, in accordance with Art 49. Available at: www.ohchr.org/en/professionalinterest/pages/crc.aspx.

[72] European Commission, 'Communication from the Commission to European Parliament, the Council, the European Economic and Social Committee and the Committee of the Regions: An EU Agenda for the Rights of the Child' (2011) COM(2011) 0060, final.

[73] European Parliament, DG Internal Policies, *EU Framework of Law for Children's Rights*, April 2012, PE462.445, 7. Available at: www.europarl.europa.eu/RegData/etudes/note/join/2012/462445/IPOL-LIBE_NT(2012)462445_EN.pdf.

[74] Case C-540/03 *European Parliament v Council of the European Union* EU:C:2006:429, 37.

[75] ibid, 38. See also Case C-244/06 *Dynamic Medien Vertriebs GmbH v Avides Media AG* EU:C:2008:85, 39.

to protect the finances of the host Member State' posited by the UK as justifying the right to reside test. A greater respect for proportionality was sorely needed to articulate the relationship between these objectives and to ensure that the host state takes account of its duty to apply EU law in compliance with the principles of the UNCRC.

Disregarding the best interests of EU national children can have damaging effects on child welfare, and may lead to an administration of EU law that is indifferent to the demands of social justice, promoting child poverty and homelessness. It also contributes to the moral vacuum at the heart of EU law, allowing for the creation of welfare cliff-edges on the basis of quite arbitrary differences, and little regard for, or even any mention of, the children in whose rights many cases and derived rights are rooted. *Teixeira*, while offering a strong and valuable set of rights to those who fit within the required factual matrix, nevertheless sets up stark differences in treatment on the basis of fairly arbitrary circumstances, while the failure to frame *Zambrano* around the children who are the basis of the claim has led to a cavalier, and parsimonious, interpretation in the UK. Both trends, explored next, contribute to the patchy nature of Union citizenship, and belie any claims of market citizenship to a fundamental status.

### V. WELFARE CLIFF-EDGES FOR FAMILIES ARE SHARPER WITHOUT PROPORTIONALITY

The incremental construction of EU citizenship-based rights has created a messy, incoherent patchwork of entitlements, punctuated with rights cliff-edges, at what can seem like quite arbitrary points. These become all the more problematic if not softened by proportionality review. Treating the right to reside condition as absolute has some counter-intuitive results: for instance, one expert informant told me about cases of former asylum-seekers she had seen, who ended up with fewer rights after their country of origin became a Member State of the EU, than they would have had had they been awarded refugee status.[76] There had been no regard to proportionality in the decision-making process and no regard for the problematic result of mandatory poverty.

It is difficult to describe the assortment of limited claims on offer to EU citizens as conferring a single status as such, or as anything that speaks to a meaningful construction of 'citizenship'.[77] Citizens enjoy very different rights of equal treatment and access to welfare benefits depending on a whole host of circumstances. If they are reliant on their worker status, then they will have to demonstrate that it counts as economic activity, which can lead to difficult cut-off points on the

---

[76] Expert interview 1.

[77] Ashiagbor suggests that the piecemeal 'social content of market rights' undermines institutional integrity (D Ashiagbor, 'Unravelling the Embedded Liberal Bargain: Labour and Social Welfare Law in the Context of EU Market Integration' (2013) 19 *European Law Journal* 3, 303, 323.

fringes of the definition of worker. For instance, there is a dramatic difference in entitlement between those whose caring responsibilities are considered *remunerated* by a care benefit[78] and those whose caring responsibilities are considered not capable of being economic activity, as in *Züchner*.[79] Moreover, there is a potentially crucial cut-off point between those whose odd jobs in return for bed and board might be capable of being economic activity,[80] and those who are considered in contrast not part of the 'normal labour market'.[81] There is a significant, but unclear, distinction between trainees who are effectively performing the activities required to be work,[82] and those who are not yet sufficiently familiar with the activities to be considered workers.[83] Those not reliant upon current worker status also face steep cliff-edges according to a variety of factors which sometimes lack logic and which undermine the coherence of the system, in particular if applied without a proportionality review. Two of the starkest cut-off points worth noting here attach to the *Teixeira* and *Zambrano* cases, discussed next.

## A. The Logic of *Teixeira*

The *Teixeira/Ibrahim*-based right to reside has proved something of a life-line for many Citizens Advice and *EU Rights Project* clients, but invoking it means picking your way through and fulfilling a series of legal conditions. Missing one flips you from full equal treatment to full exclusion—a welfare cliff-edge. The right is based on the *Baumbast* case, in which it was found that the child of an EU national migrant worker, or former migrant worker, has a continuing right to reside in the state of the former work to pursue their education. Member States must facilitate the exercise of this right 'under the best possible conditions'[84] so allowing a right to reside for the child's primary carer. *Teixeira/Ibrahim* establish that this right to reside is not dependent upon sufficient resources and so entails a right to equal treatment in respect of social assistance. The right has since been further delineated to make clear that time spent exercising this right to reside does not count towards the five years' lawful residence required for permanent residence,[85] and

---

[78] As in *Barth*: Joined Cases C-502/01 and C-31/02 *Silke Gaumain-Cerri v Kaufmännische Krankenkasse—Pflegekasse* and *Maria Barth v Landesversicherungsanstalt Rheinprovinz* EU:C:2004:413.

[79] Case C-77/95 *Bruna-Alessandra Züchner v Handelskrankenkasse (Ersatzkasse) Bremen* EU:C:1996:425.

[80] Case 196/87 *Udo Steymann v Staatssecretaris van Justitie* EU:C:1988:475.

[81] Case C-456/02 *Michel Trojani v Centre public d'aide sociale de Bruxelles (CPAS)* EU:C:2004:488, phrase at 24.

[82] Case C-188/00 *Kurz* EU:C:2002:694.

[83] Case C-3/90 *Bernini* EU:C:1992:89.

[84] Art 12 Council Regulation 1612/68/EEC of 15 October 1968 on freedom of movement for workers within the Community [1968] OJ L257/2; replaced by Art 10 in Regulation (EU) No 492/2011 of the European Parliament and of the Council of 5 April 2011 on freedom of movement for workers within the Union (codification) OJ [2011] L 141/1.

[85] Case C-529/11 *Olaitan Ajoke Alarape and Olukayode Azeez Tijani v Secretary of State for the Home Department* EU:C:2013:290.

the UK government has conceded that enrolment in reception class does count as being enrolled in school.[86]

We can distil the following conditions from EU law for invoking this right to reside: first, that one of the parents has been an EU national migrant worker; second, that the child of the (former) migrant worker is in school; and third, that the parent claiming the right is the child's primary carer. This may all sound unproblematic but it does not take long to encounter some tricky-to-justify, divergent situations. For example, a carer might be in something akin to the *Ibrahim* situation, a third country national primary carer for EU national children of an EU national citizen; she herself might be the worker, not the EU national father. She will not be able to invoke *Ibrahim*, even if she has worked much more, and contributed much more, than an EU national parent in a comparable situation, even if the family has been resident much longer, and is significantly more integrated. Now take someone in the *Teixeira* position, but whose child is not yet of school age. She may have been resident for a considerably longer period than someone who can invoke *Teixeira*, and she and her children may be more integrated, and she may have done more work. On this point, it is worth noting that many EU nationals in the UK can be resident for much longer than five years without getting their right to permanent residence recognised (see the discussion in chapter six of the implications of the minimum earnings threshold for, inter alia, *Teixeira* rights). The child may have been born in the host state, speak the language, and never have visited the state of nationality, and will have no right to reside compared to a 15-year-old child, who may have just started at a school in the host state, who has considerable links with the home state, including language, and none with the host state apart from their parent's period of work, which may have been comparatively brief. Moreover, the Court has found (in *Czop*)[87] that Article 12 of Regulation 1612/68 (now Article 10 of Regulation 492/2011), relied upon in *Teixeira*, does not apply in the case of self-employment because 'that provision applies only to the children of employed persons'.[88] This gives rise to potentially unfair and arbitrary differences in the treatment of children of Union citizens who have completed recognised economic activity, with parental status as employed/self-employed entirely determining whether those children are entitled to remain to pursue their education 'under the best possible conditions' and those not entitled to remain at all.[89] Such a difference suggests a technical adherence to literal interpretation, in isolation from consideration of the spirit and purpose of the law, or even to the exclusion

---

[86] *Shabani v SoSHD* [2013] UKUT 315 (IAC), so applies to some children before reaching compulsory school age, because of the different ages of children when they start reception class.

[87] Joined Cases C-147/11 and C-148/11 *Secretary of State for Work and Pensions v Lucja Czop and Margita Punakova* EU:C:2012:538.

[88] Ibid, 30.

[89] Though in *Hrabkova* an argument is being made before the Court of Appeal that engagement of Regulations 1612/68 and 492/2011 is not necessary for *Teixeira* to be applied by analogy to the children of self-employed EU nationals. The most recent judgment at time of writing is that of the Upper Tribunal: *Revenue and Customs v IT (CTC) (European Union law: workers)* [2016] UKUT 252 (AAC).

of considering the Court's duty to interpret the law in light of the best interests of children, or to ensure that when implementing Union law, Member States have regard to the best interests of the child.

Now, take an EU national in the *Teixeira* position but whose partner, rather than being a migrant worker, is an own-state national:

---

**Case 4: Maria**

Maria came to the UK in March 2001 as a young adult. She did on-and-off work, which got harder after she became pregnant. She became a full-time mum living with her working partner. She separated from her first partner, forming a new relationship with her British partner in 2008. She has a young child, born in 2011. She looked after her partner's five children as well as their child and her older child. She couldn't combine work with looking after seven children. She spoke perfect English and had even picked up the local accent.

*Field notes: Shortly after birth of her youngest child her partner was violent. She left him, but he emotionally blackmailed her and she went back. The last time he was 'very violent' and she had help from [a charity] with leaving him and relocating. Her children are now 11 and three; 11-year-old is in school, just started secondary school this academic year (started primary school in January 2007).*

---

The rights of the EU national children, and the EU national primary carer, were dramatically different because their father was British, reducing their claim to be the children of migrant workers. This seemed a rather arbitrary distinction, given that Maria was supporting economic activity, in her role as carer of seven children, thus subsidising the economic activity of her partner. She herself had arrived as a migrant worker in the UK. That her future rights might be severely curtailed as a result of having children with an own-state national, as compared to an EU national, in itself arguably poses an obstacle to movement, like that envisaged in *Singh*[90] or *Eind*.[91] In the event, we were able to persuade the local authority in question to reinstate her housing benefit, in recognition of her earlier work, and having retained worker status during the first few years of her oldest child's life. It was clear the local authority did not want to refuse housing benefit, and were glad of a means to award it—they felt that the length of time she had been in the UK, her degree of social integration, and her children, all weighed in favour of an award. However, the income support decision-makers stood firm on refusing her a right to reside. We did not manage to see the case through to tribunal, because Maria dropped out of contact with us.

---

[90] Case C-370/90 *The Queen v Immigration Appeal Tribunal and Surinder Singh, ex p Secretary of State for Home Department* EU:C:1992:296.
[91] Case C-291/05 *Minister voor Vreemdelingenzaken en Integratie v RNG Eind* EU:C:2007:771.

If we look at the implementing framework in the UK, there are more opportunities to be pushed off the cliff. The applicable legislation during the life of the project, regulation 15A(4)(b) of the Immigration (European Economic Area) Regulations, on the right of the *Teixeira* child's primary carer, added quite a novel extra condition: that it must be shown that the child could not continue to be educated in the UK were the carer to leave, in order for the carer to have a right to reside. This has been reproduced in the new regulation 16(4), slightly reworded to 'would be unable to continue to be educated in the United Kingdom if the person left the United Kingdom for an indefinite period'. That the child's continued pursuit of their studies would be jeopardised by the departure of their primary carer might be said to be presumed within the very existence of the *Teixeira/Ibrahim* right, so adding this condition is problematic if it means no such presumption is made. Moreover, it sets a different threshold for entitlement than that envisaged in EU law. Recall that the primary carer's right to reside is based on the legislative stipulation that 'Member States shall encourage all efforts to enable such children to attend these courses under the best possible conditions'.[92] It is not a right that only transpires where any attendance of such courses would otherwise be impossible. There is a risk that decision-makers will consider regulation 4(b) not to have been met in situations where another parent is in the UK, a finding decision-makers are positively encouraged to reach in *Zambrano* cases.

## B. The Equal Treatment and Child Welfare Gaps in *Zambrano*

*Zambrano* marked another step-change in our understanding of EU citizenship and another flurry of academic responses.[93] EU citizenship had been found to have some limited effects for non-movers (for example, with regard to challenging the application of the host state's national naming rules for non-national children born there).[94] But the core citizenship rights—of residence and equal treatment—were subject to the prior exercise of free movement rights. EU citizenship was thus

---

[92] Art 12 of Reg 1612/68, replaced by Art 10 of Reg 492/2011.

[93] Lenaerts suggests that 'Zambrano has emancipated EU citizenship from the constraints inherent in its free movement origins' (K Lenaerts, '"Civis Europaeus Sum": From the Cross-Border Link to the Status of Citizen of the Union' (2011) 3 *Online Journal on Free Movement of Workers Within the European Union* 6, 7. See also: L Azoulai, '"Euro-Bonds": The *Ruiz Zambrano* Judgment or the Real Invention of EU Citizenship' (2011) 3 *Perspectives on Federalism* 2, 31; H Van Eijken and S A De Vries, 'A New Route into the Promised Land? Being a European Citizen after Ruiz Zambrano' (2011) 36 *EL Rev* 5, 704; and A Lansbergen and N Miller, 'European Citizenship Rights in Internal Situations: An Ambiguous Revolution?' (2011) 7 *European Constitutional Law Review* 2, 287. K Hailbronner and D Thym described the case as a 'critical innovation' (in 'Case Comment: Case C-34/09, *Gerardo Ruiz Zambrano v Office national de l'emploi (ONEm)*, Judgment of the Court of Justice (Grand Chamber) of 8 March 2011, not yet reported' (2011) 48 *CML Rev* 4, 1253. Note also N Nic Shuibhne suggests *Zambrano* 'may or may not' be one of the most significant judgments in the ECJ's history (see N Nic Shuibhne, 'Seven Questions for Seven Paragraphs' (2011) 36 *EL Rev* 2, 161.

[94] Case C-148/02 *Carlos Garcia Avello v Belgian State* EU:C:2003:539.

criticised as a mobility-dependent, rather than autonomous citizenship,[95] so was meaningless to those without the means to exercise their free movement rights. As such, it risked excluding all but the well-resourced and/or well-educated, who may have more mobility options open to them. This also meant that it was not a status that children could personally rely upon at all. In a movement context, children are typically the family members of the 'primary movers' (their parents or carers), and are more likely than adults not to fit into a movement context at all, being static and economically inactive.

In *Zambrano*, the Court was faced with third country national parents (Colombian), with a Colombian older child, who had sought asylum in Belgium. It had been refused, but they were subject to a non-refoulement measure. Mr Ruiz Zambrano had found work, which was declared to the social security authorities, and subject to social security deductions. The couple had two children in Belgium, and did not complete the procedures required for children of Colombian nationals born outside the territory of Colombia to acquire Colombian nationality. The children were therefore subject to the Belgian law preventing statelessness, and acquired Belgian nationality. After he had been working for some years, a government inspection (presumably conducted by a different department to that which had been collecting his social security contributions) discovered Mr Ruiz Zambrano was in work and his employer was obliged to terminate his contract with immediate effect. He applied for unemployment benefits, which were refused on the grounds that his work had not been lawfully completed. The family was thus refused income either through work or welfare.

The proceedings on the appeal of the unemployment benefit decision led to a reference to the ECJ, asking whether the children, as EU nationals, could invoke Article 20 TFEU, which provides for a 'right to move and reside' within Member States for Union citizens. The key question was essentially whether the right to reside in the Union could be disaggregated from, and exist independently of, the right to move within it. The reference also asked whether, if there were such a right, it extended to confer a right of residence upon the primary carer, and whether that carer should be exempted from work permit requirements.

The case highlights the EU's tricky history with reverse discrimination,[96] and so underlines the rather incomplete nature of its conception of equal treatment on the grounds of nationality.[97] Reverse discrimination is a side-effect of the need

---

[95] S Currie, 'The Transformation of Union Citizenship' in M Dougan and S Currie (eds), *50 Years of the European Treaties: Looking Back and Thinking Forward* (Oxford, Hart, 2009).

[96] A Tryfonidou, *Reverse Discrimination in EC Law* (Alphen aan den Rijn, Kluwer Law International, 2009).

[97] As Van der Mei noted in 2011, when it comes to 'internal movement' compared to cross-border movement, EU citizenship may entitle citizens to equality of treatment in comparable situations, 'but does not imply that they must be regarded as being in the same position' (see AP Van der Mei, 'The Outer Limits of the Prohibition of Discrimination on Grounds of Nationality: A Look Through the Lens of Union Citizenship' (2011) 18 *Maastricht Journal of European and Comparative Law* 1–2, 62, 77.

to delineate EU competence:[98] the desire to exclude 'wholly internal' situations from the ECJ's jurisdiction can mean that own-nationals who have not moved have difficulty claiming their situation falls within the scope of EU law. As a result, they may not benefit from the entitlements afforded to non-national EU citizens (for example, in the context of family reunification, EU nationals have a right to be joined by their third country national spouse, in a way not automatically open to own-nationals)[99] or, in the context of region-specific benefits, a regional authority may exclude own-nationals from different regions of the same state from a benefit, while being obliged to include EU citizens from other Member States (unless the own nationals can claim a link to EU law through, for example, prior free movement).[100] What emerges from this picture is something quite different from a fundamental right to non-discrimination on the grounds of nationality, and something much more like a market-based right not to be discriminated against on the grounds of being a free-mover.

The Advocate General's opinion in *Zambrano*[101] was thoughtful and detailed, considering the question of reverse discrimination and the possibility of free-standing fundamental rights protection. Advocate General Sharpston suggested that the requirement for a link with the exercise of EU law in order to trigger EU fundamental rights protection should not be challenged in the instant case, but that 'sooner rather than later', the Court would need to 'confront the question of whether the Union is not now on the cusp of constitutional change'.[102] She proposed a limited challenge to reverse discrimination—that the right to equal treatment should in some cases mean a right capable of being invoked by own-nationals, where they had suffered reverse discrimination as a result of the interaction of Article 21 TFEU with national law, so violating a fundamental right protected under EU law.

The Court's judgment was startlingly brief, in light of its constitutional significance. It found that 'Article 20 TFEU precludes national measures which have the effect of depriving citizens of the Union of the genuine enjoyment of the substance of the rights conferred by virtue of their status as citizens of the Union'.[103] This was because Article 20 TFEU 'confers the status of citizen of the Union on every person holding the nationality of a Member State',[104] which included the *Zambrano* children, and that 'citizenship of the Union is intended to be the

---

[98] N Nic Shuibhne 'Free Movement of Persons and the Wholly Internal Rule: Time to Move On? (2002) 39 *CML Rev* 4, 731.

[99] See A Tryfonidou, 'Reverse Discrimination in Purely Internal Situations: An Incongruity in a Citizens' Europe' (2008) 35 *Legal Issues of Economic Integration* 1, 43.

[100] Free-moving own-state nationals can claim not to be in wholly internal situations (see Case C-212/06 *Government of Communauté française and Gouvernement wallon v Gouvernement flamand* EU:C:2008:178.

[101] Case C-34/09 *Gerardo Ruiz Zambrano v Office National de L'Emploi (ONEm).* Opinion of AG Sharpston EU:C:2010:560.

[102] ibid, 177.

[103] *Zambrano* judgment, above n 4, 42.

[104] ibid, 40.

fundamental status of nationals of the Member States'.[105] Article 20 TFEU does
have autonomous substance, and the right to move and reside can be separate
rights, creating a non-mobility-dependent right to reside within the Union. As
for the addition of the parents' right, the Court added that a right of residence
and a work permit should be granted to a third country national with dependent
minor children in the children's Member State of nationality, where refusal would
deprive the children of the genuine enjoyment of the substance of their EU citizenship rights by compelling those children to leave the territory of the Union in
order to accompany their parents.

The brevity of the decision may have been necessary as a matter of judicial
diplomacy to dodge the question of reverse discrimination, and the appropriate
distinction between what is and what is not wholly internal as a result of whether
the 'substance' of EU citizenship rights are engaged. But the result is a judgment
that devotes no time to the concept of equal treatment at all. Although the Advocate General's opinion makes clear that the national courts considered there to have
been a breach of the 'constitutional principle of equality', and the opinion itself
used the word 'discrimination' 39 times (excluding mentions in the title, headnote,
referred questions and footnotes), the judgment contains no mention of 'equality'
or 'equal treatment' and (excluding the mention in the referred question) does not
make a single reference to 'discrimination' either. Nor do questions of children's
rights, or questions of how to make children's EU citizenship meaningful, get a
look-in. Despite being a landmark ruling explicitly on EU citizenship, it is at best
'citizenship-favoured'.[106] The social justice component of the case, like the equal
treatment element, falls by the wayside. This has had significant consequences
for how the judgment has been interpreted and the ruling implemented within
national law. A narrow approach to the personal and material circumstances that
can trigger a *Zambrano* right, such as that used by the UK Home Office, has the
effect of curbing the 'substance of rights' doctrine and of tipping some *Zambrano*
carers over a rights cliff-edge. Part of the problem lies in the ECJ's own follow-up
case law in *McCarthy*[107] and *Dereci*:[108] while some commentators have welcomed
the attempt to clarify or delineate the *Zambrano* right,[109] the Court also paved
the way for Member States to take approaches so restrictive as to be problematic from a human rights perspective. In *McCarthy*, the Court established that the
right need not extend to cover third country national *spouses* of own-nationals, as
opposed to parents, apparently on the presumption that a spouse being compelled
to leave the Union does not create the same degree of de facto compulsion for the

---

[105]  ibid, 41.
[106]  S Weatherill, 'The Court's Case Law on the Internal Market: 'A Circumloquacious Statement of
Result, Rather than a Reason for Arriving at It?' in M Adams, H de Waele, J Meeusen and G Straetmans
(eds) *Judging Europe's Judges: The Legitimacy of the Case Law of the European Court of Justice* (Oxford,
Hart, 2013) 101.
[107]  Case C-434/09 *McCarthy* EU:C:2011:277.
[108]  Case C-256/11 *Murat Dereci and Others v Bundesministerium für Inneres* EU:C:2011:734.
[109]  Hailbronner and Thym, above n 88, 1270.

own-state national adult as it would for a child whose parent was compelled to leave. In *Dereci*, in the context of a third country national spouse of an Austrian national, and father of their Austrian children, who had not exercised free movement, it was found that the threatened expulsion of the third country national must create a strong presumption of de facto expulsion for the children.

While the Court added the caveat that refusal of a right to reside must also be subjected to the question of compliance with the right to family life, this case has formed the basis for finding that a would-be *Zambrano* carer cannot gain that status where there is another parent lawfully present in the UK. In *Harrison and AB*,[110] the Court of Appeal of England and Wales found that the lawful presence of the other parent meant that the child would be able to stay, notwithstanding the break-up of the family unit. In *AB*, Elias LJ noted that if the family wished to stay together, they could all move to Morocco, which would be 'hard' but there were 'no insurmountable obstacles to them doing so'.[111] A Netherlands court appears to have adopted a similar stance, finding that the Union citizen child's residence was not dependent upon the primary carer mother having a right to reside, because the child could live with the father, notwithstanding the parental separation and the fact that the mother was the primary carer with custody.[112]

This UK Home Office takes a minimalistic approach to deciding who qualifies for a *Zambrano* right, and one that has scant regard for the welfare of the children. The Home Office guidance states that decision-makers 'must refuse an application for a derivative residence card if there is another person in the UK *who can care* for the relevant person'.[113] The guidance takes a lax view as to defining a parent who 'can care' for the child. The other parent is deemed someone who 'can' care for the child, if they have had some contact in the last 12 months (which can be just an email), and have demonstrated some (undefined) financial commitment to them at some point.[114] The guidance does not invite any enquiry into the nature, duration or stability of the parental relationships the child has, and the child's wishes (and the child's best interests) are conspicuously not mentioned. The guidance acknowledges that it would be unsuitable to place the child with someone on the sex offenders' register, but offers little beyond that, stating that 'a lack of financial resources or a lack of willingness to assume caring responsibilities would not, by itself, be a sufficient basis for a person to claim they are unable to care for the relevant person'.[115]

It is hard to see how deciding that another parent, whom the child may never have seen face to face, who announces they cannot afford to care for the child,

---

[110] *Harrison v Secretary of State for the Home Department* [2012] EWCA Civ 1736.
[111] ibid, 36.
[112] ECLI: NL: 2012: BY0833, Council of State 17 Oct 2012.
[113] UK Home Office, *Derivative Rights of Residence, Version 2.0, Valid from April 2015* (London, UK Government, 2015) 69, emphasis added. Available at: www.gov.uk/government/uploads/system/uploads/attachment_data/file/488448/Derivative_rights_of_residence_v2.0_ext_clean.pdf.
[114] ibid, 70.
[115] ibid, 71.

and/or do not want to care for the child, shall be the carer, could be anything other than an egregious violation of that child's welfare. Further, it is hard to see how such circumstances could lead to anything other than the conclusion that the child was being denied the substance of their EU citizenship rights. Either they will in reality stay with their primary carer, and in so doing, be forced to leave the Union, or they will stay in a fashion violating their right to family life, imperilling their welfare, and infringing their rights to have their best interests treated as paramount (or at the very least, as pertinent). Here, we should remember that courts are required to interpret EU free movement law in a fashion that is consistent with fundamental rights, and in particular compliant with the right to family life.[116] A willingness to arbitrarily reassign primary carership was evident in *Secretary of State for the Home Department v SL*,[117] in which the Upper Tribunal judge found that the claimant had failed to show she could rely on *Zambrano* because the child's father played a role in the child's life. The judge accepted that he was not the primary carer, and he had never lived with the child, but because he had been supportive, there was insufficient evidence that he would not assume the role of primary carer, and so the child's actual primary carer, the mother, was excluded from invoking a *Zambrano* right. The failure of the ECJ to frame *Zambrano* around the rights of the children, whose EU citizenship is the very deciding point of the case, is congruent with a market citizenship framework: but they are not market actors, so are only entitled to a minimal market citizenship. Yet it precluded serious engagement with questions of social justice, of the children's best interests (which might typically require staying with their *actual* primary carer), and of children's rights to equal treatment.

In *Chavez-Vilchez*[118] the Court has qualified *Zambrano*. Member States are entitled to ask *Zambrano* carers for evidence that their departure would oblige the child to leave the territory of the EU, and they are entitled to take account of the existence of another parent, who is a Union citizen who is able and willing to become the primary carer. But while relevant this factor is not dispositive. The authorities must assess the relationship of dependency between the child and the third country national primary carer, and 'take into account' the best interests of the child.[119] That assessment should include 'the age of the child, the child's physical and emotional development, the extent of his emotional ties both to the Union citizen parent and to the third-country national parent, and the risks which separation from the latter might entail for the child's equilibrium'.[120] This is a welcome modification—the child's best interests might not be given appropriate priority but they are at least a factor. It is not clear what influence each of the factors above

---

[116] Case C-60/00 *Mary Carpenter v Secretary of State for the Home Department* EU:C:2002:434.
[117] *Secretary of State for the Home Department v SL* IA/10236/2014 UT (IAC).
[118] Case C-133/15 *H C Chavez-Vilchez and Others v Raad van bestuur van de Sociale verzekeringsbank and Others* EU:C:2017:354.
[119] ibid, 72.
[120] ibid.

has, and it is still fairly easy to imagine a system that provides only for creating a *Zambrano* right in extreme cases; an emotionally and psychologically stable child with some contact with the other parent might find it hard to mount a *Zambrano* claim. Moreover, the Court did not specify where the Union citizen parent should be—it did not refer to the presence of that parent. So it is plausible that Member States might argue that the Union citizen parent, in another Member State, able and willing to look after the child, more-or-less (but not definitively) precludes a *Zambrano* right, because the child would not have to leave the territory of the Union. It is notable that in the list of factors, the child's wishes and opinions are not mentioned; they still have very little agency as EU citizens.

But even by this, rather minimal standard—that Member States nod to other factors before placing the child with an estranged parent who is able and willing to care for them—the UK falls short. The Court did not even mention situations where the parent is not 'able and willing' to care, but the Home Office guidance suggests that the UK does not even regard such ability and willingness as essential. *Zambrano* rights exemplify the problems created with a market-based conception of citizenship—that Member States adopt a parsimonious, competitive approach in which rights must be curbed and rights-giving judgments must be given the narrowest possible interpretation. The *Chavez-Vilchez* approach does not require EU law to be interpreted through the prism of fundamental rights; instead the right to family life and the best interests of the child are factors to be taken into account, alongside, and (at best) of equivalent weight to, the other things the Member State considers relevant. So fundamental rights are refracted through the prism of the market, rather than the other way round.

## C. The Disproportionate *Zambrano* Welfare Cliff-Edge

The failure in *Zambrano* to note that the question of family life was engaged, its apparent demotion in terms of importance in *Dereci*, and its at-best treatment as a factor to be noted in *Chavez-Vilchez*, speak to a reluctance to acknowledge more than a minimal degree of autonomous content in EU citizenship. The failure to note the rights, and in particular the equal treatment rights, of the children whose citizenship is at the very heart of the case, reveals the persistence of the market citizenship model. The UK legislature responded to the apparent gaps in the judgment with alacrity, filling them with its own restrictions, and providing for discriminatory treatment that the Court had not explicitly prohibited. With one hand, the UK enacted legislation that recognised the *Zambrano* right to reside,[121] but with the other, distinguished it from all other EU law-based rights to reside and excluded it from incurring any entitlement to equal treatment for

---

[121] The Immigration (European Economic Area) (Amendment) (No 2) Regulations 2012, SI 2012/2560.

non-contributory benefits, such as housing assistance and child benefit.[122] The UK government's argument that this ensures 'fairness for the taxpayer' sidesteps the fact that *Zambrano* families have been excluded from benefits even if they are working taxpayers too.[123]

The UK legislation, in force at the time of writing, thus creates a significant welfare cliff-edge for its own-national children. In a recent challenge before the Court of Appeal of England and Wales,[124] it was found that such families were eligible for emergency, back-stop support under section 17 of the Children Act 1989. Such support is minimal, and may, for instance, involve being evicted and moved to temporary bed and breakfast accommodation. In reality, however, questions are raised about whether it provides even that, or indeed anything of significance to many non-national claimants.[125] One case in the *EU Rights Project* involved a section 17 claim, to which the local authority responded with an offer to house only the child (and to assist the mother with her fare 'back home').[126] The Court of Appeal proceeded to find that so long as support was available in theory, then *Zambrano* families were not deprived of the substance of the citizenship rights of the child. But section 17 support is different, and inferior to, normal welfare entitlement,[127] so this ruling effectively condoned discriminatory treatment afforded to UK national children in a *Zambrano* situation as compared to other UK national children, and as compared to EU national children able to invoke a *Teixeira* right.[128] This approach is not confined to the UK: a court in the Netherlands found that as long as claimants are 'not deprived of all means of subsistence', it could not be said that denying benefits such as child support (another child-directed benefit) compelled the child to leave, or jeopardised the substance of EU citizenship rights.[129]

---

[122]   The Social Security (habitual residence) (amendment) Regulations 2012 and The Child Benefit and Child Tax Credit (Miscellaneous Amendments) Regulations 2012, SI 2012/2612.

[123]   Formulation used three times in DWP, 'Access to Benefits for Those Who Will have a "Zambrano" Right to Reside and Work' (2012), *Equality Analysis for The Social Security (Habitual Residence) (Amendment) Regulations 2012* (October 2012), 3, 4, 5. Available at: www.gov.uk/government/uploads/system/uploads/attachment_data/file/220217/eia-zambrano-right-to-reside-and-work.

[124]   *Sanneh and Ors v Secretary of State for Work and Pensions* [2015] EWCA Civ 49.

[125]   The Court of Appeal acknowledged this controversy and the 'substantial cuts in public funding' in *Sanneh*, ibid, 94.

[126]   Jenna's case, ch 6.

[127]   *R (G) v Barnet LBC* [2003] UKHL 57 established that under s 17, social services do not have to meet every assessed need and can take their resources into account when identifying which needs they will meet. In *R (1.PO 2.KO 3. RO) v London Borough of Newham* [2014] EWHC 2561 (Admin) it transpired the local authority in question derived their subsistence rates from child benefit rates, which the High Court deemed inadequate.

[128]   See C O'Brien, '"Hand-to-Mouth" Citizenship: Decision Time for the UK Supreme Court on the Substance of *Zambrano* Rights, EU Citizenship and Equal Treatment' (2016) 38 *Journal of Social Welfare and Family Law* 2, 228.

[129]   ECLI: NL: 2012: BY3982, Arnhem Court, 13 Nov 2012.

At the time of writing, *Sanneh* (renamed *HC*) is being appealed to the UK Supreme Court,[130] and it may be the subject of a preliminary reference to the ECJ. If so, then it is possible that the ECJ will recognise the parallels between *Zambrano/HC* and *Baumbast/Teixeira*. In *Teixeira*, the UK had claimed that the primary carer right to reside established in *Baumbast* was subject to sufficient resources, so did not confer entitlement to benefits. The Court replied emphatically that in *Baumbast*, 'the Court did not base its reasoning even implicitly on such a condition'.[131] Similarly, the Court in *Zambrano* did not base its reasoning even implicitly on the exclusion of equal treatment rights. Whatever the outcome, *Zambrano* families have suffered discriminatory treatment and destitution for several years as a result of mandatory unequal treatment made possible by the ECJ's silence on the question of equal treatment. The UK has readily exploited that silence, deploying the default position that whatever has not been expressly required by EU law can be prohibited by national law. Thanks in part to the restrictive definition of the *Zambrano* right, such families are highly likely to be lone parent families,[132] who are in turn, more at risk than average of poverty, of being concentrated in low-paid work, and of being in need of financial support to pay for child care. Lone parents are overwhelmingly women. Birmingham Law Centre noted in 2013 that *Zambrano* families in low-paid jobs were being left without 'the kind of support available to other low income families'.[133] While we are not talking about vast numbers,[134] we are talking about vulnerable claimants—who may have been working for a considerable period of time by the point of claim[135]— and we are talking about a disproportionate impact upon women and children. The problematic, automatic exclusion of *Zambrano* families from equal treatment rights may yet be addressed, but there remains a significant risk that Member States will respond by further narrowing the gateway for establishing a *Zambrano* right in the first place through greater emphasis on needing to establish de facto expulsion and creating stringent tests for deciding whether there is no other available carer. That Member States have for several years instituted this unequal treatment policy reveals the indifference of market citizenship to social injustice and a devaluing of the citizenship of children as not-yet market actors.

---

[130] *HC-R (on the application of HC) v Secretary of State for Work and Pensions and Others* UKSC 2015/0215.

[131] *Teixeira* judgment, above n 3, 67.

[132] The UK government's equality analysis on welfare reforms notes that of the *Zambrano* residence claims, '94 percent have not made their claim with a partner, suggesting they are lone parents' (above n 115, 2).

[133] Birmingham Law Centre Blog, *Zambrano and Pryce: Does the Homelessness Duty Mean Anything?* 23 February 2013. Available at: ilegal.org.uk/thread/7425/zambrano-pryce-homeless-duty-mean.

[134] The government's equality analysis stated that 619 families had applied for a *Zambrano*-based right to reside between March 2011 (when the judgment was released) and October 2012, a period of one and a half years (above n 115, 2).

[135] The equality assessment implied that most *Zambrano* carers would be workers, pointing out that the 'the majority of non-EU nationals in the UK are employed' (above n 115, 5).

## VI. SUMMARY

If free movement rules are not subject to a proportionality review, then those who fall through the gaps in Directive 2004/38 are not protected. Groups particularly at risk are unmarried partners, lone parents and children. Each must negotiate various welfare cliff-edges, and may be pushed over regardless of need, social integration and, in some cases, substantial periods of residence and economic history. The failure to provide a proportionality safety net results in law-as-lists rather than law-as-justice.

Children are not typically expected to be economic actors, and as a result fall through the gaps in the list of approved EU migrants in Directive 2004/38, with little regard for questions of social integration, constructed citizenship or lack of links with other states. But there are sound grounds for integrating children's rights considerations into the free movement framework, in the Treaty and the Charter. Indeed, such integration may be necessary if we do not wish to see all EU national children in the UK lose any personal claim to a right to reside when the UK leaves the EU. Purely parasitic rights are not enough: children have no control over their parents' migratory or employment choices or misfortunes.

EU case law that disregards proportionality and the best interests of children sets up stark distinctions between families in similar circumstances. Welfare rights derived from *Teixeira* and residence rights derived from *Zambrano* have been implemented in UK law in such a way that they create sharp delineations. The absence of any overarching, or underlying, duty to claimants who fall between the gaps reflects the limits of market citizenship and the construction of law-as-lists. While appearing to mark a high water mark for EU citizenship, *Zambrano* actually presaged the more explicit expressions of market citizenship in the regressive phase from *Brey* onwards,[136] and highlights the social injustices that emerge from a system punctuated with welfare cliff-edges not subject to a proportionality review. What we are left with is a market citizenship, the market elements of which have in recent years been galvanised. The rationality of activation, according to which benefit claimants generally (and EU migrants specifically) are treated as economic factors of production, is explored next. This rationality has not only reinforced market citizenship, it has elevated it, to represent morality itself, hijacking notions of fairness and eclipsing concerns of social justice with constructions of economic virtue and culpability.

---

[136] E Spaventa, 'Earned Citizenship: Understanding Union Citizenship Through Its Scope' in D Kochenov (ed), *EU Citizenship and Federalism: The Role of Rights* (Cambridge, CUP, 2017) 206. Compare with G Davies 'Migrant Union Citizens and Social Assistance: Trying to Be Reasonable About Self-Sufficiency', *Research Papers in Law* 2/2016 (Bruges, College of Europe, 2016).

# 5

# *Market Citizenship and Ideological Obstacles to Social Justice*

## The Market as Morality

### I. INTRODUCTION

THE PRINCIPLES AND objectives of market citizenship infuse the EU's social rights agenda. The construction of people as means for furthering market objectives necessitates that fundamental rights of equal treatment on grounds such as sex and disability are conceived as serving the market, and are harnessed to further an activation agenda. The Union's market citizen is the mobile counterpart to the Union's static 'active' citizen, the subject of the activation agenda pursued at EU and domestic levels across many Member States. This is an economised version of citizenship, and it dilutes commitments to or concerns with social justice, through an emphasis on individual responsibility. It is insensitive to power imbalances within the labour market and, in reality, the EU's construction of 'flexicurity' places a lot more emphasis on the 'flexi' than the 'curity' component. In the context of cross-border movement, states are not hampered by the residual duties of social justice owed to their own nationals, and so EU nationals are a test-bed for an 'activation-plus' regime (explored more in chapter six).

This chapter explores the capitalist construction of equal treatment rights on fundamental grounds of sex and disability to show how fundamental rights and conceptions of equality are framed around the market ideal of activation. In particular, it examines the activating tendencies of the reconciliation agenda, and the misappropriation of the social model of disability, not to promote equality per se, but to activate disabled people. It then highlights the exclusionary aspects of the activation agenda, considers the disempowering effects of the Union's flexicurity project, the elevation of the market as the new morality, and the tensions between activation and the pursuit of social justice (such that the latter suffers in the activation-plus regime imposed on EU nationals).

## II. THE MARKET CONCEPTION OF SEX EQUALITY
## AND THE SHORTCOMINGS OF THE RECONCILIATION AGENDA

Various Advocate Generals have appealed to the social component of Union citizenship. In 2007, Advocate General Sharpston suggested that Union citizenship is capable of transforming the approach to purely internal situations, highlighting 'the arbitrariness of attaching so much importance to crossing a national border'.[1] More recently, Advocate General Wathelet has steadfastly argued for more considerations of social justice than the Court has been willing to entertain.[2]

But the Court has rejected, with increasing emphasis, a social model of citizenship beyond anything serving immediate economic ends. Market principles are infused not only throughout free movement law, but also by the framework within which the concept of 'equal treatment' on grounds such as sex and disability is constructed: market citizenship is bound up with a market-centric form of equality.[3] For example, although Mabbett suggests that the development of sex discrimination law shows the concern of the Union shifting 'from workers to citizens',[4] the EU's long-term concern with gender equality has been a matter of market imperative. It is not primarily viewed as a good in itself, and there is remarkably little concern over the economic interests of women, or any suggestion that how we shape the economy or conceive of economic benefit might be altered to take account of women's interests: the economy-as-it-is, with all its male tilts and assumptions, is what must be served for equality to be worth pursuing.

### A. The Union's 'Business Case' for Equality

The European Commission argued in 2009 that gender equality could boost economic growth by between 15 and 45 per cent.[5] Vladimír Špidla, then the Commissioner for Employment, Social Affairs and Equal Opportunities, asserted that to 'overcome the economic crisis we must use all potential and involve everybody's talents'.[6] A European Commission report on women on corporate boards in the EU noted that companies with more women on their boards had

---

[1] Case C-212/06 *Government of Communauté française and Gouvernement wallon v Gouvernement flamand* Opinion of AG Sharpston EU:C:2007:398, 141.

[2] Case C-67/14 *Jobcenter Berlin Neukölln v Nazifa Alimanovic and Others*, Opinion of AG Wathelet EU:C:2015:210; Case C-299/14 *Vestische Arbeit Jobcenter Kreis Recklinghausen v Jovanna García-Nieto and Others*, Opinion of AG Wathelet, EU:C:2015:366; and Case C-115/15 *Secretary of State for the Home Department v NA* Opinion of AG Wathelet EU:C:2016:259.

[3] D Kochenov, 'Citizenship Without Respect', *Jean Monnet Working Paper 08/2010* (New York, NYU Law School, 2011).

[4] D Mabbett, 'The Development of Rights-Based Social Policy in the European Union: The Example of Disability Rights' (2005) 43 *Journal of Common Market Studies* 1, 97, 106.

[5] European Commission, 'Gender Equality to Boost Economic Growth by 15%–45% of GDP', *Press Release IP/09/1527*, Brussels, 15 October 2009, l.

[6] ibid.

a 42 per cent higher return in sales, 66 per cent higher return on invested capital and 53 per cent higher return on equity.[7] A Commission Staff working document concluded in 2013 that 'gender equality can significantly increase the growth potential of the EU economy',[8] and the Commission launched a tellingly named 'Equality Pays Off'[9] initiative because 'getting more women into the labour market and in top jobs makes good sense for our economies and our businesses'.[10] The European Network on Gender Equality presented a 'business case for gender equality', pointing out evidence that women 'in greater than token proportions improve decision-making; improve shareholder value; and lower risk-taking'.[11]

This framing is important because it makes a number of presumptions about the desirability of furthering the aims of the market as currently conceived. It leads to a stunted and one-sided conception of 'reconciling work and family life', whereby women are simply just expected to do more. While the idea of a 'better work–life balance' is often associated with reconciliation, and sounds attractive (who would not want that?), it does not mean what it says: there is no discussion of the problems women in work face, or what that says about problems with the labour market as it currently is, or how to increase the 'life' side of the equation. Instead, better work–life balance simply means that those who do not work, or who do not work enough, have the balance wrong, and the focus is on activating them.[12] Moreover, while recognising that pay and employment penalties seem to be suffered by women working part-time, the gist of Union policies is not to improve the quality of part-time work[13] but to push them into full-time work. 'Push' being the appropriate word: the Commission's roadmap on work–life balance criticised 'tax and benefit systems that give financial incentives for the spouse earning less to withdraw from the labour market or to work part-time',[14]

---

[7] European Commission, *Women in Economic Decision-Making in the EU: Progress Report—An EC 2020 Initiative* (Luxembourg, European Union, 2012) 7.

[8] European Commission, 'Report on Progress on Equality Between Women and Men in 2012—Accompanying the Document 2012 Report on the Application of the EU Charter of Fundamental Rights', *Commission Staff Working Document* COM (2013) 271 final (Brussels, European Commission, 2013) 36.

[9] European Commission, *Equality Pays Off: The Project* [updated 2016]. Available at: ec.europa.eu/ justice/gender-equality/eu_funded-projects/equality-pays-off/the-project/index_en.htm.

[10] ibid, quoting Vivian Reding, Vice-President of the European Commission and Commissioner for Justice, Fundamental Rights and Citizenship.

[11] Eurogender, 'The Business Case for Gender Equality' *Web Discussion* (2013). Available at: euro-gender.eige.europa.eu/sites/default/files/online%20discussion%20%20The%20business%20case%20 for%20gender%20equality%20-transcript%20(3).pdf.

[12] European Commission, 'New Start to Address the Challenges of Work-Life Balance Faced by Working Families', *Roadmap* (August 2015). Available at: ec.europa.eu/smartregulation/roadmaps/ docs/2015_just_012_new_initiative_replacing_maternity_leave_directive_en.pdf.

[13] As recommended in the context of the UK, see C Lyonette, 'Part-Time Work, Work–Life Balance and Gender Equality' (2015) 37 *Journal of Social Welfare and Family Law* 3, 321.

[14] Because they might reduce the incentive for fathers to take parental leave (above n 12, 5).

combining quite strident ideological assumptions about the role of welfare and motives of female workers, with a disapprobation of part-time work, and a steer towards more punitive tax and welfare policies.

## B. Reconciliation as Assimilation and Activation

The devaluing of 'non-economic' activity fails on its own terms, in that studies show that national economies are subsidised to a very significant degree by the unpaid labour of parents and carers.[15] Indeed, Fineman has argued that the market and the state are the ones free-riding on the backs of carers and those doing family-based work, rather than the other way round.[16] Our very conception of 'dependence' built in to the free movement framework is skewed, since workers are in many senses functionally dependent upon those facilitating the work through providing care for children and adults.[17] While the idea of appreciating the economic value of care work is not unproblematic—since it suggests *more* commodification, and a shifting of the priorities of the market rather than an overthrowing of the market itself—there is a risk that in simply opposing commodification of some types of work we disguise essentialised arguments about the difference of female work.[18] A skewed agenda as to what is properly a commodity bleeds into the definition of work, and the assessment of the worthwhile contributions made by EU migrants when weighing up claims of a right to reside or claims upon the public purse. People's activities, histories and contributions are all refracted through a male prism, one that Schumpeter denounced in 1942:

> The contribution made by parenthood ... almost invariably escapes the rational search-light of modern individuals who ... tend to focus attention on ascertainable details of immediate utilitarian relevance ... the balance sheet is likely to be incomplete, perhaps even fundamentally wrong.[19]

The reconciliation agenda in focusing on women assimilating into a male-centric world of work, uses a faulty balance sheet.[20] There is little talk of addressing

---

[15] 'The economic value of the contribution made by carers in the UK is now £132 billion per year' (L Buckner and S Yeandle, *Valuing Carers 2015: The Rising Value of Carers' Support* (London, Carers UK, 2015) 4.

[16] M Fineman, 'Cracking the Foundational Myths: Independence, Autonomy and Self-Sufficiency' (2000) 8 *The American University Journal of Gender, Social Policy and the Law* 1, 13, 25.

[17] T Hervey, 'Migrant Workers and their Families in the European Union: The Pervasive Market Ideology of Community Law' in J Shaw and G More (eds), *New Legal Dynamics of European Union* (Oxford, Clarendon Press, 1995) 105.

[18] N Fraser, 'Can Societies be Commodities All the Way Down? Post-Polanyian Reflections on Capitalist Crisis' (2014) 43 *Economy and Society* 4, 541, 548.

[19] J Schumpeter, *Capitalism, Socialism and Democracy*, 5th edn (New York, Harper and Row, 1976) 158.

[20] Hervey argued that tensions between social and market objectives allowed the construction of 'social protections in a manner which perpetuates particularism and inequality' (Hervey, above n 17, 92).

job instability,[21] or the casualisation of the female workforce,[22] or the proliferation of part-time jobs[23] into which women are chivvied to ensure that they are employed.[24] The 'male tilt' of the world of work persists,[25] evident in family-unfriendly policies and costly childcare. Wacquant noted that activation policies focus on making single mothers 'work ready', instead of making jobs 'mother ready'.[26] One school of thought—'human capital' theory—suggests that women are drawn to assume caring roles in the family, and so are inclined to take up lower-paying jobs, with less status and stability as a considered compromise, because those jobs are less demanding and free up space for the caring roles.[27] But Vicki Schultz[28] has shown that human capital theory is based on a fundamental misconception: that the jobs taken up by women are somehow more 'family-friendly'. They are not. Schultz points to 'embarrassing'[29] evidence that female-dominated jobs were no more family-friendly than male-dominated jobs, while paying less. Some sectors were found to be less flexible the higher the female proportion of the workforce. Schultz argues that the belief that women make compromises to be in family-friendly work is 'part of the myth that justifies paying women lower wages'.[30] If we look to evidence from the 2015 Gender Equality Index report, we see the myth further debunked. The report included a 'flexible personal/family arrangements'

---

[21] Countouris and Freedland argue that 'Europe has to rediscover the virtues—and the economic benefits—of employment stability and of well protected, high quality, high trust work relationships' (N Countouris and M Freedland, 'Epilogue: Resocialisng Europe—Looking Back and Thinking Forward' in N Countouris and M Freedland, *Resocialising Europe in a Time of Crisis* (Cambridge, Cambridge University Press, 2013), 497.

[22] Trades Union Congress analysis of the Labour Force Survey suggests that in the UK over half of temporary workers (52%) are women and the majority of the zero hours workforce is female (55%) (see TUC, *Women and Casualisation: Women's Experiences of Job Insecurity* (December 2014). Available at: www.tuc.org.uk/sites/default/files/Women_and_casualisation.pdf). When we take account of women making up less than half of the workforce overall, we can see they are disproportionately represented in these groups: employment rates for men in Aug–Oct 2016 were 79%, for women 70% (Office for National Statistics, *Statistical Bulletin: UK Labour Market March 2017* (15 March 2017), available at: www.ons.gov.uk/employmentandlabourmarket/peopleinwork/employmentandemployeetypes/bulletins/uklabourmarket/latest).

[23] 'In absolute terms, since 2007 part-time employment has grown in Europe, while full-time employment has declined. The share of part-time workers in the EU has increased in all but two countries (Croatia and Poland), on average from 16.8 per cent to 18.9 per cent' (European Commission, 'Part Time Work: A Divided Europe', *Commission News* (04/05/2016). Available at: ec.europa.eu/social/main.jsp?langId=en&catId=1196&newsId=2535&furtherNews=yes.

[24] 'Far more women than men work on a part-time basis. In 2015, on average in the EU, 8.9 per cent of men worked part-time in contrast to 32.1 per cent of women' (ibid).

[25] N Taub, 'The Relevance of Disparate Impact Analysis in Reaching for Gender Equality', (1996) 6 *Seton Hall Constitutional Law Journal*, 941.

[26] L Wacquant, *Punishing the Poor: The Neoliberal Government of Social Insecurity* (London, Duke University Press, 2009) 86.

[27] G Becker, 'Human Capital, Effort, and The Sexual Division of Labor' (1985) 3 *Journal of Labor Economics* 1, S33, S33.

[28] V Schultz, 'Life's Work' (2000) 100 *Columbia Law Review* 7, 1881.

[29] ibid, 1893.

[30] ibid, 1895.

indicator, which measured the proportion of male and female workers who in 2010 had the 'ability to take an hour or two off during working hours to take care of personal or family matters'. The result showed a gender gap across the EU 28 of 2.7 per cent, in favour of men. The overall proportion of workers with this flexibility, and the gender gap, varied across Member States, but in no state was there a gap in favour of women.[31]

It is still predominantly thought to be women who must reconcile their competing responsibilities.[32] When it comes to caring for adults, the EU is not silent,[33] but it is inactive.[34] Failing to factor adult care into the legislative framework, while pressing women to emulate men in the labour market, is an act of denial: with a looming care crisis,[35] more transformative thinking about work is needed. As Busby and James have argued, the aims of gender equality and work–life balance have 'become completely absorbed into the overarching strategy of improving supply side factors in the pursuit of macroeconomic targets'.[36] Those macroeconomic targets determine the Union's policies on gender equality, not the other way around. The subjugation of equality concerns to economic goals determined by the majority extends beyond sex and is also evident in the sphere of disability discrimination where, again, the impetus towards 'activation' and the economically reductionist approach to citizens is evident.

## III. MARKET CITIZENSHIP AND DISABILITY

Market citizenship colours the purpose of disability equality law, setting its material and personal scope.[37] Disability equality has to be packaged to speak to a particular economic (non-disabled) agenda: in 2016, a European Parliament resolution noted evidence that 'investment in appropriate reasonable accommodation

---

[31] AL Humbert, V Ivaškaitė-Tamošiūnė, NS Oetke and M Paats, *Gender Equality Index 2015: Measuring Gender Equality in the European Union 2005–2012*, (Italy, European Institute for Gender Equality, 2015). Available at: eige.europa.eu/sites/default/files/documents/mh0415169enn.pdf.

[32] E Caracciolo di Torella, 'Men in the Work/Family Reconciliation Discourse: The Swallows That Did Not Make A Summer?' (2015) 37 *Journal of Social Welfare and Family Law* 3, 334.

[33] See, for example, the European Commission commissioned research note: R Rodrigues, K Schulmann, A Schmidt, N Kalavrezou and M Matsaganis, *The Indirect Costs of Long-Term Care: Research Note 8/2013* (Brussels, European Commission, 2013).

[34] R Horton, 'Caring for Adults in the EU: Work–Life Balance and Challenges for EU Law' (2015) 37 *Journal of Social Welfare and Family Law* 3, 356.

[35] With regard to England, Pickard projects a growing gap between supply of and demand for unpaid care, amounting to a shortfall of 160,000 care-givers by 2032 (L Pickard, 'A Growing Care Gap? The Supply of Unpaid Care for Older People by Their Adult Children in England to 2032' (2015) 35 *Ageing and Society* 1, 96.

[36] N Busby and G James, 'Regulating Working Families in the European Union: A History of Disjointed Strategies' (2015) 37 *Journal of Social Welfare and Family Law* 3, 295, 298.

[37] As argued in C O'Brien, 'Union Citizenship and Disability: Restricted Access to Equality Rights and the Attitudinal Model of Disability' in D Kochenov (ed), *EU Citizenship and Federalism: The Role of Rights* (Cambridge, CUP, 2017).

for people with disabilities is *cost-beneficial* and that, as well as promoting social inclusion, it 'increased productivity and reduced absenteeism'.[38] In 2010, the Commission addressed the European Disability Strategy 2010–20, and stressed the macroeconomic costs of lower labour market participation among disabled persons, and argued that eliminating discrimination would yield particular economic gains.[39] Non-discrimination was promoted as creating 'new or better market opportunities,'[40] and the Commission pointed to Tesco having made their website accessible, and consequently more profitable, and to the predictions that improved accessibility of facilities would lead to gains to the German tourism industry.

While it may be true that equality measures can speak to the wallets of would-be discriminators, the idea of a business case for equality—whether on grounds of sex or disability—is problematic. It suggests that where measures are not shown to be 'cost-beneficial', or may entail contested costs in the short term, that the case for equality in itself is weakened. It accepts the premise that equality is only valid or worthwhile so long as it is on the terms of those in positions of power, which is particularly problematic when it concerns minorities who must demonstrate that their interests serve those of the majority. It subjugates the interests of the disabled minority to those of a non-disabled majority. This degrades the commitment to the human right in question, and neutralises or legitimises discriminatory tendencies, thus taking the sting out of what might otherwise seem egregious exclusions on the purportedly neutral (but actually heavily loaded) notion of economic rationality.[41]

## A. Asserting the Primacy of the 'Normal' Labour Market

Disability discrimination is primarily relevant to the Union if the complainant is a worker,[42] which has been consistently defined in ECJ case law as someone performing activities under the supervision of another in return for remuneration, where those activities are genuine and effective, to the exclusion of marginal and ancillary activities.[43] Although this is a broad definition, its fringes have been

---

[38] European Parliament Resolution of 15 September 2016 on application of Council Directive 2000/78/EC of 27 November 2000 establishing a general framework for equal treatment in employment and occupation ('Employment Equality Directive'), 2015/2116(INI), 30.

[39] European Commission, 'Commission Staff Working Document: A Renewed Commitment to a Barrier Free Europe', SEC(2010) 1323 final, 16.

[40] ibid.

[41] On the shortcomings of economic actors as rational decision-makers, see E Lagerspetz, 'Rationality and Politics in Long Term Decisions' (1999) 8 *Biodiversity and Conservation* 149.

[42] Council Directive 2000/78/EC of 27 November 2000 establishing a general framework for equal treatment in employment and occupation, OJ [2000] L 303/16, has some application with regard to access to self-employment (Art 3(1)(a)).

[43] Case 66/85 *Lawrie-Blum* EU:C:1986:284 onwards. See also: C O'Brien, 'Social Blind Spots and Monocular Policy-Making: The ECJ's Migrant Worker Model' (2009) 46 *CML Rev* 4, 1107; and C O'Brien, 'Drudges, Dupes and Do-gooders?' (2011) 1 *European Journal of Social Law* 49.

much contested, with disabled people at particular risk following *Bettray*.[44] In that case, a German national in the Netherlands, who had been a drug addict, was taking part in 'social employment' (that is, rehabilitative work). The Court found that such work was not genuine and effective work if it constituted 'merely a means of rehabilitation or reintegration for the persons concerned' and if employment was 'adapted to the physical and mental possibilities of each person' and the purpose of the employment was 'to enable those persons sooner or later to recover their capacity to take up ordinary employment or to lead as normal as possible a life'.[45] This finding provoked considerable uncertainty as to how sheltered or assisted work environments might be treated and potentially excluded many disabled workers.

The case of *Fenoll* has mitigated these risks, since the Court there tried to confine *Bettray* closely to its facts, possibly even just to cases of drug addiction.[46] In *Fenoll*, the issue was not one of migrant work, but of defining worker for the purposes of the annual leave provisions (employment, rather than free movement, law), but the 'autonomous meaning specific to EU law' is the same.[47] The main question was whether persons in the French work rehabilitation centre (the CAT), were workers. The Court noted the exclusion in *Bettray*, while also pointing to the finding being limited to its particular facts, then added that while in the CAT, the tasks performed were reserved for people 'unable to work in normal conditions', it was 'nevertheless clear from the file submitted to the Court that the very concept of the regime governing the functioning of a CAT, and the activities carried out by persons with disabilities, is such that those activities do not appear to be purely marginal and ancillary'.[48] In reaching this finding, the Court noted that the framework allowed organisers 'as far as possible, to ensure that the activities entrusted to that person are of some *economic benefit* to the body concerned',[49] and that although adapted, the activities had a 'certain *economic value*'.[50] So again, the value to the non-disabled world is the guiding principle. It is curious that in this respect, disabled workers may actually be held to a tighter condition than that applied to non-disabled workers, who are simply bound to show they are performing genuine and effective activities under supervision in return for remuneration. There has been little suggestion that non-disabled workers who work in charitable sectors, or not-for-profit enterprises, or whose own activities do not contribute to

---

[44]    Case 344/87 *Bettray v Staatssecretaris van Justitie* EU:C:1989:226.

[45]    ibid, 17.

[46]    In Case C-316/13 *Fenoll* EU:C:2015:200, 38, the Court characterised *Bettray* as 'relevant only to the facts giving rise to that judgment, relating to a person who, *because of his drug addiction*, had been employed on the basis of a national law designed to provide work for persons who, for an indefinite period, are unable, by reason of circumstances related to their situation, to work in normal conditions'; emphasis added.

[47]    ibid, 25.

[48]    ibid, 39.

[49]    ibid, 32.

[50]    ibid, 40.

the financial wellbeing of the company, or who work in loss-making enterprises, or who are not very good at their job, and so represent poor value, should not be classified as workers.

Those performing adapted work may be faced with an economic utility test. This echoes the problematic assertions the Advocate General made in *Bettray*, comparing the system to schemes run by charitable foundations in which disabled people make goods for sale. According to Advocate General Jacobs, 'the purchaser generally buys the items not because he particularly needs them, but in order to contribute to the charity'.[51] The invocation of purchaser motivation is odd, as such a variable is difficult to measure in many employment situations, wherein people purchase goods for their ethical quality, or to support a friend setting up a new business, or to support local tradespeople, or because they wish to make a contribution to the museum they have just visited, or to the café whose toilets they have used. According to the Advocate General, 'in the normal employment situation … the purpose is the production of goods or services, and the job is a means to that end'.[52] But this is a narrow, mechanistic framework for identifying work and fails to acknowledge that many non-disabled people work in jobs with 'social purposes' without risk of loss of worker status. Disabled workers are thus subject to an even stronger process of instrumentalisation, to allow decision-makers to overlook their perceived deviations from (and implicit economic threat to) the 'normal' labour market.

It is only once a disabled person is shown to be a part of that labour market that equality becomes a concern for the EU. Union law on sex discrimination extends beyond the workplace to the economic realms of goods and services (the provisions on social security being limited to workers). But disability discrimination law is still limited to the sphere of employment and occupation. Disability is even defined in terms of access to the employment market—disability only being identified if it gives rise to an impaired ability to pursue employment.[53] The Commission did put forward a proposal to extend protection from discrimination on the Framework Directive grounds (disability, age, religion and sexual orientation) to the other economic aspects of the internal market (goods and services).[54] But this proposal has faced a rather tortuous journey through Council, with particular controversy over the grounds of disability.[55] It has not been killed off, however, with

---

[51] Case 344/87 I *Bettray v Staatssecretaris van Justitie* Opinion of AG Jacobs EU:C:1989:113, 33.

[52] ibid, 34.

[53] C-363/12 *Z v A Government Department and The Board of Management of a Community School* EU:C:2014:159.

[54] European Commission, 'Proposal for a Council Directive on Implementing the Principle of Equal Treatment Between Persons Irrespective of Religion or Belief, Disability, Age or Sexual Orientation', COM (2008) 426 final.

[55] The disability provisions were listed among the 'major outstanding issues' in a 2014 report (Council of the European Union Presidency, *Proposal for a Council Directive on Implementing the Principle of Equal Treatment Between Persons Irrespective of Religion or Belief, Disability, Age or Sexual Orientation: Progress Report* (Council Document 10038/14), 5).

debates continuing.[56] The draft proposal indicates a significant wariness around disability, with the word 'burden' being used 11 times in the context of complying with the disability equality measures. The treatment of accommodation measures as burdens obstructs imaginative thinking about substantive equal treatment and social restructuring. It reflects the objectives of the market: formal equality means allowing more otherwise excluded economic actors to emulate the working patterns of ideal market citizens, while holding them to the same productivity standards. But formal equality disguises structural inequalities—which play out in power relationships and institutionalised practices—that mean that treating people 'the same' results in discrimination in favour of those in positions of established privilege. Moral opprobrium directed at prejudice and 'deliberate' discrimination overlooks the problem that indirect discrimination is far more frequent, insidious and suppressing. The trouble is that tackling indirect discrimination is just harder. Moreover, a commitment to tackling it suggests a willingness to address structural inequalities and to contemplate restructuring. This imposes what the proponents of the economic status quo define as 'costs', which must be kept down.

In limiting duties to combat indirectly discriminatory provisions, criteria or practices, we fail to recognise that those provisions, criteria and practices are *disabling*—they contribute to the creation of disability. An approach that seeks to preserve the economic status quo is antithetical to a social model of disability: the market views disability as a medical aberration from a non-disabled norm, which should be adapted to fit the existing economic paradigm if possible. But the barriers that create disability are woven into the fabric of that paradigm. In light of the EU being a signatory to the UN Convention on the Rights of Persons with Disabilities (UNCRPD),[57] the Court has announced[58] that disability should be defined in line with the Convention's definition. But it has done little more than pay lip-service to it: appropriating the label, and its moralistic lustre, while continuing to work and rule in medical model terms.

## B.  Market Citizenship and the Persistence of the Medical Model

Market citizenship dictates that equality is only necessary insofar as it facilitates economic activity that serves the existing market. It adopts a medical model of

---

[56]  Council of the European Union, *Proposal for a Council Directive on Implementing the Principle of Equal Treatment Between Persons Irrespective of Religion or Belief, Disability, Age or Sexual Orientation: Progress Report* (Council Document 14284/16) 22 November 2016, 8.

[57]  UNCRPD adopted by the General Assembly 19 December 2006, and came into force 3 May 2008 (see: www.un.org/disabilities/convention/conventionfull.shtml); and Council Decision 2010/48/EC concerning the conclusion of the United Nations Convention on the Rights of Persons with Disabilities, OJ 2010 L23/35.

[58]  In C-335/11 and C-337/11 *HK Danmark, Acting on Behalf of Jette Ring v Dansk almennyttigt Boligselskab and HK Danmark, Acting on Behalf of Lone Skouboe Werge v Dansk Arbejdsgiverforening, Acting on Behalf of Pro Display A/S* EU:C:2013:222.

disability, in which impairments should be accommodated to allow for as much assimilation into the labour market as possible, but which poses no challenges to societal structures that create disability. A narrowly construed definition of work (explored in chapter six) combined with a medical model, could see disabled people more likely to be excluded from Article 45 TFEU, and thus from the core benefits of EU citizenship.[59]

The Court adopted a medical definition of disability in *Chacon Navas*,[60] namely disability as 'a limitation which results in particular from physical, mental or psychological impairments and which hinders the participation of the person concerned in professional life'.[61] In *HK Danmark*, the Court stated that this definition was no longer appropriate in light of the UNCRPD, and instead disability should be treated as 'physical, mental or psychological impairments which in interaction with various barriers may hinder the full and effective participation of the person concerned in professional life on an equal basis with other workers'.[62] Advocate General Wahl later described this as a 'paradigm shift',[63] but the problem is that the Court has repeatedly played down[64] or even neglected the 'barriers' part of the definition, resulting in a covertly medical model. In *HK Danmark* itself, there was no discussion of barriers: the focus was on the 'impairment' part of the definition.

In subsequent cases the Court has failed to consider the possibility that the disputed rules might constitute barriers, so *create* disability. This failure was particularly pronounced in *Z*. That case concerned a woman without a uterus, who was having a baby through a surrogate mother and sought maternity leave. The Advocate General and the Court were of the opinion that the medical condition in question must be disabling *in itself* and that it must cause a hindrance to employment.[65] The Advocate General identified the central question as '*does the condition* from which Ms Z suffers compromise her prospects of participating in professional life?',[66] and then found that not having a uterus did not in itself compromise her prospects. The Court found that 'it is not apparent from the order for reference that Ms Z's *condition by itself* made it impossible for her to carry out her work or constituted a hindrance to the exercise of her professional activity'.[67] But this was an opportunity to explore the 'barriers' part of the definition of disability.

---

[59] H Morgan and H Stalford, 'Disabled People and the European Union: Equal Citizens?' in C Barnes and G Mercer (eds), *The Social Model of Disability: Europe and the Majority World* (Leeds, The Disability Press, 2005).

[60] Case C-13/05 *Sonia Chacón Navas v Eurest Colectividades SA* EU:C:2006:456.

[61] ibid, 43.

[62] In *HK Danmark*, above n 58, 38.

[63] Case C-363/12 *Z v A Government Department and The Board of Management of a Community School*, Opinion of AG Wahl, EU:C:2013:604, 88.

[64] L Waddington, 'Saying All the Right Things and Still Getting it Wrong: The Court of Justice's Definition of Disability and Non-Discrimination Law' (2015) 22 *Maastricht Journal of European and Comparative Law* 4, 576.

[65] See O'Brien (2017), above n 37.

[66] Above n 63, 91.

[67] C-363/12 *Z* judgment, above n 53, 81.

The medical condition may not have been disabling in itself, but in combination with the rules excluding commissioning mothers from maternity leave, it left people with that impairment at a significant disadvantage in the labour market (or even excluded from it), given the difficulties of combining work and caring for a newborn baby. It was the interaction of the rules with the impairment that created a hindrance in working life or a disability. However, the position of the Advocate General and the Court was effectively that she would still have been able to participate in working life, so long as she modified her choices and did not have a child. Here we see threats to existing economic structures and ways of thinking being fended off through a combination of narrowly construed economic objectives imputed to equality law, and a medical model masquerading as a social one. Individuals, not the system, must adapt.

The failure to apply the social model was again evident in *Glatzel*, in which the Court stated that it did 'not have sufficient information to ascertain whether such impairment *constitutes a "disability"*'[68] thus revealing again a belief that impairments *constitute* disability. The case concerned the effects of rules about driving licences and visual acuity. The Advocate General applied the social model asserted in *HK Danmark,* acknowledging that although Mr Glatzel had learned to compensate in his daily life for his amblyopia, that condition, combined with the rules excluding him from the profession of lorry driver, could have a disabling impact upon access to the labour market. The interaction between the condition and the rules 'prevents the person from participating fully and effectively in a professional activity'.[69] The Court instead suggested that it could not rule on whether the impairment was a disability and then went on to say that even if he were disabled, the rules would be justified due to 'overriding considerations of road safety'[70] in spite of scant and out-of-date evidence.[71] The Court relied on an intuition of risk, rather than a robust logical analysis, which for instance might have required comparing the risks to those posed by other serious conditions, for which an automatic ban was not the consequence.[72] The readiness to characterise disability as inherently risky, without recourse to the maths or science of risk, is not only potentially discriminatory, it is potentially disabling.

The Court's preoccupation with the effect of impairment upon the workplace means that it has failed to recognise that in many cases there need not be an 'inherent' labour market disadvantage attendant upon an impairment, but that

---

[68] Case C-356/12 *Wolfgang Glatzel v Freistaat Bayern* EU:C:2014:350, 47, emphasis added.

[69] ibid, Opinion of AG Bot EU:C:2013:505, 39.

[70] ibid, 48.

[71] The report relied on an acknowledged 'lack of research data to determine the minimum values for visual acuity' and 'a lack of scientific studies on several aspects of eyesight for drivers of power-driven vehicles' (ibid, 60; 65).

[72] People with 'serious and irreversible renal deficiency' for example, were entitled to provide an 'authorised medical opinion' that theirs was an 'exceptional case' allowing for a Group 2 licence (for heavy goods vehicles), see Directive 2006/126/EC, Annex III Minimum Standards of Physical and Mental Fitness for Driving a Power-Driven Vehicle, 16(2).

that disability may arise as a result of 'discrimination, prejudice, stigma and an inaccessible environment, all of which serve to exclude them or limit their options', in the words of Waddington, who suggests that the Court has not yet taken seriously its own definition of disability.[73] The medical model creates an assimilation-based approach to equality, as is evident in the agenda of reconciling work and family life. And the assumptions that underpin an assimilation approach to equality have informed the EU-wide drive towards activation policies. The principle of activation is that the disabled individual needs to be assimilated into the labour market. As market citizens, the disabled, like mothers, have a duty to serve the market according to the terms set by non-disabled men. Activation is a necessary corollary to market citizenship, and the activating turn in EU policy and within Member States exhibits a tendency to make those excluded from, or marginalised within, the labour market responsible for their own exclusion. This stigmatisation of social justice measures and of benefit receipt, and the ensuing punishment of the poor, is examined next.

## IV. MARKET CITIZENSHIP: EXCLUSION, ACTIVATION AND THE STIGMATISATION OF SOCIAL JUSTICE MEASURES

Activating welfare reforms, and active labour market policies, tend to downplay the social factors at work in creating labour market exclusions, and assume that unemployment is a matter of choice susceptible to behaviour management. In Borghi's terms, they prescribe 'biographical solutions' to structural problems.[74] As such, they not only abdicate society's responsibility for social justice, they actively denigrate and stigmatise measures intended to redress social injustices.

The EU has long championed the pursuit of active labour market policies[75] which purport to tackle 'poverty traps'.[76] A 2012 Commission report made 27 mentions of inactivity or unemployment 'traps' and 11 of 'benefit dependence' in the space of 20 pages. It stated that 'generous and long-lasting' unemployment benefits 'can create unemployment traps and benefit dependence, thus entrenching long-term unemployment'.[77] The Commission's 2016 thematic fiche

---

[73] Waddington, above n 64, 591.

[74] V Borghi, 'One Way Europe? Institutional Guidelines, Emerging Regimes of Justification and Paradoxical Turns in European Welfare Capitalism' (2011) 14 *European Journal of Social Theory* 3, 321, 326.

[75] The Commission called for a move from 'passive income support measures' to 'pro-active policies' following the adoption of the employment title in the Amsterdam Treaty (see European Commission, 'Commission Communication Proposal for Guidelines for Member States Employment Policies 1998' COM(97) 497 final (Brussels, 01.10.1997)).

[76] European Commission, 'Active Inclusion: Definition'. Available at: ec.europa.eu/social/main.jsp?catId=1059&langId=en.

[77] K Stovicek and A Turrini, *European Economy: Benchmarking Unemployment Benefit Systems—Economic Papers 454* (Brussels, European Union, 2012) 6.

on unemployment benefits again argued that 'a high level of benefits can reduce the incentives to return into employment'[78] and pointed to the punitive side to activation policies as important, including 'the imposition of sanctions such as the suspension of benefit eligibility in case of non-compliance'.[79] The sub-heading of the document was 'making work pay', but the expectation is that states make unemployment pay less, since there is no discussion on how to make employment more lucrative.[80] The discourse of activation is inherently judgemental, implying that those at risk of poverty are also at risk of moral atrophy, from which they should be protected through processes of activation and responsibilisation (indeed, the language of responsibility suggesting that the inactive are *irresponsible*). In 2009, a report prepared for, and published by, the Commission emphasised the 'strong self-activity and self responsibility of the job-seeker' in activation measures dealing with unemployment.[81]

An emphasis on 'self-responsibility' can be problematic in cases of structural inequality. The Heads of the Public Employment Services of the EU released a statement announcing the importance of targeting the 'inactive ... like disabled, lone mothers, women at home, early retired, or those on sick leave' in order to reduce 'the burden for the welfare system'.[82] A 2008 report for the Commission recommended shifting more parents from 'inactivity' to 'work' by replacing 'generous child supplements and parental leave schemes' with in-work benefits and tax-credits.[83] While the 'quality' of work sometimes gets a mention,[84] the strategies deployed are aimed at increasing the quantity of those in work through reducing the choices that involve opting out. This can lead to cheap and short-term strategies (as with German measures criticised by Betzelt and Bothfeld),[85] and a failure to take account of material factors in different lives (as Nybom notes of Swedish

---

[78] European Commission, 'Unemployment Benefits with a Focus on Making Work Pay', *European Semester Thematic Fiche* 03.05.2016, available at: ec.europa.eu/europe2020/pdf/themes/2016/unemployment_benefits_201605.pdf, 1.

[79] ibid, 2.

[80] ibid.

[81] European Commission, *The Role of the Public Employment Services Related to 'Flexicurity' in the European Labour Markets—Policy and Business Analysis*, VC/2007/0927 Final report (March 2009) 37.

[82] Public Employment Services 2020 Working Group, 'PES and EU 2020: Making the Employment Guidelines Work' (2011). Available at: ec.europa.eu/social/BlobServlet?docId=3692&langId=en.

[83] M Peters, M van der Ende, S Desczka and T Viertelhauzen, *Benefit Systems and Their Interaction with Active Labour Market Policies in the New Member States—Summary Report* (Rotterdam, ECORYS, 2008) 33.

[84] Active inclusion policies should promote 'integration into sustainable, quality employment' and 'promote *quality jobs*, including pay and benefits, working conditions, health and safety, access to lifelong learning and career prospects, in particular with a view to preventing in-work poverty' (Commission Recommendation of 3 October 2008 on the active inclusion of people excluded from the labour market (notified under document number C(2008) 5737 OJ [2008] L 307/11 (1) and (4)(b)(i)), emphasis in original.

[85] S Betzelt and S Bothfeld, 'The Erosion of Social Status: The Case of Germany' in S Betzelt and S Bothfeld (eds), *Activation and Labour Market Reforms in Europe: Challenges to Social Citizenship* (Basingstoke, Palgrave Macmillan, 2011).

measures[86] while measures in the Netherlands intended to drive lone parents into work have been described as a policy of 'shock and awe').[87]

## A. Activation: Punishing the Poor

The efficacy of activation policies is deeply contested, since they are at times criticised for demonising the poor in the interests of political grandstanding.[88] As such, it is problematic that Union institutions seem to take such efficacy for granted. In 2005, Boeri pointed to research suggesting that 'help and hassle' policies of activation had no significant effect on the duration of benefit claims in the US.[89] Such policies in some cases appeared to correlate with lower earning outcomes, since those chivvied back into the workplace through administrative duress entered at a lower earning point than they might have done had they had more 'help' than 'hassle'.[90] Activation also assumes that the 'inactive' can be made active through appropriate (usually negative) incentives, but some commentators argue that employability restrictions do not simply go away[91] just because the welfare support is reduced. For instance, Berthoud has described a 'disability employment penalty' that disabled workseekers face in reduced labour market opportunities.[92]

As for the specific UK case, activation, through benefit conditionality, has been ramped up with the introduction of universal credit. The then Secretary of State for Work and Pensions, Iain Duncan Smith, has declared that UK welfare reforms represent 'a whole new concept: a contract with people who are in need of support'.[93] The Welfare Reform Act which introduced universal credit is rooted in the idea of welfare as an individual not a social contract, with 86 mentions of claimant 'commitments'[94] and 15 mentions of claimant's (benefit) responsibilities in the

---

[86] J Nybom, 'Activation and "Coercion" Among Swedish Social Assistance Claimants with Different Work Barriers and Socio-Demographic Characteristics: What is the Logic?' (2013) 22 *International Journal Social Welfare* 1, 45.

[87] T Knijn, C Martin and J Millar, 'Activation as a Common Framework for Social Policies Towards Lone Parents' (2007) 41 *Social Policy and Administration* 6, 638, 650.

[88] T Haux, 'Activating Lone Parents: An Evidence-Based Policy Appraisal of the 2008 Welfare-to-Work Reform in Britain' (2010) *ISER Working Paper* No 2010–29; J Nybom, above n 86; JM Dostal, 'The Workfare Illusion: Re-examining the Concept and the British Case' (2008) 42 *Social Policy and Administration* 1, 19; P Larkin, 'The Legislative Arrival and Future of Workfare: The Welfare Reform Act 2009' (2011) 18 *Journal of Social Security Law* 1, 11; and S Wright, 'Relinquishing Rights? The Impact of Activation on Citizenship for Lone Parents in the UK' in Betzelt and Bothfeld (2011) above n 85, 65.

[89] T Boeri, 'An Activating Social Security System' (2005) 153 *De Economist* 4, 375.

[90] ibid, 382.

[91] Van Aerschot suggests activation does not work as 'most recipients with restricted employability will never get employment' (P Van Aerschot, 'Administrative Justice and the Implementation of Activation Legislation in Denmark, Finland and Sweden' (2011) 18 *Journal of Social Security Law* 1, 33, 36.

[92] R Berthoud, 'Trends in the Employment of Disabled People in Britain' (2011) *ISER Working Paper* 2011-03, 21.

[93] Iain Duncan Smith, 3rd Reading of the Bill, HC Deb, 15 Jun 2011, col 920.

[94] Welfare Reform Act 2012, predominantly in ss 14, 44, 54, 59.

Act's explanatory notes. This commitment comes with heavy job search require-ments: claimants are required to be active for the 'expected number of hours' per week.[95] Unless there are deductions to the expected number of hours for care responsibilities,[96] or 'physical or mental impairment',[97] then the expected number of hours is 35.[98] So if a claimant is expected to be active for 35 hours, and is out of work, they will be expected to undertake job-searching activities for the full 35 hours. If they work 20 hours, they will be expected to undertake job search activities for the remaining 15 hours. Deductions may be made in certain cases, for example, for paid work, work preparation, domestic emergency or volunteering. Interestingly, if someone is unemployed and begins volunteering, they may not volunteer for more than 50 per cent of their expected hours,[99] to ensure they also spend a substantial period of time looking for work.

The requirement to always be seeking full-time work rests upon certain assump-tions about the labour market. We have seen increasing labour market flexibility, with a continued proliferation of casual and zero-hour contracts,[100] suggesting that full-time work may be even harder to get for some. We have also seen drastic public spending cuts, rather than investment in back-to-work programmes. The Depart-ment of Work and Pensions (DWP) released figures in 2015 indicating that there had been a 60 per cent cut in job centres employing disability specialist employ-ment advisers.[101] These cuts do not suggest strong investment in positive activation measures (such as support for job searches). This calls into question the wisdom of the strong negative activation emphasis in universal credit. The DWP's own longi-tudinal evaluation, published in December 2015, found that while 'universal credit claimants spent more hours on job search activity than those claiming jobseeker's allowance, it must be noted that they did not apply for significantly more jobs and a greater proportion lost confidence over time that they would find a job within the next three months'. The report stated that this may be an 'unintended consequence of the intensity of the job search required' under universal credit rules.[102]

[95]   Universal Credit Regulations 2013, SI 2013/376, reg 88.

[96]   ibid, regs 88, 89, 91.

[97]   ibid.

[98]   ibid, reg 88.

[99]   ibid, reg 95(3).

[100]   With regard to the UK, see Department for Business, Innovation and Skills, *Consultation: Zero Hours Contracts*, December 2013, 5 and 11. Available at: www.gov.uk/government/uploads/sys-tem/uploads/attachment_data/file/267634/bis-13-1275-zero-hoursemployment-contracts-FINAL. pdf. With regard to the EU, and increased casualisation and the rise in atypical work, see European Foundation for the Improvement of Living and Working Conditions, 'Very Atypical Work: Explora-tory Analysis of 4th European Working Conditions Survey' *Background Paper* EF/10/10/EN. Avail-able at: www.europarl.europa.eu/meetdocs/2009_2014/documents/empl/dv/studyveryatypicalwork_/ studyveryatypicalwork_en.pdf.

[101]   From 226 in 2011/12, to 90 in 2015/16 (J Stone, 'DWP Cuts Specialist Disability Employment Advisers in Jobcentres by Over 60 per cent', *The Independent*, 10 November 2015).

[102]   DWP, *Universal Credit Extended Gateway Evaluation: Findings from Research with Extended Gateway Claimants*, December 2015. Available at: www.gov.uk/government/uploads/system/uploads/ attachment_data/file/481865/universal-credit-extended-gateway-evaluation.pdf, 49.

Rather than question the utility of activation policies, in light of the evidence, in universal credit the government has instituted an activation-heavy regime rolling out activation not only to jobseekers but also to people actually in work to get them to try to work more and earn more. The House of Commons Work and Pensions Committee acknowledged that the imposition of such work-seeking conditions upon those in work was a break with the norm, claiming it was 'potentially revolutionary', promising progress in breaking the cycle of people stuck in low pay, low prospects employment'.[103] However, the government's longitudinal study found that while universal credit claimants in part-time work were more likely to be looking for further work than jobseeker's allowance claimants who found part-time work, universal credit claimants were not more likely to be working more hours than jobseeker's allowance claimants at 'wave 2' (three months after the first survey, which was 5.5 weeks after the claim). Actually, a higher proportion of jobseeker's allowance claimants (55 per cent) were working more than 35 hours than universal credit claimants (48 per cent).[104] Nevertheless, the same month the report was published, the government confirmed its commitment to activating those in work, noting that universal credit claimants were going to lose out as a result of cuts to the work allowance, but suggesting that claimants 'could recoup the loss from the work allowance changes by working 3–4 additional hours a week at the national living wage'.[105]

Here, the assumptions behind activation are extended so that it is not only assumed that individuals have control over whether and when they enter the labour market, but also that once in it, they have control over their hours and pay, and can readily increase them when required. Those that fail to make sufficient efforts to do so may be sanctioned, so face a reduction in their benefit for a period of time (which in the case of higher-level sanctions is at least 91 days, and can go up to 1095 days).[106] The ESRC Welfare Conditionality study has cast doubt upon the efficacy of in-work sanctions in particular, and also highlighted severe, negative outcomes of the sanction regime: sanctions had 'severely detrimental financial, material, emotional and health impacts on those subject to them'[107] with one research participant attempting suicide. In-work recipients felt that they should not be subject to the same sanction regime as out-of-work recipients, a feeling echoed in the Work and Pensions Committee report which suggested that

---

[103] House of Commons Work and Pensions Committee, 'In-Work Progression in Universal Credit', *Tenth Report of Session*, HC 549, 3. Available at: www.publications.parliament.uk/pa/cm201516/cmselect/cmworpen/549/549.pdf.

[104] DWP, above n 102, 44.

[105] DWP, *Government Response to SSAC Occasional Paper No 15: Universal Credit—Priorities for Action*, 2015. Available at: www.gov.uk/government/publications/government-response-ssac-report-on-universal-credit.

[106] Universal Credit Regulations 2013, SI 2013/376, reg 102.

[107] S Wright, P Dwyer, J MacNeill and ABR Stewart, *First Wave Findings: Universal Credit*, May 2016, 1. Available at: www.welfareconditionality.ac.uk/wp-content/uploads/2016/05/WelCond-findings-Universal-Credit-May16.pdf.

those in work 'self-evidently do not lack the motivation to work'[108] and pointed to submissions that 'conditionality is most effective where claimants lack motivation or have negative attitudes towards employment'.[109] In contrast, the barriers to earning more when actually in employment were thought to be 'structural or due to personal circumstances rather than motivational'.[110] The Committee had recommended in March 2015 that the government not proceed with in-work sanctions until it had 'robust evidence' that in-work conditionality would be effective. There is, as yet, no such robust evidence but in-work sanctions were introduced anyway.

Sainsbury noted in 2010 that in times of recession, activation may amount to 'an attack on the unemployed at a time when they are least able to do anything about it',[111] but the new turn in the UK is towards making targets of the employed, but poorly paid, in variable hours and low-security work, who do not command the labour market bargaining power to adjust their position as required. An example of a worker whose degree of labour market disempowerment resulted in exploitation and abuse of rights, is the case of Ernesto. The facts of the appalling conditions in which he lived rather make a mockery of the idea that he could command changes in the details as to hours in his employment contract:

---

**Case Study: Ernesto**

This client was a Bulgarian man in his 20s. He came to the UK after the expiry of transition measures and experienced exploitation and denial of basic rights with two employers in quick succession.

*Field notes: Went through client history—he arrived in UK and started working for hotel on 26 August. He left as the accommodation was awful—client said he felt 'treated like an animal'. He showed me photos—five beds in very small space—about the size of a bureau interview room. One bed propped up on kitchen worktop/edge of another bed as physically no space on the floor. In same space was the kitchen/food prep area. Photo showed very dirty and mouldy. Photo of toilet/bathroom facilities—filthy and mouldy. I advised client on possibility of reporting the hotel to environmental health, gave details.*

The conditions of the accommodation were unacceptable and presented a threat to his health and to his safety. Ernesto left and found new employment, through an agent, at a restaurant. The agent charged him £300. The employer provided accommodation and was told a deduction would be made from his wages. After a few weeks he was summarily dismissed and told to move out of the flat in a week. Much of the advice was about how to manage the housing situation and to enforce his right not to be subject

---

[108]   House of Commons Work and Pensions Committee, above n 103, 26.
[109]   ibid, 21.
[110]   ibid, 24.
[111]   R Sainsbury, '21st Century Welfare: Getting Closer to Radical Benefit Reform?' (2010) 17 *Public Policy Research* 2, 102.

to an illegal eviction, informing him that his landlord had to go through the correct procedures, and give appropriate time. The employer was trying to pursue an unlawful eviction. Then the employment agency got involved, further pressurising the client to leave and issuing an ultimatum.

*Field notes: The recruitment company that had put him in touch with restaurant had phoned him and said unless he and his partner left the flat by 12.30pm today the police would be called—alleged that client's painting of a room constituted criminal misconduct ... Client had a contract with [the restaurant], nothing in writing re dismissal and no court order concerning eviction had been served.*

We had to give advice on what to do if he had already been locked out while coming to the Citizens Advice office. I gathered the details of his employment with the restaurant, in order to help him later present a case for retaining worker status during this gap. On looking at the pay details, it seems that the restaurant had effectively offered a contract with unlawful deductions: the deduction for rent went above the total allowable offset, leaving him below the minimum wage. Ernesto chose not to pursue this, his concerns were (a) getting another job and (b) not getting evicted before finding other accommodation.

Ernesto had little control over his erratic employment record and poor treatment at the hands of unscrupulous employers. The inappropriate emphasis on personal responsibility and assumptions of individual control echo Levy's description of activation as a 'thin, neo-liberal strategy' which 'attributes unemployment to personal failings or excessively generous benefits, rather than broader social and economic factors'.[112] When Levy was writing, the emphasis was simply getting into any form of work, so that those subjected to activation measures could be 'forced to take substandard jobs at substandard wages, on pain of losing their benefits', leading to the conclusion that 'activation transforms Marshallian citizens into a reserve army of the unemployed, mobilised on behalf of capital and against the rest of the workforce'.[113] The difference under the universal credit system is that the reserve army now includes those in work but on low pay or low/variable hours who may be forced to seek to take several sub-standard jobs. While the rationale that more people should earn more may seem in itself reasonable, the universal credit system simply assumes that it is in the worker's gift to increase her own earnings. Activation mechanisms do not include addressing the flaws in a labour market that employs people in insecure positions, with few or, in some cases, no guaranteed hours and on low pay. Activation stands in opposition to Stuart White's 'fair work test', which requires different forms of participation to

---

[112] JD Levy, 'Between Neo-Liberalism and No Liberalism: Progressive Approaches to Economic Liberalization in Western Europe' in B Eichengreen, D Stiefel and M Landesmann (eds), *The European Economy in an American Mirror* (Abingdon, Routledge, 2008) 315.
[113] ibid, 311.

be treated equitably, providing recognition and respect for invisible work, such as care, to avoid arbitrarily penalising some individuals for 'meeting their contributive obligations in one way rather than another'. White's test also calls for contribution equity, which means imposing equivalent contribution requirements on *all* citizens, including asset-rich citizens and high earners, rather than constructing responsibility solely around low earners.[114]

## B.  The EU: Activation and the Market as the New Morality

While commentators have criticised the ability of activation policies to respond to economic crisis,[115] the European Employment Strategy has typically spurred Member States to wield the activation stick as the only response to a tough economic climate[116] since welfare systems 'should be designed to reward return to work for the unemployed' and should link job searching 'more closely' to benefits.[117] The EU policy of flexicurity places rather more emphasis on 'flexi' than on 'curity', with Member States required to make workers absorb labour market fluctuations and create expectations that workers move quickly between jobs, and take on responsibility for retraining and job searching for example, without any great responsibility placed upon Member States to provide the resources to create adequate welfare cushions and positive active labour market supports.

The 'flexi' element of flexicurity refers to the flexibility afforded to employers, rather than to employees: flexibility to hire, fire, change shift patterns and contractual terms, stipulate zero-hours contracts to keep employees on call, and so on. In the face of mixed evidence, the European Commission has nevertheless applauded the UK's moves to create 'clearer work incentives' and even expressed concerns that universal credit might not go far enough if it created an incentive for second earners to reduce their hours. The Commission noted with approval the plans to 'mitigate these risks' by introducing more 'work search conditionality' into the benefit.[118] The Commission has chivvied the UK to be more punitive

---

[114] S White, *The Civic Minimum: On the Rights and Obligations of Economic Citizenship* (Oxford, Oxford University Press, 2003).

[115] See above n 88, also Sainsbury, above n 111.

[116] The Public Employment Services Working Group suggested in 2011 that there needed to be a 'shift from passive to active labour market policies and the mutual obligation approach' (above n 82, 7).

[117] Council of Ministers of the European Union (EPSCO), *Joint Employment Report*, Doc 7396/11, 8 March 2011, 23. Available at: register.consilium.europa.eu/doc/srv?l=EN&f=ST%207396%202011%20INIT.

[118] European Commission, 'Commission Staff Working Document: Assessment of the 2013 National Reform Programme and Convergence Programme for United Kingdom Accompanying the Document Recommendation for a Council Recommendation on United Kingdom's 2013 National Reform Programme and Delivering a Council Opinion on United Kingdom's Convergence Programme for 2012–2017', COM(2013) 378 final (Brussels, 29.5.2013) 21.

before, encouraging the UK to further lower the age of a child at which a lone parent is required to seek work.[119] The UK obliged.[120]

Within the rationale of activation, benefit receipt is characterised as an aberration to be rectified and benefit recipients are 'othered' as having interests at odds with those of the market. People who are out of work are viewed as distortions to the market, rather than as market actors themselves.[121] It is this reification of the market, and the elevation of its precepts above the interests of individuals, as though they are laws of nature, that chimes with the driving policy forces of the EU. As Weiler noted back in 1991, the creation of a 'single market' represented a 'highly politicized choice of ethos, ideology, and political culture: the culture of "the market"'.[122] Activation thus makes sense as an EU approach as constructed by those with greatest market power.[123] The use of market norms to reassess welfare will not promote greater redistribution of property since, as Dworkin notes, market norms assume 'the adequacy of the scheme already in place'.[124] The invocation of responsibility serves to legitimate inaction in the face of potential social injustice, echoing Somek's summary of Weber's prediction that 'responsibility' would provide such a rationalisation since it 'serves consistently the interest of those who are too avaricious to give'.[125]

At EU level, the culture of the market holds even greater sway than at national level, since nation states still provide some degree of buttress against untrammelled market logic. The free movement regime is more readily subjected to activation principles than national welfare rules and the characterising of EU nationals as production factor labour is seen as legitimate. Theirs is a true market citizenship, with roots in the idea of a 'homo economicus',[126] whose emphasis is upon individualistic choice. As Peebles noted in 1997, 'it is only as a citizen-worker that ... one is granted the many rights accorded to commodities in the treaties'.[127]

---

[119] European Commission, 'Commission Staff Working Paper: Assessment of the 2011 National Reform Programme and Convergence Programme for the United Kingdom Accompanying the Document Recommendation for a Council Recommendation on the National Reform Programme 2011 of the United Kingdom and Delivering a Council Opinion on the Updated Convergence Programme of the United Kingdom', 2011–2014 SEC(2011) 827 final, 14, 16.

[120] Above n 118, parents of school age children are subject to conditionality, while parents of three to four-year-olds are required to undertake preparation for work. See reg 2(2) of the Social Security (Lone Parents and Miscellaneous Amendments) Regulations 2012, SI 2012/874.

[121] DWP, 'Summary: Interventions and Options', *Impact Assessment of Welfare Reform Bill 2009* (14 January 2009), 4.

[122] JHH Weiler, 'The Transformation of Europe' (1991) 100 *Yale Law Journal*, 2403, 2477.

[123] A Somek, 'Europe: From Emancipation to Empowerment', *LSE Europe in Question Discussion Paper Series*, LEQS Paper Number 60/2013 (April, 2013), 38.

[124] R Dworkin, *Law's Empire* (Oxford, Hart, 1998), 310.

[125] A Somek, *Engineering Equality* (Oxford, Oxford University Press, 2011) 87.

[126] M Everson, 'The Legacy of the Market Citizen' in J Shaw and G More (eds) *New Legal Dynamics of European Union* (Oxford, Clarendon Press, 1995).

[127] G Peebles, 'A Very Eden of the Innate Rights of Man? A Marxist Look at the European Treaties and Case Law' (1997) 22 *Law and Social Inquiry* 581, 608.

Such steps as had been made since then towards an EU social citizenship were faltering and led to an at best nebulous right to a modicum of equal treatment, through the entitlement to proportionate unequal treatment. These appear to have been rolled back by the cases leading up to and including *Commission v UK*.[128]


## V. SUMMARY

Activation is more than an isolated policy: it is a structural agenda, that shapes how the Union conceives of fundamental rights such as equal treatment on the grounds of sex and disability, while simultaneously promoting a restructuring of welfare that disproportionately disadvantages women and disabled people, and requires their assimilation to the male, non-disabled, 'normal' labour market. Equal treatment is valued insofar as it furthers the objectives of the single market. The reconciliation agenda rather misleadingly calls upon the phrase 'work–life balance' when the aim is to increase the numbers of people in work, rather than to increase the weight given to life for workers. Similarly, the Union is keen to activate the disabled. A market citizenship framework asserts the importance of the 'normal' labour market and so relies upon a medical model of disability that does not challenge the economic or social status quo.

Activation carries with it some ideologically loaded assumptions about the 'inactive' and, like market citizenship, rewards the economically successful while denigrating, negating and punishing the poor. It is a scheme in which the market is elevated to the role of morality itself, and in which social justice measures are marginalised and the pursuit of social justice itself is stigmatised as facilitating moral turpitude. But in a national context, Member States recognise the necessity of maintaining some such measures, even if they are curbed and vilified. In the context of EU nationals, however, market citizenship gives Member States rather freer rein to take activation to its logical conclusion.

This leaves us with a market citizenship in which EU nationals must be performing economic activities in order to be entitled to the rights stemming from free movement law. This limitation was in recent decades softened by the breadth with which economic activity was defined (though still not broad enough to encompass family care responsibilities).[129] But an activation-plus approach in the UK directed at EU nationals means that they might not benefit from such a broad definition, and are at risk of being found not to be doing enough of the right kind of economic activity. The construction of rights as a corollary of economic utility

---

[128] Case C-308/14 *Commission v United Kingdom* EU:C:2016:436.
[129] Case C-325/09 *Secretary of State for Work and Pensions v Maria Dias* EU:C:2011:498 and Case C-77/95 *Bruna-Alessandra Züchner v Handelskrankenkasse (Ersatzkasse) Bremen* EU:C:1996:425.

is an act of commodification. Such commodification has long been controversial, but is apparently more palatable—or even seen as morally imperative—in the context of non-nationals. EU nationals are perceived as less entitled to benefit from national networks of solidarity of host states and must 'earn' their membership through economic virtue. This rationale, premised on inequality, is explicit in the UK welfare reforms from 2014 onwards targeting EU nationals. The UK reforms are explored next as an example of activation untrammelled by the trappings of duties owed to own-nationals: an activation-plus regime.

# 6

# Activation-Plus: Welfare Reforms and Declaratory Discrimination

*The government is determined to cap welfare and reduce immigration.*[1]

## I. INTRODUCTION

THE FREE MOVEMENT framework is premised upon unequal treatment. The UK has created an activation-plus regime where only economically active EU nationals have any entitlement. But equal treatment *just* for the economically active EU nationals means there is no real equal treatment for *any* EU nationals. There are a number of ways that the economically active are disadvantaged. They may fall foul of restrictive interpretations of economic activity, and so be excluded in spite of working, or they may have a fairly fluid status, moving in and out of work, and so regularly be at risk of exclusion. While economically active, they are still on a precipice that affects health and well-being[2] and makes them vulnerable (creating pressures to stay in exploitative work or to stay in abusive relationships to avoid loss of worker or family member status, for example). The stratification of rights according to economic activity necessitates an evidential burden—a need for checks and testing creates administrative hurdles for all EU national workers not faced by own-state nationals, and contributes to a culture of administrative hostility and suspicion. The UK's programme of reforms targeting EU nationals does all of these things. Moreover, it implements a stated intention to discriminate, based on discriminatory (and inaccurate) perceptions of EU nationals as benefit tourists, and also states an intention to reduce free movement. These announcements are declaratory obstacles to movement.

---

[1] DWP, 'Further Curbs to Migrant Access to Benefits Announced', *Press Release*, 8 April 2014. Available at: www.gov.uk/government/news/further-curbs-to-migrant-access-to-benefits-announced.

[2] C Bambra, T Lunau, KA Van der Wel, TA Eikemo, and N Dragano, 'Work, Health and Welfare: The Association Between Working Conditions, Welfare States and Self-Reported General Health in Europe' (2014) 44 *International Journal of Health Services* 113, 130; J Benach, A Vives, M Amable, C Vanroelen, G Tarafa, and C Muntaner, 'Precarious Employment: Understanding an Emerging Social Determinant of Health' (2014) 35 *Annual Review of Public Health* 229.

This chapter outlines the concept of declaratory discrimination established in EU employment law. It argues that the state should be held to at least the same obligations as employers and that the UK government has embarked on a programme of declaratory discrimination underpinning the welfare reforms introduced to target EU nationals. It then extends the concept to declaratory obstacles to movement, drawing upon the case law on the free movement of goods. Several of the specific reforms are examined as obstacles to movement, and the publicity and guidance accompanying them as declarations of discriminatory intent. The three-month waiting period for benefits[3] applied to returning UK nationals effectively reverses *Swaddling*,[4] creating a penalty for UK nationals who exercise free movement. A number of the reforms target EU national jobseekers, reducing entitlement to housing benefit,[5] and introducing a narrowly applied, genuine prospects of work test for entitlement to jobseeker's allowance for more than three months.[6] The implementation of this test reveals the problems that arise when decision-makers rely solely on guidance that instructs them to infringe EU law.

The reduction in entitlement for jobseekers makes the cliff-top steeper, so that being defined as a jobseeker entails significant disadvantages. This has been accompanied with measures that narrow down the definition of worker, so that more people are likely to fall into the jobseeker category, and go over the welfare cliff-edge. Here, it is worth revisiting some of the shortcomings in the EU definition of work, and the invisibility of unpaid care, before going on to analyse the problematic UK approach. Two developments in particular are problematic: (1) the creation and use of a minimum earnings threshold[7] which establishes a presumption of marginality for work at quite a high threshold of work (23 hours per week at the national minimum wage when introduced); and (2) the UK courts' decision to negate all work carried out during years of transition for A8 nationals, where they have not fully complied with the initial worker registration scheme.[8] Both have had significant consequences for EU nationals' claims not only to be workers but to later claims to permanent residence. The combination of those rules has had a significant detrimental impact upon accession state national women fleeing abusive relationships, so this chapter concludes with an argument that domestic

---

[3] The Jobseeker's Allowance (Habitual Residence) Amendment Regulations 2013, SI 2013/3196; Child Benefit (General) and Tax Credits (Residence) (Amendment) Regulations 2014.

[4] Case C-90/97 *Robin Swaddling v Adjudication Officer* EU:C:1999:96.

[5] Housing Benefit (Habitual Residence) Amendment Regulations 2014, SI 2014/539.

[6] The requirement for compelling evidence of a genuine prospect of being engaged after six months of job seeking was introduced in The Immigration (European Economic Area) (Amendment) (No 2) Regulations 2013 Sch 1: amending reg 6(2)(b) of the Immigration (European Economic Area) Regulations 2006 and inserting reg 6(2)(ba). The six-month period was reduced to three months in The Immigration (European Economic Area) (Amendment) (No 3) Regulations 2014, SI 2014/2761. The 'genuine prospects of work test' was introduced in DWP, *Decision-Maker Guidance Part 3* 'Habitual Residence and Right to Reside—IS/JSA/SPC/ESA' (June 2015) 073080.

[7] DWP, *Decision-Maker Guidance*, ibid, 073031.

[8] *Zalewska v Department for Social Development (Northern Ireland)* [2008] UKHL 67.

abuse is a social security risk but that EU and domestic social security frame-
works, afflicted with a male tilt, fail to recognise it as such. Taken together, the
pre-existing gaps in the EU framework with the new cavities created by punitive,
exclusionary welfare reforms, make the disappearance of proportionality review
all the more concerning since they create automatic cut-offs that are indifferent to
social injustice and, in some cases, are manifestly absurd.

## II. DECLARATORY DISCRIMINATION

The concept of declaratory discrimination, and its prohibition, was established in
the employment law case of *Feryn*,[9] which dealt with allegations of race discrimination contrary to Directive 2000/43.[10] In that case, an employer had announced
publicly that he would not employ Moroccans, to accommodate his customers'
preferences. In an interview for the newspaper *De Standaard*, he said 'we aren't
looking for Moroccans. Our customers don't want them. They have to install
up-and-over doors in private homes, often villas, and those customers don't want
them coming into their homes'. In an interview on national television he said:
'People often say "no immigrants". ... I must comply with my customers' requirements ... We must meet the customers' requirements. This isn't my problem.'[11]

The ECJ received questions about the bearing of such announcements and
whether they were sufficient to create a presumption of discriminatory recruitment practices, without more evidence on the actual practices. The Court found
that the statements were sufficient to create a presumption of discriminatory
recruitment practices which would then put the onus on the firm to show that
'the actual recruitment practice does not correspond to those statements'.[12] But
it also found that those statements were not merely evidence of discrimination
elsewhere in the process, they were *acts of discrimination themselves*, and that those
announcements were part of the recruitment process. As Advocate General Poiares Maduro noted, to find otherwise would mean that such statements might
actually prove the most exclusionary tactic at an employer's disposal. If they were
permitted to 'differentiate very effectively ... simply by publicising the discriminatory character of their recruitment policy as overtly as possible beforehand', then
the 'most blatant strategy of employment discrimination might also turn out to be
the most "rewarding"'.[13] The statements must be viewed as part of the recruitment

---

[9] Case C-54/07 *Centrum voor gelijkheid van kansen en voor racismebestrijding v Firma Feryn NV*
EU:C:2008:397.

[10] Council Directive 2000/43/EC of 29 June 2000 implementing the principle of equal treatment
between persons irrespective of racial or ethnic origin OJ [2000] L 180/22.

[11] Case C-54/07 *Centrum voor gelijkheid van kansen en voor racismebestrijding v Firma Feryn NV*
Opinion of AG Poiares Maduro EU:C:2008:155, 3 and 4.

[12] *Feryn* judgment, above n 9, 32.

[13] *Feryn* AG Opinion, above n 11, 17.

process because the 'greatest "selection" takes place between those who apply, and those who do not'.[14]

As the provision on direct discrimination in Directive 2000/43 mirrors that in Directive 2000/78, and the *Feryn* principle pertains to the concept of non-discrimination rather than to the specific ground of race, the prohibition on (direct)[15] declaratory discrimination in *Feryn* applies across all prohibited characteristics. That is how the UK interprets it.[16] These instruments apply to employers, but states themselves should be held to at least as high standards when it comes to creating discriminatory barriers to the labour market. Indeed, announcements by the state are likely to have an even stronger dissuasive effect—even a labour market distorting one—upon potential applicants to the labour market in their territory, than announcements by any single employer. If we consider the wording of *Feryn*, it is possible to map it onto announcements by the state: the case prohibits discriminatory statements which are strongly likely 'to dissuade certain candidates from submitting their candidature and, accordingly, to hinder their access to the labour market'.[17] A Member State that makes its hostility to EU nationals known through public announcements would seem to also strongly dissuade those candidates from applying for jobs within its territory, so hindering access to the labour market.

While constructing the state as an actor in the process of private recruitment might require an imaginative step that has not yet been taken in EU law, the state does have (well-established) responsibilities to not create obstacles to movement. Declaratory discrimination can constitute a declaratory obstacle to movement. Again, if we look at the wording of *Feryn*, we can see how it might apply in a barriers-to-movement context:

> The fact that an employer declares publicly that it will not recruit employees of a certain ethnic or racial origin, something which is clearly likely to strongly dissuade certain candidates from submitting their candidature and, accordingly, to hinder their access to the labour market, constitutes direct discrimination.[18]

The same logic can be deployed as follows: the fact that a Member State declares publicly that it wishes to reduce the number of EU nationals in its territory, something which is clearly likely to strongly dissuade certain candidates from submitting their candidature and from moving, accordingly, to hinder their access to the labour market, and to hinder the exercise of free movement rights, constitutes a discriminatory obstacle to movement.

---

[14]  ibid, 15.
[15]  The Court made no mention of whether the same principle might apply to indirectly discriminatory declarations; the UK appears to have interpreted *Feryn* as applying to direct discrimination only (Equality Act 2010, explanatory notes, s 13, fn 63).
[16]  ibid.
[17]  *Feryn* judgment, above n 9, 25.
[18]  ibid.

In the UK, the waves of welfare reform targeting EU nationals create a picture of state-sanctioned xenoscepticism towards EU nationals[19] and, accompanied by a declared desire to reduce the number of EU nationals in the UK, form a programme of declaratory obstruction of movement. For the avoidance of doubt, the plan for reform was unveiled when then-Prime Minister David Cameron penned an article in the *Financial Times*, in November 2013, entitled 'Free movement within Europe needs to be less free'.[20] There followed a stream of announcements on new measures, accompanied with press releases adopting accusatory language towards EU nationals. It was not a tabloid newspaper, but the government itself, that announced it was 'accelerating action to stop rogue EU benefit claims',[21] that it was ensuring that 'migrants don't take advantage of the British benefits system',[22] and that the Prime Minister had 'made it clear that abuse and clear exploitation of the UK's welfare system will not be tolerated'.[23] The language of 'rogue' benefit claims, of migrants 'taking advantage' and of 'abuse and clear exploitation' is derogatory, to say the least. It conjures up the association of threat with EU nationals—one that is poorly substantiated. The announcements and measures are conspicuously unencumbered with evidence that there is a significant issue with 'rogue' or abusive claims. As it happens, the way the right to reside test has been operating for years would make it extremely difficult for the economically inactive to apply at all.

Such evidence as there is does not suggest that there is a benefit tourism problem. Studies indicate that EU nationals are net contributors to the UK public purse,[24] so even adopting an instrumentalist, production-factor labour approach, rather than one prioritising social justice, the argument that EU nationals should be treated differently because they pose a threat to the public purse fails on its own terms. Here it is worth noting that Daniel Korski, deputy director of the policy unit in David Cameron's government, in giving an account of the UK–EU negotiations preceding the 2016 referendum, said that the government had tried to 'argue that the UK faced a unique set of circumstances ... [but] we struggled to

---

[19] C O'Brien, 'The Pillory, The Precipice and The Slippery Slope: The Profound Effects of the UK's Legal Reform Programme targeting EU migrants' (2015) 37 *Journal of Social Welfare and Family Law* 1, 111.

[20] D Cameron, 'Free Movement within Europe Needs to be Less Free' (2013) *The Financial Times*, 26 November.

[21] DWP, 'Accelerating Action to Stop Rogue EU Benefit Claims' (2013) *Press Release*, 18 December. Available at: www.gov.uk/government/news/accelerating-action-to-stop-rogueeu-benefit-claims.

[22] DWP, 'Tough New Migrant Benefit Rules Come into Force Tomorrow' (2013) *Press Release*, 31 December. Available at: www.gov.uk/government/news/tough-new-migrantbenefit-rules-come-into-force-tomorrow.

[23] DWP, 'Minimum Earnings Threshold for EEA Migrants Introduced' (2014) *Press Release*, 21 February. Available at: www.gov.uk/government/news/minimum-earningsthreshold-for-eea-migrants-introduced.

[24] C Dustmann and T Frattini, 'The Fiscal Effects of Immigration to the UK', *Centre for Research and Analysis of Migration Discussion Paper Series* CDP No 22/13 (November 2013); J Wadsworth, S Dhingra, G Ottaviano and J Van Reenen, 'Brexit and the Impact of Immigration on the UK', *LSE CEP Brexit Analysis* No 5 (May 2016).

provide evidence to support our case'.[25] When the Commission consulted the UK government in 2013 as part of its study into the costs of free movement, the DWP responded that it had no evidence of benefit tourism.[26]

Yet the spectre of benefit tourism was used to drive through punitive welfare reforms explicitly aimed at EU nationals. One of the changes introduced, the Minimum Earnings Threshold, explored below, was announced in a press release that stated the measure was 'part of the government's long term plan to ... reduce immigration'.[27] Given the measure is specifically one directed at EU migrants, this can only mean that it will reduce the immigration of EU nationals. An announcement of an explicit desire to reduce free movement, coupled with measures intended to bear out that objective, can be construed as a declaratory obstacle to movement and potentially dissuasive to would-be free movers.

## A. Declaratory Obstacles to Movement

The case law on obstacles to movement tends to draw the remit of possible obstacles rather broadly, with the Court readily finding measures to be potential obstacles in the context of goods—with measures considered equivalent to those having quantitative restrictions (MEQRs) where 'they are capable of hindering, directly or indirectly, actually or potentially, intra-community trade'.[28] Discriminatory adverts might create a potential hindrance or disincentive to trade. The *Buy Irish*[29] case concerned an advertising campaign to encourage the sale and purchase of Irish products. The Irish government took a series of measures to promote Irish products, including giving 'financial and moral support' to the Irish Goods Council, which was responsible for the 'Buy Irish' advertising campaign. The ECJ found that the actions of the Irish Goods Council could not be divorced from the original programme of the government, which was therefore responsible for the 'discriminatory' campaign (discriminatory because by emphasising Irish produce, it disadvantaged goods from other Member States). The same reasoning would apply a fortiori to derogatory statements about produce from other Member States, or statements seeking to dissuade customers from buying their products. If we adopt a *Buy Irish* approach in the context of the free movement of people, then here we have no difficulty ascertaining whether the UK government is responsible

---

[25] D Korski, 'Why We Lost the Brexit Vote' (2016) *Politico*, 20 October 2016. Available at: www.politico.eu/article/why-we-lost-the-brexit-vote-former-uk-prime-minister-david-cameron/.

[26] 'When asked by Factcheck for estimates of how big the problem of benefit tourism actually is, and whether it had got better or worse since the introduction of the "right to reside" test in 2004, the DWP stated that there was "no information available"' (GHK ICF for the European Commission, *A Fact Finding Analysis on the Impact on the Member States' Social Security Systems of the Entitlements of Non-Active Intra-EU Migrants to Special Non-Contributory Cash Benefits and Healthcare Granted on the Basis of Residence—Final Report* (October 2013; revised December 2013) 10.5.2.

[27] Above n 23.

[28] Case 8/74 *Procureur du Roi v Benoît and Gustave Dassonville* EU:C:1974:82, 5.

[29] Case 249/81 *Commission of the European Communities v Ireland* EU:C:1982:402.

for the statements, since it has issued them. Those statements should be construed as potentially dissuasive to EU nationals—as well as promoting a derogatory picture of EU nationals which compares unfavourably with British nationals—and so as potential obstacles to movement.

The fact that EU nationals have continued to move to the UK does not in itself mean that there is no barrier. In the context of goods, the threshold for identifying a potential barrier is fairly low. In *Gourmet*,[30] the Swedish government claimed that in spite of the contested advertising rules prohibiting the advertising of alcohol, consumption of imported wine and whisky had increased, while consumption of domestically produced vodka had decreased, so the rules were not a barrier. Nevertheless, the Court found that without the rule, the consumption of imported beverages might have increased even more.[31] In the cases following *Keck*,[32] the breadth of measures that could require justification in the context of goods expanded further.[33] The free movement of goods imposes a principle that must be interpreted broadly, creating a low threshold[34] to establish a prima facie barrier, and placing the burden upon the Member State to disprove that barrier through evidenced justification.

We might expect measures adopted in order to reduce immigration to be subject to justification tests generally applied to restrictions on free movement: that they pursue a legitimate objective, are proportionate, necessary and appropriate. To be legitimate, the objective cannot be purely protectionist, and in theory should not be purely economic.[35] A stated objective to reduce free movement could not easily be squared with EU law, and so could not be regarded as legitimate in itself. The objectives of reducing the welfare burden might be legitimate (though also might be a purely economic aim), but the burden would have to be shown to be a problem in fact, rather than in rhetoric, which is not straightforward, given the weight of evidence to the contrary.

There is a strong onus upon Member States to show that any measures restrictive of the movement of goods are proportionate and do not go beyond what is necessary. In *Commission v Austria*,[36] restrictions on lorry traffic on a part of a motorway were imposed, with Austria seeking to justify them with the objective

---

[30] Case C-405/98 *Konsumentombudsmannen (KO) v Gourmet International Products AB (GIP)* EU:C:2001:135 EU:C:2001:135.

[31] ibid, 22. See S Reynolds, 'Explaining the Constitutional Drivers Behind a Perceived Judicial Preference for Free Movement Rights' (2016) 53 *CML Rev*, 643.

[32] Joined Cases C-267/91 and C-268/91 *Criminal proceedings against Bernard Keck and Daniel Mithouard* EU:C:1993:905.

[33] E Spaventa, 'Leaving *Keck* Behind? The Free Movement of Goods After the Rulings in *Commission v Italy* and *Mickelsson and Roos*' (2009) 34 *EL Rev* 6, 914, 923.

[34] So low as to be based on 'judicial hunches or intuitions rather than clear criteria and objective evidence' (D Wilsher, 'Does *Keck* Discrimination Make Any Sense? An Assessment of the Non-Discrimination Principle within the European Single Market' (2008) 33 *EL Rev* 1, 3, 3).

[35] An economic aim 'cannot constitute a reason relating to the general interest that justifies a restriction of a fundamental freedom guaranteed by the Treaty' (Case C-398/95 *Syndesmos ton en Elladi Touristikon kai Taxidiotikon Grafeion v Ypourgos Ergasias* EU:C:1997:282, 23).

[36] Case C-320/03 *Commission of the European Communities v Republic of Austria* EU:C:2005:684.

of environmental protection. The Court found that the Austrian authorities had not shown that this objective could not be achieved through a means that was less obstructive to free movement,[37] and found the measure to be insufficiently connected to the objective.[38] In *Commission v Netherlands*,[39] the Court found that for discharging the burden of proportionality, Member States could not simply 'refer to two alternative measures which, in its opinion, are even more discriminatory than the requirement laid down', and that they had to show not only that the 'measure at issue is proportionate to the objective pursued but also to *indicate the evidence capable of substantiating that conclusion*'.[40]

We might deduce from this that rules that create barriers to free movement should be based on evidence that shows that they are necessary. Such evidence is in short supply in the context of measures seeking to reduce free movement or reduce welfare entitlements of EU nationals in the UK. Those measures should not go beyond what is necessary, so the UK should show that it has considered alternative means to achieve the objective. The Court has been quite ready to scrutinise and unpack legislation that poses a restriction on the free movement of goods, and to, in effect, make policy decisions on what would be 'better' measures. However, in the context of discriminatory statements and declaratory obstacles to movement, it is difficult to identify a legitimate (and not purely economic)[41] objective. If such an objective could be excavated from the scrapheap of rhetoric, political posturing and misguided generalisations, then the government would need to provide evidence that the measure would deliver on that objective. But the government's own projections were very hazy on possible 'gains' resulting from the measures.[42] The next few sections consider the specific problems of both declaratory and classic discrimination attaching to some of the new measures, which form part of a programme of declaratory obstacles to movement. The legislation itself is also a form of declaration, being a means for the government to articulate its disdain for EU nationals and for free movement.

## B. The Objective to Reduce Free Movement

In 2013, the then UK Prime Minister David Cameron heralded the launch of a programme of reforms when he declared a need for making free movement

---

[37] ibid, 89.

[38] ibid, 82.

[39] Case C-542/09 *European Commission v Kingdom of the Netherlands* EU:C:2012:346.

[40] ibid, 82, emphasis added.

[41] Though on the requirement for non-economic objectives, 'the relevance of economic arguments to restrictions on the free movement of EU citizens occupies an especially misty normative space', N Nic Shuibne and M Maci, 'Proving Public Interest: The Growing Impact of Evidence in Free Movement Case Law' (2013) 50 *CML Rev* 4, 965, 998.

[42] The impact assessment for the three months' residence requirement for jobseeker's allowance listed each cost as 'n/a' and did not provide an estimate for gains 'due to the lack of detailed data and

'less free'.[43] There followed wave upon wave of changes to tackle the phenomenon of benefit tourism by EU nationals, although this had not been shown to be a genuine mischief. This chapter will consider particular sets of change. The first is the re-erection of obstacles to movement for UK nationals, reversing *Swaddling* in the imposition of a three-month waiting residence period for jobseeker's allowance, child benefit and child tax credit. Some of the changes seek to punish those who fall out of work: the removal of housing benefit from EU national jobseekers; the reduction of periods of jobseeker's allowance claim for non-nationals; the 'genuine prospects of work' test; and the removal of translation services from job centres. These changes all make the welfare cliff-edge steeper: if you lose worker status and fall off, you lose protection quickly. They have particular impacts upon people in insecure, low status work and create worrying consequences for women and children. They have been coupled with changes that curb the definition of worker, so making it more likely that EU nationals will be pitched over the now-steeper cliff-edge. This has had a significant effect on the treatment of part-time work in the UK (though other Member States adopt not dissimilar mechanisms), and has also created noteworthy detriments for women and children. Finally, brought together, and grouped with the UK position of self-sufficiency and the operation of the right to reside test, these changes mean that EU nationals face status gaps, making *Teixeira*-based rights to reside[44] harder to establish (and permanent residence rights harder still) and these changes highlight the gap created by the failure to recognise domestic abuse as a social security risk. The absence of proportionality, or of citizenship-based rights, within the framework leads to profoundly socially unjust exclusions, of people resident for very long periods of time, with little regard for the need to prevent poverty or destitution.

## III. CREATING CLASSIC OBSTACLES: REVERSING *SWADDLING*

Among the first wave of changes was the three-month wait for jobseeker's allowance for new arrivals. This appears to draw upon the exception in Article 24(2) of Directive 2004/38 that Member States need not provide social assistance for the first three months of residence. However, it stretches the definition of social assistance. Indeed, if jobseeker's allowance were pure social assistance, then the UK would not be obliged to pay it to EU national jobseekers at all. But in *Collins*,[45] the ECJ treated jobseeker's allowance as a benefit for facilitating access to the job

---

the uncertainties regarding future migration patterns', (DWP, 'The Jobseeker's Allowance (Habitual Residence) Amendment Regulations 2013' *Impact Assessment* (16 December 2016), 3. Available at: www.legislation.gov.uk/ukia/2013/230/pdfs/ukia_20130230_en.pdf).

[43] Cameron, above n 20.
[44] Case C-480/08 *Maria Teixeira v London Borough of Lambeth and Secretary of State for the Home Department*, EU:C:2009:642.
[45] Case C-138/02 *Brian Francis Collins*, EU:C:2004:172.

market. There, the ECJ found it was not possible to exclude such benefits from the equal treatment provisions in Article 48 EC (now Article 45 TFEU). Member States were entitled to require claimants to demonstrate a connection with the labour market, which might be shown through genuinely seeking work in the Member State for a reasonable period, but such a requirement cannot go beyond what is necessary 'in order for the national authorities to be able to satisfy themselves that the person concerned is genuinely seeking work in the employment market of the host Member State'.[46]

A three-month wait may well go beyond what is necessary to establish genuine jobseeking. The UK government's impact assessment of the three-month rule stated that 'more than a quarter of new jobseeker's allowance claims end within a month and over half within three months'.[47] The process of determining whether jobseeking is genuine should result in genuine jobseekers becoming entitled, but this rule results in *more than half* of all jobseekers being excluded, all of whom were genuinely seeking work, as borne out by their finding it. The three-month wait has been extended to child benefit and child tax credit for jobseeking claimants— benefits which are confirmed to be 'pure' social security, so there is no question of their being social assistance within the exemption of Article 24(2). Such benefits are significant for women on low incomes: their exclusion makes it difficult for EU national lone parents to contemplate moving to the UK to seek work (as opposed to moving having already secured a job), and the absence of financial support also makes the logistics of jobseeking difficult, since without support it is difficult to pay for childcare to attend interviews, for instance. The effect is to preclude the majority of new arrivals from benefits, making it harder for non-nationals to access the labour market.

The three-month wait applies to UK nationals who have worked in other EU Member States (that is, returners). This is a striking rejection of the ECJ's ruling in *Swaddling*[48] that a set residence period of eight weeks (or simply requiring an 'appreciable period of residence') went too far in the case of determining habitual residence of own-state nationals. The duration of residence could not be 'an intrinsic element of the concept of residence'.[49] In particular, the Court added, when an employed person returns to his state of origin after exercising free movement rights, and has a clear intention (at the time of applying for benefits) to remain in the home state, 'he cannot be deemed not to satisfy the condition concerning residence … merely because the period of residence completed in his state of origin is too short'.[50] Yet while an eight-week residence requirement went too far, the UK has exceeded it, with the new three-month rule, which is applied without exception and without regard to other indicators of habitual residence.

---

[46] ibid, 72.
[47] Above n 42, 5.
[48] Above, n 4.
[49] ibid, 30.
[50] ibid.

This constitutes a potential obstacle to movement imposed by the home state upon its own nationals, who may be disadvantaged as a direct result of having exercised free movement rights:[51]

---

**Case Study: John**

John was a UK national who completed a four-month internship in Belgium. He left before the new rules took effect, but on his return he was denied jobseeker's allowance until he had been back for three months. This case on the face of it was one of the more straightforward cases—it engaged the three-month rule, and presented a clear challenge to that rule's legality. In practice it was one of the longer, more administratively complicated cases. It was not resolved through reconsideration and we had to go to the First-tier Tribunal twice.

*Field notes: Client refused jobseeker's allowance because 'the information you have provided shows that you have not resided in the UK or the CTA for three months prior to the claim' (decision letter). The Decision-Maker was in the 'EU Right to Reside Appeals' team, based in Wick. Submission drafted based on: (1) breach of the Swaddling principle; (2) creation of an obstacle to the exercise of free movement rights; and (3) a duty to aggregate periods of residence under Article 6, Regulation 883/2004.*

The SSCS1 (notice of appeal) was completed and submitted, and we went to tribunal.

*Field notes after the hearing: Judge said at outset we could not proceed. Said that she needed the DWP to advance a counter-argument; checked with DWP rep whether it was the case that they had not engaged with our grounds of appeal at any stage. Point was conceded. DWP rep had turned up with a copy of the Collins case. Judge pointed out this was not referred to in any of DWP's documents, rep did not seem sure why he had it: '[John] raises detailed and arguable grounds of appeal. S of S has not responded to these grounds of Appeal. The Tribunal was not in a position to proceed until the S of S responds to the points of law raised and in the interests of justice the S of S should be given further opportunity to prepare a detailed argument'.*

The decision not to proceed was surprising: the DWP's failure to submit a reasoned response to the grounds in the SSCS1, and sending a representative who did not know what arguments he was supposed to make, and did not know why he had been given a copy of a case, rather than telling against the respondent, resulted in awarding them more time.[52] The second First-tier Tribunal hearing was scheduled four months after the first. We had a different judge. It began inauspiciously, as noted in the post-hearing field notes:

*Field notes: The judge started out by noting that we were asking for domestic law to be disapplied and saying 'I'm just the bottom of the pecking order', and that these things*

---

[51] As in Case C-18/95 *FC Terhoeve v Inspecteur van de Belastingdienst Particulieren/Ondernemingen buitenland* EU:C:1999:22.

[52] The judge gave a second reason for adjourning—she wanted full copies of all cases I had excerpted. This was unusual (see ch 7).

> *would be for the European Court of Justice to decide. DWP's rep pointed out that he did*
> *nevertheless have the power to disapply UK law where it conflicted with EU law (just*
> *that the DWP didn't think it did). I ran through my responses to the DWP reply to our*
> *appeal documents ... DWP rep argued that the Commission guidance could not be relied*
> *upon, and that aggregation was not relevant. The judge at one point agreed that he did*
> *not think the case would be decided on aggregation (effectively encouraging me to not*
> *take up much time on the subject).*
>
> *At the end of the hearing, judge reiterated that he thought whatever he decided would*
> *be irrelevant as it would be higher courts that decided the issue. I offered to produce the*
> *additional submissions and evidence in writing to aid the decision-making process. Judge*
> *accepted the offer ... Outside the hearing, DWP rep spoke to me to say he would have*
> *advised against an additional submission, as it would enable DWP to pick through it(!)*
> *as they were treating it as a test case. I said I was happy for them to have the opportunity*
> *to do so and wanted our arguments on the record ...*

The judge appeared quite sceptical about the idea that he could (indeed, was obliged) to
disapply UK law not compliant with EU law, such that the respondent's representative
interjected to confirm our representation of the law on that point. Even so, the judge
repeated his belief that this was a decision the higher courts would make. The suggestion
that any finding by him would be 'irrelevant' if it were subject to appeal, is itself a fairly
curious interpretation of appeal rights. If the First-tier Tribunal makes a decision that
led to further litigation, that original decision takes on some considerable importance.

In the hearing itself, the Secretary of State's representative, (who was different to the one
who had turned up to the first hearing), explained the perceived relevance of the *Collins*
case. In short, he argued that *Collins* meant that *Swaddling* no longer applied, because in
*Collins* the Court found that the claimant could be required to spend a period of time
jobseeking before getting benefits. Here is an extract from my written summary of the
argument I made at the hearing:

> *There is no basis for suggesting that* Collins *and* Swaddling *are incompatible.* Collins
> *dealt with a non-national, whose only link with the UK labour market was a period of*
> *casual work 17 years prior to the claim. The requirement that such claimants show a link*
> *with the labour market, for example through a short period of workseeking, is reasonable*
> *in such a context. It does not deal with claimants who are UK nationals and who already*
> *have significant links with the labour market.*
>
> *The facts of this case reflect the situation dealt with in* Swaddling *whereby the state of*
> *origin should not prevent an own state national who has exercised free movement rights*
> *in another Member State from potentially being habitually resident on their return to the*
> *state of origin ... Reliance upon a blanket residence rule during the first three months of*
> *re-established residence, to the exclusion of other factors, thus conflicts with* Swaddling.
> Collins *does not address or change this ratio ...* Swaddling *remains good law ... The*
> *European Commission's recently published Guide on applicable legislation, which states*
> *on page 41 that 'this understanding of the term "residence" has a Union-wide meaning'*
> *and refers to* Swaddling.

We also made a final argument about aggregating periods of residence, under Article 6,
Regulation 883/2004. The judge's announcement, before hearing my arguments, that

the case would not be decided upon by aggregation was surprisingly dismissive.[53] The judge did find in favour of our client, but the statement of reasons avoided challenging the regulations at the heart of the case. He found, contrary to the arguments of both parties, that the client had not been 'resident' in Belgium at all: 'I find he was living in England for the whole period ... The situation was similar to someone going on a four-month world cruise. They continue to be living in England but occupying the space on the ship to enjoy the facility of the cruise ...'.

Therefore the regulations were not engaged. The client was happy to get the award, but frustrated that the judgment meant that he couldn't pursue it any further, *'as I really wanted to fight this ridiculous regulation'*.

For families, the three-month curfew applied to child benefit and child tax credit can make a dramatic difference. The measure creates a disadvantage stemming from the exercise of movement, and is a potential obstacle to movement, since UK nationals may be dissuaded from exercising free movement if they know they will face financial difficulties on their return (a risk exacerbated in the case of women who, if they return with children, would risk their financial well-being). Child benefit and child tax credit are directed at protecting child welfare, and UK national children, if they are not dual nationals, would have no other Member State in which to claim a 'special relationship of solidarity and good faith',[54] and from which they are entitled to expect protection. A rule that disentitles them from that protection, when they may be unable to receive it elsewhere, imperils their welfare and creates a barrier to movement for women with children, or to women who may have children while in another Member State.

## A. Absence of Justification

These measures were accompanied by statements suggesting an aim of discouraging movement, and painting a discriminatory picture of migrants. The DWP's impact assessment repeatedly stated that the purpose was to discourage those from coming to the UK 'with the primary aim of claiming benefits'. But there was no evidence that there were EU migrants with that primary aim. The assessment also stated, at the point at which it noted that any savings must be offset against alternative provisions or entitlements (such as local authority support where children were concerned), that 'savings would be increased if the policy discouraged those who would otherwise have claimed benefits coming to the UK'.[55]

---

[53] On reflection, it was a good thing that the case was not decided on aggregation, as that argument now seems to be a dead end in the UK. The Upper Tribunal has heard a case on this point and decided that 'mere' residence cannot be aggregated under Art 6, Reg 883/2004, only residence which counts as equivalent to a period of insurance (which it never does in the UK). See *Secretary of State for Work and Pensions v MM* [2016] UKUT 547 (AAC).

[54] Case C-135/08 *Janko Rottman v Freistaat Bayern* [2010] ECR I-01449, 51.

[55] Above n 42, 5.

This is a telling turn of phrase: savings will not be made just by discouraging *benefit tourists*, but by discouraging migrants who 'would otherwise have claimed benefits', a much wider group that includes 'genuine' migrants, genuinely seeking work, and who would have claimed benefits to which they would have had a genuine entitlement. The assessment includes a section entitled 'Problem and Solution' but this does not outline what the problem is. It states that the (then) 'current system allows individuals to make a claim to benefits from the date of arrival in the UK, and to become entitled to income related benefits provided they satisfy the habitual resident test'.[56] While the 'problem' appeared to be the possibility of immediate claims, the same sentence notes that claimants still had to satisfy a habitual residence test. On the same page, the report notes that decision-makers assessed a 'wide variety of factors to determine whether someone is factually habitually resident. These include evidence of intention to remain and attachment to the UK'.[57] As a consequence, each case was 'treated on its own merits, in the light of the person's individual circumstances'.[58] Although the policy change introducing a three-month wait was supposed to 'ensure that migrants have established a genuine link with the labour market',[59] decision-makers were entitled, obliged even, to take into account a range of factors to ensure that link anyway. Under these circumstances, it is difficult to escape the sense of political grandstanding: measures to tackle a non-existent problem, in order to be seen to be doing something, with the added 'bonus' that these acts of declaratory discrimination might also create barriers and dissuade people who might claim benefits (poor people and women) from moving.

When the three-months wait was extended to child benefit and child tax credit, the government issued a press release stating that 'the Prime Minister has made it clear that abuse and clear exploitation of the UK's welfare system will not be tolerated'.[60] This is strident, combative, and emotive language, typically employed by tabloids, but being used by the government to suggest that 'abuse and clear exploitation of the welfare system'[61] is occurring at the hands of EU migrants and must be stopped. The same press release also noted that the 'government is determined to cap welfare and reduce immigration as part of Britain's long-term economic plan'.[62] In the context of measures only affecting EEA nationals, an aim to 'reduce immigration' means reducing free movement. The explicit statement of such an aim could amount to a declaratory obstacle to movement.

The government made high-profile claims that around 40% of recently arrived EU nationals in March 2013 were on benefits.[63] However, these claims were not

---

[56]  ibid, 4.
[57]  ibid.
[58]  ibid.
[59]  ibid.
[60]  DWP, n 1.
[61]  ibid.
[62]  ibid.
[63]  D Cameron, 'Speech on Europe' at Chatham House, 10 November 2015. Available at: www.gov.uk/government/speeches/prime-ministers-speech-on-europe. Covered by, inter alia: *The Independent*

accompanied with a statistical breakdown. Repeated freedom of information enquiries, and complaints from the head of the UK Statistics Authority, led to the release of a 'deeply unconvincing post-hoc explanation',[64] based on a range of rather weakly substantiated assumptions and including a number of 'up-lifts' (and the figures included in-work benefits). The case that migrants were arriving to take advantage of the British benefits system was not made. The measures present declaratory obstacles to movement without adequate justification. The next section explores the targeting of EU national jobseekers in particular: following the introduction of the three-month wait for benefits, the government changed the law to deny EU national jobseekers housing benefit, and to impose a strict time limit on their jobseeker's allowance entitlement.

## IV. MAKING THE CLIFF-EDGE STEEPER: PUNISHING THOSE WHO FALL OUT OF WORK

The UK government's distaste for EU national jobseekers (notwithstanding the rather low numbers involved)[65] was made more explicit in further changes. Those on income-based jobseeker's allowance are 'passported' onto automatic eligibility for housing benefit in the UK. One of the reforms introduced in 2014 severed this connection, but only for EU nationals, so that EU nationals relying on a jobseeking right to reside would not be entitled to housing benefit. This measure was 'sold' as just affecting recent arrivals, and only those who have not worked: '*New* migrant jobseekers are also now unable to claim Housing Benefit … EEA nationals who have been working in the UK, and are subsequently made redundant and claim jobseeker's allowance, will not be affected by this measure'.[66]

But it is not just new arrivals who are affected. This measure applies to all EU jobseekers. As such, it captures former workers who have not retained worker status or gained recognised permanent residence rights, some of whom may have been long-term residents with long, but punctuated, employment histories. It also captures former partners of EU migrant workers. Spouses of migrant workers

---

(C Cooper, 'David Cameron's Claims of 40% of Migrants on Benefits Based on Figures Beset by "Uncertainty", Government Analysis Admits', 10 November 2015); *The Times* (S Coates, B Waterfield and M Savage, 'Almost Half of Migrants from EU are on Benefits', 10 November 2015); the BBC ('EU Reform: Curbing EU Migrants' Benefits Access', 10 November 2015); and *Channel 4* ('Factcheck: Do 43% of EU Migrants Claim Benefits?'), 10 November 2015.

[64] J Portes, 'EU Migrants and Benefits: The Government Continues to Stifle Debate by Hiding the Data' *National Institute for Social and Economic Research*, 18 January 2016, available at: www.niesr.ac.uk/blog/eu-migrants-and-benefits-government-continues-stifle-debate-hiding-data#.WOO8PlPys2J.

[65] The UK was the only country in a European Commission study with lower unemployment rates for EU nationals than for its nationals (European Commission, *Fact Finding Analysis*, above n 26, see table 3.3).

[66] DWP, 'New Rules to Stop Migrants Claiming Housing Benefit', Press Release, 20 January 2014. Available at: www.gov.uk/government/news/new-rules-to-stop-migrants-claiming-housing-benefit, emphasis added.

retain their rights to reside as family members of migrant workers after separation, following *Diatta*,[67] but unmarried partners do not. In cases of separation, there may well be a period of jobseeking while the leaving partner re-establishes themself elsewhere, or where they may not recently have been working due to caring for small children. A lone parent in this situation will not continue to be treated as a family member, even though she is caring for the EU migrant worker's children. She may derive rights from *Teixeira/Ibrahim*, but only if she has a child in school (and then, as shown above, the UK authorities seek to curtail these rights). A woman with pre-school children in an abusive relationship with an EU migrant worker faces an appalling choice: (1) to retain her right to reside as a family member (and in some cases as a worker too) by keeping her children in the abusive situation; or (2) to leave, and so lose a right to reside. For those in work, relocation will often mean stopping work at least temporarily, and they may well not retain worker status for a number of reasons. If the stress of the trauma means she did not register with the job office quickly enough, or if her previous work is reclassified as 'not-work' (due to the minimum earnings threshold, see below, or due to *Zalewska*,[68] also below). She may have a right to reside as a jobseeker, but this now means she cannot pay rent to house her children.

The government's equality analysis and impact assessment both noted the risks posed to families by the withdrawal of housing benefit from EU national jobseekers. The impact assessment noted in the final paragraph that the proposal increased the risk of 'difficult circumstances' for the 'vulnerable, such as families with children',[69] and the equality analysis stated that nearly one in four of those who would be affected by the measure had dependent children and that lone parents 'could face an increased risk of homelessness'.[70] However, the DWP claimed that the United Nations Convention on the Rights of the Child (UNCRC) had been taken into account and that such families would not be left without state support because they could 'claim jobseeker's allowance (incapacity benefit) for a period and in certain circumstances they may be able to apply for support from the local authority'.[71] This is a dismissal of a risk of destitution and homelessness that bears greater scrutiny. Let us take the first suggestion, that families facing an increased risk of homelessness will not be without state support, since they can claim jobseeker's allowance for a period. This would not reduce the risk of homelessness: jobseeker's allowance would not cover the cost of rent, let alone any other costs. In January 2017, the local housing allowance (the amount of

---

[67] Case 267/83 *Aissatou Diatta v Land Berlin* EU:C:1985:67.

[68] Above, n 8.

[69] DWP, 'The Removal of Housing Benefit from EEA Jobseekers', *Impact Assessment*, 27 February 2014, available at: www.legislation.gov.uk/ukia/2014/67/pdfs/ukia_20140067_en.pdf.

[70] DWP, *Equality Analysis for Removal of Access to Housing Benefit for EEA Jobseekers*, 27 February 2014, available at: www.gov.uk/government/uploads/system/uploads/attachment_data/file/322808/equality-analysis-eea-jobseekers.pdf.

[71] ibid.

rent eligible for housing benefit funding) for a lone parent in York in need of two bedrooms was £123.58 per week.[72] In Scarborough, it was £103.56. The weekly rate of jobseeker's allowance for someone 25 or over was £73.10.[73] Even if the family did not spend money on anything other than rent (like food, gas, electricity, water, transport, or clothes), there would still be a significant rent shortfall. This would lead to rent arrears, possession proceedings and homelessness. If we turn to the second suggestion, to fall upon local authority support, that too seems wanting. Local authority support for housing is a fall-back and seems in many cases to be little more than theoretical (or at best inadequate). It is provided under section 17 of the Children Act 1989 and in certain circumstances under the Care Act 2014.[74] The Court of Appeal noted the question of the adequacy of local authority support in *Sanneh*, stating it was 'well known that there have been substantial cuts in public funding' and that 'there have been a number of first instance decisions on the operation of section 17 in practice'.[75] There are significant questions to be asked about the capacity of local authorities to accommodate the shortfalls created in welfare changes for EU nationals. It should be noted that the Secretary of State for Work and Pensions is generally required to consult with the Social Security Advisory Committee before making changes to benefits within the ambit of the Social Security Administration Act 1992,[76] and is also specifically required to refer proposed changes to the housing benefit regulations to organisations 'representative of the authorities concerned'.[77] The Secretary of State did not undertake these consultations 'as it appears to him that by reason of the urgency of the matter it is inexpedient to do so'.[78]

The purported urgency appears to relate to the then imminent lifting of transition measures applied to A2 nationals—from Bulgaria and Romania—who would enjoy full free movement from 1 January 2014. David Cameron's *Financial Times* article opened by stating 'on 1 January, the people of Romania and Bulgaria will have the same right to work in the UK as other EU citizens. I know many people are deeply concerned about the impact that could have on our country. I share those concerns.'[79] However, this would be a curious reason for urgency, the date of the end of transition measures having been known since 1 January 2007 at the latest. In response to a legal challenge to the legitimacy of the regulations, the government also argued that the urgency was necessary to 'dovetail' the change with

---

[72] UK Directgov, *Local Housing Allowance Rates*, available at: lha-direct.voa.gov.uk/search.aspx.
[73] UK Government, *JSA—What You'll Get* (last updated 1 April 2017), available at: www.gov.uk/jobseekers-allowance/overview.
[74] Which replaced the relevant sections of the National Assistance Act 1948.
[75] *Sanneh and Ors v Secretary of State for Work and Pensions* [2015] EWCA Civ 49, 94. On the adequacy of s 17 support, see *R (1PO 2 KO 3 PO) v London Borough of Newham* [2014] EWHC 2561, 47, 49.
[76] Under s 172.
[77] Social Security Administration Act 1992 s 176.
[78] Preamble, Housing Benefit (Habitual Residence) Amendment Regulations, SI 2014/539.
[79] Cameron (2013), above n 20.

other reforms, when presented with an argument in court that any urgency was of the Secretary of State's own making.[80] The Upper Tribunal noted that the decision to remove housing benefit passporting from EEA jobseekers had not been taken until January 2014, which was 'late in the day', in light of the intention to dovetail with the other changes.[81] But lateness did not make the policy decision unreasonable, or negate the appearance of urgency, and so the challenge failed, meaning that the Secretary of State was entitled to invoke the exemptions to consultation provided for in urgent cases,[82] and the new regulations were held to be validly made.

## A. Declaring Obstructive Intent and Incentivising Discrimination

In the government's response to the Social Security Advisory Committee's 2014 report on the housing benefit changes for EU nationals, the language of simply discouraging those seeking solely to rely on benefits is dropped, and it becomes clear that the desire is to dissuade jobseekers without certain work prospects from coming to the UK. The response states that the measure is 'part of a package of measures which this Government has introduced to … *discourage migration* from people who have little or no connection with the UK *who do not have a firm offer or imminent prospect of work*'.[83] This phrasing suggests that the UK government wishes to discourage migration from EEA nationals who wish to *seek* work. Here, the government is publicly declaring a desire to obstruct movement for the purposes of seeking to enter the labour market. Workseekers must be well-heeled if they are to be welcomed: the report goes on to say that those coming to seek work 'should ensure that they have sufficient resources to pay for their accommodation needs, as well as other support that they or their family may need while here'.[84] The declaratory obstacle to movement created by the announcements of the measure have been underlined by a public warning campaign held in other EU states. The government report noted that the 'the Department for Communities and Local Government (DCLG) has funded a voluntary sector-led "Before You Go" awareness campaign in home countries about the dangers of coming to the UK without appropriate support such as a job, accommodation or some money in case there are short-term difficulties'.[85] Actively promoting *not* exercising free

---

[80] *IC v Glasgow City Council and Secretary of State for Work and Pensions* [2016] UKUT 0321 (AAC). 41.

[81] ibid, 42.

[82] s 173(1)(a) of the Social Security Administration Act.

[83] DWP, *Response to the Report by the Social Security Advisory Committee* 'The Housing Benefit (Habitual Residence) Amendment Regulations 2014 (SI. 2014 No. 539)' (November 2014), 3, para 3. Available at: www.gov.uk/government/uploads/system/uploads/attachment_data/file/376103/PRINT-HB-Habitual-Residence-Amendment-Regs-2014-SSAC-report.pdf, emphasis added.

[84] ibid, 3.

[85] ibid, para 7, 4.

movement rights, and employing the language of 'dangers', and publicising the UK's exclusionary and discriminatory policies, to put people off migrating, all contribute to a real, and not very remote, declaratory obstacle to movement.

As an objective, aiming to dissuade poor jobseekers from exercising free movement rights is not only problematic, but it is also an inadequate explanation—it does not explain why the measure extends to *all* EEA jobseekers rather than just new arrivals. People who did have actual job offers and imminent prospects of work, and become workers, are affected if they later become jobseekers. Should they have been dissuaded from exercising their free movement rights, even with jobs in hand, just in case the unforeseen happened? If so, then we are into the territory of full-blown obstacles of movement for *workers*. Such obstacles may arise from the unintended consequences of the measure. The Residential Landlords Association, in responding to the Social Security Advisory Committee's consultation on the measure, raised concerns that it could make even working EEA nationals seem less attractive as tenants to landlords who, aware of the possibility that they might be left unable to pay rent, might discriminate against them when offering tenancies.[86]

The measure thus not only discriminates and contributes to a programme of declaratory discrimination and declaratory obstacles to movement on the part of the state, it creates financial incentives for individuals to discriminate against EU nationals in the provision of services. A recurring theme in this research is that measures supposedly targeting the 'economically inactive' have significant repercussions for the economically active too: there is no such thing as equal treatment *just* for the economically active. An increased risk of discrimination in securing housing is itself another potential obstacle to movement faced by workers, in particular low-paid workers, in low-status, low-security jobs. It also encourages a culture of exclusion with regard to jobseekers, such that some decision-makers react primarily to a person's jobseeker status and fail to consider their other rights to reside:

**Evidence Submission:** An adviser submitted an anonymised decision letter to the EU Rights Project; it concerned an EU national's claim to a Teixeira-based right to reside, in order to claim universal credit. The decision included the following sentence:

*I have also considered the fact that you have shown that you have a child in general education but you cannot derive rights as her primary carer as long as you have another right to reside and this includes that of a jobseeker.*[87]

---

[86] Social Security Advisory Committee, *Report on The Housing Benefit (Habitual Residence) Amendment Regulations 2014 (S.I. 2014 No. 539)*, 30 June 2014, 2.23, 20. Available at: www.gov.uk/government/uploads/system/uploads/attachment_data/file/376103/PRINT-HB-Habitual-Residence-Amendment-Regs-2014-SSAC-report.pdf.

[87] Evidence submitted, not referred for advice, submission 3.

The rules on universal credit explicitly exclude EU nationals relying on a jobseeker-based right to reside from any universal credit entitlement. This decision suggests that these rules are encouraging decision-makers to treat EU national jobseekers as being automatically excluded from universal credit simply by virtue of being a jobseeker, regardless of other existing rights to reside. But there is no basis for finding that a jobseeker-based right to reside eclipses, or negates, other, stronger rights to reside which carry greater entitlement:

> **Evidence Submission:** One advice worker informant submitted anonymised evidence to the *EU Rights Project* on client experiences of the genuine prospects of work test,[88] and noted:
>
> *We are even seeing cases rejected where the person has another right to reside and have seen cases rejected where the claimant has a permanent right and also where they have Baumbast/Texeira rights. There seems to be no attempt to establish if the person has another right to reside and numbers of claims are being ended where right to reside is pretty obvious.*[89]

The government's response to the report indicates an unwillingness to recognise any element of transnational solidarity. It suggests that EEA nationals who may end up being in low-paid, low-security jobs, and at risk of becoming workseekers at some point, migrate and work at their own risk. The 'best option for those EEA migrants who are unable to find work, who lack savings or support networks and who are at real risk of ending up destitute is to return home'.[90] In the case of long-term UK residents this is tricky: they may not have another 'home' to which to return, a problem compounded where children are concerned, who may have entirely constructed their home, as well as their citizenship, in the host state. Yet there is little hint that successful integration is recognised and the language of 'returning home' reveals a persistent 'othering' process. UK authorities have nevertheless fired up the migrant centrifuge, to repel them back to their home states, adoptingd the somewhat euphemistic term of 'reconnection': the London 'reconnections service ... helps vulnerable rough sleepers from the EU return home', and 'local authorities themselves may help reconnect those who are destitute as an alternative to rough sleeping'.[91] As seen in the case study below, 'reconnection' seems to be favoured over discharging accommodation duties:

---

[88] See below.
[89] Evidence submitted, not referred for advice, submission 2.
[90] Above n 83, para 7.
[91] DWP, above n 83, para 6.

---

**Case Study: Jenna—Recourse to the Local Authority**

This case was referred to the *EU Rights Project* for second-tier advice. Jenna had come from Bulgaria just over a year ago with her partner and daughter, who was then 12. They were living in her partner's brother's home, and shortly after the birth of their second child, Jenna's partner announced that he wanted to separate. He moved out and his brother told Jenna to move out too:

> *Adviser notes: Client is desperate to get some housing for herself and her children and would also like to know if there is any benefit assistance she can access. Client is not in receipt of any benefits at the moment and is relying on friends for food.*

The adviser went with her to the housing team at the local authority, to declare homelessness:

> *Adviser notes: We were told immediately that client would not qualify for any LA housing/homelessness assistance, and she was advised that perhaps she should return to [Bulgaria]. A possible source of assistance suggested by Housing Options was Social Services who they said might offer care for her child, but not for her—they might be able to help with her fare back to [Bulgaria]. Provided client with a Food Voucher to get her through the next few days.*

I suggested that the adviser explore the client and partner's work history/plans. If either had worked in the UK, or were planning to do so, that could trigger a Teixeira right to reside for the child and her primary carer. At that point, her partner was planning to return to Bulgaria, and it looked likely to be difficult to get any information from him about any past jobs, so we also had to explore possible residual support, beyond advice to go back to Bulgaria.

---

Many EEA nationals choose not to be 'reconnected', for a variety of reasons. Many have been resident in the UK for a long time and have no family or work connections in their home state.[92] Homeless Link expressed scepticism about the idea that people would leave the UK once their housing benefit entitlement ended, noting that many A8 nationals had chosen to sleep rough during the period of transitional arrangements when they were not entitled to full equal treatment under UK law.[93] St Mungo's Broadway noted that in 2014, '819, or 40%, of the people counted sleeping rough in London were EEA nationals', and that that proportion had increased since the introduction of the new measures.[94] The automatic disentitlement of EU national jobseekers from housing benefit can result in a significant threat to social justice, especially when not subject to a proportionality review. The change reveals a very minimal approach to transnational solidarity within the UK and, insofar as it may be condoned by the ECJ's case law, it exposes

---

[92] Above n 86, para 2.6.
[93] ibid, 2.5.
[94] ibid, 2.17.

the rather weak protections for social justice or solidarity within EU law as it is currently adjudicated.

## B. Automatic Exclusions and Disproportionality: Law-as-Lists Rather than Law-as-Justice

The especially acute impact of the measure upon lone parent families means that the effects are gendered and are detrimental to children. The DWP's own equality analysis recognised that while single males and single females were affected, 'it is possible that the measure will have a disproportionate impact on females as they are more likely to have primary child care responsibilities, which may act as a barrier to moving into work'.[95] It noted that lone parents 'could face increased risk of homelessness'. The significant majority of lone parents are female.[96] In responding to the Social Security Advisory Committee's consultation on the measure, the Salvation Army argued that:

> Families and others who would wish to make a life here are now less likely to do so because of the risk of becoming destitute between periods of employment. Accordingly, we predict an increase in single men working here temporarily, living in basic conditions, and sending money home rather than spending their earnings in the economy.[97]

Women's Aid raised the particular risk of women being trapped in abusive situations, noting that if they have children it makes it harder to find work in a new location immediately.[98]

The ECJ's apparent abandonment of proportionality as a nugget of Union citizenship-based rights again has significant consequences. Stripping EU jobseekers of housing benefit impacts not just upon new arrivals. It would affect people who have been working full time and consistently for over four years, if they subsequently become jobseekers. For example, they might become unemployed and then initially seek work under their own steam and using their own resources, which would mean that they lose the opportunity to retain worker status. It also affects very long-term residents who have fallen through the gaps in the Directive and not been able to establish a claim to permanent residence as a result (think of Mariella, who had lived in the UK for over 55 years, and Elsa who had lived in the UK for over 14 years and had British children, and the *Sequeira Bathala*[99] case, all covered in chapter four). For such former workers, a commitment to proportionality might mean assessing the weight of contributions made, social integration, the 'near miss' of permanent residence, and the disproportionate effects of insisting on a particular condition in secondary law—the requirement to be 'duly registered' as a work seeker—akin to the

---

[95] DWP, n 70, 7.
[96] ibid.
[97] Above n 86, 2.3.
[98] ibid 2.15.
[99] *Secretary of State for Work and Pensions v Sequeira-Batalha* [2016] UKUT 511 (AAC).

disproportionate insistence on comprehensive sickness insurance in the state of residence in *Baumbast*.[100]

Former workers may also find themselves affected thanks to the stringent approach to establishing retained worker status once people move out of work. In their response to the Social Security Advisory Committee's consultation on the removal of housing benefit from EEA jobseekers, Wavertree Citizens Advice noted that many former workers were treated as losing worker status, and so were instead classified as jobseekers if they did not *immediately* claim jobseeker's allowance.[101] The submission noted that the decisions were frequently overturned on appeal, but 'the vast majority of EEA migrants refused housing benefit on these grounds simply do not challenge these decisions due to language barriers, difficulty accessing specialist advice services with interpreters and even a fear that by challenging authority they may be jeopardising their right to stay in this country'.[102] Reliance on appeal mechanisms to avoid making appropriate decisions in the first place is poor practice when it comes to the principles of administrative decision-making. The Parliamentary and Health Service Ombudsman has published the 'Principles of Good Administration'.[103] The fourth principle is 'acting fairly and proportionately':

> When taking decisions, and particularly when imposing penalties, public bodies should behave reasonably and ensure that the measures taken are proportionate to the objectives pursued, appropriate in the circumstances and fair to the individuals concerned ... If applying the law, regulations or procedures strictly would lead to an unfair result for an individual, the public body should seek to address the unfairness. In doing so public bodies must, of course, bear in mind the proper protection of public funds and ensure they do not exceed their legal powers.[104]

Reliance upon an appeals system to redress disproportionate decision-making fails to address concerns of the (now closed) Administrative Justice and Tribunals Council that more must be done to get decision-making 'right first time'.[105] Proportionality does not represent a radical extension of EU competence or the imbuing of Union citizenship with excessive power: it is a basic domestic principle of good administration and is essential for administrative justice. As such, the ECJ's shying away from it is unfortunate and unwarranted, and the cleaving of domestic decision-makers to the letter of the law in EU cases represents a discriminatory departure from their own (supposed) good practices. It seems that decision-makers are too readily steered by problematic (and discriminatory) decision-maker guidance, rather than by principles of administrative justice.

---

[100] Case C-413/99 *Baumbast and R v Secretary of State for the Home Department* EU:C:2002:493.

[101] Above n 86, 2.10.

[102] ibid.

[103] Parliamentary and Health Service Ombudsman, *Principles of Good Administration* (London, PHSO, 2009).

[104] ibid, 9.

[105] Administrative Justice and Tribunals Council, *Right First Time* (London, Ministry of Justice, 2011). The report presented 'evidence of poor decision-making' (10) and commented on the 'unknown cost of poor decision-making' (17).

The next section explores another change imposed upon EU national jobseekers—the time limiting of jobseeker's allowance coupled with a genuine prospects of work test—and, in particular, looks at how rights have been distorted and infringed through reliance upon guidance documents, to the extent that such documents effectively become the law.

## V. THE GENUINE PROSPECTS OF WORK TEST

Along with removing housing benefit from jobseekers, and excluding them from jobseeker's allowance for the first three months of residence, the UK government also put a six-month time limit on claims of jobseeker's allowance, which it quickly reduced for workseekers (who have not retained worker status) to three months, and introduced a 'genuine prospects of work test' for those who reached the limit.[106] This test draws upon the principle in EU law that jobseekers are allowed a right to reside beyond three months where they are actively jobseeking and have a 'genuine chance of being engaged'.[107] *Antonissen*[108] gave us some guidance on what might be an appropriate point for 'checking' whether someone has a genuine chance of employment, which was in that case six months. The Court did not indicate whether an earlier test would be acceptable. In *Commission v Belgium*,[109] the Court interrogated national legislation which meant that jobseekers in Belgium might face automatic expulsion after three months, and deemed it incompatible with EC law, since jobseekers should have a chance to show they had a genuine chance of finding employment. The fact that the test was conducted after only three months was not explicitly addressed and so it might be that the ECJ agreed in principle that three months was an appropriate point at which to conduct an enquiry, just not to conduct automatic expulsion.

There is no guidance on how a Member State may test for a 'genuine chance of employment'. The UK's genuine prospects of work test theoretically makes use of this margin of discretion. But it does not test for a genuine chance of employment and instead requires evidence of a *practical certainty* of imminent employment. Only a few narrow types of evidence are considered relevant, and only certain types of work are considered to create relevant prospects (ie work that passes the minimum earnings threshold test). Moreover, those who do pass the test are granted a maximum of up to three months' extension of worker status, even though there is no basis in EU law for such a limit.[110] Under *Antonissen*, Member States may not

---

[106] The Immigration (European Economic Area) (Amendment) (No 3) Regulations 2014, SI 2014/2761 in combination with The Immigration (European Economic Area) (Amendment) (No 2) Regulations 2013, SI 2013/3032 and The Immigration (European Economic Area) (Amendment) Regulations 2014, SI 2014/1451.

[107] ibid.

[108] Case C-292/89 *The Queen v Immigration Appeal Tribunal, ex p Gustaff Desiderius Antonissen* EU:C:1991:80.

[109] Case C-344/95 *Commission of the European Communities v Kingdom of Belgium* EU:C:1997:81, 17.

[110] Above n 6, 073099 and 073139.

deprive a jobseeker of a right to reside so long as they are continuing to seek work and have a genuine chance of engagement. These factors make it unusually difficult to pass the genuine prospects of work test, which suggests it is not a test set up in good faith to identify those with a genuine chance of work.

The legislation introducing the genuine prospects of work test introduces a new concept: 'compelling evidence' of a genuine prospect of work.[111] This, in itself, is a UK invention with no basis in EU law and it does not mean what it says: the guidance[112] explicitly states that much 'compelling evidence' can be ignored. The guidance requires a specific type of evidence of near-certainty of the right kind of employment.[113] According to the guidance, compelling evidence must be one of two specific types. First, an actual written job offer, which must provide sufficient detail for the decision-maker to see that it is genuine and effective work. This is a peculiar interpretation of *Antonissen*, since that case required that a person must *still be actively seeking employment* and have a genuine chance of engagement. If actually having a job offer is appropriate evidence of the second arm of that test (a chance of engagement), this renders the first arm of the test (to still be actively seeking work) pointless. Secondly, it is evidence of a change of circumstances in the last two months that makes imminent employment likely, where the applicant is awaiting the outcome of job interviews. Until recently, evidence—even compelling evidence—of a chance of employment was to be disregarded if it did not meet these criteria. A guidance memo issued in 2014 stated: 'The DM [decision-maker] should note that it is irrelevant whether the evidence is compelling if the change in circumstances does not meet the "date of change" requirement'.[114] This suggests a deliberate limiting of discretion to narrowly circumscribed circumstances with little relationship to testing for evidence of a genuine chance of work.

One project informant, an advice worker in London, reported the following incident:

> More depressingly, [client] had a genuine prospects of work test last week and the assessor refused to take copies of the Home Office documentation he'd brought demonstrating his alternative right to reside (permanent residence). I'd talked him through the process on the phone so he knew what he needed to show her but she was adamant that she didn't need to see it so it won't have got to the Decision Maker.[115]

The same informant reported several months later that she had since 'seen numerous cases where the DWP has stopped their benefits after a genuine prospects of work test when their … records should have shown a permanent right to

---

[111] The Immigration (European Economic Area) (Amendment) (No 2) Regulations, SI 2013/3032, reg 6(7).

[112] Above n 6.

[113] ibid, 073099.

[114] DWP, 'Habitual Residence and Right to Reside: JSA' *Memo DMG* 15/14, para 15. Available at: webarchive.nationalarchives.gov.uk/20140801115640/https:/www.gov.uk/government/uploads/system/uploads/attachment_data/file/324534/m-15-14.pdf.

[115] Evidence submitted, not referred for advice, submission 4.

reside'. These included 'a disabled pensioner who'd also been subject to a genuine prospects of work test even though DWP held information showing he had a permanent right to reside. I sent Inverness their own award letter for the "gap" they claimed broke the continuity of lawful residence'.

For one client, the adviser had 'provided a detailed letter explaining his right to reside and his birth certificate (under 21) and his father's HO (permanent residence card)'. The client was refused a right to reside and when the adviser spoke to the decision-maker afterwards she was told that 'it was because he hadn't used the word "alternative right to reside" during the interview which is just ridiculous'.[116] Another case involved a 'very vulnerable' client, and the adviser wrote a letter asking the DWP to investigate a possible permanent right to reside, but 'the work coach decided it was "not relevant" and chose not to forward my letter'.[117] This was followed by a negative genuine prospects of work test decision, and when the adviser challenged the decision-maker to investigate as originally requested, 'departmental/HMRC records showed a permanent right to reside'. The adviser concluded that 'having "work coaches"' who should be the information gatherers decide what is and isn't relevant is really quite worrying'.

Evidence submitted to the project includes an account of a client who did have a job offer but not a start date and so was found not to have a genuine prospect of work and, as a result, was facing homelessness, which would have prevented her from starting the job she had secured:

---

**Case Study and Evidence Submission: Rina**

*Adviser notes: She had a job offer when she was assessed but she didn't have a start date. She passed the interview in February and did the three-day training course. The HR admin process has been slow-going but when she had her genuine prospects of work test, she'd done the interview, the training, the DBS check and had two of three references back. Still they decide it isn't a genuine prospect of work ...*

As a result of this decision, the adviser noted:

*She lives in a homeless hostel and is at imminent risk of losing her accommodation now her benefits have stopped. She's got nothing to live on and is relying on the food bank and borrowing from fellow (homeless) residents when she can. The DWP have acknowledged her vulnerabilities but it doesn't seem to be speeding things up. I've lost count of the number of times I've been told it's next on the pile.*

*Her mandatory reconsideration application sat with the specialist decision-making team ... for two weeks, only to be told today that they can't change it so it's now gone off to Wick for the mandatory reconsideration to be carried out ... my client has no income and if she's made street homeless she might not even be able to start the job, or maintain it if she does.[118]*

---

116    Evidence submitted, not referred for advice, submission 5.
117    ibid.
118    Evidence submitted, not referred for advice, submission 6.

The failure to treat an actual job offer as evidence of a genuine prospect of work had the perverse effect of jeopardising that client's chances of being able to take up the job, since it is difficult to hold down a job when homeless. The likelihood is that people in this situation may feel forced to relocate, or leave the country, in spite of being about to start a job (which seems like a considerable obstacle to the free movement of labour).

The genuine prospect of work test is not a genuine test for a genuine prospect of work at all, as evidenced by the failure to take account of real prospects, and by it being extremely hard to pass. The same adviser who saw Rina noted that she had taken on five genuine prospect of work cases in that same week alone. Clients within this study who have been able to challenge genuine prospect of work test decisions at tribunal have found that First-tier Tribunal judges take a broader approach to a genuine prospect of work, and recognise the guidance as non-binding. Some, as reported by this adviser, have been critical of the guidance:

---

**Case Study: Stefan**

This Polish client moved to the UK in 2006. He worked in a variety of jobs without significant breaks in employment, then became unemployed in 2014 and claimed jobseeker's allowance. After six months he was deemed to have no genuine prospect of work and refused benefits. He had two periods of registered work but these did not cover 12 months and the rest of his work was unregistered. The adviser sought second-tier advice and support with drafting grounds. We argued that reliance upon *Antonissen* was inappropriate for someone who was seeking to retain worker status having worked for over 12 months, while also noting that genuine prospect of work guidance was too narrow.

*Adviser notes from the tribunal: The tribunal judge was clearly very surprised when he then (finally) understood how narrowly the DWP were interpreting genuine prospect of work. He asked where this was set down in the legislation and on being told it was in the DM guide, asked what was the status of the DM guide. The presenting officer explained it was a departmental policy document and the judge seemed unimpressed.*

---

However, the application of potentially unlawful guidance to cases unless and until they reach the First-tier Tribunal is an obstacle to justice for the many clients who do not appeal, or do not pursue their appeal to that point, due to lack of support or help with appeals, and/or lack of understanding of possible grounds of appeal.

The genuine prospect of work test has been subject to challenge in a case before the UK Upper Tribunal (*MB*).[119] It was found that the test in principle was lawful, but that it should be applied to be in line with *Antonissen*, so it should test for a genuine but realistic chance which must be less than certainty. Judge Ward

---

[119] *Secretary of State for Work and Pensions v MB* [2016] UKUT 0372 (AAC).

found that a genuine chance is more than a merely 'illusory of speculative' one,[120] and 'significantly higher than just "not hopeless"'.[121] But the Decision-Maker Guidance requires more than a 'genuine chance' of employment. It requires practical certainty of employment. It establishes a completely different—and much higher—threshold of probability and practical certainty.

## A.  Reliance Upon Problematic Decision-Maker Guidance

In *MB*, the judge argued that the legislation itself was not at fault, and that the requirement for evidence to be 'compelling' should be interpreted as not adding anything to the *Antonissen* test. He cautioned against decision-makers making too much of that word, because they may confuse compelling evidence with a compelling chance. What the evidence actually tests for, as set down by *Antonissen*, has not changed and the compelling evidence requirement 'cannot raise the bar for what constitutes a genuine chance (or chances) of being engaged higher than it falls to be set in accordance with *Antonissen* … Insistence on "compelling" evidence may, if care is not taken, all too easily result in raising the bar above the level I have found to be required'.[122] The judge also noted problems with reliance upon the guidance, though noted that he was not ruling on the legitimacy of the guidance itself. But such guidance could not be used to amend or add anything to the *Antonissen* test or to narrow down legislation. Tribunals should be 'alive to the risk that, because the guidance is framed in the limited way in which it is, genuine prospect of work test interviews may have been conducted, and/or the Secretary of State's submissions to the tribunal written, by reference to a restricted palette of issues'.[123] This restricted palette is evident in the restricted nature of the questionnaire, which is directed at the types of evidence described in the guidance.

The questionnaire for the genuine prospect of work test[124] is very directive and confined to the two types of compelling evidence. The first question is: 'Have you been offered a job to start in the near future?' If the answer is no, the respondent is to go to question two: 'Have you made arrangements to start up your own business?' If not, proceed to question three: 'Is there anything you have done to increase your prospects of being offered a job imminently?' If not, the respondent proceeds to question four, which is about children in education. If there are none, question five is simply: 'Is there anything else you would like us to consider?' The questionnaire does not ask in great detail about jobseeking, or other kinds of evidence of prospects of work. The kinds of evidence disregarded in cases sent to the *EU Rights Project* include voluntary work, references, applications, interviews,

---

[120]  ibid, 38.
[121]  ibid, 42.
[122]  ibid, 57.
[123]  ibid, 61.
[124]  Obtained on request from a Jobcentre Plus.

and job offers for fixed-term contracts, part-time job offers, being in part-time work and, retrospectively, having after the period of claim, got a job. Decision-makers have also ignored other possible avenues of a right to reside when conducting the genuine prospect of work test:

---

**Case Study: Enrique**

Case referred for second-tier advice. Evidence submitted includes a first instance decision that stated: 'At the genuine prospect of work test interview in answer to Q1 [the client] stated he had not been offered a job. In answer to Q2, [he] stated he had not made any arrangements to start up his own business to become self-employed. The information provided … at the interview was considered against the guidance laid out in paragraphs 73099 and 73100 of the Decision-Makers Guide (page 12) to establish whether [he] had provided compelling evidence which demonstrates he is continuing to seek employment and has a genuine prospect of work'.

---

This suggests that the guidance is heavily relied upon, becoming determinative of outcomes, and of the law, so does restrict what decision-makers to consider compelling evidence:

---

**Case Study: Alessandro**

This client (referred for second-tier advice) had had his jobseeker's allowance stopped on the grounds that he did not have a genuine prospect of work. He had been living, and mostly working, in the UK for over 10 years. His work history in the UK included 12 jobs. At the point when his benefit was stopped, he had a job interview scheduled five days later—but still an imminent interview was deemed insufficient evidence of a genuine prospect of work—possibly because it was not one of the two 'types' of compelling evidence considered 'relevant' in the guidance. His adviser also pointed to 'his good command of the English language, his readiness to be flexible in the type of work and number of hours he is happy to do'.

---

The Upper Tribunal ruling makes clear that evidence other than that within the guidance, and other than that elicited by the questionnaire, may be relevant. In particular, decision-makers should not limit themselves to just looking at qualifications at the point of the test, but should note qualifications soon to be gained.[125] However, the prior period of jobseeking can be taken into account in weighing up the likelihood of the claimant getting work. Decision-makers are also entitled to be sceptical about the comments about employment prospects from employment

---

[125] *MB* above n 119, 46.

advisors, who may be unrealistically positive.[126] Following the Upper Tribunal ruling, the guidance has been amended, to include a non-exhaustive list of types of
evidence that may be taken into account.[127] However, this list comes after the section appearing to still require one of the two types of compelling evidence from
the old guidance. The section states that compelling evidence must be provided
and then states 'this may be', and lists two bullet points: the first is 'a genuine offer
of a specific job' and the second is the old change of circumstances condition, as
result of which the applicant is awaiting the outcome of job interviews. Between
the two is the word '**or**', in bold font.[128] This appears to be an exhaustive list of two.
As a result, the later list reads as though various forms of evidence may be considered, but only insofar as they point to either of those scenarios.

It seems that even claimants who have a genuine offer of a specific job may not
be able to demonstrate that they have a genuine prospect of work, if they cannot
provide evidence to show that it will pass the minimum earnings threshold. The
guidance requires evidence that the work will be 'genuine and effective' work. The
new test for genuine and effective work has two tiers (explored in more detail in
the next section): the first is assessing whether a minimum level of earnings has
been consistently met for three months; and if not, then the assessment moves to
the second tier, assessing whether work is genuine and effective. But due to lack
of guidance on this second tier, and the lack of evidence a claimant can provide
about a job that has not yet started, then in the context of the genuine prospect
of work test, this is likely to be reduced to a question of predicted earnings. Such
guidance as there is on the second tier suggests the key questions are of duration,
pay and hours.[129] The guidance on genuine prospects gives example scenarios,
including someone with a zero-hours contract due to start in two weeks. In the
scenario, it is determined that 'although he has a job offer, there is no compelling
evidence that the work will be genuine or effective because the income, hours per
week and duration cannot be confirmed'.[130] He has therefore 'not provided compelling evidence to show a genuine chance of being engaged' and so 'no longer has
a right to reside as either a retained worker or a jobseeker and is a person from
abroad'.[131] This is despite the fact that the job in practice may involve long hours.
The prospective work may be above the earnings threshold, but if there is a lack of
clarity in advance due to variable hours, it will be very difficult to adduce prospective evidence to displace the (problematic) presumption that it is marginal. The
result is perplexingly that actually having a job may not be sufficient evidence of
a chance of a job.

[126]  ibid, 94.
[127]  Above n 6, 073100.
[128]  ibid, 073099.
[129]  ibid, 072816 and 073050.
[130]  ibid, 073100, example 5.
[131]  ibid.

## B. Undue Conditions Placed on Retained Worker Status

Just as the genuine prospect of work test is applied to people who have secured jobs, it is also applied to people who actually have worker status through the provisions on worker status retention. It is difficult to find a basis in EU law for applying the genuine prospect of work test to those who have retained worker status (rather than had jobseeker status) for six months. Article 7(3) of Directive 2004/38/EC provides for the retention of worker status in the event of unemployment in the following circumstances:

(b)  he/she is in duly recorded involuntary unemployment after having been employed for more than one year and has registered as a job-seeker with the relevant employment office;

(c)  he/she is in duly recorded involuntary unemployment after completing a fixed-term employment contract of less than a year or after having become involuntarily unemployed during the first twelve months and has registered as a job-seeker with the relevant employment office. In this case, the status of worker shall be retained for no less than six months.

The new UK rules state that those who have retained worker status having worked for less than 12 months (so under Article 7(3)(c)) cannot retain worker status for any longer than six months. The 'floor' provided in the Directive is thus a 'ceiling' in domestic legislation. This approach is adopted in many other Member States,[132] calling into question whether the spirit of the Directive's provision is sufficiently respected. Those who exhaust their allowed six months of retention in the UK may subsequently be treated as jobseekers, but only if they pass the genuine prospect of work test first. There is arguably no basis in EU law for testing prospects of work at that point, which is *before* a claimant has exercised a right to reside as a jobseeker.

Former workers who have retained worker status having worked for more than 12 months (under Article 7(3)(b)) are subject to an extendable six-month limit under UK rules; after six months they must pass the genuine prospect of work test to continue retaining worker status. Again, there is no basis in EU law for a six-month limit for those retaining worker status under Article 7(3)(b). Nor is there a basis for requiring evidence of genuine prospect of work for extending that limit. Applying the genuine prospect of work test to those with retained worker status is particularly problematic when we consider how difficult it is to pass the test. It creates a very significant hurdle to retaining worker status for longer than six months. The *EU Rights Project* has worked with a significant number of advisers around the country who have worked with clients before receiving notification of the test,[133] and not one client encountered by all advisors consulted has passed the

---

[132] C O'Brien, E Spaventa and J De Coninck, *Comparative Report—The Concept of Worker Under Article 45 TFEU and Certain Non-Standard Forms of Employment* (Brussels, European Commission, April 2016).

[133] So they were not just working with people who seek advice *because* they have failed the test.

test at first instance. A test that is very hard to pass is unlikely to accurately test for a genuine prospect of work.

The changes increase the likelihood that EU nationals will lose retained worker status, and jobseeker status, and so have status gaps. They also make it harder for EU nationals to seek work, and even to take up work already offered. The lack of appetite for the promotion of employment of EU nationals is evident in another change: the removal of routine interpretation services from job centres. In a government press release, the government announced that ministers wanted to 'call time' on routine interpretation 'and stop subsidising unemployed migrants who do not learn English, hindering their ability to find a job and integrate into British life'.[134] Again, these statements are potentially acts of declaratory discrimination, suggesting that EU migrants were being subsidised, and refusing to learn English and to integrate into British life. In theory, according to the equality impact assessment,[135] withdrawal of interpretation services should increase employability. However, it is difficult to imagine how making it harder to access services that help people find work will actually help them find work.

### C. Preventing EU Nationals from *Finding* Work

Interpretation will still be offered in some cases. The policy addressed to job centre workers states that: 'You should arrange for an interpreter if it is clear that the person's command of English, or Welsh, is not good enough for you to deal with them properly and it is in the Department's interest to do so'.[136] This suggests that if it is not 'clear' that their English is not good enough, the job centre should assume they can proceed without interpretation. There is an instruction to muddle through: 'Where an individual asks for an interpreter you should discuss the request with them. If it becomes apparent that you can conduct business with them without the need for an interpreter, you may proceed without an interpreter'.[137] So basic communication may be deemed sufficient, even though that may result in misunderstandings that could have serious ramifications for the claimants concerned, and may simply dissuade them from engaging with the job centre in the first place. The equality impact assessment makes a number of grand, unsubstantiated claims about the effects of removing interpretation: that it should 'improve integration of migrant communities and strengthen a cross British identity'; that it will 'advance equality of opportunity and foster good relations between different communities'; and it will help 'people to compete equally

---

[134] DWP, above n 1.

[135] Obtained through a Freedom of Information Request: DWP, 'Equality Analysis for Withdrawal of Routine Interpreting and Translating Services from New Jobseekers' (Social Justice Change and Delivery Team, DWP, 17 January 2014).

[136] Obtained through a Freedom of Information Request: DWP, *Interpreting Services Policy*, sent 22 July 2014.

[137] ibid.

in the labour market and not allowing them to slip into benefit dependency and social exclusion'.[138] No evidence is given to back this up. There is however evidence to suggest the opposite. The Cities for Local Integration Policy Network found that translation provided in public services, including for job searching, served to help integration.[139] The National Institute for Economic and Social Research has found that those who do not speak English are less likely to use public services. They may become even less likely to do so without interpretation services. This might reduce the direct cost of services, but could 'result in exploitation of migrants where they are not aware of their rights and of available support':[140]

**Evidence Submission:** An evidence submission from an advice service supervisor in the Midlands to the *EU Rights Project* highlighted that language difficulties were obstructing claimants' access to benefits, rather than promoting their access to work.

*Supervisor notes: We have identified a particular trend relating to migrants struggling with the security questions posed by the DWP, HMRC and Local Authorities. Clients have been denied benefits for several months due to a language difficulty ... we had 15 instances between January 2015 and March 2015 where clients who came to see us needed an interpreter and were not provided with one by the DWP/HMRC.*[141]

Such experience does not bode well for the removal of most interpretation from job centres. Rather, it increases the risk of screening EU nationals out of the welfare system, rather than integrating them into it. The policy makes it harder for some EU nationals to access services to find work. However, we should not overplay the change, since in practice, in the experience of advisers consulted in the *EU Rights Project*, interpretation services were not 'routinely' offered anyway.[142] As such, the change might not be all that noticeable for some, but it does send out a message about the state's general distaste for EU nationals with poor English skills even though, under EU law, a language requirement cannot be imposed unless justified by an overriding reason of general interest.[143] It indicates a declared obstacle to the labour market in the stated policy: 'there is an expectation that all new jobseeker's

---

[138] DWP, above n 135.

[139] Cities for Local Integration Policy, *Equality and Diversity in Jobs and Services for Migrants in European Cities: Good Practice guide* (Dublin, European Foundation for the Improvement of Living and Working Conditions, 2008).

[140] H Rolfe, T Fic, M Lalani, M Roman, M Prohaska, and L Doudevapage, 'Potential Impacts on the UK of Future Migration from Bulgaria and Romania' (2013) *National Institute of Economic and Social Research Report*, April, 31.

[141] Evidence submitted, not referred for advice, submission 7.

[142] Participants in the reflective focus group expressed this view.

[143] UI Jensen, 'The Language Requirements under EU Law on Free Movement of Workers', *Analytical Note 2013 For The European Network on Free Movement of Workers within the European Union* (October 2013—updated February 2014). See Case C-424/97 *Salomone Haim v Kassenzahnärztliche Vereinigung Nordrhein* EU:C:2000:357, 57.

allowance claimants will have a level of English which enables them to compete and be successful in the UK labour market'.[144] The equality impact assessment emphasises the language expectations and states that removing routine access to interpreting and translation services 'from the outset of jobseeker's allowance claims helps to reinforce this message'. The message about what is expected has a flip-side: who is unwelcome.

## D. The Perils of Being Defined as a Jobseeker

With entitlements for jobseekers decreasing dramatically, and being subject to strict time limits and tests, the cliff-edge is set to steepen further with universal credit, a new benefit rolled out in the UK to replace income-based jobseeker's allowance, income support, income-based employment and support allowance, housing benefit, working tax credit and child tax credit. The government announced in 2015[145] that universal credit would be classed as social assistance and so EEA national jobseekers would be excluded from it in its entirety. The government argued that universal credit is 'a wide-ranging anti-poverty measure rather than a benefit solely designed to address a specific social risk such as unemployment or incapacity for work'.[146] This is the position adopted in the universal credit regulations.[147] Since income-based jobseeker's allowance, the only non-contributory benefit that is currently treated as a benefit facilitating access to the labour market, is subsumed into universal credit, that leaves EEA national jobseekers without any claim to a non-contributory benefit for facilitating access to the labour market, and makes the precipice that beckons on being found to be a jobseeker rather than a worker even steeper. This may yet be subject to challenge as it is not impossible to divide benefits into elements to which claimants are entitled under EU law, and those which they are not, as evident in the splitting of the 'care' and 'mobility' elements of disability living allowance in the ECJ case of *Bartlett*[148] on the subject of its exportability. Similarly, it is not inconceivable that the individual jobseeker element of universal credit could be disaggregated from the elements more readily defined as social assistance.

It may be possible to characterise universal credit as a combination of components, some social assistance and some social security, in recognition of its

---

[144] DWP *Interpreting Services Policy* (2014).

[145] DWP, above n 135.

[146] Social Security Advisory Committee, *Minutes of the Meeting with DWP*, 4 March 2015, 2.3(f). Available at: www.gov.uk/government/uploads/system/uploads/attachment_data/file/429954/ssac-minutes-march-2015.pdf.

[147] reg 9(3)(aa)(i) and (ii) exclude a right to reside as a jobseeker or family member as a jobseeker for the purposes of qualifying for entitlement to universal credit under reg 9(2), which requires a right to reside (see Universal Credit Regulations 2013, SI 2013/376).

[148] Case C-537/09 *Ralph James Bartlett and Others v Secretary of State for Work and Pensions* EU:C:2011:278.

compound nature, combining multiple purposes and multiple original benefits. It would then be possible to argue that the jobseeker part of universal credit is a *Collins* benefit—that is, a means-tested cash benefit to facilitate access to the labour market. However, without a change in approach at ECJ level, such a construction may not fare well, given the recent suggestions in case law (explored above in chapters three and four) that means-tested benefits, because they at heart exist to preserve human dignity, are to be treated as social assistance and withheld from jobseekers.

As the distinction between the rights of workers and non-workers becomes starker, so the definition of work becomes more important. In EU law, for many years, it was argued that the importance placed on economic activity as a gateway to equal treatment was offset by the breadth of the definition of economic activity. An EU migrant had to be doing some work to get equal treatment, but the threshold to be recognised as doing work was low. However, national rules in many Member States—especially the UK—are making it harder to claim the status of worker, mainly for those in low-pay, low-status jobs with variable hours. A narrowed definition of work, explored next, makes it more likely that people will fall over the now steeper cliff-edge, meaning that workers may find themselves excluded from equal treatment rights, exacerbating the risk of in-work poverty, and alienating workers from the fruits of their labours. As Marx observed of developing capitalism, poorly paid work results in greater objectification, in which the workers are more means of production than rights-acquiring citizens.[149] Their labour 'produces for the rich wonderful things—but for the worker it produces privation'.[150]

## VI. MAKING THE CLIFF-TOP NARROWER: A FLAWED AND NARROWING DEFINITION OF MIGRANT WORK

The definition in ECJ case law of migrant work for the purposes of Article 45 TFEU has been both broad and vague.[151] The Court has typically taken an expansive approach, while emphasising that the term has a 'Community meaning'[152] not to be amended at will by Member States as otherwise 'the effectiveness of Community law would be impaired, and the achievement of the objectives of the Treaty would be jeopardized'.[153] The basic definition emerging from the

---

[149] The 'worker becomes all the poorer the more wealth he produces ... [and] becomes an ever cheaper commodity', see K Marx and F Engels, *Economic and Philosophical Manuscripts of 1844* (Radford, Wilder Publications, 2011) 67–83.

[150] ibid.

[151] Common Market Law Review Editorial, 'The Free Movement of Persons in the European Union: Salvaging the Dream while Explaining the Nightmare' (2014) 51 *CML Rev* 3, 729.

[152] Case 75–63 *Mrs MKH Hoekstra (née Unger) v Bestuur der Bedrijfsvereniging voor Detailhandel en Ambachten* EU:C:1964:19, 1.

[153] Case 53/81 *Levin v Staatssecretaris van Justitie* EU:C:1982:105, 15.

*Lawrie Blum*[154] case is of someone who performs activities under supervision of another in return for remuneration. In *Levin*,[155] the Court found that this extended to people in part-time work and/or people who earn less than the income level considered in that state to be the minimum required for subsistence. To exclude part time workers from the definition of worker would impair the effectiveness of Community law, since part-time work 'constitutes for a large number of persons an effective means of improving their living conditions.'[156] In *Kempf*,[157] the Court found that this applied to part time workers who sought to supplement their income through welfare benefits ('financial assistance drawn from public funds'). The key components of a work relationship—the *Lawrie Blum* criteria—hold good, excluding activities on 'such a small scale as to be regarded as purely marginal and ancillary'.[158] The work must therefore be 'genuine and effective', but in *Kurz*, the Court stated that when determining whether someone is a worker, 'neither the sui generis nature of the employment relationship under national law, nor the level of productivity of the person concerned, the origin of funds from which remuneration is paid or the limited amount of remuneration can have any consequence'.[159] Apprentices must be included in the definition if they perform genuine and effective activity, a conclusion that cannot be 'invalidated' by low productivity, not carrying out full duties, only working a 'small number of hours per week' and receiving 'limited remuneration'.[160] The concept of worker 'must not be interpreted narrowly.'[161]

The Court found in *Rinner Kuhn*[162] that 10 hours per week could constitute work, and then in *Genc*,[163] that a contract for five and a half hours per week might constitute genuine and effective work, and the possibility should not be ruled out. The authorities should not look only to the number of hours and rate of pay, but also to 'the right to 28 days of paid leave, to the continued payment of wages in the event of sickness, and to a contract of employment which is subject to the relevant collective agreement' and take account of the duration of employment, being 'almost four years'.[164] Though broad, the definition of worker has notable exclusions. The continued requirement of remuneration (even though this may in some cases not be wages, but may be payment in kind for odd jobs),[165] serves

---

[154] Case 66/85 *Lawrie-Blum* EU:C:1986:284.
[155] Above n 145.
[156] ibid, 15.
[157] Case 139/85 *R H Kempf v Staatssecretaris van Justitie* EU:C:1986:223.
[158] ibid, 10–11.
[159] Case C-188/00 *Bülent Kurz, né Yüce v Land Baden-Württemberg* EU:C:2002:694, 32. This was reiterated in Case C-456/02 *Michel Trojani v Centre public d'aide sociale de Bruxelles (CPAS)* EU:C:2004:488.
[160] *Kurz*, ibid, 33.
[161] ibid, 32.
[162] Case 171/88 *Ingrid Rinner-Kühn v FWW Spezial-Gebäudereinigung GmbH & Co. KG* EU:C:1989:328.
[163] Case C-14/09 *Hava Genc v Land Berlin* EU:C:2010:57.
[164] ibid, 7.
[165] Case 196/87 *Udo Steymann v Staatssecretaris van Justitie* EU:C:1988:475.

to screen out a lot of reproductive work (child care and care for old or disabled adults). Before moving on to examine the UK's modifications to the EU definition of work, the next section looks at the gendered effects of the ECJ's definition and, in particular, the exclusion of unpaid care.

## A. The Invisibility of Unpaid Care Work

The difference in treatment between familial care and non-familial care can be striking: an adult paying a non-familial carer with his benefits meant that the carer was performing, according to Advocate General Tizzano, 'undoubtedly "genuine and effective" activities' within the meaning of (then) Article 39 EC.[166] The Court chose not to follow this approach,[167] simply finding that the citizenship provisions meant that the carer resident in another Member State was entitled to equal treatment with resident carers. The Court thus argued that it could answer the questions 'without it being necessary to take a position … on the issue of whether the third parties [the carers] concerned are to be regarded as workers within the meaning of Article 39 EC'.[168] It was an unusual approach at the time, to decide the case on citizenship provisions where a possible answer lay in the worker ones. Now, as the Court is erasing citizenship from its adjudication, it seems unthinkable. But the reason may lie in the Court's phrasing: it wanted to avoid 'taking a position' on the worker status of informal, or semi-formal carers, precisely because the distinctions currently riven through EU law lack logic, entrench existing gender-power differentials and affect many people. The Court has already answered the question with regard to family carers in *Züchner*.[169] In that case, a woman sought to rely on protections from sex discrimination, as her husband's sickness insurance would only pay a carer's allowance where the carer had had to give up work to care, as entitlement to the relevant sickness insurance payment only arose where there was 'no person living in the household who can assist and care for the patient to the extent necessary'.[170] In excluding unpaid household members from entitlement to care benefits, Mrs Züchner argued that it was primarily the female members of the family who would be disadvantaged. In order to do so, she had to show she fell within the scope of Directive 79/7/EEC on equal treatment for men and women in matters of social security[171] (that is, that she was a worker).

---

[166] Joined Cases C-502/01 and C-31/02 *Silke Gaumain-Cerri v Kaufmännische Krankenkasse—Pflegekasse* and *Maria Barth v Landesversicherungsanstalt Rheinprovinz* Opinion of AG Tizzano EU:C:2003:649, 130.

[167] Cases C-502/01 and C-31/02 *Gaumain-Cerri* and *Barth* Judgment EU:C:2004:413.

[168] ibid, 32.

[169] Case C-77/95 *Bruna-Alessandra Züchner v Handelskrankenkasse (Ersatzkasse) Bremen* EU:C:1996:425.

[170] ibid, 4.

[171] Council Directive 79/7/EEC of 19 December 1978 on the progressive implementation of the principle of equal treatment for men and women in matters of social security OJ [1979] L6/24.

She pointed to the intensity of the activities required to care for her husband, who had become paraplegic following an accident, the level of competence required (she had undergone training) and argued that the care work 'by virtue of its nature and scope, can be assimilated to an occupational activity'.[172] She also pointed out that were she not providing the care, it would have to be provided by someone on a paid basis. The Court acknowledged that the term 'working population' in the Directive was very wide and added that the various activities required of carers/providers of services to disabled persons 'call for a degree of competence, are of a certain scope and must be provided by an outsider in return for remuneration if there is no-one else … who will do so without payment'.[173] But there was no mention of the loss of opportunity to engage in paid employment for carers in Mrs Züchner's position—an opportunity that might be most useful at the point her husband was removed from the labour market. The Court simply found that an interpretation that purported to include unpaid members of the family undertaking those activities 'would have the effect of infinitely extending the scope of the Directive'.[174]

The language of 'infinite extension' betrays the limits of the ECJ's imagination: including some unpaid carers in some worker protections is portrayed as not merely simply unthinkable, but as impossible as, in effect, an extension to everyone. This 'floodgates' reasoning is familiar and is deployed time and again when challenges to discrimination, or to prevailing power dynamics, are proposed.[175] In *Dias*,[176] the Court conceived of periods of unremunerated child care as, at best, equivalent to periods of absence as addressed in *Lassal*,[177] so that periods of less than two years should not be treated as affecting the acquisition of permanent residence. This appears to automatically condone the approach taken in the Court of Appeal in England and Wales that a right to reside is lost in such periods. The Court of Appeal had stated that the periods in which she was 'not working' were due to 'reasons which are perfectly understandable socially but which had nothing whatever to do with her occupational activity: indeed precisely the reverse'.[178] Her looking after her six-month-old child rather than returning to work was a 'perfectly comprehensible but voluntary decision to care for her child herself rather than to work'.[179] The treatment of women undertaking care for infant children as exercising a choice 'not to work' stems from a floodgates fear similar to that in *Züchner*—a belief that the term 'worker' must be delimited,

---

[172] Above n 169, 9.
[173] ibid, 14.
[174] ibid, 15.
[175] C O'Brien, 'Social Blind Spots and Monocular Policy-Making: The ECJ's Migrant Worker Model' (2009) 46 *CML Rev* 4, 1107.
[176] Case C-325/09 *Secretary of State for Work and Pensions v Maria Dias* EU:C:2011:498.
[177] Case C-162/09 *Secretary of State for Work and Pensions v Taous Lassal* EU:C:2010:592.
[178] *Secretary of State for Work and Pensions v Dias* [2009] EWCA Civ 807, 22.
[179] ibid, 20.

and so must self-evidently be delimited in a way that happens to uphold current power dynamics:

> The circumstances of a parent, of either sex, who gives up employment to care for a child but anticipates a return after some as yet unknown time are very common. The breadth of the concept of 'worker' has to recognise a balancing of the interests of migrants and of host states and their taxpayers.[180]

This reasoning suggests that these circumstances should be excluded because they are 'very common'. It might however be suggested that it is precisely because they are very common, that a definition of work that systematically disadvantages women ought to be rethought. The interests of 'taxpayers' are paramount, because of the sacralising of economic activity, but unpaid carers (for children and for adults) subsidise the economy, and thereby taxpayers, to a considerable degree,[181] which may be considered an equivalent contribution. In many cases this contribution is in the form of caring for an own-state national child or adult. But the fixation upon an economic nexus, in which what is 'economic' has been fixed according to a traditional male model of work, has ill-served women in the context of right to reside decisions, if they have not yet acquired, or have not been able to provide evidence to acquire, permanent residence.

Courts in the UK have also emphasised that the exclusion of such care requirements from attracting a possible right to reside holds good even when the circumstances are not that common (for example, where the child is very sick or disabled). In a startling paragraph, Commissioner Rowland[182] decided that a woman, on becoming pregnant, assumes the risk of having a very sick child in need of extra care, and of being excluded from the job market as a result, while simultaneously not being able to return to her home state due to the child's condition, so being left without resources for herself or her child. Hence he decided it was the woman's responsibility to decide whether to avert that risk by leaving the country on discovering the pregnancy:

> [I]t was not the claimant's fault that her child was ill and that it might have been impossible for her to travel to Holland while the child was ill in hospital, *but she had known she was pregnant* and presumably knew that she would be without support if she were to be unable to work through childcare responsibilities and were to receive no support from the child's father and so it cannot be said that she had not previously had the opportunity to return to Holland where she would have been entitled to benefit.[183]

---

[180] ibid, 21.

[181] 'The economic value of the contribution made by carers in the UK is now £132 billion per year' (L Buckner and S Yeandle, *Valuing Carers 2015: The Rising Value of Carers' Support* (London, Carers UK, 2015), 4.

[182] The Office of the Social Security and Child Support Commissioners became the Upper Tribunal (Administrative Appeals Chamber) in 2008.

[183] CIS/3182/2005, 17.

This suggests a significant obstacle to freedom of movement for women. While some cases like this involving new-born babies might be averted through *St Prix*, allowing women to retain worker status during 'reasonable' periods of pregnancy and maternity,[184] that does not help those who cannot invoke *St Prix* for any reason, or whose reason for temporary exclusion from the labour market is more clearly related to care or a child's medical needs than to pregnancy or maternity. *St Prix* might however provide the basis for arguing that the categories provided for retaining worker status are not exhaustive, and that the primary law-based right to move and reside, in Article 45 TFEU takes precedence and should be interpreted expansively and with other Union objectives (such as equality between men and women) in mind.

While flawed, the definition of migrant work has hitherto been wide. But part-time workers combining work and care are at greater risk in the UK of being found not to be workers at all. There were signs in the UK, prior to the introduction of the minimum earnings threshold, that decision-makers might disregard periods of work, such as in the decision-maker's language in Irina's case:

---

**Case Study: Irina**

Irina had worked for 77.5 months, punctuated by two short periods of jobseeking. She was refused income support, and in his response to the ensuing appeal [which pre-dated the minimum earnings threshold], the Secretary of State for Work and Pensions listed those periods of work, and yet went on to say: '[Irina] has not gained Worker Status in the UK, she has worked in the UK but has not gained or retained worker status'. This was a blank statement. There was no explanation or basis for this finding, especially in light of the Secretary of State's own findings on the length of the periods of work. She had earned enough not to need benefits during those periods. The ease with which work was disregarded without reason was puzzling and symptomatic of a tendency I noted in other cases,[185] to refuse first, and ask questions later (on appeal). This tendency may be exacerbated by the introduction of the UK's new definition of worker, which introduces a presumption that work below a high threshold is marginal.

---

## B. The Minimum Earnings Threshold

In March 2014, the UK government provided a framework for decision-makers to refuse to recognise worker status—the minimum earnings threshold.[186] In theory, it is a two-tier test, with an earnings threshold applied to allow some people to automatically acquire worker status and a second-tier test for those who fall below the threshold to determine whether the work they perform is 'genuine

---

[184]   Case C-507/12 *Jessy Saint Prix v Secretary of State for Work and Pensions* EU:C:2014:2007.
[185]   See ch 8.
[186]   Above n 6.

and effective'.[187] This second tier appears to be a means to make the test EU-compliant. However, prior to this test, decision-makers already applied a 'genuine and effective' assessment to workers. The only possible, logical reason for introducing the threshold is to reduce the number of people who are defined as workers. This objective is more-or-less explicit. The press release announcing the measure stated that 'European Union case law means the definition of a "worker" is very broad, meaning some people may benefit from this even if, in reality, they do very little work'.[188] The measure is presented as a deliberate circumvention of EU law. Moreover, the press release added that the measure was 'part of the government's long-term plan to cap welfare and reduce immigration'.[189] It could only be conceived as such if it *reduces* the number of people defined as workers. Again, the government is erecting a declaratory obstacle to movement—announcing a desire to reduce the number of EEA nationals migrating to the UK and also indicating that those who do migrate now face a greater risk of being denied worker status.

As there is very little focus on the second tier of the test, and no indication that it introduces anything new, the only way the overall test can reduce the number of those found to be workers is if the first tier—the earnings threshold—is more decisive than it would have been in a genuinely 'two-tier' test. There is a significant risk that the first tier is fairly determinative, not least since it informs decision-makers about what is key to 'genuine and effective' work. The press release itself elides the two tiers, treating the earnings threshold as definitive of *genuine* work, stating that '*to show they are undertaking genuine and effective work* in the UK an EEA migrant will have to show that for the last three months they have been *earning at the level* at which employees start paying National Insurance'.[190]

There is a risk, apparent in evidence collected under the *EU Rights Project*, that decision-makers will take the steer to focus on earnings and hours worked, making them all-but determinative. Indeed, the test was heavily publicised as a 'Minimum Earnings Threshold',[191] not as a new genuine and effective test. The decision-maker guidance further adds to such concerns. There is not much specific guidance about the dividing line between genuine and effective work and marginal and ancillary activity, but the focus in the second tier is still upon criteria similar to those used in the first tier:

> When determining whether or not someone is a worker, the following can be relevant considerations: (1) whether work was regular or intermittent; (2) the period of employment; (3) whether the work was intended to be short-term or long-term at the outset; (4) the number of hours worked; and (5) the level of earnings.[192]

---

[187] ibid.
[188] DWP, above n 23.
[189] ibid.
[190] ibid, emphases added.
[191] In the government press release, ibid, and in Cameron, above n 20.
[192] DWP, above n 186, 073050.

Factors 4 and 5 (hours and pay) are effectively repeats of the first tier. The only other factors seem to be duration, regularity and whether the work was intended to be long-term. The factors relevant to the first tier are used again and played off against these other factors so that in 'some cases the decision-maker will have to weigh, for example, low hours against long duration of work as part of their over-all assessment of whether work is genuine and effective'.[193] The fact of failing the first tier may be weighed up against other positive factors, such as long duration. This steers decision-makers to use tier one to inform the genuine and effective assessment at tier two. The effect is to create a presumption of marginality for those who fall below the threshold, who must adduce not only evidence of the genuine nature of their work, but evidence that 'genuine and effective' aspects of the work outweigh the fact of failing the minimum earnings threshold. They face a significant burden of displacing that marginality presumption.

The DWP has issued a 'jobseeker's allowance three months residency and work information' form for decision-makers, questions 4–14 of which deal with 'work information'.[194] They focus on hours and pay. The only other factors sought are duration, whether the work is permanent/temporary, and whether fixed-term, casual or seasonal. This form is likely to steer decision-makers to focus on earn-ings, and to find that if someone earns below the threshold, then if the contract is temporary and fixed term, it must be marginal and ancillary (contrary to guidance given by the ECJ).

## C. Part-Time Work and the Presumption of Marginality

The presumption of marginality is evident in the treatment of part time work in the decision-maker guidance, which states that 'work that is part time or low paid is not necessarily always marginal and ancillary'.[195] As a statement of probability '*not necessarily always*' means 'usually'. It operates from an assumption that the reader would be inclined to treat part time work as 'necessarily always' marginal, and then offers a slight challenge to that assumption. What we are left with is a rebuttable presumption (but one which is *almost* always not rebuttable). This is a significant steer to decision-makers: 'not necessarily always marginal and ancil-lary' is a very different statement of probability to that implied by the ECJ when it stated that it constituted 'for a large number of persons an effective means of improving their living conditions',[196] and to an assessment in which a limited amount of remuneration 'cannot … have any consequence in regard to whether or not the person is a worker'.[197]

---

[193] ibid.
[194] Supplement to forms HRT2/HRT2[R] 'Jobseeker's Allowance 3 Month Residency and Work Information' (obtained from Jobcentre Plus on request).
[195] Above n 186, 073052.
[196] *Levin* judgment, above n 155, 15.
[197] *Kurz* judgment, above n 159, 33.

The presumption of marginality kicks in at a relatively high threshold. The minimum earnings threshold of £155 is equivalent to 21.5 hours per week at the minimum wage for the 2016/17 financial year (and even more hours for workers below the age of 25).[198] It is not just in the 'fringe' cases crossing the paths of the ECJ, wherein people have worked for 5.5 or somewhere around or less than 10 hours a week, that the presumption is made, and must be displaced. It is in the case of substantial periods of part time work including for lone parents and disabled persons who may be working as much as is practicable. It is worth noting here that the UK benefits system recognises reduced work capacity for UK nationals, and decision-makers cannot, for instance, require a lone parent on jobseeker's allowance to work more than 16 hours per week.[199] But there is no sliding scale to the threshold for lone parents or disabled workers, and those who fall below the threshold are all subject to the same decision-making process and guided by the same guidance. Women and disabled people are at greater risk of nationality discrimination in its application:

**Evidence Submission**[200]

One account submitted to the *EU Rights Project* as evidence was an adviser's experiences of helping a lone mother working 16 hours per week deemed not to be a worker, so she and her children (two school-aged, one pre-school-aged) were refused housing benefit, child benefit and child tax credit. She started working as a sex worker in order to pay her rent and had to leave her young children unattended at night.

The UK does not seem to be alone in establishing a threshold at which the presumption of work shifts to a presumption of marginality (where the evidential burden shifts), yet it does seem to set the highest threshold. In response to questionnaires issued as part of research conducted with the EU Commission's Free Movement and Social Security Coordination network (FreSsco), the national expert for Belgium interviewed key informants[201] and found that a 12 hour per week threshold is used, with a 'quasi-irrebuttable' presumption that work below this threshold is marginal and ancillary. According to the Finnish national expert, Finland uses a high threshold, requiring 18 hours of work per week, or 80 hours in four weeks (with hours completed in all four weeks) as well as an earnings threshold of €1,165 per month.[202] Denmark uses a 10–12 hour per week threshold[203]

---

[198] 22.3 hours for those aged 21–24; 27.9 hours for those aged 18–20; 38.75 hours for those aged under 18; and 45.6 hours for those on an apprenticeship wage.

[199] reg 13(4)(c) of the Jobseekers Allowance Regulations 1996.

[200] Evidence submission 10, not referred for advice.

[201] Above n 124.

[202] Act on the Application on Residence-Based Social Security Legislation (s 2a) or the Act on Health Insurance (see ibid, 25).

[203] The Danish Immigration Service states that normally there is the condition that the employment amounts to 'at least 10–12 hours' per week, although it is not possible to fix a lower

and the Netherlands uses alternative thresholds of either earnings exceeding 50 per cent of the social assistance standard (approximately €670), or hours equal to at least 40 per cent of the normal full-time working time (which may vary from sector to sector).[204] In most cases, respondents reporting thresholds also added that those falling below the thresholds would be subject to discretionary case-by-case assessments. However, the crucial concern is how this discretionary assessment (or second tier) of the process works in practice, and whether requiring claimants to displace a presumption of marginality results in most other relevant factors being eclipsed by the focus on earnings and/or hours. One advice worker in the North West of England has reported to the project that 'anyone earning less than the threshold is automatically refused housing benefit',[205] with the possibility of revision upon appeal. Another advice worker, in London, commented:

> Often the minimum earnings threshold is being misunderstood/wrongly applied. Regularly I'm hearing clients report that they've been turned away and told they're not eligible for assistance because they're not workers simply because they're earning below the threshold, without even a cursory consideration of whether their work is genuine and effective.[206]

The guidance gives a strong steer to give disproportionate weight to hours and earnings, so that some decision-makers confuse the 'genuine and effective' work test with the threshold itself:

---

**Case Study: Pavel**

This case was referred to the *EU Rights Project* for second-tier advice. Pavel was working 16–20 hours per week on the minimum wage, and had been working for over six months. He was also about to start a new job that would give him a minimum of 24 hours of work per week. He applied for housing benefit and was turned down.

*Field notes: [The decision-maker] said they find his employment 'genuine but not effective as ... you do not have sufficient resources to support yourself not to become a burden on the state'.*

---

This is a strange interpretation of the rules and it is not clear what the basis in law is for finding work to be 'genuine but not effective'. It also shows an elision of the concept of effective work with the threshold, and reflects a misapplication of EU law, in suggesting that work can only be genuine and effective where a worker poses no 'burden on the state' (a position in direct conflict with that of the

---

limit (New to Denmark, *Residence in Denmark for Union Citizens and EA Nationals*, available at: www.nyidanmark.dk/en-us/coming_to_dk/eu_and_nordic_citizens/eu-eea_citizens/residence_in_denmark_for_union_citizens_and_eea_nationals.htm).

[204] Above n 124, B.10(2) Aliens Circular (*Vreemdelingencirculaire*).
[205] Evidence submitted to the project: submission 4.
[206] Evidence submitted to the project: submission 8.

ECJ in *Kempf*). The idea that the decision involves assessing a person's ability to support themselves and their family also surfaced in a focus group discussion. One participant reported the following exchange:

> I had one [EU national client] working for 24 hours a week under the national minimum wage and he had eight children, their response was, 'well how can he provide for his family?'[207]

Other decision-makers seem generally confused about what the test means, with one attempting to find a definition from a dictionary and applying it in a way that would have absurd results:

---

**Case Study: Birgitte and Mateo**

This case was referred to the *EU Rights Project* for second-tier advice. This couple had both been working on and off in the UK for over three years. The decision-maker did not consider whether Birgitte's overall work record made her a worker, instead looking at each separate temporary job, and finding that each one was marginal and ancillary, notwithstanding that taken together they added up to a considerable period of work. The moves between jobs also counted against her.

*Extracts from decision letter: During the time of making my decision you have supplied me with various contracts of employment … Due to you changing your employment so regularly this has also influenced my decision as to why I am satisfied your employment has not been genuine and effective.*

This decision-maker also adopted a bizarre interpretation of marginal and ancillary:

*Extract from decision letter: 'ancillary means adj "The ancillary workers in an institution are the people such as cleaners and cooks whose work supports the main work of the institution" this is interpreted as seasonal workers and working on short-term temporary contracts [weekly]'.*

---

I felt a certain amount of sympathy for a decision-maker resorting to a dictionary to look up 'ancillary', as this indicates how little guidance there is as to its meaning beyond failing the earnings threshold. But the result was a ludicrous interpretation that has nothing to do with EU law. If all work performing functions 'ancillary' to the main purpose of institutions was marginal and ancillary work, then huge swathes of the workforce would be excluded from the definition, regardless of the intensity, duration or genuine nature of their activities. It would exclude, as the decision-maker intimates, all cleaners and cooks, and also clerical staff, and fund-raising staff. If we conceive of universities as primarily places of teaching, then it would exclude non-teaching researchers, too.

Being subjected to a poorly administered tier two test creates a disadvantage. In practice, since part-time work under the minimum earnings threshold falls

---

[207] Reflective focus group.

automatically below the tier one threshold, and so falls to be decided as a tier two case, this disadvantage seems to be particularly detrimental for lone parents. If they are doing part-time work, they are now more likely to be told that they are not workers. In some cases, workers may have been residing and working in the UK for many years, and are being told that swathes of past periods of work are now being characterised as 'not-work', either because of being part-time, or because of variable hours. They were not jobseeking at the time (because they were working), so those past periods are not only treated as not-work, they are treated as periods in which there was no right to reside at all, either. Those periods thus create status gaps which could be particularly detrimental to those seeking at some point to rely on having accrued permanent residence. They are also being treated as negating claims to *Teixeira/Ibrahim* rights. Where someone seeks to invoke their status as the primary carer of the school child of a former migrant worker, they are now at greater risk of being told that they were never actually migrant workers in the first place and so their children have no derivative rights (and, therefore, neither do they).

Some are caught by a mixture of provisions that have the effect of negating substantial work histories: if they have recently been doing part time work since having a child, that is being redefined as not-work, so they may seek to rely on prior periods of full-time work to invoke permanent residence. However, if they are A8 nationals and have moved frequently between jobs, there is a very significant risk—thanks to the effects of the worker registration scheme—that all their work up until the end of the transition measures will also be effectively 'deleted' from their record, so that long-term working residents are being treated as though they have never worked at all.

### D. Using the Workers Registration Scheme to Negate Work During Transition

The *Zalewska* ruling on periods of work under the transitional provisions applied to A8 nationals has also had the effect of negating substantial periods of work. In that case, the House of Lords had to decide upon the treatment of work completed by A8 nationals where they/their employers had failed to comply with the registration requirements of the scheme. In contrast to the approach to the later A2 accession, the UK did not derogate from Article 39 EC on the accession of the A8 states, but kept its labour market open to nationals from the new states. The 2004 Act of Accession included provisions permitting a derogation from Articles 1–6 of Regulation 1612/68 permitting Member States to temporarily regulate access of A8 nationals to their labour markets.[208] The UK did not make

---

[208] Act concerning the conditions of accession of the Czech Republic, the Republic of Estonia, the Republic of Cyprus, the Republic of Latvia, the Republic of Lithuania, the Republic of Hungary, the

use of this derogation, but the obstacle it did introduce was the workers registration scheme for A8 nationals.[209] It limited A8 nationals' access to welfare during their first year of work. As such, it was not a derogation from access to the labour market, under Articles 1–6 of the Regulation, but a departure from the principle of equal treatment with regards to access to social advantages (under Article 7 of Regulation 1612/68) for those who have been permitted access. There was no basis within the accession agreements for such a derogation: a permitted restriction to accessing the labour market is not the same thing as treating people differently once you have allowed them in. The ECJ found in the case of *Sotgiu*[210] that once people have been granted access to the labour market, then it is not open to Member States to discriminate against them. Nevertheless, this is what the UK did. The scheme required all A8 workers to register their work with the scheme, and excluded them from equal treatment rights in the event that they became unemployed, until they had completed a continuous period of 12 months of registered work.

The problem that many A8 nationals encountered was that employers frequently did not fully understand the obligations to register the work. Those that worked in short-term or temporary work did not themselves always realise that they needed a new certificate each time they started a new job, thinking that having registered at the start, and continuously working for over 12 months since, that they had complied with the requirements. Employers often did not realise this either: the project received evidence that big public sector employers also failed to comply properly or to advise their EU national employees appropriately, so jeopardising their employees' residence rights.

This had significant consequences for those employees who fell out of employment any time during the period in which the transitional provisions applied (until 2011), since they were told that, if they could not show compliance with the registration requirements for a continuous period of 12 months, then all subsequent work was to be regarded as unlawful work, as not-work, and so a period during which the worker did not have a right to reside. As such, they would not be able to retain worker status under Article 7(3), since there was no status to be retained, and they could not claim permanent residence even if they had worked for over five years. In *Zalewska*, the claimant had worked for a continuous 12 months, having originally registered as required, but part-way through had changed employer and did not re-register. She was therefore treated as not having worked for the required 12 months in order to get normal worker status, which she needed in order to claim benefits when she left the family home due to domestic violence.

---

Republic of Malta, the Republic of Poland, the Republic of Slovenia and the Slovak Republic and the adjustments to the Treaties on which the European Union is founded OJ [2003] L236/33; Annexes V, VI, VIII, IX, X, XII, XIII, and XIV.

[209] Accession (Immigration and Worker Registration) Regulations, SI 2004/1219.
[210] Case 152/73 *Giovanni Maria Sotgiu v Deutsche Bundespost* EU:C:1974:13.

The House of Lords approved this approach, although by a narrow majority. In a strong dissenting judgment, Baroness Hale argued that any aims for reducing benefit tourism were achieved by the 12 month rule, not by the administrative requirements of (re-)registration, and to find otherwise created 'disproportionate perils' with consequences that were 'much more serious' than they would have been had she committed a criminal offence.[211] As a result, those in positions similar to the claimant in *Zalewska* have found themselves unable to claim benefits, not only once 12 months of work has been completed, but also after further significant periods of work have been completed. Currie reports that the 'scheme's rules had a particularly harsh impact on individuals who had remained continuously in work but had not been registered throughout the whole employment period'.[212] The finding has continued to have effects for people who have since wished to claim permanent residence, if they need to rely on a period than includes some time worked before the expiry of the transitional provisions on 30 April 2011:

---

**Case Study: Jonas**

This case was referred to the *EU Rights Project* for second-tier advice. The DWP's response to the appeal contains the statement that 'any employment carried out during the Accession Period of 01/05/04 to 30/04/11 must still be shown to have been registered in accordance with The Accession (Immigration and Worker Registration) Regulations 2004 to be treated as lawful'. After the first month of employment 'they were in unlawful employment until the issue of their Worker Registration Certificate'.

---

Curiously, Upper Tribunal Judge Rowland reopened the discussion regarding *Zalewska* and proportionality. In *JK*,[213] he found that the strict registration requirements of the workers registration scheme *should* be applied proportionately. In that case, the claimant was the family member of a Polish worker who had been a student in employment for 12 months prior to accession, and so assumed that he was covered by the transitional measures and exempted from the Worker Registration Scheme requirements. He had then continued to work in unregistered work. It seems that his student visa ran out before the date of accession, and that he returned to Poland to avoid being an overstayer, so was not in the UK on the 30 April 2004, then came back to the UK after accession. This, argued the Secretary of State, meant that he was not covered by the transitional measures, and was subject to the Worker Registration Scheme, and by not registering his work had failed

---

[211] *Zalewska* judgment, above n 8, 53, 58, 51.
[212] House of Lords Select Committee on the European Union, 'Written Evidence from Dr Samantha Currie, University of Liverpool' in *EU Enlargement: Written Evidence*, 13 November 2012, 9. Available at: www.parliament.uk/documents/lords-committees/eu-select/EU%20Enlargement/EU%20enlargement%20-%20written%20evidence%20(2).pdf.
[213] *JK v Secretary of State for Work and Pensions (SPC)* [2017] UKUT 179 (AAC).

to comply with it. As a result he was not a qualifying worker during most of the period of work relied upon.

However, in a surprising turn of events, *the Secretary of State* argued that it would be disproportionate not to find that he had accrued permanent residence rights, even though he could have readily invoked *Mirga* and *Zalewska*.[214]

Judge Rowland agreed, pointing to 'incontrovertible evidence of his employment and jobseeking for seven years' to the worker's wish to settle, and fact of having settled, in the UK, adding that he had 'clearly believed, for a perfectly understandable reason, that he did not need to apply for a registration certificate in respect of his work'.[215] The Judge emphasised the minimal, and unintentional nature of his non-compliance, since it was 'only … [his] failure to have his work registered in compliance with the Regulations that has led to his employment not being regarded as lawful and therefore to his failure to meet the terms of the Directive'.[216]

The House of Lords seemed to, by a narrow majority, consider such outcomes lawful, noting (and quoting Judge Rowland himself—then Commissioner Rowland) that the Worker Registration Scheme (WRS) would lead to hard cases, where the consequences of not qualifying are serious. *Zalewska* had been a case in which a woman had worked for over 12 months, but had failed to re-register on moving between jobs, then claimed income support after leaving her work and home and moving into a Women's Aid hostel with her daughter due to domestic violence—but there was no duty to apply the requirements of the Scheme proportionately; Lord Brown expressed misgivings with subjecting the scheme at all to a proportionality review.[217]

In *Mirga* the Court of Appeal was adamant that *Zalewska* precluded any such review of the terms of the scheme. Laws LJ said it was 'wholly impossible to read *Zalewska* as an *ad hominen* decision … the majority were addressing the WRS in principle',[218] and that a proportionality challenge to the terms of the WRS 'plainly cannot stand with the *Zalewska* decision'. The Supreme Court reached the more muted, but not much less nuanced conclusion that 'the provisions of the 2003 Accession Treaty, were consistent with EU law',[219] and that it was not possible to become a qualified person until the WRS had been complied with.[220] Lord Neuberger suggested that the consequence of the 2004 Regulations was that 'so

---

[214] It is not clear why the Secretary of State took this position; it could be that he wished to avoid opening up the other avenues of claim suggested, such as the possibility of retaining self-employed status on becoming involuntarily unemployed (the worker had, after the work discussed here, become self-employed, and later unemployed).

[215] *JK* judgment, above, n 213, 25.

[216] ibid, 22.

[217] *Zalewska* judgment, above n 8, 65.

[218] *Mirga v Secretary of state for Work and Pensions* [2012] EWCA Civ 1952 16, 17.

[219] *Mirga and Samin v Secretary of State for Work and Pensions and Anor* [2016] UKSC 1, 55.

[220] ibid, 31.

long as the A8 Regulations were in force, A8 nationals could not become "qualifying persons" under the EEA Regulations unless and until they had performed registered employment for a continuous period of at least 12 months'.[221]

Judge Rowland has however interpreted *Zalewska* as being confined to its facts, arguing that the House of Lords did not decide that the regulations establishing the WRS were 'intra vires for all purposes but merely that it was not necessary for them to be disapplied for the purpose of Mrs Zalewska's case'. He reflected that otherwise the consequences of not subjecting the regulations to a proportionality requirement was that 'a failure ever to register can result in several years of employment being disregarded when considering whether the person concerned has acquired a right of permanent residence'.[222] As the Secretary of State supported this outcome, it is unlikely to be appealed in this case, meaning that it poses an intriguing juxtaposition in the case law. It opens the way to making proportionality challenges to *Zalewska*-based loss of worker status for those who were in work, and so to claims for permanent residence. But it leaves us with the question of when a failure to comply with the WRS requirements is 'perfectly understandable', as in the man who misunderstood the law in *JK*, and when those cases in which it is 'impossible ... not to feel a measure of sympathy' for those affected but in which the scheme should lead to hard cases and serious consequences, as in the working woman subjected to domestic violence. It could be that *JK* is simply read as a very exceptional case, as not completely excluded by Lord Neuberger in *Mirga*,[223] and that regard to proportionality remains the rare exception to the rule.

The use of transition measures in the UK between 2009 and 2011 is currently under challenge in *TG*,[224] on the grounds that the UK failed to show there was any evidence of a threat of serious disturbance to the labour market to warrant their continued application after the initial five-year period.[225] The Upper Tribunal found the use of transition measures from 2009 onwards to be unlawful, and this has been appealed to the Court of Appeal. This could have significant implications for EU nationals caught by *Zalewska*, potentially rendering two years' worth of work lawful again.

Judge Ward in *TG* pointed to a number of factors that could lead to non-registration—'language difficulties and the frequent participation of A8 nationals in short-term work obtained through agencies'[226]—and to evidence as to confusion among A8 nationals about their employment rights and responsibilities. He cited the Migration Advisory Committee Report from 2009, which noted that

[221] ibid.
[222] *JK* judgment, above n 213, 24.
[223] See ch 4.
[224] *TG v Secretary of State for Work and Pensions (PC)* [2015] UKUT 50 (AAC).
[225] The Annexes to the 2004 Act of Accession, above n 200, provide that Member States may 'at the end of the five year period ... in case of serious disturbances of its labour market or threat thereof and after notifying the Commission, continue to apply these measures until the end of the seven year period following the date of accession'.
[226] *TG*, above n 205, 115.

'for an immigrant earning the national minimum wage, [in 2009] and working a 35-hour week for 48 weeks, £90 represents around 1 per cent of annual gross pay.'[227] The report in turn references a study of 217 A8 respondents—of the 72 who failed to register, 21 had 'never heard' about the scheme.[228] Several of those affected by *Zalewska* were in full-time, continuous work and not made aware that there was a failure in the registration process until after the expiry of transitional provisions, so had no opportunity to lodge claim for permanent residence until five years of continuous work had been clocked up from 1 May 2011 onwards. The next case study again highlights the need for a proportionality review of these measures (their possible reduction following *TG* notwithstanding), especially in cases where large periods of work are discounted, and workers have clocked up nearly five years of work since May 2011, so seek to rely on a large amount of unregistered work to plug a very small gap:

---

**Case Study: Jonas—nearly five years' worth of work since the end of transition measures**

In this case, referred to me for second-tier advice, an A8 client had evidence of work for a period of eight years. He claimed JSA, but after six months was found to fail the genuine prospects of work test. He had two periods of registered work in his first year, but not covering 12 months, and all subsequent work was unregistered. So, he had completed nine months of registered work, and then remained employed for a further near seven years. The majority of this fell outside of the transition measures, and the vast majority of the required five-year period fell outside of the period of transition. He had completed four years and 10 months' work since the end of the lawful application of transition measures (using the dates required by Judge Ward in TG).

*Field notes extract: In short, the obstacle to permanent residence is the Supreme Court case Zalewska, where it was found that unregistered periods of work do not count as work ... It may be that if we can sufficiently distinguish it, the courts will be amenable to a proportionality-esque approach. The way I would distinguish it is as follows:*

— *The majority of the necessary five-year period of work falls after May 2011—ie after the end of the transition measures. The vast majority of the necessary five-year period of work—four years and 10 months—falls after May 2009, ie after the end of the lawful application of transition measures according to the Upper Tribunal in TG.*

---

[227] ibid, referencing Migration Advisory Committee, 'Review of the UK's Transitional Measures for Nationals of the Member States that Acceded to the European Union in 2004', *Migration Advisory Committee Report*, April 2009, 5.9. Available at: www.gov.uk/government/uploads/system/uploads/attachment_data/file/257240/review-transitional.pdf.

[228] ibid, 5.7, referencing B Anderson, M Ruhs, B Rogaly and S Spencer, *Fair Enough? Central and East European Migrants in Low-Wage Employment in the UK* (York, Joseph Rowntree Foundation, 2006).

> — *It would be disproportionate to disregard all of his work prior to the end of the lawful application of transition measures, given that the claimant need only rely on it to represent two months to complete his five-year period.*
> — *The claimant did complete over nine months of registered work at the start of this period. We would ask that this period be taken into account, in conjunction with the period of work completed post-transition to total five years and seven months.*
> — *The intervening period of unregistered work should not be treated as disrupting the continuity of his work record. To do so would be disproportionate, given he made contributions during this period.*
>
> *In terms of … the genuine prospects of work test, I would be minded to challenge the application of Antonissen criteria, given that he should have been treated as having retained worker status, having worked for more than 12 months prior to that point … Antonissen is not authority for assessing a retained worker's chances of work. Article 7(3)(b) of Directive 2004/38 does not lay down any time limit for retention of worker status for those who have worked for more than a year, so an automatic six-month test should be challenged as contrary to EU law.*

I sent these suggestions to the adviser who made submissions to the tribunal. The First-tier Tribunal judge decided that the claimant did not have permanent residence rights, but also found that the decision that the claimant did not have a genuine prospect of work was incorrect, in light of his work history. With regard to *Zalewska*, the judge stated that 'the position was as set out by the DWP'. On simply accepting the DWP's position, we see an unwillingness, evident in other tribunal judges, to consider the disapplication of UK law where there is a possible EU law infringement. The Secretary of State chose not to appeal but time-limited the award to three months. The adviser had to complain to the government's complaint resolution team on the failure to implement the judge's decision. The complaint was sent to the team's head office and the adviser was then quickly contacted to say the full amount would be paid to the client after all.

For claimants in less steady work, or whose work has become less secure or more part-time since the end of transition measures, this resetting of the permanent residence clock is even more problematic, since it may be a long time before they reach the required continuous five years. Significant periods of work have thus, as with the minimum earnings threshold, been re-characterised as not-work, in a way that creates a significant detriment to those who face interruptions in their work history, and may require reliance upon benefits. This creates acute problems for those in low-paid, low-security work, and also for women whose work history may be punctuated by periods of child care, and/or care for sick or disabled children hindering the immediate rejoining of the workforce, or relocation due to domestic abuse.

Early plans on the introduction of universal credit and work-hours requirements would have further served to disadvantage female workers. The Regulations provide for permitted exceptions from full work conditionality for lone parents, and for people with caring duties, and for disabled claimants. The government originally planned to exclude EEA nationals from the permitted exceptions so that EEA nationals and the family members who were lone parents, or persons with disabilities, or had caring duties, would be excluded from reductions in conditionality afforded to UK nationals in the same situations (so would be subject to the full conditionality requirements, 35 hours per week of work/work and work search related activity).[229] Following correspondence with the Social Security Advisory Committee, the government has repealed the relevant provision[230] so that EEA national workers are entitled to make use of the reductions. However, given the stark distinction between the treatment of those found to be workers, and those found to be work-seekers and completely excluded from universal credit, the route by which decision-makers identify genuine and effective work will be crucial. As yet, there is no guidance on this. It may be that the minimum earnings threshold will continue to be applied, but this would conflict at the outset with the now-permitted reduced conditionality in some circumstances. For example, lone parents with children under the age of one are subject to no work-related requirements, while lone parents with children aged one to three years are subject only to a work-focused interview requirement (not to a requirement as to hours of work or workseeking). An EEA national in either position would be excluded from universal credit if they were not a worker, so must be working, and be working enough to be considered to be a worker, which may mean passing the minimum earnings threshold, which is significantly different treatment to that afforded to UK nationals. In other words, they may be entitled to exercise a right to reduced conditionality if they are eligible for universal credit, but may be found ineligible in the first place due to a higher conditionality imposed by the minimum earnings threshold.

The combination of rewritten definitions of work and the exclusions permitted in *Teixeira* and *Zalewska* has resulted in difficult and distressing scenarios that highlight a significant social security risk not covered in EU provisions: the predominantly female risk of domestic abuse. The next section examines this effect, and highlights the shortcomings of the EU's existing framework of social security risks, which covers predominantly male risks.

### VII. THE FAILURE TO COVER THE SOCIAL SECURITY RISK OF DOMESTIC ABUSE

Domestic abuse is a social security risk that affects the status not only of women who are not married to their EU national partners, but also of EU national women who marry, or become partners with, own-state (here, British) nationals.

---

[229] (Now repealed) reg 92(1) and (2).

[230] Under the Universal Credit (EEA Jobseekers) Amendment Regulations 2015, SI 2015/546, reg 3.

They cannot rely upon their status as family members of their working spouses, if those spouses are British, and their children cannot rely on their status as the children of EU migrant worker fathers, if their fathers are British. Everything turns upon being able to show that the woman fleeing domestic violence has a right to reside in her own right, which is becoming more difficult in terms of the increased amount of evidence required of past work. Attempts to demonstrate a right of permanent residence are hampered not only by a narrowing definition of work, but also by the disqualification of relevant work years through *Zalewska,* as evidenced in the following two cases:

---

**Case Study: Anita**

This case was referred to me for second-tier advice. Anita had been in the UK for over a decade. She had a two-year old daughter and was fleeing domestic abuse. She was refused income support.

*Adviser notes: 'Although she has worked for many years continuously in the UK her pre-2011 employment years were not authorised and cannot contribute towards years for permanent residence. The DWP have turned down her claim on Mandatory Reconsideration'.*

Three years after arriving in the UK she married a British national. They had a daughter four years later. Our letter of appeal noted the following:

*She left her husband ... following years of enduring a violent and controlling relationship. She eventually moved away ... with the assistance from the ... Police Domestic Violence team early this year and she continues to move around for fear that her husband may find her ... [Anita] would be working if it were not for the destabilisation and itinerant lifestyle that fleeing domestic violence has caused. She does not have any local connections or support where she is now living temporarily and cannot afford child-care.*

Several years of Anita's work history were negated as a result of Zalewska. We argued that she should be able to retain worker status on the grounds that St Prix[231] had established that the grounds for such retention were not exhaustively listed in Article 7(3) of Directive 2004/38. We argued that domestic abuse was one such ground:

*Our client has only ceased work due to the upheaval caused by domestic violence, which has forced her to give up the opportunity to work whilst she ensures her and her child's safety. Such a social security risk is predominantly a female one ... These exceptional circumstances should not deprive her status of 'worker' within the meaning of Article 45 TFEU (paras 37–40) as [Anita] intends to return to work or search for work within a reasonable period once her life has resumed a semblance of security and stability.*

This argument was successful at the First-tier Tribunal. However, it involved persuading the judge to take a relatively creative approach to Article 7 of Directive 2004/38, which would not have worked with some judges, and certainly would not yield results at the first instance decision-maker level, or at mandatory reconsideration (which is also done

---

[231] *St Prix* judgment, above n 184.

by a first instance decision-maker). As an First-tier Tribunal decision, it does not set a precedent, and so the domestic violence gap in the right to reside provisions remains. Moreover, the judge was primarily persuaded by the 'exceptional' nature of her circumstances, as noted by the adviser: 'the judge acknowledged [Anita's] exceptional circumstances, stating that [Anita] has retained her worker status despite not working recently, on the grounds of proportionality, that you raised'.

Even if that had been a precedent-setting decision, a decision that turns on exceptionality does not plug a significant general gap in the law, and would be harder to deploy in support for other clients. The case that immediately followed, another referral for second-tier advice, suggested to me that the circumstances were not all that exceptional:

**Case Study: Paulina**

Paulina was a Latvian national who arrived in the UK in early 2005. She worked continuously for nearly nine years. She had obtained a Worker Registration Certificate early on, but did not know of the need to re-register when moving between jobs, which she did before having worked for 12 months for the registered employer. After five years in the UK she married a British national, and they later had two children. When her children were three and two, she felt compelled to leave her husband due to domestic abuse; she did not have police records to support this as most of the abuse was of a coercive and controlling nature. She had applied for income support and been refused.

We requested mandatory reconsideration, on the same grounds as for Anita, arguing that she should retain her previous worker status, interrupted by domestic abuse, and also drawing upon *TG* (the dispute about when the worker registration scheme ceased to be lawful). We suggested that looking just from 2009 onwards, Paulina had four years and seven months of work to rely upon, and that therefore a refusal to take account of her prior full four years of unregistered work, to supply the necessary five months to view her as having attained a permanent residence-based right to reside,[232] would be disproportionate. We also argued in the alternative that the periods of work negated as a result of *Zalewska* could nevertheless be treated as periods in which she had a right to reside as a self-sufficient person, since she was earning enough to support herself. The lack of comprehensive sickness insurance should not be a bar in light of the proportionality required by Baumbast, and in light of her economic activity, and her paying tax and national insurance.

*Extracts from our submission:*

—   *On permanent residence, we would argue that Zalewska (2008) UKHL 67 should be distinguished. In the instant case, much of the most recent period of work falls after the end of the worker registration scheme, while the vast majority of the period*

---

[232] Under reg 15(1)(a) of the Immigration (European Economic Area) Regulations 2006.

> *pertinent to the claimant's five years of permanent residence falls after the scheme ceased to be lawful. The Upper Tribunal has recently ruled that the extension of the scheme beyond April 2009 was unlawful in TG v SSWP (2015) UKUT 50 (AAC)). She thus completed four years and seven months of work past the point at which the scheme can be applied—from 1 May 2009 to December 2013.*
> — *It would be disproportionate to refuse to take any account of the four full years of work prior to this point (2005–09), when she need only rely on it to represent a period of five months, in addition to her four years and seven months of post-scheme work.*
> — *This especially so given the disproportionate disadvantage this would cause in circumstances of domestic abuse and control, forcing an EU national who has been lawfully working in the UK to choose between staying in and keeping her children in an abusive situation, or leaving and facing destitution, because of a temporary period which she requires support, before returning back to work.*
> — *In the alternative, [Paulina] could be considered to be permanently resident as an EEA national who has 'resided in the United Kingdom in accordance with these Regulations for a continuous period of five years' under regulation 15(1)(a), as having been self-sufficient in accordance with regulation 4(1)(c) and so a qualified person under regulation 6(1)(d) of the Immigration (EEA) Regulations 2006. Her work has prevented her from being reliant upon out-of-work benefits.*
> — *The requirement for comprehensive sickness insurance must be applied proportionately, as in Case C-413/99 Baumbast, especially in circumstances where the claimant is/has been working, and in this case, unlike in Baumbast (where the worker was working outside of the EU) she has actually been making contributions to the UK for nearly nine years.*

The mandatory reconsideration did not result in a change of decision, and Paulina was still refused income support. However, we were successful at the First-tier Tribunal, with an even stronger judgment than we got for Anita. The judge found that Paulina did have permanent residence.

## VIII. SUMMARY

The UK welfare reforms targeting EU nationals make them subject to an activation-plus regime which elevates the key principles of activation—conditionality and responsibilisation[233]—and disregards concerns for social justice. These reforms came wrapped in rhetoric denigrating the non-existent ill of benefit tourism, and disparaging EU national jobseekers and low-paid

---

[233] So emphasising the 'conduct' lever of conditionality (the other two levers being category and circumstance). See J Clasen and D Clegg, 'Levels and Levers of Conditionality' in J Clasen and N Siegel (eds), *Investigating Welfare State Changes: The Dependent Variable Problem in Comparative Analysis* (Cheltenham, Edward Elgar, 2007) 171.

workers. They add up to a programme of declaratory discrimination by the state and create declaratory obstacles to movement: just as it is an obstacle to movement to produce own-state produce, it is also an obstacle to movement to denigrate non-national workers and workseekers.

On top of declaratory obstacles, the substance of the reforms also create classic obstacles, which extend to own-nationals as well, as seen in the reversal of *Swaddling* through the imposition of a three-month wait for UK national return-ers claiming benefits. The UK has also created an obstacle by steepening the welfare cliff-edge for those EU nationals who fall at any point into jobseeker status (removing housing benefit entitlement, and potentially accelerating home-lessness) which in turn makes it harder to get back into the labour market. The accompanying government statements made clear an intention to dissuade not only benefit tourists, but jobseekers more generally from moving to the UK—an intention borne out through publicity campaigns waged in other Member States to put people off coming. The removal of interpretation services in job cen-tres indicates an unwillingness to facilitate jobseeking of non-nationals and the requirements for jobseekers to learn a set standard of English is an obstacle that it is not open to employers to impose.

An increased distaste for EU national jobseekers is also evident in the introduc-tion of the genuine prospect of work test. This is a misnomer, since it does not genuinely test for prospects of work, but looks for certainty or near-certainty of the right kind of work with fixed hours and pay. This test, and how it is imple-mented, underlines the problems that arise from decision-makers' over-reliance on government guidance. In many cases, the guidance assumes the status of law, since it is the only expression of law with which decision-makers are familiar.[234] The importance of the practical implementation, rather than the written law and policy, is pronounced when it comes to the minimum earnings threshold, since a genuinely two-tier test that adopted a broad approach to genuine and effective work would be EU law-compliant. What emerges from the evidence is a presump-tion of marginality. The EU definition of worker was already somewhat gendered, with an exclusion of familial care (even if 'remunerated' through care benefits) and childcare. But the UK modifications to the definition of work have had drastic consequences for women, as part time work is increasingly treated as marginal and ancillary, high amounts of evidence are required, and short-term, fixed-term, temporary, casual and zero-hour contracts are all more likely to be deemed mar-ginal, even when a string of fixed-term jobs represents a long period of employ-ment. Lone parents with young children and limited child-care are struggling to demonstrate that their part time work is genuine and effective. This is combined with the negation of significant periods of past work, even if full-time, due to the non-fulfilment of the technical requirements of the worker registration scheme.

---

[234] See ch 9, 'we don't look at the law'.

People who have failed to re-register when moving between jobs will see all subsequent work until the end of transition measures deemed unlawful and so discounted. They may have worked full time for well over five years, but had this disregarded due to *Zalewska*, then had a child and moved to part-time work, and had that disregarded due the threshold. A group of women acutely disadvantaged by these rules, and the free movement framework generally, are those who have experienced domestic abuse. The failure to recognise domestic abuse as a social security risk belies the male tilt of the EU framework, and constitutes one of several significant gaps in the residence Directive (others include care work, childcare, and long-term residence (as the spouse/partner of a *host* state national worker, for example)).

The Directive is not the only source of gaps or the only subject of skewed implementation. Regulation 883/2004 was intended to replace, modernise and simplify[235] the preceding social security coordination law, as Regulation 1408/71 had been much amended and supplemented with a good deal of case law. But navigating and activating that regulation is anything but simple. The next chapter focuses on some problems encountered in identifying specific rights and obligations, and in actually seeking to rely upon them. It suggests that poor domestic treatment of the regulation is not just the fault of Member States, but is related to a lack of clarity, and some unnecessary complexity, within the EU coordination rules themselves.

---

[235] Recital (3) of Regulation 883/2004.

# 7

# Resisting Competence for Market Citizens: Shortcomings in the Social Security Coordination Framework

The government does not collect information on the number of provisional benefit payments made on the basis of either Article 6 or 7 of Regulation (EC) No 987/2009.[1]

## I. INTRODUCTION

THE SOCIAL SECURITY coordination regime is complex and incomplete. In spite of the Coordinating Regulation's aims to simplify and tidy up the law, there are still many situations in which the law is unclear. This chapter explores the difficulties regarding the determination of competence, and the tendency of Member States to deflect competence where possible. First it looks at the problematic constellation of rules with respect to pensioners, and the inappropriate categorisation of carers allowance, disability living allowance, personal independence payment and attendance allowance as sickness benefits. This is not just a matter of labelling: the categorisation has very significant consequences for the family members of pensioners, and the denial of care benefits for the carers of older family members can have gendered effects. Second, the analysis turns to problems with exportation, both to and from the UK. The focus is on the practical problems that arise domestically, but these imply a lack of successful coordination and oversight at EU level, which is necessary because of national welfare states' tendencies to resist non-resident claims made upon them. The final section looks at the issue of interim payments and argues that the EU legal provisions are inadequate, setting unnecessary conditions which are open to Member State manipulation, with the result that in the UK, getting an interim payment, even in a drawn-out case lasting 18 months, is virtually impossible. Taken together, these issues point to the shortcomings of a system built around a conception of people as market citizens allocated to welfare markets—it is a system, but one (like the recent treatment of Directive 2004/38) that relies upon clear demarcation

---

[1] Response to Freedom of Information request. There may not be much information to collect.

of responsibilities as a matter of legal literalism, rather than requiring the social justice dimension of decision-making to be taken into account. The result is that when the demarcation is not clear, Member States engage in a process of competence denial, rather than a consideration of socially just outcomes or of the circumstances of the citizens at the heart of the dispute.

## II. COMPETENCE, CARE AND DISABILITY: THE INAPPROPRIATE LABEL OF SICKNESS BENEFIT

Regulation 883/2004 provides a guide for the allocation of competence in Article 11 on the 'determination of legislation applicable', but when people might have multiple statuses, it is not always clear which holds sway. The priority rules do not spell out, for example, how a person's status as a family member of a migrant worker should interact with their status as the family member of a different migrant worker in a different state, or as a pensioner, or as the family member of a pensioner. Nor is it clear under what circumstances different Member States might be competent for the same person, but for different aspects of their social security entitlement (for example, when pensioners are subject to a complicated regime in which the pension-paying state(s) are competent in some respects, and the state of residence in others). Articles 23–25 make the pension-paying state competent for sickness benefits in kind, and Article 29 states that the state responsible for sickness benefits in kind is also responsible for cash sickness benefits.

In seeking to bring a wide range of benefits under the social security coordination regime, the ECJ has inappropriately classed a number of benefits as sickness benefits. In *Molenaar*,[2] the Court found that care benefits should not be excluded from the coordination system. The Commission had argued that they were covered but could not be exclusively linked with any one particular branch of benefit in Regulation 1408/71[3] because they had 'characteristics in common with the sickness, invalidity and old-age' social security benefits. The Court found instead that they were 'essentially intended to supplement sickness insurance benefits ... in order to improve the state of health and the quality of life of persons reliant on care'.[4] In *Jauch*,[5] the Austrian government argued that the care benefit at issue had more in common with social assistance than with sickness benefits, but the Court reiterated the line from *Molenaar* that 'even if they have their own particular characteristics, such benefits must be regarded as sickness benefits'.[6] This was again

---

[2] Case C-160/96 *Manfred Molenaar and Barbara Fath-Molenaar v Allgemeine Ortskrankenkasse Baden-Württemberg* EU:C:1998:84.
[3] Regulation (EEC) No 1408/71 of the Council of 14 June 1971 on the application of social security schemes to employed persons and their families moving within the Community OJ [1971] L 149/2.
[4] *Molenaar* judgment, above n 2, 24.
[5] Case C-215/99 *Friedrich Jauch v Pensionsversicherungsanstalt der Arbeiter* EU:C:2001:139.
[6] ibid, 28.

affirmed in *Hosse*,[7] in which the Court rejected the classification of the care benefit as a special non-contributory benefit, treating it instead as pure social security (a sickness benefit). Care is, and should be recognised as, a social security risk and care benefits treated as social security rather than social assistance. But doing so by defining them as sickness benefits is problematic. In *Tolley*,[8] care benefits were described as benefits 'granted objectively on the basis of a statutorily defined position and are intended to improve the state of health and quality of life of persons reliant on care [and] have as their essential purpose supplementing sickness insurance benefits'.

The dismissal of differences between different systems through the formulation 'even if they have their own particular characteristics' is a failure to recognise that some care benefits do not conform to the core definition. Carers allowance in the UK is awarded on the basis of a legally defined position. It is only available to those caring for people who qualify for disability living allowance, personal independence payments or attendance allowance. But it only supports the health and quality of life of those being cared for indirectly: it is not paid to the person claiming those benefits, but to the carer. The carer does not automatically get it as a result of the cared-for person's degree of care needs—there are conditions attached to amount of work they can do, and there is an income ceiling. It is essentially a benefit given in recognition of a person's reduced capacity to work as a result of their caring obligations. It qualifies the carer for credited national insurance contributions, to help with their record for later pension claims. In short, it recognises a significantly different social security 'risk'—that of caring, as compared to that of being sick—to a different social security subject (the carer, rather than the cared for person). The classification of care benefits as sickness benefits, to enhance the quality of life for the cared-for person, is itself a gendered act, since it avoids making the carer the subject of the legislation, and care is a predominantly female social security risk.[9] The next section explores an example of how female workers can be disadvantaged by this male tilt.

## A. Care Benefits and the Gendered Social Security Risk

It may be that in disregarding the idiosyncrasies of different care benefit systems, and sweeping them under the sickness benefits banner, the Court is attempting to

---

[7] Case C-286/03 *Silvia Hosse v Land Salzburg* EU:C:2005:621.

[8] Case C-430/14 *Secretary of State for Work and Pensions v Tolley* EU:C:2017:74, 46.

[9] 'Women are more likely than men to assume care responsibilities for elderly or dependent family members with long-term care needs and are thus far more likely to reduce their working hours or exit employment altogether' (European Commission, 'Labour Market Participation of Women', *European Semester Thematic Fiche*, 26 November 2015, 2.2); 'Across the 16 OECD countries reviewed in this study, close to two-thirds of informal carers aged over 50 years are women' (F Colombo et al, 'The Impact of Caring on Family Carers', *Help Wanted? Providing and Paying for Long-Term Care*) (Paris, OECD, 2011) 86.

stave off attempts to categorise those benefits as special non-contributory benefits, which would otherwise result in disentitling cross-border claimants or claimants without a 'right to reside'.[10] However, carers allowance could not easily be classified as a special non-contributory benefit, as it is not means-tested. There is a limit to what a claimant can earn and the amount of hours they can work, but the amount is not determined by income, there is no limit on capital/savings, and it counts as an overlapping benefit with other non-means-tested benefits (so you cannot claim carers allowance and a state retirement pension). Finding carers allowance not to be a sickness benefit should not result in it simply being reclassified as not pure social security. We need a rethink about classification of risks, and in particular an acknowledgement that the categories currently recognised are simply regurgitations of those thought suitable in 1971 (albeit the list of 'matters covered' now includes 'pre-retirement benefits' and 'paternity benefits'). The list of risks is out of date and is structured, much like the worker retention provisions in Directive 2004/38, around 'male' risks. It is disappointing that in reconfiguring the coordination regulation, no further attempt was made to address the inadequate forcing of care benefits into the sickness category. The European Parliament has acknowledged the gendered nature of care responsibilities throughout the EU; a motion for a resolution noted that 'over 20 million Europeans (two-thirds of whom are women) care for adult dependent persons, which prevents them from having a full-time job and therefore increases the gender pay gap and leads to a higher risk of poverty in old age for women who are approaching retirement'.[11] Care is gendered. The absence of a care category of benefits in the coordination regime is gendered and this has consequences, as shown in the following case study:

---

**Case Study: Jeremias**

This client was terminally ill and was dependent on the care of his son. His son had been an EU migrant worker in the UK for over 21 years, his daughter-in-law was also an EU migrant worker. The claimant himself had lived in the UK for eight years without claiming benefits. He received a (small) state pension from his state of origin (a southern EU state). His application for attendance allowance in the UK was refused, on the grounds that he was receiving a pension from another Member State. This triggered the rules in Regulation 883/2004 linking pensions to sickness benefit competence, implemented into UK law in section 65(7) of the Social Security Contributions and Benefits Act 1992, which states:

*A person to whom either Regulation (EC) No 1408/71 or Regulation (EC) No 883/2004 applies shall not be entitled to an attendance allowance for a period unless during that*

---

[10] Following the finding in Case C-140/12 *Pensionsversicherungsanstalt v Peter Brey* EU:C:2013:565 that special non-contributory benefits can be made subject to such conditions. However, note its recent approval of a right to reside requirement imposed also on 'pure' social security benefits in *Commission v UK*, explored in ch 4.

[11] European Parliament, 'Motion for a Parliament Resolution on Women Domestic Workers are Carers in the EU' 2015/2094(INI) 5 April 2016, AJ.

> period the United Kingdom is competent for payment of sickness benefits in cash to the person for the purposes of Chapter 1 of Title III of the Regulation in question.

This case was primarily about challenging the categorisation, and consequent refusal, of attendance allowance, but highlights the related categorisation problem of carers allowance, which is dependent upon the cared-for person's eligibility for a qualifying benefit (disability living allowance, attendance allowance or personal independence payments). The refusal of attendance allowance had a significant knock-on effect for his family, who were now ineligible for carers allowance. The assumption that someone in this situation could claim an equivalent care benefit from the state paying the pension is flawed in a number of respects. There may be no close equivalent benefit, or the nearest equivalent may be a compound, means-tested benefit, treated as a special non-contributory benefit, so not exportable. The pension-paying state may award care benefits according to the carer's circumstances, and find that they are not the competent state for the *carer* who is working elsewhere (which was the situation in Jeremias's case). In any case, the level of benefits in the pension-paying state may be incommensurate with the cost of living, and lost earnings, in the state of the carer's work and residence. If carers allowance were not treated as a sickness benefit for the cared-for person (the pensioner), then his daughter-in-law could have argued for eligibility for carers allowance on the basis that she should be treated the same as a carer for a claimant who was in receipt of a UK pension. This would mean that her father-in-law should have been assessed and, if it were found that he would have been entitled to attendance allowance, save for the cross-border element (that is, that he had an underlying entitlement but could not claim because of his pension), then *her* situation is the same in all relevant respects as that of someone caring for a UK pensioner, in terms of degree of care, degree of disability and degree of reduced labour market activity on grounds of caring. Alternatively, if the pensioner's eligibility for a disability benefit in the pension-paying state were established, then she might have argued that that eligibility ought to be treated as discharging the qualifying benefit criterion, as an 'equivalent benefit' under Article 5 of Regulation 883/2004:

> Where, under the legislation of the competent Member State, the receipt of social security benefits and other income has certain legal effects, the relevant provisions of that legislation shall also apply to the receipt of equivalent benefits acquired under the legislation of another Member State or to income acquired in another Member State.[12]

As it is, even had Jeremias successfully claimed an equivalent disability benefit from the pension-paying state, his daughter-in-law would still have been unable to rely on Article 5 to show that she met all the eligibility criteria for carers allowance

---

[12] Art 5, Regulation (EC) No 883/2004 of the European Parliament and of the Council of 29 April 2004 on the coordination of social security systems OJ [2004] L 200/1.

because of its categorisation as a sickness benefit. As the pension-paying state did not award care benefits to cared-for people, but to carers, then she was deemed to have no claim in her own right to claim a care benefit from that state, on the basis of another person's pension there, since she was a social security subject in her own right, having been working and insured in the UK for many years. Her inability to claim carers allowance had significant consequences: the family was incurring significant extra costs in support required on her working days and in travel for emergency care requirements on her working days. They could not easily meet these costs and she decided that she would cut her hours down further or even stop working. A policy that excludes people from being able to claim benefits to support care work has a disproportionate impact upon women. UK government statistics in 2015 showed that 72 per cent of carers allowance claimants were women.[13] This exclusion could incur unwanted consequences such as exacerbating problems of poverty and social exclusion, marginalisation in the work place and, in cases like this, creating a penalty for long-term migrant workers when they work and so creating an obstacle to the exercise of free movement rights.

Jeremias's case also highlights the problem with the categorisation of the primary benefit at issue—attendance allowance—bringing into question the appropriate categorisation of disability benefits more generally and of disability living allowance and personal independence payments specifically. All are currently deemed sickness benefits. Disability living allowance, attendance allowance and carers allowance have been subject to litigation to establish whether or not they were special non-contributory benefits. The UK had deemed them to be so, and treated them as non-exportable. In the ensuing cases,[14] the Court found that, except for the mobility component of disability living allowance, they were not special non-contributory benefits, and did so by virtue of finding them to be sickness benefits. But these should not have been the only two choices on offer. Again, this approach reveals the inadequacy of the existing categories. The next section outlines the main problems with treating disability benefits, and especially disability benefits for pensioners, as sickness benefits.

## B. Disability Benefits as Sickness Benefits

Disability is not sickness, and benefits to help meet the extra costs associated with disability are therefore not meaningfully 'sickness' benefits. In *Chacon Navas*,

---

[13] DWP, 'Quarterly Benefits Summary', *Great Britain Statistics to February 2015*, available at: www.gov.uk/government/uploads/system/uploads/attachment_data/file/452513/statistical-summary-august-2015.pdf.

[14] Case C-299/05 *Commission of the European Communities v European Parliament and Council of the European Union* EU:C:2007:608 and Case C-537/09 *Ralph James Bartlett and Others v Secretary of State for Work and Pensions* EU:C:2011:278.

the Court stressed that disability and sickness were two separate concepts.[15] While in *HK Danmark*, the Court modified that when finding that sickness may lead to disability, the difference between the two was maintained, and the long-term nature of disability as compared to sickness was emphasised.[16] Sickness is a social security risk, in that it stops a person from working temporarily, while 'invalidity' tends to cover permanent exclusion from the labour market. The ECJ, the UK and the Commission were all in agreement on this approach to sickness, for the purposes of Regulation 1408/71 in *Stewart*:

> As the United Kingdom government and the European Commission correctly submit, a sickness benefit, within the meaning of Article 4(1)(a) of Regulation No 1408/71, covers the risk connected to a morbid condition involving temporary suspension of the concerned person's activities.[17]

Disability living allowance and personal independence payments are not income-replacement benefits for people too sick to work, facing a 'temporary suspension of activities'. They can be paid to people *in work* and are not subject to income limits. They arguably more closely reflect the purpose of invalidity benefits described in *Stewart* as 'to cover the risk of disability of a prescribed degree, where it is probable that such disability will be permanent or long-term'.[18] The conditions for entitlement include that the claimant have a 'substantial' and 'long term' condition. The government guidance[19] on eligibility refers to the definition of disability under the Equality Act 2010 which defines 'long term' as of 12 months or more. Alternatively, given that invalidity carries with it again a suggestion of exclusion from the labour market, it might be more accurate to characterise these benefits as representing a different kind of social security than that structured around 'risks' to a person's capacity to work. They might instead be conceived of as measures to address the indirectly discriminatory costs that arise from disability.

In *Tolley*, the Court confirmed the categorisation of disability living allowance as a sickness benefit on the grounds that sickness benefits are 'granted objectively on the basis of a statutorily defined position and are intended to improve the state of health and quality of life of persons reliant on care'.[20] But people may actually claim sickness benefits—as in benefits to mitigate the social security risk

---

[15] Case C-13/05 *Sonia Chacón Navas v Eurest Colectividades SA.* EU:C:2006:456, critically analysed in: L Waddington, 'Case Note: Case C-13/05, Chacón Navas' (2007) 44(2) *CML Rev* 487; D Hosking, 'A High Bar for Disability Rights' (2007) 36(2) *Industrial Law Journal* 228; and M Bell, 'The Implementation of European Anti-Discrimination Directives' (2008) 79(1) *The Political Quarterly* 36.

[16] C-335/11 and C-337/11 *HK Danmark, acting on behalf of Jette Ring v Dansk almennyttigt Boligselskab and HK Danmark, acting on behalf of Lone Skouboe Werge v Dansk Arbejdsgiverforening, acting on behalf of Pro Display A/S* EU:C:2013:222, 39.

[17] Case C-503/09 *Lucy Stewart v Secretary of State for Work and Pensions* EU:C:2011:500, 37.

[18] ibid, 38.

[19] The DWP web page *PIP: Eligibility* (available at: www.gov.uk/pip/eligibility) states that you must have a 'health condition or disability', which links to the UK government's 'Definition of Disability under the Equality Act 2010' webpage (available at: www.gov.uk/definition-of-disability-under-equality-act-2010).

[20] *Tolley* judgment, above n 8, 46.

of being too sick to work—without having any need of care. It seems that in an apparently well-meaning attempt to bring care benefits within the compass of social security coordination, and to avoid them being classified as social assistance or special non-contributory benefits, the ECJ has embarked on a misclassification that has become self-perpetuating. Indeed, the reasoning in *Tolley* does not go far beyond 'It's a sickness benefit, because we said so'; the Court noted the similarities between disability living allowance and an invalidity benefit, and the dissimilarities with sickness benefits 'strictu sensu'.[21] But found that it had previously (in *De Cuyper*)[22] determined that benefits for people reliant on care 'have as their essential purpose supplementing sickness insurance benefits',[23] and that it had also previously found (in *Commission v Parliament and Council*)[24] that even though the essential purpose of disability living allowance is *not* supplementing sickness insurance benefits, it should still be treated as a sickness benefit anyway. 'Accordingly'[25]—in other words, because the Court had said so—it must be treated as a sickness insurance benefit.[26]

As such, care benefits must be sickness benefits, because they improve the life and quality of people on sickness benefits, and then disability benefits must be sickness benefits because they improve the life and quality of people who qualify for care benefits. In this, the Court has been led astray by the terminology of disability living allowance and its 'care component' (which, in reality, is not a 'care benefit' at all and is paid to people who do not have carers). While the classification of disability living allowance and personal independence payments as sickness benefits is inadequate, that of attendance allowance is more manifestly inappropriate. Attendance allowance is also not an income-replacement benefit, and is likely to be mostly paid to people out of the labour market in any case, since the minimum age for eligibility is 65 (the current state retirement age). As of February 2015, 69 per cent of recipients were aged 80 or over.[27] Claims tend to be long-term: 84 per cent of attendance allowance claims in payment in May 2016 had lasted for over a year (and 47 per cent over five years).[28] Again, we are not dealing here with the social security risk of being temporarily sick to work, in the context of a group of people not expected to work on account of having already encountered the 'risk' of state retirement age. Attendance allowance might more realistically be an invalidity benefit or, like disability living allowance and personal independence

---

[21] ibid, 54.

[22] C-406/04 *Gérald De Cuyper v Office national de l'emploi* EU:C:2006:491

[23] *Tolley* judgment, above n 8, 46.

[24] *Commission v Parliament and Council* judgment, above n 14.

[25] *Tolley* judgment, above n 8, 51.

[26] See T Royston and C O'Brien 'CJEU welcomes opportunity to repeat itself' in 'Cases' (2017) (24) 2 *Journal of Social Security Law* (forthcoming).

[27] DWP, 'AA Recipients at February 2015', *Quarterly Benefits Summary—Great Britain Statistics to February 2015*, 20. Available at: www.gov.uk/government/uploads/system/uploads/attachment_data/file/452513/statistical-summary-august-2015.pdf.

[28] From the DWP 'Cases in Payment' dataset at *Stat-Xplore*, I extracted a table of duration of AA claim by age.

payments, a 'disability benefit', falling into a class not yet catered for. In Jeremias' case, I made the further argument that in cases of terminal illness it is especially inappropriate to classify attendance allowance as a sickness benefit, as it is patently not a situation of temporary exclusion from the labour market:

---

**Case Study: Returning to Jeremias**

We drafted a submission for the First-tier Tribunal and that was successful. The judge followed the Upper Tribunal's approach in an earlier case,[29] which dealt with a claim in the opposite direction. In that case the spouse of someone receiving a benefit classified as a 'pension' for the purposes of the coordinating regulation, from the UK, while resident in another Member State, sought to rely on the provisions that make the pension-paying state competent for sickness benefits, in order to claim carers allowance from the UK. The judge there stated that, notwithstanding Article 29 of Regulation 883/2004, it was still necessary to use Article 11 to identify the competent state, which in the claimant's case would be the state of residence (in that case, Spain). The judge applied the same logic to the case in hand, to find that under Article 11, the competent state was 'clearly' the UK. In Jeremias's case the judge seemed to think that the DWP could not have their cake and eat it: if the state of residence was competent in such cases, then here that was the UK.

The Secretary of State appealed the decision to the Upper Tribunal. I composed a submission drawing upon the distinction between 'sickness' and 'invalidity' benefits in Stewart, to argue that attendance allowance should be treated as an invalidity benefit, or in the alternative, that at least in cases of terminal illness it should be treated as an invalidity benefit. Here, we drew again upon Stewart, in which the ECJ had found that the same benefit was capable of fitting in different branches of social security for different purposes. Here are some excerpts from the submission:

— *The criteria for eligibility for attendance allowance concern permanent or long-term disability; due to the age criterion, many of the conditions are degenerative, and some terminal.*

— *The decision-maker's guide (Chapter 61—attendance allowance and disability living allowance: vol 10 amendment 34 June 2012) describes attendance allowance at 61001 as: 'a benefit designed to help severely disabled people who need: (1) attention from another person; or (2) supervision from another person; or (3) another person to watch over them'. The initial classification of it as a sickness benefit cannot preclude attendance allowance being an invalidity benefit in certain circumstances.*

— *The Court in Stewart found that in some circumstances, short-term incapacity benefit, which would otherwise be a sickness benefit, could be an invalidity benefit: 'in circumstances, such as those in question in the main proceedings, where it is established, at the time of the claim, that the claimant has a permanent or long-term disability, short-term incapacity benefit in youth has, in view of the continuity between it and long-term incapacity benefit, the characteristics of an invalidity benefit within the meaning of Article 4(1)(b) of Regulation No 1408/71' (para 45, emphasis added).*

---

[29] CG/4143/2012 Decision of the Upper Tribunal, unreported, 8 November 2013, UTJ Jacobs.

> — *As an alternative the Upper Tribunal may find that attendance allowance should in circumstances of terminal illness, be considered an invalidity benefit. Our client has been found to suffer from a permanent disability.*
>
> *The Upper Tribunal Judge did not accept this reasoning. He found that the earlier case[30] was based on a mistake and that the UK was not the competent state. His reasoning on the subject of Stewart was brief, finding the case to be 'distinguishable' because a claimant of incapacity benefit in youth 'will probably never be able to function ... productively in the labour market'.*

But if labour market productivity is the deciding factor, then it must be highly unlikely that the majority of attendance allowance claimants will re-enter the labour market. There are no figures to suggest that attendance allowance is more likely than incapacity benefit in youth to be short-term, bearing in mind that 84 per cent of attendance allowance claims last over a year, and 69 per cent of recipients are over 80. Incapacity benefit in youth may have been awarded to young people who would never enter the labour market, but young people with short-term conditions were also eligible and could claim for short periods (for example, if temporarily incapacitated as a result of a car crash). Both benefits require some degree of long-term condition, since the eligibility criteria for both stipulate that a claimant must have had the relevant disability for six months before claiming (unless terminally ill).

In any case, the possibility of the benefit fitting into different categories in different circumstances was not explored. In *Stewart*, the Court *had* to consider a benefit's different manifestations because the fuller title for the benefit was '*short-term* incapacity benefit in youth'. The Court had to explain how a self-proclaimed 'short-term' benefit could in some cases actually be a 'long-term' one, and did so:[31] '[In] *circumstances, such as those in question* ... where the claimant has a permanent or long-term disability, short-term incapacity benefit in youth has ... the characteristics of an invalidity benefit'.[32] The key point was that it depended on the circumstances of the claimant and the nature of the disability.

The classification of attendance allowance, disability living allowance, personal impendence payments and carers allowance always as sickness benefits is thus inadequate and inaccurate. Thanks to the operation of Article 29 in Regulation 883/2004, it can have counter-intuitive consequences as to the determination of the state responsible for disability and caring benefits. A coordination regime premised on market citizenship, itself premised upon restricted entitlements and activation-plus principles, promotes competence-avoidance and an adherence to legal literalism rather than an attempt to respect the spirit of free

---

[30] ibid.
[31] *Stewart* judgment, above n 17, 42.
[32] ibid, 45.

movement and equal treatment. This is especially so, because the *coordinators* are the Member States themselves, passing the buck back and forth (with exceptional cases referred to the Administrative Commission).[33] The difficulties clients encounter when attempting to export benefits from one state to another indicate a need for more EU-level mechanisms of coordination or means of more routine oversight and enforcement.

## III. PROBLEMS EXPORTING BENEFITS

Benefit exportation is not straightforward. Chapter eight analyses administrative obstacles encountered both in terms of equal treatment and social security coordination, but the present section suggests that some of these failings, experienced domestically, point to a greater failing in the social security coordination framework as a whole. Member States are not always efficient or conscientious coordinators. Some greater supranational oversight is required, as is also evident in the following section on interim payments. Two cases—one dealing with exportation to the UK, one from the UK—highlight a crucial problem claimants face: that is, that challenging decisions on cross-border benefit receipt is made considerably more difficult by being resident in a different state. Under such circumstances, claimants are at a notable disadvantage not least since advice available to them in the state of residence will not necessarily pertain to the welfare and appeals systems in the state of claim. Such advice as is offered through the EU's portal is generic. It is here that more coordinating activity is required, and more support at EU level is necessary, if Member States are to be held to account.

## A. Seeking to Export to the UK: Trying to Challenge Another State's Decision

The existing coordinating rules do not help to coordinate where claimants fall between two stools since one system sets a time-limit entitlement, while the other sets a longer past presence requirement, resulting in a substantial coverage gap:

---

**Case Study: Sophie and Louis**

Sophie was a Belgian national, in receipt of an education benefit for children with disabilities, and a supplement to that benefit for her EU national son, Louis. Her EU national husband, Louis's father, was resident, working and paying tax and national insurance in Belgium. Sophie had brought Louis to the UK as she wanted him to go to school in the UK. Sophie was not working, as caring for Louis out of school hours was very demanding, and she needed to be on call during school hours every day anyway.

---

[33] Art 72(a) of Reg 883/2004 and Arts 5(4) and 6(3) of Reg 987/2009.

> She wanted Louis to be able to continue receiving the education allowance. The family had a meeting with decision-makers (including doctors) at which they were told that the benefit and the supplement would be awarded for a fixed term of a year only. The doctors described it as a period of 'exceptional payment' after which the benefit would then stop, as the choice to educate Louis in the UK meant the family forfeited any further rights to the benefit.
>
> Client notes from their memorandum of the meeting (translated):
>
> *[The doctor] told us that this amount was allocated on an exceptional basis, because the fact of enrolling our child abroad resulted in the loss of all our rights.*
>
> Sophie was told that once the fixed term expired she would have to be subject to the UK system.

It seems that in part the problem arises through potentially overlapping benefits but with different conditions and categorisations. The nearest cognate benefit to the education allowance for disabled children in the UK is disability living allowance for children,[34] but unlike the education allowance, this is not a family benefit (as discussed above, disability living allowance has been treated as a care benefit, and so a sickness benefit for the purposes of social security coordination).[35] It is subject to a past presence condition that the child has been resident in Great Britain for two of the last three years. As a result of the forfeiture of the family benefit, combined with the past presence test for disability living allowance, Sophie and Louis faced a year's gap in which they would receive no equivalent benefit. This appeared to be a failure of the coordination system to actually coordinate:

> **Case Study: Returning to Sophie and Louis**
>
> It was difficult to know how to go about challenging the decision, as Sophie had not been given any information about appealing it, and I could not readily acquaint myself with the Belgian welfare appeals processes. In the hope that a letter of appeal would be treated as a request for an appeal with grounds, I put together a letter for the client to use with the Belgian decision-makers challenging the decision, noting that the benefit fell within the definition of family benefit at Article 1(z) of Regulation 883/2004: *'"family benefit" means all benefits in kind or in cash intended to meet family expenses, excluding advances of maintenance payments and special childbirth and adoption allowances mentioned in Annex I'.* The EU Commission has classified the education allowance as a family allowance. As a family benefit, I argued that it should be subject to the rules on exportation, as per Article 67 of Regulation 883/2004:
>
> *Members of the family residing in another Member State: A person shall be entitled to family benefits in accordance with the legislation of the competent Member State,*

---

[34] Disability living allowance has only been replaced by personal independence payments for claimants over the age of 16.

[35] *Tolley* judgment, above n 8.

*including for his/her family members residing in another Member State, as if they were residing in the former Member State.*

The competent state, we argued, was Belgium, due to Louis's father's work there. He had been working in Belgium for 11 years and worked 35 hours per week. Sophie was not working, and was in fact precluded from working by the terms of the entitlement to the education allowance. So the only state of insurance was Belgium. The priority rules outlined in Article 11(3) of Regulation 883/2004 give first priority to the state of employment and insurance:

> *Article 11(3): Subject to Articles 12 to 16: (a) a person pursuing an activity as an employed or self-employed person in a Member State shall be subject to the legislation of that Member State.*[36]

We further attempted to invoke EU citizenship, arguing that refusal of the benefit created an obstacle to movement in the context of education, contrary to D'Hoop,[37] in which the ECJ had stated that it would be 'incompatible with the right of freedom of movement were a citizen, in the Member State of which he is a national, to receive treatment less favourable than he would enjoy if he had not [exercised his right of] freedom of movement'.[38] The Court added that that consideration was 'particularly important in the field of education'.[39] I argued that the citizenship case law showed that the criteria of access to a benefit should not be too exclusive and should represent the genuine links between a claimant and the competent state, and that a place-of-school criterion is likely to be disproportionate, being too exclusive and excluding other representative elements, again invoking *D'Hoop*,[40] and also Joined Cases C-11/06 and C-12/06 *Morgan and Bucher*.[41]

> *Extract from letter: In the current case the connection is even stronger—Ms D'Hoop was not working in Belgium when she made her claim. Here, the claim is made in respect of the family member—a child—of someone living and working in [Belgium] ... To refuse renewal of the disability benefit and the supplement on the ground that the child in question is receiving education in the UK would be to create an obstacle to movement. While no justification has been put forward, it is submitted in any case that any legitimate objective cannot be proportionately pursued if established with reference to a single criterion not representative of genuine economic and social links with the competent Member State.*

Making a call upon EU citizenship may seem optimistic enough given its rather waning light in the ECJ.[42] But I put forward an even more optimistic argument that

---

[36] Also note the European Commission's summary on competence for family benefits: http://europa.eu/youreurope/citizens/family/children/benefits/index_en.htm#benefits-differ. Generally, the primary country responsible for providing the benefits is the country where your family's right is based on work (you or your spouse are employed or self-employed).

[37] Case C-224/98 *Marie-Nathalie D'Hoop v Office National de L'Emploi* EU:C:2002:432 39; also Case C-192/05 *K Tas-Hagen and RA Tas v Raadskamer WUBO van de Pensioen- en Uitkeringsraad* EU:C:2006:676.

[38] *D'Hoop* judgment, ibid, 30.

[39] ibid, 32.

[40] ibid, 39.

[41] Joined Cases C-11/06 and C-12/06 *Rhiannon Morgan v Bezirksregierung Köln and Iris Bucher v Landrat des Kreises Düren* EU:C:2007:626, 46.

[42] As argued in chs 3 and 4.

Member States have a duty to implement EU law in a non-discriminatory fashion, pointing out that the obstacle to movement in question had a disproportionate impact upon disabled people. Here I pointed out that the situation fell within the scope of the Charter of Fundamental Rights.[43]

Sophie's case showed that trying to activate what might seem like clear-cut coordination rules can be a cumbersome, opaque process in which domestic decisions appear to be at odds with coordination duties, and ironically, cross-border benefit decisions are made more difficult to challenge by being resident in another country. This case appeared to point to a failure of national authorities to consider the classification of the education allowance within the coordination regime, combined with the different conditions attaching to potentially overlapping benefits in the host state, but which fell under a different branch of the coordination regulation and were subject to past presence conditions, leaving the claimants stuck between two regimes and entitled to neither.

The interaction of different provisions, within the coordination regime, and within two (or in some cases more) domestic welfare systems, combined with the lack of guidance on situations that do not fall neatly into Article 11, creates substantial problems, and Member States are little incentivised to find the correct solution for the claimant, and are ready to tolerate situations in which claimants fall through the gaps of entitlement. An EU-level commitment to social justice is necessary to protect those people, especially at times of heightened vulnerability.

### B. Seeking to Export from the UK: Refuse First, Ask Questions Later

The claim processing machinery in the UK seems to promote a refuse first, ask questions later response whenever a claim contains a cross-border dimension: there is a presumption against competence for non-residents, and so a presumption against exportation. In Stanislaw's case, excerpted below, this was particularly frustrating and distressing, since we had attempted to make the original claim through the DWP's 'exportability team' to ensure it was assessed properly first time. But we never managed to establish whether that team existed. He had to make a claim through the normal procedure, and with depressing predictability, was refused because of not meeting the residency requirements, even though we had presented our request as one of exportation from the outset. It was a distressing decision, not least since it added to the delay the whole claim faced, and time was of the essence, given that the context was of terminal illness. The claim ended up being a posthumous one:

---

[43] So engaging the non-discrimination provision, Art 21.

**Case Study: Stanislaw—A Case of Terminal Illness and Bereavement**

Stanislaw was referred to me for direct advice and support. He and his wife Agata had been working in the UK for five and a half years. His wife had recently had their second child, and while she was on maternity leave, they went on holiday to visit their family back in Hungary. While there, Agata was admitted to hospital and diagnosed with cancer. She had to stay in Hungary to receive treatment, and Stanislaw stayed with her, taking unpaid compassionate leave from his job, to help take her to and from the hospital, and look after the two children. Agata was swiftly diagnosed as having terminal cancer. She died while I was working on the case.

While she was ill, I suggested that we apply for personal independence payments for Agata for the period during which she needed care. It is an exportable benefit, and while she was on maternity leave, she was employed in the UK, so should have been eligible. The claim was refused on the ground of not meeting the residency requirements. This signals a problem with the first instance decision-making machinery—we had made clear it was an exportation claim for someone who was a worker in the UK (she was on maternity leave and still employed). We tried to make a claim through the 'exportability team' since: (a) that is what the government website advises claimants to do; (b) they would presumably be au fait with dealing with cross-border cases; and (c) it would allow us to support Stanislaw to make the claim, rather than him having to phone the standard claim line on his own from Hungary. It turned out to not be possible to contact the exportability team (see the discussion of this case in chapter eight on administrative obstacles and communication difficulties), and we were advised that Stanislaw would have to phone the standard number, which possibly contributed to the inadequacy of the decision-making that followed:

> *Field notes: Client has sent FOA [a form of authority, giving me permission to act on the client's behalf] form; phoned DWP personal independence payments line and spoke with J. Asked what had happened to the claim. Was told it had been disallowed due to not meeting residence requirements. Client has been sent two letters [dated four days apart], both saying the same thing. I requested a mandatory reconsideration on the grounds that the UK was the competent state at the material time and it is an exportable benefit. Also notified them of wife's death. Received phone call from S at DWP's personal independence payments. She said that they had received our representations and re-made the decision in the client's favour. She needs the client to fill in another form about his wife's hospital admission. Asked for best address to send it to.*

The flawed decision was quickly reversed, but only after intervention—an intervention that many people in Stanislaw's position, being in a different country, would find difficult to make. That was, of course, not the end of the dispute. We also faced problems regarding a further form that for some peculiar reason could only be posted, not emailed or faxed (though the client was between addresses and worried about it going missing in the post), and confusion about how to fill it in, since it did not ask about hospital treatment outside of the UK.

Social security is not so well-coordinated as we might like to think. Member States' intergovernmental tendencies, and their conception of each other's nationals as market citizens, contribute to a process of responsibility-shifting and a blinkered approach to the cases before them. A distaste for exportation can lead to a refuse-first attitude, such that even when a clear entitlement has been made out, a claimant might have to meet at least the extra hurdle of an appeal before the possibility of entitlement is considered. Once entitlement in principle has been established, entitlement in practice may be more complicated because of the lack of clarity on how specific domestic benefit conditions should interact with facts and events in another Member State.

The complexity of the coordination rules can appear to give Member States a wide margin of discretion, so might make them quite malleable in circumstances where states seem to wish to avoid competence. Just as Member States have little incentive to get exportation decisions right first time, they have little incentive to ensure clients receive provisional payments. Here, it is not just lack of EU oversight that is the problem, but shortcomings in the Union measures themselves, that have allowed them to be subject to narrow (to the point of cynical) implementation in UK law.

## IV. THE IMPOSSIBILITY OF CLAIMING PROVISIONAL PAYMENTS IN THE UK

Regulation 987/2009[44] provides, at Article 6, for the provisional allocation of competence and provision of benefits 'where there is a difference of views between the institutions or authorities of two or more Member States concerning the determination of the applicable legislation'. The preamble suggests that the purpose is to avoid a loss of protection while different Member States are discussing the person's status and working out which is the competent Member State: 'provision should be made for provisional membership of a social security system' in order to 'ensure that the person concerned is protected *for the duration of the necessary communication between institutions*'.[45]

Article 6 stipulates an order of priority for the provisional application of one Member State's social security system: first, the state of employment/self employment; second, the state of residence; and third, the state in which the application was made if activities are pursued in that and another state. While Article 6(1) provides for the provisional application of legislation, Article 6(2) provides for provisional benefit entitlement:

> Where there is a difference of views between the institutions or authorities of two or more Member States about which institution should provide the benefits in cash or in

---

[44] Regulation (EC) No 987/2009 of the European Parliament and of the Council of 16 September 2009 laying down the procedure for implementing Regulation (EC) No 883/2004 on the coordination of social security systems OJ [2009] L 284/1.

[45] Recital (10), Reg 987/2009, OJ [2009] L 284/2, emphasis added.

kind, the person concerned who could claim benefits if there was no dispute shall be entitled, on a provisional basis, to the benefits provided for by the legislation applied by the institution of his place of residence.[46]

Where it is concluded that the state making provisional payments, or providing provisional benefits in kind, is not the competent state after all, Article 6(4) and (5) allow for the provisionally competent state to claim reimbursement from the actually competent state. The basic concept of provisional payment is a familiar one, in the form of 'interim' payments in domestic welfare law.[47] They reflect the principle that claimants should not be disadvantaged as a result of lengthy administrative wrangling involved in processing claims (a risk which is even higher in cross-border cases). Significant delay—as explored in the next chapter—can be the biggest barrier to accessing rights, and the mechanism for provisional payments mitigates the damage done by such delay. However, the problem with this mechanism is the phrase 'where there is a different of views between ... two or more Member States'. This is too narrow, and does not reflect the intention of the preamble.

The preamble recognises that thorough examination of a person's circumstances by several Member States will be necessary 'to determine' the competent institution, and that a claimant should be protected 'for the duration of the necessary communication between institutions'.[48] Such communications, and ensuing delay, will be necessary even where there is no official difference in views. There is just a lengthy period of time in which Member States attempt to formulate their views and come to agreement. There may also be a difference of views in practice, with neither state considering themselves competent, but that has not been expressed as such (for example, if Member State A says to Member State B 'please pay benefit X to this claimant' and Member State B just responds to say 'benefit X does not exist here'). Communications can be protracted, and authorities from different states can be talking at cross-purposes for some time. In the UK, people making claims that oblige the UK authorities to seek information from another state, are likely to be told that it could take a long time to process their claim.[49] But in the communications from the DWP there is no mention of the possibility of being awarded provisional payments.

## A. The UK Authorities' Condition of its Own Invention

The problem of requiring an official 'difference in views' between Member States before provisional payments are possible is exacerbated by the confusing

---

[46]  Art 6(2) Reg 987/2009; OJ [2009] L 284/5.
[47]  Social Security (Payments on Account of Benefit) Regulations 2013, SI 2013/383, regs 4 and 5.
[48]  Recital (10), Reg 987/2009, OJ [2009] L 284/2.
[49]  Here it is worth noting that HMRC sets itself a target average claims processing time for international claims that is more than four times as long as that set for national claimants (92 days as opposed

provisions depending on whether there is a difference of views as to competence, or a difference in views as to which rules take priority where both states might consider their legislation to be applicable. Article 60(3) of Regulation 987/2009 provides that a state may find that it is competent but its legislation is not applicable by priority right. In such a case, it should forward the application to the state whose legislation is applicable, and if 'the institution to which the application was forwarded does not take a position within two months of the receipt of the application, the provisional decision referred to above shall apply'.[50]

The UK authorities have interpreted this as meaning that where the UK makes a decision that another state is competent for a benefit, unless it receives notification of the other state disputing that decision within two months, that decision becomes unilateral and there is no possibility for claimants to receive provisional payments from the UK. HMRC, responsible for child tax credits, working tax credits and child benefit, have adopted the condition that another Member State must make a decision on competence within two months of the UK contacting them. If not, then according to the UK, the UK decision on competence prevails and the claimant will be denied any opportunity to claim provisional benefits. The HMRC Child Benefit Technical Manual states:

> If the other Member State does not make a decision on whether to accept competency within that two month period, the UK's provisional decision would apply and that Member State must pay its benefits in full from the date of the claim and notify the UK of the date and the rate of payment.[51]

However, this approach is problematic for a number of reasons. First, there does not seem to be a clear demarcation between claims to be treated as though another state is competent, and claims to be treated as though the UK legislation is applicable but not to be applied. Even if there were a clear demarcation between those claims that fall within Article 68(3) and those which do not, but do fall within Article 6, there is no clear logic for treating them differently with regard to eligibility for provisional payments. The decision has the same effect: that the UK has deemed itself not competent to pay benefits and is communicating with another Member State, with all the delay that is likely to entail. Secondly, there has to have been some investigation and communication with the other Member State in

---

to 22 days). As an 'average', that target allows for some lengthy outliers (see HMRC, 'Single Departmental Plan 2015–2020', *Corporate Report* (London, HMRC, 2017), 2.2.

[50]  Art 60(3) Reg 987/2009, OJ [2009] L 284/21.

[51]  HMRC, *HMRC Child Benefit Technical Manual* CBTM10208; 'European Law: Priority rules in the event of overlapping entitlement to family benefits—Article 68(3) of Regulation (EC) 883/2004 and Articles 6 and 60 of Regulation (EC) 987/2009'; the same wording is used in HMRC, *HMRC Tax Credits Technical Manual* TCTM02835; 'Entitlement: Tax credits and European Law: Priority rules in the event of overlapping entitlement to family benefits—Article 68(3) of Regulation (EC) 883/2004 and Articles 6 and 60 of Regulation (EC) 987/2009'.

the first place, to show that the priority rules have been observed.[52] Those rules outline the order of priority in the case of overlapping benefits provided on a different basis, and of benefits overlapping on the same basis. To show that the UK had determined priority according to Article 68, it must show that it has established the possible benefit entitlement, and the basis on which that entitlement arises. Simply asserting that the UK is not competent because of residence or work elsewhere is not enough, without showing that that residence/work carries with it an entitlement to family benefits in that Member State. Consequently, the UK cannot make that priority decision without having communicated with the other Member State, and that communication carries with it a delay that should be mitigated through a provisional payment. Thirdly, the EU provisions do not link the payment of provisional benefits to a two-month deadline for responses. It would be (indeed, is) deeply problematic to make it so conditional. If Member State B does have a different opinion about competence or the legislation that should take priority, that state is unlikely to pay the benefit just because confused communications meant that it did not officially dispute competence within two months. In such circumstances, it would be the claimants who suffer as a result (if not permitted provisional payments). Far from screening off provisional payments, the Regulation suggests that the procedures for deciding another state's legislation is applicable by priority apply *without prejudice* to the rules on provisional payments.[53]

The UK interpretation of these rules results in subjecting provisional payments to an illogical and highly exclusionary extra condition of its own invention: if the UK says it will not pay, either claiming lack of competence, or acknowledging competence but claiming its legislation is not applicable, then it will not be responsible for interim payments unless it receives within two months evidence that the Member State it has deemed competent denies competence. As explored next, this condition defeats the very object of provisional payments.

## B. A Disproportionate Interference with Social Justice

The effect of the UK approach has been to screen out provisional payment claims, and to exclude those claims likely to be the most complicated, and take the most time, and so likely to result in the greatest hardship for the claimants. For example, a case that involves a Member State that is particularly slow to respond, or involves confused communications between the states, and in which it takes Member State B a long time to take a 'position' on competence or priority right, will fall foul of the two-month rule, and see claimants disentitled from provisional payments. An example of this arose in Sarah's case:

[52] As contained in Art 68 of Reg 883/2004.
[53] Art 68(3)(a) of Reg 987/2009.

**Case Study: Sarah**

Sarah had returned from Portugal with her four children. Her husband had followed and continued to pay national insurance in Portugal, but started to pay tax in the UK. She was told that she was not entitled to claim child benefit in the UK because of her husband's national insurance payments to Portugal. The Portuguese authorities had told her that because their family benefit was determined by the payment of tax on employment, which was paid in the UK, she was not entitled to it.

When I first saw Sarah, she had made her first claim more than a year previously. After eight months, her claim had been refused, which she appealed. It was only after she had submitted an appeal that she was told that the UK would be seeking information from the other Member State. HMRC then warned her that it could take 'some time' before they were able to make a decision based on that information.

On chasing the appeal up, we were told that the Portuguese authorities had not provided an adequate response to the request for information, slowing things down further. We requested a copy of the information request sent to Portugal, and a copy of their response. The request had been sent using the electronic F-001 form, as required of Member States seeking social security coordination information from other states to determine competence.[54] The form originally sent by the UK authorities stated:

*Article 67 of EC regulations 883/04 apply. [Sarah] resides in the UK from [date] she is not employed. All of her family live in the UK. Her husband ... lives in the UK but works for a [Portuguese] company. He is paying [Portuguese] NI and is therefore covered by the [Portuguese] social security scheme. The UK has made a provisional decision that Poland [sic] is competent by priority right to pay full rate Family Benefit and the UK will consider a supplement. Please consider the attached claim under Article 60 of EC Regulation 987/09.*

The response received from the [Portuguese] authorities was (this is the translation provided by HMRC): 'Further to your request via Form F001, dated [date], we would like to inform you that the referenced person does not obtain nor has applied for family benefits through this Office'. HMRC followed this up with a further F001 with the additional comment:

*'You told us in your reply dated [date] that neither [Sarah] or her husband have applied for Family Benefits in [Portugal] however we sent you a copy of their UK claim form which should be treated as a claim by yourselves under Article 60 of EC Regulation 987/09. I have enclosed another copy of the claim for your information.*

---

[54] 'The Structured Electronic Document (SED) F001—Request for determining competences and F002 Reply for determining competences have been developed for establishing competence': European Commission *Commission Staff Working Document* 'Impact assessment: Initiative to partially revise Regulation (EC) No 883/2004 of the European Parliament and of the Council on the coordination of social security systems and its implementing Regulation (EC) No 987/2009 Accompanying the document Proposal for a regulation of the European Parliament and of the Council amending Regulation (EC) No 883/2004 on the coordination of social security systems and regulation (EC) No 987/2009 laying down the procedure for implementing Regulation (EC) No 883/2004' SWD/2016/0460 final/2—2016/0397 (COD).

> *Please take the necessary action to process the claim and advise us of the outcome as soon as possible.'*
>
> The authorities of two different states appeared to have been talking at cross-purposes, with Portugal interpreting the F-001 as an enquiry about whether there were overlapping benefit claims and the UK treating the F-001 form as a means to request Portugal to process the claim. Sarah felt frustrated.
>
> *Excerpt from client communication:* 'The CB office have not even asked the [Portuguese] *authorities if we are entitled to any benefits in [Portugal] and have just told them to proceed with the claim. It is very confusing for the [Portuguese] office to reply to … I'm in disbelief.'*

The misunderstanding may have arisen in part from the nature of the form itself, which is called a 'request for determining competence'. Arguably a request for information should contain clear questions or open the door to communication over a claim in order that the first Member State can make a decision as to competence or priority right. It is not clear that the form should be used for a unilateral announcement of one state's decision as to competence/priority right; so the recipient state is not necessarily on notice that the 'request' is actually a decision that they are expected to dispute (according to UK rules, within two months) or to act upon by processing a claim and paying benefits. Moreover, different Member States may struggle to know how to deal with/process an attached claim form drawn up to reflect the entitlement conditions of another Member State's benefit. It may take longer than two months to gather further information just to establish whether there is in principle a valid claim for an equivalent benefit in that state, let alone to make a decision as to competence.

Again, we run up against mal-coordinated coordination mechanisms, which require a Member State that finds another state's legislation to be applicable as of priority right, to forward the application to that state without delay. Sarah's case showed that this procedure can work poorly in practice if state B does not understand what is required of it, and highlights how easily communication problems between states occur (which are all the more likely to create delays and mean state B takes longer than two months to reach a decision).

## C. Inviting Communication Problems

The requirements regarding provisional decision-making stipulate a 'difference of views'. It may be that using the F-001 form to invite a rejection of claim, rather than purely as a fact-gathering tool, is the quickest way to ascertain whether such a difference exists, and therefore whether a provisional decision must be made. However, if that was the intention of the UK authorities, then again, clear statements and questions are needed, to indicate that a decision as to competence/priority right is required. The case study shows that the F-001 form itself does not invite such a statement of view, and the UK's mode of filling it in did not do so either. It should also be noted that the UK's filling in had a whiff of 'cut and paste' about it, since in the brief statement of decision as to competence it referred to Poland. In Sarah's case, we complained about the communication failings, noting that HMRC had failed to contact Portugal in the first place, resulting in a flawed first instance decision and extra delay, and arguing that the delay increased the duty to make provisional payments:

---

**Case Study: Returning to Sarah**

We complained to HMRC about the continued delay with Sarah's case, noting that the initial refusal was flawed, since the claim appeared to have been refused by default, with no recourse to further information gathering, and HMRC only seeking that information from [Portugal] once an appeal had been lodged. HMRC responded to this with a concession and apology: 'It is accepted that while necessary checks were ongoing, HMRC disallowed your client's claim on an incorrect basis ... The position should have been that ... we needed to obtain further information ... before making any decision'. We highlighted the unreasonable delay overall in processing Sarah's claim, especially in light of the children whose welfare was at issue. We pointed to the coordination requirements for making provisional payments. We were told:

*It is our position that interim payments may only be considered in instances where there is a dispute as to competency that cannot be resolved within the specified timeframes ... In your case, as the [Portuguese] authorities did not take a position on the child benefit provisional competency decision within two months, a provisional decision was made by HMRC that [Portugal] was competent to pay child benefit to your client.*

---

The UK's interpretation and implementation of the provisional payments provisions struck me as both bizarre and exclusionary. It takes the two months given to states to dispute decisions on competence 'by priority right' in Article 60 Regulation 987/2009 and makes it a precondition for any provisional payments, under Article 6 of the same regulation, to be paid at all. The overall effect of not paying interim payments unless and until the other Member State has taken a clear position on competence within two months was that claimants lose out as a result of miscommunication. Portugal had not taken a clear position, because the authorities did not understand that that was what they were being asked to do, and because that is not what the UK asked them to do. The Portuguese authorities thought they were being asked about overlapping claims, while the UK had just asked them to process a claim. In the midst of this confusion, the need for a clear statement on competence was lost. This is all within the context of a client who had been waiting for over a year for benefits—a case in which the UK had signally failed to forward the application to Portugal 'without delay'. The policy aim of this is illogical: it results in excluding claims which are more likely to take a long period of time (and which may have already taken a long period of time) from the possibility of receiving provisional payments. Claimants who come from a Member State whose authorities are slow to respond to, or misunderstand the purposes of, communications, would likely find that there was no clear position within two months and so have no access to benefits, even though theirs were the cases that might yet last months or years. It seems open to Member States to start the two-months clock ticking even before sufficient information has been shared for anyone to have reached an informed decision.

This cannot have been the intention of the EU legislature. Judge Jacobs in the UK Upper Tribunal expressed similar misgivings about UK practices, stating: 'I have been troubled recently that the correct approach was not being taken to disputes about the competent state'.[55] In *HR*, he found that were there was 'a difference of view between Sweden and the UK as to their competence to pay Mrs R's sickness benefit' so that it 'must be paid provisionally by the UK as the state of residence, pending a resolution of the difference of view'.[56] No mention is made of a two-month limit. Moreover, once there is a difference of view, the state of claim—in that case, the UK—becomes 'immediately but provisionally liable to make payments under Article 6'.[57] If the UK has made a decision but has no 'acceptable evidence' of a difference of view, then it should refuse the benefit, but submit the claim to the other state, which 'may generate a difference of view, to which Article 6 will apply and the UK may become provisionally liable'. Again, no mention is made of a two-month deadline. Judge Jacobs noted that a problem arises with the definition of 'difference of view', and took issue with the position of the Secretary of State for Work and Pensions that documentary evidence of a refusal from another state was required. The judge argued that prior communication is not necessary before a difference of view could be said to arise because 'the claimants involved are, by definition, (i) in need of financial assistance and (ii) disabled or incapacitated and often elderly', so it was 'unlikely that the Article is designed to allow states to undertake lengthy discussions before a difference of view can arise'.[58] Documentary evidence 'may be setting too demanding a standard' because claimants often get and act upon information or advice given verbally: 'claimants often enquire of the DWP whether they may be entitled to a particular benefit and act on the information given. That information is not necessarily, or even usually, put into writing'.[59] He suggested that a difference of view was an objective fact that could exist even if one state was not aware of it (for instance, if a state's rule made clear what their position would be). The difference of view is 'an objective fact, not

---

[55] *Secretary of State for Work and Pensions v HR* (AA) (European Union law: Council regulations 1408/71/EEC and (EC) 883/2004) [2014] UKUT 571, 11.
[56] ibid, 15.
[57] ibid, 27.
[58] ibid, 18.
[59] ibid, 19.

a matter of what a particular state knows at a particular time'.[60] He emphasised that the purpose of the provisional payments was to:

> ensure that the time taken to identify the responsible state does not disadvantage anyone. The claimant is protected by the provisional application of the law of the place of residence. And the paying state is only required to pay if the claimant satisfies the conditions of entitlement under domestic law and, if so, is then protected by the right to reimbursement if the other state is eventually held responsible.[61]

However, this approach seems to have only been very lightly adopted within DWP guidance. Guidance released after this judgment still required evidence of a 'dispute',[62] whereas Judge Jacobs was explicit that a 'difference of view' was different to and 'more general than disagreement or dispute'.[63] Also, the new guidance does not tell us what constitutes 'acceptable evidence of a dispute', leaving open the risk that decision-makers look and wait for an official decision before considering the possibility of provisional payments (remembering that decision-makers look only at the guidance and not at the original cases). The HMRC policy on not making provisional payments until an official decision has been received, and only if such a decision is received within two months, was not here at issue and so was not discussed or challenged. However, the issue of provisional payments has been appealed to the Court of Appeal,[64] and it may be that a sufficiently high profile decision in the context of DWP benefits could result in a change of practice within HMRC as well. The current HMRC guidance does not make the position on provisional payments clear, but by implication, suggests that it will only consider liability for a 'supplement' once it has received notice of the other state's commencement of payment. If it does not hear from the other Member State within two months then the HMRC position is that 'the UK's provisional decision would apply and that Member State must pay its benefits in full from the date of the claim and notify the UK of the date and the rate of payment. The UK would then consider whether a supplement payment is appropriate'.[65]

The omission of a mention of a duty to make provisional payments if it receives evidence of a difference of view (or an adverse decision from the other state as to competency), the suggestion that it is only the other state that must make payments once two months have elapsed, and the statement that the UK would 'then' consider whether to make a supplement payment (*after* not only receiving

---

[60]    ibid, 17.

[61]    ibid, 24.

[62]    DWP, *DMG Memo 27/15—Action to Take Once Competency Has Been Decided* (DMA, Leeds, 2015). Available at: www.whatdotheyknow.com/request/380407/response/937713/attach/4/m%20 27%2015.pdf. Replaced by DMA, *Advice for Decision Makers: Memo ADM 21/15—Action to Take Once Competency Has Been Decided*, DMA, Leeds, 2015. Available at: www.gov.uk/government/uploads/ system/uploads/attachment_data/file/475981/adm21-15.pdf.

[63]    *HR* above, n 54, 18.

[64]    C3/2016/0358 *Secretary of State for Work and Pensions v Fileccia*.

[65]    HMRC, above, n 50.

a decision, but notification of the 'date and rate' of payment by the other state), all appear to preclude consideration of provisional payments. I was somewhat suspicious that the two-month rule must screen out the vast majority of potential provisional payment claims where information from other Member States is needed and possible competence disputes are at issue, to the extent that the duty to provide provisional payments was being avoided, and EU law infringed. I tried a number of avenues to press both HMRC and DWP to share the numbers of provisional payments they had made since the relevant provisions came into force. I met with little success.

## D. The UK's Reluctance on Granted Provisional Payments

In order to ascertain how faithfully the UK was implementing its duty to provide provisional payments, we need to know how many claims were made that resulted in the issuing of F-001 forms (that is, the amount of claims that could possibly give rise to a provisional payment claim and then the amount of provisional payments made). I sent a Freedom of Information request to DWP and HMRC. This was turned down, as explained in the case study below, and I requested a review of that decision, to no avail. I also worked with a member of the House of Lords, who tabled written parliamentary questions seeking the same data. She did not receive an answer either:

---

**Case Study: Returning again to Sarah**

We responded to the HMRC statement of policy on interim payments, arguing that it failed to properly implement EU law and created a disproportionate detriment for those people most in need of provisional payments (claims likely to take a while to resolve). Because, as HMRC acknowledged when contacting Sarah to let her know they were writing to Portugal, cross-border information-gathering can take a long time, I had suspicions about the amount of interim payments they could actually have made since the implementation of Regulation 987/2009 in the UK. As such, as well as making further representations, I sent a Freedom of Information Request, asking for the number of claims for child benefit and child tax credit that had resulted in submitting information requests through the electronic F-001 form. Of those, I asked how many had led to provisional payments under Article 6 of Regulation 987/2009. Here is how HMRC responded to our further arguments:

*Excerpts from the FOI response: HMRC have still not heard from the [Portuguese] authorities despite sending reminders ... Until HMRC receive a response ... they are unable to act in relation to the period [of non-payment] ... It is available to your client to contact the [Portuguese] authorities directly in order to enquire as to when a response will be provided ... [interim] payments are available in law only where there is a dispute between two or more Member States as to which of them is the competent authority.*

> *There is no such dispute here as HMRC has established that [Portugal] was the compe-*
> *tent state ... and [Portugal] has not disputed that decision.*

There was no consideration of evidence that might demonstrate a difference of view in the absence of an actual statement rejecting competence from Portugal (and a stated requirement of a 'dispute between two or more Member States'). Our Freedom of Information request was refused, as HMRC claimed that they would have to look at every child benefit and child tax credit claim made since 1 May 2010. This seemed unlikely: provisional payments would only arise where there were questions of competence, and where there were such questions, an F-001 form would have been sent. As this is done electronically, it seems highly likely that there is a means to count the number of F-001 forms sent. I requested an internal review of the FOI decision, and the refusal was upheld, as although 'the records are annotated with this information, there is no function that enables this information to be extracted separately. Therefore the only way the information can be obtained is by manually examining each tax credit and child benefit record for the available period'.[66]

Vexed by the failure to reveal how many interim payments have been made, and concerned that the number might be so low as to in itself reveal that EU law is not being properly implemented or respected, I followed up the FOI request, by asking Baroness Ruth Lister to table written questions in the House of Lords. She submitted the written parliamentary questions asking how many F-001 requests had been submitted to other Member States since 1 May 2010,[67] and in how many of those cases Article 6 provisional payments had been made.[68]

The government's responses was essentially 'we don't count them':

> *HMRC does not keep a record of the number of F001s issued.[69] ... The Government does*
> *not collect information on the number of provisional benefit payments made on the basis*
> *of either Article 6 or 7 of Regulation (EC) No 987/2009 ... In domestic guidance there*
> *is the facility for a decision-maker to make an award of benefit where the evidence is*
> *incomplete, with a revision of that award undertaken, if appropriate, once the required*
> *evidence is received. This would cover claims made under Article 7. Each claim to benefit*
> *is assessed on a case-by-case basis.[70]*

Whatever the number of provisional payments made (if any), the domestic rules appear to create unwarranted barriers to claiming interim payments thus effectively creating penalties for claimants with cross border social security histories which constitutes a potential obstacle to movement. Those domestic rules have been made possible by unclear and unnecessarily complex coordinating

---

[66] Extract from letter received.
[67] HL 3326 Tabled on 17 November 2016.
[68] HL3327 Tabled on 17 November 2016.
[69] Baroness Chisholm of Owlpen, date and time of answer 1 December 2016 at 15:35.
[70] Lord Freud, date and time of answer 1 December 2016 at 16:30.

provisions at EU level. At a close level of detail, it is not clear why there needs to be a distinction between issues on which there is a difference of view as to competence compared to where there is a difference of view as to the application of legislation by priority right. If such distinction is necessary, and a two months deadline for Member State responses in the latter case is justified, then more clarity is needed on the consequences for claimants of: (a) delays caused by a failure of the state of application to seek an opinion from another state in good time; and (b) the absence of a clear statement of 'difference of opinion' within that two month period. We also need to know what conditions, if any, should be attached to a claimant who meets the essential criteria when it comes to provisional payments. At a more general level of coordination, it is not clear why a 'difference of view' is necessary at all, if the main aim is protecting claimants who would otherwise go without benefits for a long period of time due to protracted communication and decision-making mechanisms. It should be possible to trigger provisional payments in cases of actual or likely delay, and if, as in Sarah's case, there is at least evidence that the claimant is not receiving any benefits from anywhere, especially if the main aim of the provisional payments is to ensure claimants are not left without protection during long periods in which Member States must communicate and work things out.

## V. SUMMARY

The existing coordination instruments are complex, contradictory and incomplete, which leaves them open to imaginative and exclusionary domestic interpretation. If we recall the different rulings of Judge Jacobs on the proper construction of the rules on sickness benefits and pensions, the fact that the same Upper Tribunal judge can come to diametrically opposed conclusions based on the interpretation of the same piece of legislation, within the space of a few years, is some indication of how poor a job Regulation 883/2004 does of creating clarity in vaguely complex cross-border situations.

The construction of other Member States' nationals as market citizens contributes to a parsimonious approach on the part of Member States, who use legal literalist readings of the law to limit their obligations and comfortably reach decisions that leave claimants without protection. Member States have little incentive to ensure the system is well-coordinated and to view claimants' situations in terms of the combined effects of different regimes. As a result, claimants can be left caught between regimes and protected by neither. This risk is exacerbated by shortcomings in the coordination framework itself, such as the damaging effects on pensioners' families, living and working in a host Member State, of the mis-classification of disability and care benefits as sickness benefits, or the mis-match of eligibility time-limits in one state and past presence conditions in another. Because Member States are the primary coordinators, there is a risk in exportation cases that without closer scrutiny, domestic decision makers might tend to refuse first and ask questions later (that is, once the refusal has been appealed).

That there is an apparent default of restricted entitlement in cross-border situations is evident in the UK's policy on provisional payments—a policy that makes it extremely difficult, if not virtually impossible, to actually receive them. This is not a faithful implementation of the duty set down in EU law, but part of the problem is that that duty is not as clear, or as wide, as it should be. In requiring a 'difference of view' before triggering the possibility of provisional payments, the Regulation is open to a wide range of approaches as to what constitutes a difference of view and how it should be evidenced. It fails to adequately protect claimants in cases of major delay, perhaps suggesting that the EU legislature is not fully alive to the factors that create the greatest risks of hardship for EU citizens who exercise their free movement rights.

Delay for many is tantamount to refusal without appeal, since at least if you have a decision against them, you can appeal. If you are still just waiting, then you are in legal limbo, and possibly in financial dire straits, for a significant period of time. Delay is just one of the many administrative barriers to justice experienced by EU nationals. The next chapter argues that the decision-making processes and procedures applied to EU nationals in the UK verge upon maladministration, and have created hardship and social injustice.

# 8

# *Market Citizenship and Administrative Barriers to Justice*

You just feel when you get a case, you just think, somebody comes to you and they say, European, migrant, benefits. You just know it's going to be complex, a bit of a minefield, that things are going to go wrong.[1]

I mean everything has problems, but everything is just more exaggerated, the waits are longer, the mucking about is longer, the level of ignorance is bigger, it's the same thing but exaggerated.[2]

## I. INTRODUCTION

AS THE MECHANICS of social security coordination show, how rights work in practice is to a large extent determined by administrative processes. These are not neutral facts of life: they are in turn shaped by policy and steering from the state. Most claims for benefits do not involve litigation: first-tier decision-makers are the gatekeepers of EU citizenship rights, which presents a number of problems for access to justice, not least being the complexity of the areas of law at issue.[3] This chapter will consider the role of 'street-level bureaucrats' in defining EU citizens' rights, and how changes in the legal environment, and policy messages from the state, might influence how they exercise their discretion.

Lipsky noted that street-level bureaucrats mould the law[4] and suggested that they might exercise too much discretion. However, this project has argued that street-level bureaucracy takes place in the context of a programme of declaratory discrimination such as to give strong steers to decision-makers and to limit the scope of their discretion (for example, through questionnaires on the genuine prospect of work that confine questions to the evidence sought by the decision-maker guidance). The demise of proportionality at ECJ level reflects what

---

[1] Preparatory focus group.

[2] Reflective focus group.

[3] Here I draw on Mashaw, who emphasised the need to look to first instance decision-makers and the 'routine administrative action by low-level administrators' (J Mashaw, *Bureaucratic Justice: Managing Social Security Disability Claims* (New Haven, Yale University Press, 1985) 16.

[4] M Lipsky, *Street-Level Bureaucracy: Dilemmas of the Individual in Public Service*, 30th anniversary expanded edn (New York, Russell Sage Foundation, 2010).

has actually been the practice in terms of first-tier decision-making for years: decision-makers are not, and have not been, encouraged to consider the proportionality of their decisions at first instance, but to focus instead on narrow categories of rights to reside. Of course, simplified or swift decision-making could end up being arbitrary in either direction—so a lack of attention to detail could in some cases work in the claimants' favour. As my data comes from those who have sought help, they are more likely to have experienced problems, so I do not have much experience of accidental generosity.

While decision-makers shape the law, they do so in a complex and nuanced process, in which they themselves are manipulated and constrained. As Lipsky put it, 'if the public wants to affect public service policy delivery, it must look not to the behaviour of individual workers but to managers and policy-makers'.[5] This project was interested in the importance of the policy environment and the administrative culture shaping decision-making through procedural constraints. The systems, policies, procedures and practices that influence, restrict or instruct decision-makers are not ideologically neutral, but reflect legal and political priorities. Even stipulations about the format of claimant communications can have significant ramifications for access to justice and so reveal something of the systemic commitments to such access. The *EU Rights Project* found three key types of administrative obstacle to justice: (1) constrained and inaccurate interpretations of the law (getting it wrong); (2) a lack of institutional responsibility for sound procedure in decision-making (not caring about getting it right); and (3) a lack of institutional accountability, evident in mechanisms that insulated law, policy and practice from challenge (stopping claimants from putting it right).

Decision-makers' interpretation of the law is subordinated to the prevailing administrative culture. When adopting definitions for key terms in legislation or guidance—such as deciding what counts as marginal work, deciding whether someone has signed on at the job centre without undue delay, and deciding whether someone has a genuine prospect of work—these decisions are often underpinned by poor decision-maker knowledge and understanding of the relevant law, and are susceptible to government steers as to appropriate assessments. I was told that decision-makers 'don't look at the law', which means that non-statutory guidance documents are effectively elevated to the status of law. These documents, combined with directive questionnaires and strident government communications, restrict the palette of issues on which decision-makers actually decide.

The lack of institutional responsibility for getting decision-making right was evident in processes that responsibilised claimants at every stage, such as requiring particular types of evidence to be presented in particular ways, requiring claimants to present in person, or to make written submissions, and stipulating formats for forms of authority. The duty upon the authorities to gather evidence or ask

---

[5] ibid, 212.

questions in our cases only came into play after appeals had been lodged, so the law was being implemented in these cases through a refuse-first approach. There was also a lack of concern about, or responsibility taken for, communications and applications not being recorded, identity documents going missing, and other administrative errors. All of these implementation problems contribute to delay— one of the biggest administrative obstacles to justice EU nationals face.

Law, policy and practice were insulated through mechanisms that kept the decision-making process opaque and remote from the client. The systems put in place for clients make it difficult to contact the relevant authorities and require repeated communications. Even tribunal judges, when appearing to overturn a decision in the client's favour, can insulate the law by avoiding challenging the problematic law in question (as happened in John's case, discussed in chapter six). Insulating processes thus occur at all levels: they make it difficult to have open and transparent discussions about the 'working out' of decisions, they make it harder to hold decision-makers accountable, they obscure fundamental tensions between domestic law, policy and practice, and the state's obligations under EU law.

EU nationals caught in the system are market citizens, entitled to no more than the state can be forced to eke out. Nick O'Brien suggests that the 'test of any system of administrative justice will be its contribution not only to free citizenship, but to equal citizenship also'.[6] The differential treatment of EU nationals indicates short-comings both in administrative justice and in 'equal' EU citizenship. Decision-makers are steered by heavily publicised government policy, and directed through the government guidance, to be restrictive in their acts of interpretation, proce-dural implementation and insulation. These processes simultaneously reflect and recreate the social justice gap in the free movement framework.

## II. GETTING IT WRONG: SYSTEMIC CONSTRAINTS ON INTERPRETATIONS OF THE LAW

One of the key systemic constraints on accurate administration of EU nationals' benefit claims is the level of training of administrators. For most EU national wel-fare claimants, the place that EU welfare law becomes manifest is in the hands of administrative decision-makers. Yet those decision-makers might not even be aware that they are engaging with EU law at all, and even fewer will know or understand the legislation or case law in question. Poor understanding does not just affect the substance of actual decisions: it can have an earlier, chilling effect on rights, as when an administrator gives the wrong advice about entitlements, they effectively assume the role of de facto decision-maker, and prevent people from asserting them in the first place.

---

[6] N O'Brien, 'Administrative Justice: A Libertarian Cinderella in Search of an Egalitarian Prince' (2012) 83 *The Political Quarterly* 3, 494, 500.

## A. Poorly Informed Administrators as De Facto Decision-Makers and Gatekeepers

[Someone on the HMRC helpline] used to insist to me that in order to get their child tax credit, they had to have their child benefit in place, which was of course totally wrong. He used to say me, I've been doing that for 10 years, I know! You know? He stopped doing it. We did make some complaints.[7]

Poor understanding can lead to administrators giving erroneous advice. An example of misleading advice came to light in two cases dealt with first-hand through the *EU Rights Project*. Claimants with ongoing appeals whose circumstances change are entitled to continue to pursue the appeal on the issue of the past entitlement, which can amount to a significant period in protracted cases, while making a separate, fresh prospective claim on the basis of new circumstances. In two early cases, decision-makers advised me—one in very strong terms—to not pursue both an appeal and a new claim, but to simply inform those handling the appeal about the change of circumstances. This would result in a revised decision, but only with prospective effect, in effect cancelling the appeal with regard to past entitlement:

---

**Case Study: Sarah**

This client had been refused child benefit after 'a lot of to-ing and fro-ing' with correspondence. The ground given was that although she and her children, all UK nationals, were resident in the UK, her husband was paying national insurance contributions in Portugal. She had not received any family benefits since moving back to the UK. She submitted an appeal. While we were pursuing the appeal, she was considering starting work, and so we spoke to HMRC. We outlined that in this case there would be a change of circumstances, and she would want to submit a fresh claim based on new circumstances, while keeping appeal alive regarding 'old' circumstances. Here are my notes of the conversation with the person on the helpline:

*Field notes: Initially told if does both—new claim and appeal—there might be a delay. Told repeatedly that 'the best thing is not to submit a new claim but to tell the people handling her appeal that her circumstances have changed'. Then told if she makes a new claim her appeal might be cancelled (I emphasised that client would make clear she wants her appeal to stay live). Also told if she makes a new claim the clock would start again on 26 weeks timescale. M said she was speaking to her manager who asked her to reiterate that a new claim would 'do more harm than good'. Explained we did not want to invite reconsideration of decision based on change of circumstances as she would lose money appealed for (the period from the point of original claim) now. Told 'highly unlikely it would be returned anyway', said that 'if she wasn't entitled, I don't see how they would change their decision'.*

I was troubled by this exchange for a number of reasons. The inaccurate advice was accompanied with an emphatic warning that we would 'do more harm than good'

---

[7] Reflective focus group.

which understandably made the client nervous. Fear is a powerful tool to stop people exercising their rights, and this message did not just come from the person answering the call, but from her manager as well, which gave the warning added weight. It was important that the appeal was kept alive, because this represented over a year's worth of benefit for four children, and the client could not easily afford to write off that money. Just pursuing a new claim would be to abandon the old entitlement. But even when I explained this to the adviser, I was still being steered away because it was 'highly unlikely' her appeal would succeed. Here, the adviser was pre-empting a tribunal and acting as a (rather obstructive) gatekeeper to a fair hearing. The assumption that 'she wasn't entitled' so there would be very little reason for them to change their decision belies a deep misunderstanding of why the appeals system exists in the first place. In response to a written complaint, HMRC said [Excerpt from response to complaint]:

> We have listened to our recording of the call ... and accept the advice she was given was clearly incorrect. We will ensure this is addressed by the senior manager responsible and we will remind all of our advisers of the correct advice in this situation.

This turned out not to be an isolated incident. In the very next case referred to the *EU Rights Project*, Irina was refused income support, child benefit and child tax credit as she had been found not to have a right to reside for a period between jobs. We appealed on the grounds, inter alia, of permanent residence. In the meantime, she found another job, and we wished to submit a new prospective claim for child tax credit and child benefit while the appeal on past entitlement was ongoing, based on the change of circumstances (being in work):

**Case Study: Irina**

Irina had been working in the UK for seven years. When she left her most recent job, she claimed jobseeker's allowance for one month, and was then told she could no longer claim it, and should claim income support because she was seven months pregnant. This was refused on the grounds of her not having a right to reside. This decision had direct knock-on effects—after her baby was born she received a letter refusing her a sure start maternity grant—because she had been refused income support:

> About your claim for a sure start maternity grant ... We have decided that you are not entitled to a payment. This is for the following reason(s): you are not receiving universal credit, income support, income-based jobseeker's allowance, income-related employment and support allowance, pension credit, working tax credit or child tax credit being paid at a higher rate than the appropriate maximum family element.

She was also refused child benefit and child tax credit. She later started work again and so was entitled to make new claims while appealing the old ones. We phoned the HMRC helpline, and the first person we spoke to agreed that a fresh claim and appeal were the best way forward. He triggered the sending of a new claim form and passed us onto the appeals department, who then told us that we should not do this:

*Field notes extract: [Phoned HMRC] Was passed on to F, who initially told me client should EITHER make a new claim, OR appeal the old one. I explained that client wanted to do both, as new claim would reflect change of circumstances, but that she believes she should be entitled on basis of old circumstances as well. At this point the client was a bit shaken as she thought it was a choice between appealing or claiming from now on. She said if that was the choice, she would just claim from now on: 'I need the money—I don't want to wait and lose even more if appeal does not work'. I persisted with F, however, who agreed to note client wants to appeal in tandem with a new claim.*

This message came from the appeals department—from the section in HMRC that ought to have a sound grasp on the rules of procedure for appeals, and yet they misunderstood the basic access to justice issue at stake. In Sarah's case, it was surprising on the first occasion, but it was troubling for it to happen again in another case, with another decision-maker, soon afterwards. On raising this with the reflective focus group, the issue struck a chord with two of the participants:

I have had that. That was with tax credits appeals … When I spoke to them I did my best to put them right! But they were putting me off helping the client make an appeal, and you have to explain it to them.

I've had that. And I think that, and I think, well hang on … have [I] got it wrong! But I stand my ground then I go and check it!

In the face of strong pressure, advisers can be intimidated into doubting their own grasp of the relevant law or rules. My field notes from Sarah's case showed that I was unnerved by the attitude of the helpline adviser, and I did double check with the advice session supervisor that I was not doing 'more harm than good'. Concerns about wrong advice, and pre-empting appeals, were also evident in a case referred to the project for second-tier advice. The adviser was noted that a DWP helpline adviser was pressuring the client not to assert rights:

**Case Study: Julia**

This case was referred to me for second-tier advice. Julia was in her early twenties and was severely disabled (she was in a wheelchair and needed full time care). She had arrived with her step-father and brother in the UK over two years before the referral, to join her mother who was already working in the UK. The mother stopped work to care full time for Julia. Her step-father and brother worked full time to support the family. Julia had never worked but there were a number of possible family member routes to a right to reside for her.

Adviser notes: '*When I called to request a mandatory reconsideration for this case, the helpline advisor was reluctant to lodge it, insisting that 'if she has never worked then there*

> *is no way she can get employment support allowance'. The advisor was very insistent on this point and I feel that had the client or a family member called the helpline themselves, they would have been put off and wouldn't have lodged the mandatory reconsideration'.*

Here we see how it is not just the interpretations of *official* decision-makers that matter, in imposing their own interpretations before any claim has been made or evidence submitted, people answering official helplines become de facto decision-makers and act as gatekeepers to accessing rights. Once clients got past that hurdle, and actually submitted a claim, they next faced the difficulty of dealing with interpretations of the law that might have very little to do with legislation or case law.

## B.  Systematic Inaccuracy: 'We Don't Look at the Law'

One of the more startling moments of the project was when I spoke to a decision-maker on behalf of a client to challenge a particular decision, which was based on a straightforward mistake:

> **Case Study: Elena**
>
> The decision-maker had not taken account of the fact that the client, though separated, was still married to a migrant worker. I thought this was a fairly simple error, and so tried calling the decision-maker (who was a standard IS decision-maker, not on the EU decision-making team) to see if it could be easily resolved. I referred to the relevant ECJ case and the UK implementing legislation. I was told 'We don't look at the law. Just the guidance.' I suggested that the two were different and this was why the decision was wrong, and was told 'Well, if it goes to appeal, maybe our appeal section can look at the law.'

This suggests that the law is interpreted and recreated without reference to the text of the law. That approach elevates the status of the guidance to the law-in-effect, which in turn makes errors in the guidance more concerning. While the UK Upper Tribunal has made clear that the guidance cannot legitimately be used to alter the nature of EU law-based rights, it is bound to alter them when it is the only expression of those rights in use. I mentioned this incident to the reflective focus group, and one participant suggested it was an old problem:

> [laughing] Sadly, I remember being told that 20 years ago! We just look at the guidance. We don't look at the law … And I said, that's why you've made the wrong decision! … They really didn't have any idea, in a way, it hadn't really entered their minds, that the law and the guidance could be different. In a way, they treated it as though it was the law.

It is perhaps, therefore, not surprising that the process of interpretation of the law is affected by the poor knowledge and understanding of the legal materials and issues at play. The decision issued in Elsa's case was based on some quite glaring errors of law:

---

**Case Study: Elsa**

This case concerned an EU national who had been resident in the UK for over 14 years. She had a long and complicated work history, punctuated by periods of work-seeking and childcare. She had two school-aged children, one of which was a British citizen. Her homelessness application was refused in a decision that featured several errors of law: '*You were not working when either of the children entered into the UK, and you had not worked whilst either of your children have been in education in the UK* (Ibrahim/Teixiera *does not apply)*'. However, the relevant test is not whether she was working when her children entered the UK, or whether she was working while they were in school. The relevant test is set out in the Immigration (EEA Regulations); regulation 15A of the 2006 Regulations provides for a right to reside to a child who is the child of an EEA national who *resided* in the UK at the same time as the EEA national was a worker, and who was in education at the same time the EEA national parent was *resident* in the UK. Regulation 15A(4) then provides for a right to reside for the primary carer of a child with this kind of right to reside, where not to allow the primary carer to stay would mean that the child could not continue to pursue their education in the UK. The decision continued:

> In terms of you [sic] children being British, you are an EU citizen so you will not gain a retained right of residence because of them, as firstly their father lives here which enables them to remain. Also the cases Ibrahim, Teixeira and Zambrano do not apply as you are an EU citizen. Also they are not applicable as the father is British and even though that is an EU country these requirements only apply where the applicant's family member is exercising their EU rights which he is not as he is remaining in his country of origin.

It was difficult to know where to begin with spelling out the mistakes in this section. I started with '*the cases Ibrahim, Teixeira and Zambrano do not apply as you are an EU citizen.*' *Ibrahim* and *Teixeira* do apply when the parent is an EU citizen; indeed, they *only* apply when at least one of the parents is an EU citizen. As for '*you will not gain a retained right of residence because of them, as firstly their father lives here*', the fact of residence of a separated parent has no bearing on whether a *Teixeira* right is triggered. Moving on to '*they are not applicable as the father is British*'—neither the nationality of the absent parent or of the children is relevant for triggering a *Teixeira* right, which provides for a right of residence for the school-aged child of an EU national migrant worker or former migrant worker, and then also for that child's primary carer, all based on Article 12 Regulation 1612/68, and the child's right to access education 'under the best possible conditions'. What matters is that the children are the children of an EEA national who has exercised their right to reside as a migrant worker. The letter did acknowledge that the client was an EEA national who had completed periods of migrant work in the UK. I drafted a reply to the decision-maker outlining these arguments in a series of bullet points, and requesting a revision of the decision. The decision was duly revised within a few weeks and the client and her children were granted housing assistance.

Poor understanding of the law leads to flawed first instance decisions, such as failing to recognise *Teixeira*[8] rights or family member rights. Even when such rights are acknowledged, they might not hold sway. In one piece of evidence, discussed in chapter six, a decision-maker refused to give effect to *Teixeira* because of a mistaken belief that being a jobseeker discredits other possible rights to reside ('you cannot derive rights as her primary carer as long as you have another right to reside and this includes that of a jobseeker').[9] Lack of knowledge, and reliance upon incomplete, non-statutory instruments as though they are the law, speaks to basic training needs among decision-makers. As well as narrow interpretations of individual rights to reside, I encountered a failure to consider alternative avenues to a right to reside, even when presented with the evidence, and in some cases, even when presented with the explicit claim. The disregard for material factors, and confinement of decision-making to a restricted palette of issues, reflects the direction in which decision-makers have been told to travel. The fact that there are such training needs among decision-makers tells us something about the institutional commitment to getting things right for these claimants, and indicates a significant social justice gap.

## C. Administrative Regard to a Restricted Palette of Issues

Narrow guidance, a disinclination to 'look at the law', and a barrage of statutory messages about excluding EU nationals from benefits, combine with questioning tools focused on specific aspects of specific rights to reside to confine the discretion of first instance decision-makers. In some cases, it was clear that the possibility that a person might have permanent residence had not been considered, in others, it was dismissed cursorily without a detailed consideration of the evidence.

---

**Case Study: Irina**

The failure to take account of Irina's claim to permanent residence was strange. In the Secretary of State's response to our appeal of the income support decision, he noted (dates have been changed for anonymity purposes, but the periods are exactly the same):

*From the information provided, the following was established:*

*She is a [Greek] national and she originally came to the UK on 03/06/06;*

*She did not arrange any employment before coming here;*

*She has done some work since her arrival in the UK: Restaurant A 03/06/06 to 03/12/09; Restaurant B 03/01/10 to 03/01/11; Restaurant C 03/03/11 to 14/02/13 [after restaurant C she had claimed jobseeker's allowance for one month and then*

---

[8] Case C-480/08 *Maria Teixeira v London Borough of Lambeth and Secretary of State for the Home Department*, EU:C:2009:642.
[9] Evidence submission 3.

claimed income support on 20/03/13] ... *In this case, although [Irina] has lived in the UK for over five years, she has not yet acquired a right of permanent residence under regulation 15(1)(a) and (c) of the Immigration (EEC) Regulations 2006, as her departmental records do not reflect five continuous years in employment. Nor has she gained or retained Worker Status.*

This position was perplexing. There was no apparent basis for the last line, that she had not 'gained or retained worker status', given that there was no dispute about her periods of work, and no questions raised about whether that work was genuine and effective (in light of the lengths of time involved, and given that she had earned enough to support herself without claiming any benefits until falling out of work in February 2013). Nor is it clear why the phrase 'she has done some work' was used. The periods outlined by the Secretary of State constitute 77.5 months of work—well over the 60 months required for permanent residence. There were two breaks between jobs, but these were short: one of less than one month (a break that also included Christmas), and one of less than two months. During the first break, Irina had not claimed benefits (she secured her next job quickly and used her savings to tide her over) and during the second break, of less than two months, she had registered with the jobcentre and received jobseeker's allowance for a few weeks before finding her next job. Here are some excerpts from my submissions to the tribunal:

*The 'gap' from 04/12/09–02/01/10, during which [Irina] was workseeking, and indeed secured a job within weeks, should not be treated as a gap, as [Irina] retained worker status. This is notwithstanding not applying for jobseeker's allowance, as according to the Upper Tribunal in* VP v Secretary of State for Work and Pensions (JSA) *[2014] UKUT 32 (AAC); 'Periods of less than one month are covered under regulation 7(3) anyway, even if not certified'.*

*In order to be covered under 7(3)* [retention of worker status] *the recognised test for involuntary unemployment is whether the worker remained available to the labour market—see the Upper Tribunal decision in* MK v Secretary of State for Work and Pensions (IS) *[2013] UKUT 629 (AAC). [Irina] clearly did remain so available, given her swift finding of alternative employment.*

*During the gap from 04/01/11–02/03/11, [Irina] should be treated as retaining worker status as she registered as a jobseeker without undue delay. This test is outlined in MK and requires continued attachment to the labour market, through, for example, active job seeking. Again her genuine job search activities are evidenced by her swift finding of alternative employment.*

We could have added that the UK courts have already given a steer on how to treat separate periods of temporary work segmented with short periods of unemployment. In *NE v Secretary of State for Work and Pensions*, Judge Rowland held that where 'short periods of temporary work are not separated by longer periods of no work, it will often be appropriate to regard the person concerned as having become a worker rather than a workseeker'.[10] However, I did not encounter

---

[10] *NE v Secretary of State for Work and Pensions* [2009] UKUT 38 (AAC) (13 February 2009) 10 [9].

any case in the course of the project in which a first instance decision-maker had treated such periods as overall periods of work. Even when, as in Irina's case, the stretches of work were lengthy, in permanent jobs, with very few and very brief intervals between jobs, decision-makers treated this as discontinuous. As noted below, the DWP submissions at appeal stage on different possible rights to reside felt cursory to the point of complacence:

---

**Case Study: Back to Irina**

It was striking that the decision-makers did not enter into consideration of retained worker status even at appeal stage, simply stating that discontinuous employment disqualified her from a permanent residence claim. I was surprised when, at the outset of the hearing, the tribunal judge stated that the DWP had 'looked at this case very carefully and thoroughly'.[11] But the failure to explain why she was not considered to have permanent residence on the vague basis of not 'reflecting five continuous years of employment' was particularly inadequate because her periods of work were substantial and barely broken by short periods in which she had a clear claim to retain worker status. If the default is that discontinuous employment negates permanent residence claims, even in a case where the client's record—as accepted by the DWP—was really quite complete, then that approach will disproportionately create a detriment for people in low-status, insecure or casual jobs (people who are more likely to have a punctuated record and to move between jobs). HMRC's child benefit refusal had also revealed a failure to take account of a possible permanent right of residence; it stated:

> *To have the right to reside you must either be: lawfully working; self-employed; self-sufficient and comprehensively insured. By self-sufficient you must have the means to support yourself above the level of UK basic social assistance for the duration of your stay in the UK; and receiving a qualifying benefit, for example JSA. As none of the above applies to your circumstances, you do not have the right to reside in the UK and as such you are not entitled to child benefit for [Georgios].*

The letter did not even mention permanent residence as affording a possible right to reside. At the tribunal, the Secretary of State had not sent a representative. The judge accepted our two main arguments: first, that Irina had retained worker status since her last period of employment; and secondly, and most significantly, that '[Irina] has demonstrated that she has been a qualified person for a continuous period of five years'. Irina was able to present this decision to support her appeals on other benefits (which were retrospective only as she had already found work). This decision also gave her further protection if she should fall out of work in the future. But it should not take a tribunal ruling for such factors to be considered (or at least, it should not take a tribunal ruling at which a client has specialist representation). When I asked Irina how she would have felt representing herself, she responded: 'Oh my God! I couldn't do it—I couldn't say the things you said. I couldn't write the things. I don't know the laws and the rules. I didn't know about the five years'.[12] Her original appeal, which she had hand-written

---

[11] An observation made all the more surprising by the decision-maker having left '(delete as appropriate)' in the body of the decision.

[12] Field notes, immediately after the hearing.

before coming to Citizens Advice, expressed her confusion and sense of unfairness. That the gaps were barely gaps is reflected in her own representation: 'I have been living in the UK since 03/06/06 and always worked ... I don't understand why in your decision you wrote I do not have a right to reside in the UK'. The original decision had included irrelevant detail about reasons people might be excluded, and no explanation of the specific right to reside decision, and so she had not been able to engage with any particular point of law.

In other cases where workers had strings of short-term jobs, with workseeking in between, the overall periods seemed even less likely to be viewed as work, and the possibility of permanent residence did not seem to get any attention unless and until raised at appeal:

**Case Study: Alessandro**

This case was referred to me for second-tier advice, after the client had failed the genuine prospects of work test and been found not to have a right to reside. He had lived in the UK for seven years with a long, punctuated work history (12 periods of work were recorded, for 11 different employers). During eight of the intervening periods he had sought work, but not claimed benefits, having found work quickly. He had claimed jobseeker's allowance for two periods, and it was this second period that had ended with a genuine prospects of work test after six months. His history merited a careful assessment of whether he had accrued a right to permanent residence, but the decision-maker did not consider that, steering him straight down the genuine prospects of work test route instead. Because he had moved around a lot, he did not have payslips for all jobs and so evidence was a problem. We put together a challenge asserting that he should be deemed to have permanent residence, giving authority for how to address the perceived 'gaps' between his jobs.[13]

The failure of decision-makers to look at the possibility of permanent residence creates a substantial access to justice problem for claimants who do not even know that is a possible basis of challenge. It relates to deeper, and a more general problem, of a failure to identify the key relevant factors to eligibility, and making adverse decisions without having sought or considered relevant evidence. The next case highlighted a failure to consider permanent residence that might be attained through a family member's five years of continuous work:

---

[13]   The decision-maker reversed the decision as to a genuine prospects of work test without the case reaching a full appeal, so reinstating his JSA entitlement, but meaning we did not get a finding as to permanent residence.

---

**Case Study: Anton**

This was a case referred for second-tier advice. Anton was a 19-year-old college student, who had lived and studied in the UK since he was 11. He had arrived as the family member of an EU national migrant worker (a parent). The parent continued working in the UK for 'at least 6/7 years—possibly longer'.[14] She had a mental breakdown and left the UK. Anton was refused income support and housing benefit. The adviser noted that a charity was housing him: '[They] will let him keep his room despite the arrears but he's left with just £10 every two weeks from [a sibling]. He's been living off nothing for months now'. At the point of referral there had already been two further reconsiderations of the decision (so three decisions in total), all refusing benefits. But what was needed was an argument based on permanent residence derived from the mother's more-than five-year continuous period of work. I gave some advice on adducing the material details and presenting the case. This resulted in a relatively quick reversal of the decision, as the adviser reported to me:

*The DWP ended up agreeing to reconsider their decision for the third time and the decision was changed in the client's favour (permanent residency accepted and income support and housing benefit arrears paid in full). We ended up with three mandatory reconsideration notices but at least we didn't have to wait to go to appeal.*

---

Anton's case should never have taken four decisions to get to the point where a decision-maker noticed that he might have a permanent residence claim through his mother's work and permanent residence rights. Another case sent to the project, not for a referral but as evidence, reveals not only a failure to investigate, but an apparent refusal to countenance an explicit claim to permanent residence on the basis of a family member's status, and a placing of the responsibility to identify, assert and properly name the right to reside upon the claimant:

---

**Evidence Submission: Jean-Philippe**[15]

*Adviser notes: The benefit centre is also very reluctant to look at alt R2R [alternative right to reside] at the HRT [habitual residence test] for JSA so even when you demonstrate an alt R2R at the interview you're classified as a jobseeker. Therefore, having to do battle for housing benefit entitlement and being subject to a genuine prospect of work assessment when you've already demonstrated another R2R. I have made numerous complaints about this and only if you have time to doggedly pursue the case will they revise the decision. In their view, the client can just wait for the genuine prospects test to demonstrate it again and they seem to fail to understand why that outcome is not desirable. These aren't vague cases where someone asserts they have an alt R2R; for [Jean-Philippe's] HRT interview, I'd provided a detailed letter explaining his R2R and his birth certificate (under 21) and his father's HO (permanent residence card) etc. When I spoke to the DM on the phone about this case, she suggested it was because he hadn't used the word 'alternative right to reside' during the interview, which is just ridiculous.*

---

[14] Adviser notes as submitted.
[15] Evidence submitted, not referred for advice, submission 8.

Inaccurate decision-making seems to be a 'feature' of the system. It is made all the more inevitable by procedures and practices that encourage screening out other rights to reside, and a focus on the key priority of benefit restriction. The failure to explore claimants' different possible statuses speaks to a lowered sense of institutional responsibility for getting decisions right; when constructed as possible intruders upon our welfare state, EU nationals must bear the responsibility of refuting the presumption of unlawful residence. The next section explores the processes of decision-making that normalise poor administration, error and delay, and a refuse first, ask questions later approach.

### III.  NOT CARING ABOUT GETTING IT RIGHT: PROCEDURAL DEFICIENCY AND REDUCED INSTITUTIONAL EXPECTATIONS

In making cursory pronouncements on rights to reside, without feeling the need to substantiate them or to check other possible rights, decision-makers are constructing their role as reactive implementers of the restrictive intentions of policymakers. Where there are possible status gaps, they will be treated as gaps, rather than trigger investigations into the various possible explanations or exceptions. This approach of reactive implementation reflects a lowered sense of institutional responsibility for getting decisions right in the first place, and a shifting of responsibility upon the claimant at all stages of the process. It lends itself to an approach of refusing first, and only addressing questions of detail on appeal, and it is expressed in simple, small acts and omissions, like not saying sorry.

### A.  Refuse First, Ask Questions Later

> You apply, you get back a decision. But if there is any 'weirdness' in the case the answer will be no.[16]

> If they need to clarify, you know, further information and evidence they should ask for that, rather than just making the decision that you're not entitled, [and then] sending that notice to the claimant, who probably doesn't understand at all what it is that they've failed to establish![17]

We saw the poor, almost automatic reasoning in Irina's case—a blank statement that she had not gained or retained worker status, despite the notice having acknowledged evidence to the contrary, and not having advanced any explanation. Sarah's case also appeared to be one of refusal-by-default, as HMRC had refused the claim for child benefit without first seeking the necessary information from Portugal, and only sought that information on receipt of her appeal. A number of advisers referring cases to the *EU Rights Project* mentioned that

---

[16] Expert interview 2.
[17] Expert interview 1.

their case had 'gone to Wick' (the remote outpost—see the image below—at which the EU specialist decision-making team has its postal address) only after a mandatory reconsideration had been requested:[18]

**Figure 1: The remote EU decision-making team location of Wick**

---

[18] In the case studies of Rina, Tulio and Julia.

It was not until a refusal was contested that an expert decision-maker was consulted. In Julia's case (summarised next), the adviser noted that she had spoken with the EU decision-making team to contest a refusal of employment support allowance because the decision-maker had failed to take account of Julia's family member status. She was told that the guidance deemed it irrelevant, and it was only once the decision was formally contested, and it 'went to Wick', that this avenue might be considered:

---

**Case Study: Julia**

Julia was an EU national in her early twenties and was severely disabled (she was in a wheelchair and needed full-time care). She had arrived with her EU national stepfather and brother in the UK over two years before the referral, to join her mother who was already working in the UK. The mother stopped work to care full-time for Julia. Her stepfather and brother worked full-time to support the family. Julia was refused employment support allowance. The adviser stated: 'It seems very unfair that [Julia] should be excluded from this benefit—all her family are here in the UK and she is dependent on them for her care needs'. In correspondence with the adviser, I suggested putting together a case based on her status as an 'extended family member' of her brother, under regulation 8(2) of the Immigration (EEA) Regulations 2006, since she was a relative, he was a worker, she was a member of the household, if there was evidence of 'dependence' upon him. The adviser phoned the decision-maker to ask for a reconsideration on this basis.

*Adviser notes: I have verbally asked the DWP EU decision-making department to consider whether she can derive rights from her brother but the decision-maker I spoke with said his guidance book stated that this is not possible. He has now referred the case to Wick and advised they will spend a couple of months looking at it and then give their response.*

---

Again, we had a decision-maker confining himself to the decision-maker guidance, and departure from the guidance, and referral to the law, only being possible once a case is subject to a mandatory reconsideration request and sent for specialist decision-making. Refusing a benefit before seeking necessary information is problematic for a number of reasons: not only does it create significant hurdles for EU nationals, in the form of appeals through which many will choose not to go, but it can also put them off applying in the first place. Oskar's case showed how stressful the process can be, and how that can have a chilling effect on the later exercise of rights:

---

**Case Study: Oskar**

This case was a first-hand case in the *EU Rights Project*. Oskar had been in the UK for six years; after more than two years of working full-time he had a stroke, which left him permanently incapable of work. This meant he should have attained permanent residence under Article 17(1)(b) of Directive 2004/38, which provides for permanent residence rights for those who have resided and worked for more than two years and then become permanently incapable of work. This was given effect in UK law[19] which provided for permanent residence for 'a worker or self-employed person who has ceased activity',[20] having terminated their work as a result of permanent incapacity and who has resided in the UK for at least two years.[21] He had been refused ESA initially, though he had had support from a charity and successfully appealed it. When I saw him, we talked about applying for personal independence payment, and he was worried about doing so, because he was nervous that decision-makers might query his employment support allowance award.

*Field notes: Explained possibility of applying for personal independence payment, client very nervous about it, worried a negative decision would affect his employment support allowance claim. Said 'The last time, it was very difficult … It was hard, it was a fight. But the person who helped me was very good, he helped and we got it finally.' He said: 'I will be OK without, I can manage, is just worry about the money we need for my son, it's not about me.' Said 'It is all too much. Too much stress. Too many things to think about … I need to just do one at a time. I don't, don't feel I can.'*

A quickness on the part of decision-makers to refuse first and ask questions later (if there is an appeal) can make even an initial application unattractive, especially where clients are worried that new applications will lead to reconsiderations of awarded benefits, as in Oskar's case. Moreover, for clients surviving on minimal income, a refusal screens them out of possible claims for short-term benefit advances (available where a decision has not yet been made on a DWP administered benefit, if it seems likely the conditions will be satisfied, and the claimant is in financial need).[22] They are not available if an adverse decision has been made and an appeal is underway.[23] One expert commented in interview that 'effectively no EU national client … ever gets a short-term advance'.[24]

An assessment that only seeks relevant information after a refusal has been contested is procedurally deficient. To a degree, it seemed that this deficiency was a feature of the system, not only because first instance decision-makers were reliant upon incomplete guidance, but because the information gathering tools were incomplete. For example, the genuine prospects of work test questionnaire gathers information on a 'limited palette of issues', and in Elena's case, it seemed that the decision-maker did not have the facility to record her marital status as 'separated but still married':

---

[19] reg 15(1)(c) of the Immigration (EEA) Regulations 2006 (the regulations in effect at the time).
[20] As defined in reg 5(3)(a) and (b)(i).
[21] In the Immigration (European Economic Area) Regulations 2016, the relevant provisions are regs 15(1)(c) and 5(3)(a).
[22] Social Security (Payments on Account of Benefit) Regulations 2013, SI 2013/383.
[23] ibid, reg 4(2).
[24] Expert interview 2.

---

**Case Study: Elena**

The failure of the decision-maker to ask whether Elena was married had significant results. She also had a possible permanent residence claim, having worked in a series of consecutive temporary jobs for four years, followed by two years in a permanent job, followed by another one and half years in casual work. She had completed the required 12 months of registered work at the outset, as required by the worker registration scheme rules, as an A8 national, and this was not disputed by the Secretary of State for Work and Pensions at any point. But on separation from her abusive husband she was found not to have a right to reside. She was refused housing assistance, even though she had primary care of a young child. We made an application for income support and emphasised the basis of Elena's claim as the spouse of a migrant worker.

*Field notes: Spoke to S at the contact centre. [Elena] made the application over the phone. I spoke to S afterwards to stress we believe she should be entitled as the family member of a migrant worker (her husband).*

The application, after some delay and a lost claim,[25] was refused.

*Field notes: Read through income support refusal letter. It states that there was not sufficient evidence to find a right to reside derived from her 'estranged partner'. [Elena] is still married, she does have a marriage certificate ... Phoned the number on the refusal letter—explained that client is the spouse of a migrant worker. Woman I spoke to said 'but they've separated' and that she didn't see what difference it made if they were married. Explained that did not matter—she was entitled to a right to reside as the spouse of a migrant worker. I was told 'We don't look at the law, just the guidance'. Was told that if appealed, the appeals section would maybe look at the law. She said it was unlikely a DM would change without an MR [mandatory reconsideration]—but said she would ask DM to phone me back. Could take some hours.*

I also asked for a call from the EU Decision-Making team, since I did not have the means to contact them.

*Field notes: Phone call received from EU DM in response to contact. She said that JCP was not aware that client was married. She agreed that being married to an EU worker meant that client is eligible to income support. She said that client would need to provide evidence.*

It seems that the problem arose because, in spite of our emphasising that Elena's marriage to a migrant worker was the basis of her claim, the decision-maker, using the drop down menu for 'marital or civil partnership status' had recorded 'separated'. It was not clear whether there actually was an option for 'separated but still married'.

---

Poor evidence-gathering and inadequate guidance contribute to a procedurally problematic refuse-first approach. The area of EU law-based rights to benefits is unusual in this respect: the mandatory reconsideration/appeals procedure is normally an opportunity to review the decision about the facts of the case (whether

---

[25] See the section below on administrative error.

someone is sufficiently incapable of work for benefit, on the basis of medical evidence, for instance). In the context of EU law, it is in many cases the stage at which the first principles of a claim are established. Administrative justice is, in such cases, deferred to the second stage, which for many claimants, will mean that it is never realised at all. One participant in the preparatory focus group noted that clients might not know to pursue claims once they had received a refusal. Some might make fresh claims if they later receive advice and support, albeit too late to actually appeal an original flawed decision:

> I've had two where they've been turned down for separate benefits and they haven't pursued it, and it's over a year later they try again with our help, that it makes you wonder how many people have been ... have tried, been turned down for all sorts of benefits.

The same participant noted that people without advice were less likely to challenge refusals, and that it was often a significant life change that led to advice ever being sought:

> It's often pregnancy or having a child that prompts EU migrants to actually access advice. Whereas if that same client had not been expecting or having a baby, or had a baby, then how long would they have gone on not claiming the benefits they were entitled to.

It is not appropriate to treat a refusal as something EU nationals should just go through in order to access a decision that will take account the first principles of their benefit eligibility, because those refusals are taken seriously and at face value. If we return to Stanislaw's case, explored in chapter seven in relation to benefit exportation, we received first instance refusals (or stoppages) of all benefits claimed, on grounds that did not take account of the first principles of eligibility. It was not only personal independence payment that was refused at first instance, on the grounds of not being resident. The family's child benefit and child tax credit were stopped once it was clear they had been out of the country for more than a few weeks, and Stanislaw's later claims for bereavement payment and widowed parent's allowance were also refused. We contested each of these decisions, and each one was reversed without having to go to a formal appeal, so it should have been possible for the decision-makers to make the right decision first time. What was needed was an identification of the circumstances under which claims with a cross border element would be permissible (that is, the first principles of eligibility, and a decision on that basis or, if the decision-maker felt that more information was needed, to seek that information out, rather than to refuse by default).

A process that only takes account of legal grounds for eligibility, and/or seeks information to establish whether those grounds exist, after an initial refusal, would be deficient, and an obstacle to justice and that would be the case even if everything went smoothly in the application/refusal/appeals cycle. As it is, the extra layer—of contesting a refusal—is the more onerous because for some cases, each stage is fraught with administrative errors, and in the cases I saw, the presumption was that it was the client's responsibility to put things right by sending evidence again, or by submitting new claims, and so on.

## B. Claimants Bear the Brunt of Administrative Errors

Elena's case was a disturbing example of how a claim with a fairly straightforward basis could be made complicated and protracted by administrative error. It was a good example of the expectation that the claimant can 'make good' on the errors of the DWP, because I had witnessed and taken part in the original application over the phone from the Citizens Advice office, yet the application went missing from DWP's records, and after significant delay it was simply up to the claimant to start the process again:

---

**Case Study: Elena**

Elena's case was fraught with obstacles, one of which was the contact centre apparently misplacing her claim.

*Field notes: Spoke to S at the contact centre. She made the income support application over the phone. I spoke to S afterwards to stress we believe she should be entitled as the family member of a migrant worker (her husband). Phone call took approximately 45 mins: 'She should receive a statement in the post, she should check and complete it, and sign and send it back. The statement may also include requests for further info'.*

Twenty days later she had not received any such statement and so contacted the income support department.

*Field notes: She had not received the statement … and rang the helpline to find out what has happened. The call centre denied any knowledge of her claim … The client rang J at the Contact Centre from the bureau. She told the client that as she had not received the statement within four working days of the claim she would need to reapply. No explanation was given as to why her claim had gone missing. Client rang income support and spoke to C to make a new claim. Client was told the statement should be sent out today and she should receive it next week.*

The client received a refusal, and we lodged a request for mandatory reconsideration. 30 days after making the second claim, we received a phone call from the EU Decision-Making team:

> *EU DM [EU decision-maker] said that an internal email had earlier been sent to establish whether relevant evidence was already held on the DWP system but that none had been established. She said that the record showed that client's claim … had not been received by her. EU DM said that client should start the process again and produce the necessary evidence. She agreed to get back in touch with bureau should she discover that DWP already has evidence on record. She did not refer to mandatory reconsideration.*

---

We faced the prospect of a third application, due to the loss of the client's application and subsequent loss of client's evidence. The failure to offer explanations or apologies, and the assumption that the client was responsible for putting things right, all pointed to a failure to acknowledge departmental responsibility for errors. Another example of this kind of error was the loss of identity documents:

---

**Case Study: Johannes**

This was a first-hand case study. Johannes came into the Citizens Advice office for help because he needed his child's identity documents back. He had sent the birth certificate to the child tax credit office, and they had not yet returned it. He had sent the child's identity card to the child benefit office, but they had said they did not have it.

*Field notes: Phoned child benefit to ask about child's ID. Told the case 'was closed' yesterday, but there were no notes on file regarding the document; call back number was taken, adviser said she would look into it and get back to me within about 25 mins.*

Johannes then received a request from the child benefit office for the child's birth certificate.

*Field notes: Client cannot send original birth certificate, as tax credits still have this (as they also have the P60) from the original application. Client does have a copy of the birth certificate issued in Estonia, but does not want to send this (he needs it for passport application, and also says tax credits already have the original). Explained on the form that tax credits have the birth certificate, and child benefit office were sent ID card and do not know where it is.*

---

Missing identity documents, lost applications and missing evidence, all created extra burdens for claimants who had to deal with the losses and, where relevant, submit further applications and repeatedly submit evidence. These errors also contributed to what is possibly the most substantial and commonplace administrative obstacle faced by EU nationals—that of delay.

## C.  Normalising Delay

Delay for many is tantamount to a refusal without a right of appeal, because if you have an adverse decision you do at least have the opportunity to appeal it. As one national welfare specialist put it in interview, 'the really awful thing is, once they get a decision saying no, they maybe get advice and can go somewhere, but advisers are really bad at dealing with delay'.[26] There is an institutional acceptance of delay in these cases, evident in the difference in targets for national compared to international claimants. The target claim-processing time is four times as long for

---

[26] Expert interview 2.

international claimants (an average of 92 days, whereas for national claimants, an average of 22 days)[27] and because they are only 'averages' they permit significant deviations. Delays could be exceptionally protracted and could result in a total loss of access to justice, since the claimant in question may have been effectively forced to leave the UK in the interim, then dropping the case.

Throughout the project, clients and advisers encountered delays at each point in the claims/decision/reconsideration/appeals processes. Sarah's case, explored in chapter seven on resisting competence and the impossibility of claiming provisional payments, was an example of extreme delay. There had been an enormous wait to get a decision in the first place, which was a refusal, and it transpired that during this period of time the UK had not communicated with the other relevant Member State (Portugal):

---

**Case Study: Sarah**

When I started advising Sarah, she had been waiting for over a year without child benefits. It was almost another full year before her claim was resolved, without HMRC budging at any point on their rules excluding her from provisional payments. Nine months after I began work on the case, we issued a letter before action, indicating that we were considering judicial review, and copied this to the treasury solicitor. It was the solicitor who got back in touch with us, to let us know that their client (HMRC) had 'taken the time to review' Sarah's position and that CB was going to be paid in full for the entire period at issue.

---

Delay causes real and avoidable hardship. One focus group participant said that advising EU national clients involved 'prepping them for the nightmare process that will take months'.[28] One focus group participant noted: 'We're often at the end of our tether when we get to someone, let alone somebody who has got no money and no way to put food on the table for their families and children, and have been put off and put off'.[29] An informant submitted a précis of a case that, like Sarah's, involved the UK seeking further information from another Member State, but HMRC would not tell her what information was sought. The adviser noted that HMRC had said they 'would not process her claim until they have it' and no mention was made of provisional payments. 'Meanwhile' the adviser reported, 'she is struggling on very little money'.[30] One of the national specialists interviewed also picked up on the problem of delay when the UK contacts other Member States: 'There are ongoing issues about family benefits and children in another Member

---

[27] HMRC 'Single Departmental Plan 2015–2020', *Corporate Report* (updated February 2017), 2.2 ('How HMRC is doing'). Available at: www.gov.uk/government/publications/hmrc-single-departmental-plan-2015-to-2020/single-departmental-plan-2015-to-2020.

[28] Preparatory focus group.

[29] Reflective focus group.

[30] Evidence submitted, not referred for advice, evidence submission 6.

State … and it's partly that's just massive delays … Some of them it's literally been years.'[31]

Some focus group participants expressed frustration at the lack of urgency with which different stages of claims were addressed; rather than 'refusing first, asking questions later', in some cases it is instead, 'delay first, ask questions later':

> The client gets a letter saying 'thank you for your claim, please don't contact us for 16 weeks, we will contact you when we need something'. So they're already waiting for more than three months, for HMRC—whether it's the child benefit office or the tax credits office—to come back to them and say, we need your passport, we need this, we need this, so there seems to be initial three months acceptable delay before they even start looking at what they need.[32]

While delays in looking at applications, in reaching decisions, and in obtaining information from other Member States were all predictable at the outset of the project, one source of delay I had not expected was the slowness of HMRC in some cases to do anything with an appeal once they had received it (neither revisiting the decision, nor submitting it to a tribunal for a hearing). Advisers in this situation can feel a bit stuck and some do not know that the First-tier Tribunal does have case management powers that include the capacity to direct HMRC or DWP to send an appeal they have received to the tribunal.[33] In one case I advised calling upon the tribunal to exercise these powers, but this was not straightforward:

---

**Case Study: Karina**

This client, in a case referred for second-tier advice, was contesting the stopping of a tax credit award, and contesting HMRC's finding that there had been a substantial overpayment, for which they were seeking recovery. Nothing had been done with her appeal for four months when her adviser contacted the First-tier Tribunal, to request that a judge issue directions to HMRC to submit the appeal for listing. The client was deeply distressed about it, and the delay compounded the stress. The request had been received by a clerk to the tribunal, who it seemed was unaware of the tribunal's case management powers in this respect.

*Primary adviser's notes: We appealed the tax credit decision … We wrote a complaint letter [four months later] about the delay in producing a submission [to the tribunal]. There was no response. A second complaint was made [a month after that] in which we explained that we would ask [the] tribunal to send directions to tax credits to produce a submission. We wrote to [the] tribunal … when we contacted them a few weeks later to find out if our request was accepted, we were told by A from the switchboard that they never heard [of] this procedure. We received a letter from tribunal saying they could not approach the agency about an appeal that they know nothing about.*

---

[31] Expert interview 1.
[32] Reflective focus group.
[33] See *FH v Manchester City Council* (HB) [2010] UKUT 43 (AAC) and *Social Security Decision* R(H) 1/07.

This unofficial gatekeeping was problematic. A representative of the tribunal was expressing a basic misunderstanding of the tribunal's powers, and limiting the tribunal's actions accordingly. We drafted letters before action, both to the Tax Credits office to expedite their sending the appeal to the tribunal, and also the tribunal itself, requiring it to exercise its powers and also requiring the letter to be placed before a judge. We further required assurance that the First-tier Tribunal would 'review their procedures for responding to delayed submissions from public authorities where such delay prevents a claimant's case being heard'.[34] I aired this experience with the reflective focus group. To them it was a familiar story:

> Facilitator: Another thing that I've come across ... are people who've submitted their appeals and it's not transpired into anything because HMRC ... sit on it, rather than submitting it to the First-tier Tribunal.
>
> C: That's all of our appeals.
>
> Facilitator: Really?
>
> C: The lot.
>
> D: I reckon I've had about a hundred.

One participant noted the difficulty she had persuading the tribunal to exercise its powers in this way:

> That's what I had, took me three goes! On the very first one I did, three goes! And then my colleague gave me an email address, so I emailed it to them, in great big letters—'for the attention of the duty judge'—and I got a response then, and after that, the other two they've just done it. So you do need to keep pushing and pushing to get them to accept it, but that's another social policy issue. In that goes to admin, they see that there's no appeal there so they just go away. I've had three letters saying, sorry no client record. And that's all they said.[35]

Gatekeeping here obstructs justice not only by contributing to delay, but also by insulating law, policy and practice from challenge. The next section explores in more detail the means by which decision-makers (including where acts of gatekeeping make people de facto self-appointed decision-makers) can create a cocoon around the decision-making processes (for example, through obstructing communications, and/or acting without due transparency, to render the process less accessible to claimants and less susceptible to challenge).

## IV. STOPPING CLAIMANTS PUTTING IT RIGHT: SYSTEMIC INSULATION OF LAW AND PRACTICE

Decision-makers operate within systems that help mould the law—or stop it being remoulded—by insulating it from challenge through practices that render

---

[34] Letter before action, Karina's case study.
[35] Reflective focus group.

the decision-making process opaque and remote from the claimants and their advisers. Communication difficulties proved a significant shielding factor for policy and practice, as we struggled to get through automated helplines, to get interpretation, or to speak to (or otherwise contact) decision-makers, making them less accountable. In some cases, decision-makers in different departments had no easy means of contacting each other.

## A. Obstacles to Communication: Language, Accents and Automated Helplines

In some cases, communication difficulties arose from a failure to provide adequate interpretation, as in Oskar's case, in which we were offered an interpreter but one failed to materialise:

---

**Case Study: Oskar**

First-hand *EU Rights Project* client. Oskar was disabled following a stroke that had rendered him incapable of work. He was very anxious (his word) and was conscious of the extra difficulties he had in making himself understood in English. He had not wanted to pursue a personal independence payment on our first meeting, but asked after a few meetings whether he could make a claim.

*Field notes: Rang payments line, on hold for while. Got through and asked for interpreter. On hold. Then got cut off. Rang again, client concerned about time, so decided he didn't want interpreter, so began claim with adviser. I acted as interlocutor, where client wanted some things explaining, or the helpline adviser needed things repeating. There were a few points where the client said he didn't understand but adviser not obviously noticing. However, at points of declaration and statement of terms it was clear that the client needed these rephrasing.*

---

Absence of interpretation can lead to lengthy delays. People claiming employment and support allowance are initially placed on the 'assessment rate' of the benefit, which is lower than the full rate, for a maximum of three months, after which an assessment takes place, and if the client is deemed entitled to the benefit, they then get the full rate.[36] But this depends on an assessment taking place in the appropriate timescale which, for some clients, depends on interpretation being arranged and actually being provided (and being provided in the right language):

---

[36] At the time of writing the assessment rate for over-25s is £73.10 per week, compared to £102.15 if in the work-related activity group, or £109.30 in the support group.

---

**Case Study: Michal**[37]

This case was submitted as evidence, not referred for advice. Due to repeated DWP failures to secure interpretation for an assessment, Michal was instead on the assessment rate for 16 months.

*Adviser notes: [Michal] has been on the assessment rate of employment and support allowance for 16 months … The delay in having his WCA [work capability assessment, to determine whether the claimant meets the medical conditions for his entitlement] is due to [assessors] not arranging interpreters. He has had numerous appointments but they have all been cancelled in advance due to not having an interpreter available or sometimes he has arrived for his appointment and they have provided an interpreter for the wrong language so they were unable to conduct the assessment. On one occasion, he attended the appointment but the interpreter was not there so the assessment could not take place. He then received a letter asking why he had not attended the appointment and the threat of a sanction if he did not reply by the deadline.*

---

Language, and even just accent, proved a considerable hurdle for clients trying to navigate their way through the HMRC automated helpline. Johannes had not managed to get through to speak to someone, and had given up and come to the Citizens Advice office to ask someone else to make the call for him. As a native English speaker with no heavy accent,[38] I struggled to navigate my way through the automated helpline in Johannes's case:

---

**Case Study: Johannes**

This was a first-hand *EU Rights Project* case. We were trying to get through to both the child benefit office and tax credit office to address information requests they had sent, and to chase up documents that had gone missing once sent to them.

*Field notes: Automated answer machine—had to go through eight questions, with several repeats, client made clear he had found it difficult, as his accent was poorly understood when he tried, and it gave no opportunity to rephrase or ask to rephrase. He had got stuck at same point, repeating, getting nowhere then being cut off. The last question for us [with me answering] was a cut-off question without warning—was asked whether the claim was made less than/more than five weeks ago. As there was a follow-up claim, we said 'less than' and the automated response was 'we can't deal with queries if claim made less than five weeks ago, thank you for calling' then we were cut off. This was despite the fact we were calling in response to their request for information. To get through we then went through the process again, answered the final question as 'more than' on the basis of the original date of the first claim.*

---

[37] Evidence submission 9.
[38] One colleague termed my accent 'generic mild Northern'.

I kept on having difficulties with automated helplines in other cases. In Irina's case, the helpline did not understand my saying the words 'child benefit' and we cycled round four times before getting through:

---

**Case Study: Irina**

On trying to contact HMRC to lodge Irina's appeals and to make new claims on the basis of Irina having started work, I encountered a problem with the automated helpline.

*Field notes: Phoned HMRC about child benefit, to explain client still wanted to appeal refusal [for period since initial decision] as well as making new claim. Difficult to get put through to correct person due to automated response—supposed to use a few words. Machine kept asking if it was about a 'tax credit decision'—when I said no, it cycled back to the start. It eventually recognised 'child benefit'—over five minutes since first asking.*

---

Although we did eventually get through, the fact that I had had to repeat myself four times did not inspire confidence. Clients acting on their own behalf might not be so persistent, or even if they were, might not get through at all if they are prevented by their accent or language difficulties. It was not just the HMRC helpline that was an obstacle in this sense, in Elena's case, the income support automated system hung up on me:

---

**Case Study: Elena**

This client was in distress—she had just separated from an abusive husband and had been told she and her small child would be made homeless as a result of the DWP's right to reside decision. We were trying to contact income support to put this right.

*Field notes: Made phone call with her to income support claim line, first call, went through the automated system. We then got the on hold, then message. After some time, we got the recorded message that 'the other person has hung up'. Rang again, got stuck in the system this time—it could not understand me when I gave the postcode—third time, it gave up and put us on hold.*

---

Participants in the reflective focus group also reported considerable difficulty in navigating the automated helplines, and noted that an inability to get through, to communicate a change of circumstances for instance, could result in severe consequences for the clients:

> You end up pronouncing everything out ... And my client could not have done that ... but in this case it was reporting a change of circumstances for tax credits. If she'd had given up and not been able to get through, she would have had a massive overpayment,

she may have even been investigated for fraud … so to me, it was, although it's a helpline and it seems very small in the big grand scheme of things, this was an enormous barrier that I immediately saw for my clients.

[Those] same clients are actually the least likely to be able to write well enough in English, that they could write in a change of circumstances. They may actually speak quite good English, but maybe with very strong accents which means that they can't get through it, but that doesn't mean they can write in good enough English to be able to communicate a change in circumstances effectively. So using the telephone is very helpful to them, but only if they can get through.

Another participant in the same focus group noted the problem that the helplines do not have 'safety nets', in the form of a fall-back option to speak to someone: 'there wasn't even anything saying if you're having difficulties please hold and we'll put you through to someone'.

### B. Obstacles to Communication: Departments Who Will Not Speak to Us

At a number of points, I was frustrated by refusals on the part of decision-makers to give out numbers—this happened even when they called and I was not present to take the call. An advice supervisor would speak to them and ask how I could get back in contact. If they refused to give a number it added considerable delay to the case.[39] It also added to the sense that decision-making was somewhat opaque and remote. Mandatory reconsiderations with an EU dimension typically went to the EU decision-making team in Wick (see above). Given that the team did not routinely provide phone numbers, email addresses, or fax numbers, its geographic location seemed symbolically remote. One focus group participant said that she had had difficulty getting the Wick team to share phone numbers, noting that they never put them on their letters and exclaiming 'there was no way you get in touch with Wick … it was like trying to get in touch with God'.[40] Another argued that the combination of distant decision-making machinery she could not contact, with things going missing and information not being recorded, together created a Kafkaesque system: 'you almost feel, you know, if you were a great fan of Kafka, you would feel it was a kind of system that was built up in order to produce those sort of outcomes'.[41]

Offices that are difficult to contact are one thing, but I experienced a rather new level of remote decision-making when the exportability team seemed to vanish. As examined above in chapters two and seven, EU law sets clear requirements for social security benefits to be exportable. As such, in Stanislaw's case, we wanted to make it clear from the outset that he and his wife were claiming under the

---

[39] As happened in Stanislaw's case when someone from the child benefit office rang me when I was not in the Citizens Advice office, but would not leave a number for me to call back.
[40] Preparatory focus group.
[41] Preparatory focus group.

exportability rules: we were keen to avoid mistaken refusals leading to appeals as there was extra time pressure on the family. Stanislaw was in Hungary, with his terminally ill wife, who was on maternity leave. They were both still employed in the UK and so needed to make cross-border claims for benefits. The government web page on exporting the relevant benefits suggested that we contact the 'exportability team'. We did not have much success in establishing whether such a team in fact existed:

---

**Case Study: Stanislaw**

In attempting to follow government guidance on claiming exportable benefits, we were sent round in a loop on an automated helpline, and found that the advertised email address for the 'exportability team' had been taken out of service:

*Field Notes: Gave client details for making personal independence payments claim, and also details about contacting the exportability team. Offered to draft initial email, to send to client who can then send it on, though personal independence payments team would then be dealing with him … Email from client saying the email address for the exportability team was wrong. Checked by sending an email myself; received message saying the email address was out of service. Looked up exportability team; phoned the number. Got sent round in a loop on automated line—if phoning about PIP told to phone other number—general PIP claim number. No other option—hung up and went round the loop again until chose an option that led to a 'speak to an adviser' option.*

*Spoke to P who gave me the same exportability email address. I said that we had already used it and it hadn't worked. He tried it out, and received an auto message and agreed that it said the address was defunct. He seemed surprised and confused—said it must have only just happened. Went on hold—he spoke to colleagues, who confirmed email address had disappeared but that there was no replacement or forwarding address. I asked if there was any way to speak to the exportability team, explaining that the DWP website states if claiming PIP from abroad should speak to them, and also adding that there is a 'contact that exportability team' web page. P said I should phone that number—I explained that was the number I had phoned, and was now speaking to him. He said they did not have any internal transfer numbers to the exportability team. The only advice I was given was for the client to phone the general PIP claims line from abroad, even though this meant the client making the claim himself without advice or support. P apologised for this and said he would raise the issue as a complaint.*

I spoke to the client after he had made an application over the phone.

*Field notes: It sounds as though he had a medical interview over the phone, and that in spite of his inability to speak English, no [Hungarian] interpretation was provided. He has heard nothing since.*

The person answering the number given for the 'exportability team' had suggested we try ringing it because he did not know that he was the person answering that number. No one in his office had an explanation for the disappearing email address or an alternative mode of contact for the exportability team. Moreover, the people answering the number given for the exportability team had no internal number for contacting the exportability team themselves. As a result we were faced with the extremely difficult situation of a client having to make an application himself over the phone from a different country without an adviser or other support present. We had further communication difficulties when trying to deal with the family's child benefit and child tax credit claims, which had been stopped while they were out of the UK.

*Field notes: Made phone call, to HMRC re child tax credit and child benefit, but after being sent round the automated loop got kicked off as line too busy ... Client not heard anything back ... Phoned to chase it up. 10 mins on hold, then decided instead to write to them again ...*

When the client returned to the UK, some time after his wife had died, he had with him a mandatory reconsideration letter, that it turned out had been sent to him in Hungary, instead of to us as his representatives. This had caused a significant delay, and meant that we were in theory slightly out of time to appeal.

*Field notes: Had to submit an appeal for tax credits late as the [mandatory reconsideration] letter was sent directly to client in [Hungary]—delaying its arrival, and inevitably delaying how it would be dealt with. Have requested that our appeal be treated as in time, as [mandatory reconsideration] should have been sent or copied to us, since we submitted the request on behalf of client.*

While it was frustrating that we could not get in touch with the exportability team, it seemed farcical that those people answering the telephone number associated with the exportability team had no means of contacting them either. The failure to have adequate communications between different branches of the same decision-making process was another common communication failure.

## C. Obstacles to Communication: Departments That Cannot Speak to Each Other

In several cases, the decision-making process involved a series of parties (for example, Job Centre Plus, the income support decision-making team, and the EU decision-making team). Each branch seemed strangely separated from the others: they did not have internal numbers to contact each other or email addresses or fax numbers. It should be noted that the habitual residence questionnaire that first-instance decision-makers use includes the option 'refer to EU Team Wick' and a box to click to 'email Wick EU Team',[42] but given we were told the offices were totally separate and email was not possible, it seems this option is not used, and does not provide decision-makers with an actual email address for other, later

---

[42] Habitual residence questionnaire, obtained on request from the EU decision-making team.

uses. Nor did they have a linked-up electronic system for client case records, so that when a client submitted evidence to Job Centre Plus, it would not show up on the EU decision-making team's electronic records. Instead it had to be sent through the internal mail to reach other decision-makers. We were told that the internal mail could be 'a lot' slower than normal post:

---

**Case Study: Elena**

We hit something of an administrative wall in trying to put things right in Elena's case, due to different branches of the decision-making process not sharing information and apparently not having any means to speak to each other:

*Field notes: Phoned adviser-only numbers for income support claims and appeals, both [numbers] disconnected. Phoned standard existing enquiries line … spoke to C on team X. He said there were no notes on the system of the conversation I had had with the EU decision-maker. I was told that that office is 'totally separate'—they do not have access to the notes file so they cannot update them. I asked if I could speak to the EU decision-maker. I was told they cannot connect to 'that office'. So have requested a call back—which will be from an income support decision-maker—and I will have to ask that person to put in a request for a call back from [Betty] or someone in the European decision-making team. We need to ascertain whether the current claim is being processed: whether they have acknowledged that she has a right to reside; whether the copy of marriage certificate taken has been accepted/put on file; or whether client's case is subject to the normal mandatory reconsideration process—and in either case how long it will take.*

Each time Elena was asked to resubmit evidence, she did so. Under pressure from the decision-makers, she even made contact with her abusive husband to ask him to submit the necessary evidence of his earnings, which he did. But the dislocation between the Job Centre, the income support team, and the EU decision-making team, seemed to delay things further, especially in terms of amassing her submissions. The EU decision-maker was rather sanguine about this, noting that the transmission systems were slow and things came to her in 'dribs and drabs'.

*Field notes: Client phoned, said she tried to make appointment with Job Centre Plus, phoned national line, received call back. Was told she did not need to come in, as they had already taken her marriage certificate copy and sent it. Her husband went into his local Job Centre Plus, spoke with A. Presented passport and payslips, explained for client's claim, wrote down her name and national insurance number. They took copies, said they would be faxed, and would not take long, and signed the receipt I'd written for him to take. Client received call from income support two days later saying they had still not received any further details. Phoned EU decision-maker, explained client and husband had presented everything. She said there were no updates on the system, apart from a mention of documents. She said she thought they would be in transit—as the internal mail can be very slow, and is slower than Royal Mail. Them not having arrived by now would 'not be exceptional'. Said 'things come in in dribs and drabs'. And also added that they may have been sent directly to income support but income support know she is waiting for them.*

> On complaining about the length of time the process was taking, and hardship being caused, the decision-maker suggested that the client had been at fault. When I pointed to the client's original application—made through the Citizens Advice office, with me—had gone missing in the hands of DWP, I was told not to 'dwell on the past'.
>
> *Field notes: Pointed out original claim made months ago. EU decision-maker said 'It's not all our fault. We have been waiting for her to provide evidence'. I explained client had made her claim over the phone and was not invited then to submit evidence, and did not receive a written request for evidence. I added that things had gone wrong before EU DM's decision—with the first claim going missing etc. EU decision-maker said at one point 'Let's not dwell on the past'.*

The disconnect between different offices, and in particular, the inability of first instance decision-makers to contact the EU decision-making team, made for a frustrating and highly inefficient process. This issue resurfaced in a case referred to me for second-tier advice:

> **Case Study: Tulio**
>
> Tulio had a complicated migratory history, and had been in and out of the UK for over 30 years, having married a British woman, from whom he was since divorced. He had serious medical needs and for the last couple of years had been receiving a lot of community mental health support in the UK. His employment and support allowance was suddenly stopped. The adviser referring the case to the project for second-tier advice pointed to his strong links with the local mental health services, and noted a letter had gone missing from the DWP's system early on in proceedings. She was told that the benefit had been stopped because one local authority had not sent the necessary details to another local authority when the client moved. The person on the helpline agreed to fax over the relevant forms for the adviser to fill in and then did not send the fax.
>
> *Field notes: Some days later, Tulio's adviser got back in touch with DWP and asked them to email the forms. DWP agreed but then did not send the email. Four months after the adviser asked for a mandatory reconsideration she received a phone call from an EU decision-maker, and asked why it was taking so long, reminding the decision-maker that the client was vulnerable. She was told 'that he didn't know as his job is only to decide whether the client has a right to reside and he is not part of the employment and support allowance team'.*

The fragmentation of the decision-making process, combined with communication firewalls between the different decision-making offices, made it hard to have clear and open conversations in some cases about what was going on, and made it very difficult to try and correct simple errors. It made decision-makers less accountable and kept the process inefficient and cumbersome. It added to bureaucratic hurdles, such as those explored next, in that multiple records had to be kept and updated, which were not synchronised with each other, and created obstacles for clients where different offices demanded different means of discharging the same requirement (the child benefit office and child tax credits office, both in HMRC, requiring separate forms of authority for a third party (an adviser) to act, and then placing obstructive stipulations on how an unfilled form could be sent to a client).

## D. Bureaucratic Hurdles

As with the other obstacles noted in this chapter, bureaucratic hurdles do not just affect EU nationals. But, as the focus group participant quoted at the start of the chapter suggested, there are just more of them—in the form of extra checks and extra evidential requirements—and they can be harder to surmount, because they are ill-adapted to cross-border situations (for instance, in refusing to send a form of authority for the client to sign by any means other than through the post):

---

**Case Study: Stanislaw**

Stanislaw's case at various points felt dominated by the issue of forms of authority. It was frustrating because the client was doing his best to make clear to HMRC that he wanted us to act for him, especially since he would find it difficult to act for himself while in Hungary, and while looking after his children and dying wife. The main problem we had was that the forms of authority seemed to go missing once posted to HMRC, and HMRC refused to accept Citizens Advice's forms of authority—signed by the client and his wife—or to send their own forms of authority through any other means than by post. This kept slowing things down, not least since the client was in Hungary during much of the case.

*Field notes: Spoke to A … Told they cannot speak with me—and no record of FOA on file (client thought he might have sent it directly there). Asked for email or fax so we can send FOA and speak today—told not possible. Has to be by post. At one point we tried phoning the client to put the phones together to get verbal authority, but the line was too faint.*

At a later point another adviser got back in touch with the Tax Credits office and was told that the client had sent a copy of his FOA, rather than the original one, which was not acceptable. The adviser asked whether it was possible that the original FOA had gone to the child benefit office instead of the tax credit office. A problem we had was that the postal address for both was the same, and sometimes one office would open a form of authority and send a copy to the other. She was told that this was likely what had happened. Nevertheless, the client was required to send another FOA from Hungary. When we were told by DWP that the same client had been found to be entitled to a posthumous award of personal independence payments for his wife, they also said he would need to fill in another form about her hospital treatment. We asked whether that form could be sent by email, as the client was between addresses in Hungary and worried about missing the post, and were told 'no'.

---

> *Field notes: Explained client 'between addresses' [in Hungary]—she suggested she could leave it and phone me back in two weeks. I asked if instead, to speed things up, she could email the form to the client. Was told they do not have that facility. Then asked if she could post c/o client's friend, who would scan and email to client (client would print it, fill it and post it to her). She said that would be acceptable.*

This struck me as odd—they could accept a form that had been emailed to the client, but not email it directly. It seems strange that a department that boasts of an (impossible to reach) 'exportability team' does not have the 'facility' of email. Aside from forms of authority, and other forms, which all had to be sent in the post, and then returned by post, Stanislaw also encountered another bureaucratic hurdle, in the rules imposed on claimants wishing to notify HMRC of a change of circumstances:

**Case Study: Returning to Stanislaw**

Stanislaw faced an unfortunate obstacle in the form of HMRC security questions which prevented him from being able to notify them of his wife's death, information crucial to their claim and records.

*Field notes: Apparently client tried calling child benefit office and tax credits office to notify of wife's death, but as the claims are in her name, and she normally dealt with them, he couldn't answer the security questions, so the people on the helplines refused to speak with him—so he couldn't notify them of her death. Have complained about this in letters as situation frankly ludicrous, in the light of a dead claimant and bereaved husband.*

This was made all the more bizarre by the fact that once we finally had the correct FOA lodged with the correct department, HMRC would speak to me on his and his wife's behalf, and I was able to notify them of her death.

The paperwork hurdles in John's case—challenging the three-month residence rule applied to a returning UK national—were substantial. The judge directed me to submit all of the cases I had referred to in full. This resulted in a protracted and burdensome bundle-preparation process, which seemed both unusual and unfair to impose upon appellants represented by a charity:

**Case Study: John**

*Field notes: [The judge] also said she wanted each of the cases I had referred to in the skeleton/grounds to be submitted to the tribunal seven days in advance. I had not done this as it has not been required in the past—usually submit a key case and provide required*

*excerpts, and bring full copies of everything on the day … So she said she would issue direc-*
*tions for me to submit all cases in full, then require DWP to make a submission engaging*
*with the grounds. She would direct that DWP send a rep to the re-listing. I offered to hand*
*in my full lever arch file directly to the tribunal, but they refused to take it and said I should*
*post it to Leeds. I note this as it is a bit of an extra administrative (and costs) hurdle. No*
*explanation as to why they would not put it on the system, or if necessary, post it themselves.*

There followed a series of communications with the Courts and Tribunals service, with
extra bundle requirements. I submitted one full bundle, which took three hours to com-
pile, with relevant sections highlighted, and a contents page. The tribunal clerk phoned
to ask me to submit three full bundles in total. This was surprising, because again it put
all of the costs and time burdens upon the appellant party. I was told that the tribunal
used to do the photocopying but that this would take too long. I repeated the process
with two more bundles. The clerk then phoned to say that the pagination on some of
the pages of the latest two bundles did not match that of the first. After examining my
records, it transpired that this this was because in the interim, the format of one of the
cases had changed. After some discussion, the clerk was persuaded to make the required
pagination corrections for me. The final bundle, including cases, legislation, other materials, correspondence and forms, was 778 pages long. Posting the bundles securely cost
over £30 in total.

At times it felt that bureaucratic requirements led the law, rather than the other
way round. Johannes's case was an example of bureaucratic processes dictating
HMRC's actions: he had been sent a form, which would gather already provided
information, and which would turn out to be unnecessary because it had been
triggered by his wife not having a national insurance number, but she was about
to get one. Nevertheless, the form had to filled in, according to HMRC, 'because
we have sent it':

**Case Study: Johannes**

In Johannes's case, it was not just the complexity of the forms in question that created
an obstacle—it was the repetition. He had been sent a request to provide a lot of information that he had already given. We were told that this was because his wife did not
have a national insurance number. However, she was waiting for it, and would have it
in a couple of weeks.

*Field notes: Client has received a combined letter and form from HMRC 'request for further*
*information' [because his wife did not have national insurance number]. Rather lengthy,*
*13 pages, asks for a lot of info provided on original application. Also asks for a number of*
*ID documents (client's and wife's passports; child's birth certificate and identity document,*
*both of which have been sent to HMRC and gone missing) … Suggested we phone tax cred-*
*its office and explain client's wife should have a NI number [in a couple of weeks], ask if*
*they could wait and see if further information/docs actually required at that point, given we*

> *were told last week that the request was triggered because wife had no national insurance number. Phone tax credits adviser line, spoke to X. He said they could not review the request for information, regardless of acquisition of national insurance number, that it has to be filled in and returned 'and I know this sounds a bit silly, but it has to be filled in because we have sent it'. Suggested that it may be that no further info needed, if they have regard to info already provided. X stated they could not refer to the original form, that 'it is our process and we have to stick to it'. Asked if we could speak to a case worker/claims handler to explain and avoid re-sending info and important docs. Told no, 'we get lets of enquiries and we cannot pass everybody through'—suggested what if we wanted to complain about the administration of the claim; still wouldn't pass us on, but said we could complain in writing.*

The adherence to internal procedures, even in the face of evidence that they are no longer necessary, speaks to a routinisation of checking on rights to reside that perhaps goes beyond that which is permitted in EU law. Article 14 of Directive 2004/38 prohibits 'systematic' verification of whether Union citizens and their family members fulfil the conditions of residence rights set out in that Directive. As well as the rather systematic/tautological nature of requiring evidence because evidence has been required, there are other indications that verification—and the bureaucratic processes that go with it—is increasingly systematic, in the new approach to HMRC compliance checks and with regard to cross-border benefit claims.

HMRC compliance checks are more intensive checks issued in some cases on top of the normal checks/requests for information. HMRC guidance states that these should only be triggered either as part of a random programme or because there are grounds to suspect that the award is wrong.[43] But in 2014, the UK government announced that the restrictions on EU nationals' benefit eligibility were to be 'augmented by additional HMRC compliance checks to improve detection of when EEA migrants cease to be entitled to these benefits'. The announcement appeared in the budget policy costings document and added that 'the checks will apply to all EEA migrant claims'.[44] The Budget itself made clear that these checks would be applied to 'new claims and existing awards'.[45] The government has since confirmed that it has indeed been carrying out 'increased compliance

---

[43] HMRC, 'How to do a Compliance Check: Starting a Compliance Check: Case Selection' *HMRC Compliance Handbook*, at CH206200. Available at: www.hmrc.gov.uk/Manuals/chmanual/CH206200. htm. See also The Tax Credit Act 2002, s 16 (2)(a)–3(b).

[44] HM Government, *Budget 2014: Policy Costings*, March 2014, 49. Available at: www.gov.uk/government/uploads/system/uploads/attachment_data/file/295067/PU1638_policy_costings_bud_2014_with_correction_slip.pdf.

[45] HM Treasury, *Copy of the Budget Report: March 2014 as Laid Before the House of Commons by the Chancellor of the Exchequer When Opening the Budget'* HC 1104 (HM Treasury, 19 March 2014), para 1.197. Available at: www.gov.uk/government/uploads/system/uploads/attachment_data/file/293759/37630_Budget_2014_Web_Accessible.pdf.

checks ... targeted at EU/EEA nationals'.[46] When it comes to cross-border benefit claims, for child benefit or tax credits where children are resident in another Member State, then a House of Commons research note makes clear that on top of the 'checks with the "competent authority" in the Member State to verify the information provided by the claimant', there are, in all cases, 'a wide range of checks on entitlement and an annual review'.[47] Such verification sounds 'systematic' and can create significant, bureaucratic hurdles.

Checks that impacted particularly harshly upon women were those imposed by the DWP and HMRC upon claimants to provide the necessary details of their ex-partner's or husband's work, in cases of separation and domestic abuse. Although the authorities had access to this information themselves, they failed to take steps to acquire it, placing the burden solely upon the abused women. This was something I encountered first hand with Elena's case. I asked the EU decision-maker three separate times to seek out the information she needed, and each time she agreed, but then the next time I spoke to her would say she had not sought this information and it would be easier for the claimant to provide it. One national expert noted this was a problem for women in refuges and said they 'cannot obtain evidence of their violent partners' work ... but it's a no-brainer, if [DWP] have a NINO [national insurance number], they should be seeking the records themselves'.[48] Another national expert in interview said that in cases of separated spouses:

> We get the impression that the department puts the onus on the claimant to provide evidence of their spouse's right to reside, when obviously in many cases that's just not feasible, they just might not be able to get that! And certainly, you know, the government as a whole, might be able to, quite easily, check that. And that's definitely an ongoing problem.[49]

The creation of administrative obstacles, the fetishisation of procedure, and the sacralisation of the right to reside commandments can mean that the humans at the centre of the claims—such as the women and children fleeing from dangerous men—get lost from view and concerns about social justice can be eclipsed by the desire to see the correct box ticked.[50] In this way, an obstructive administrative

---

[46] P Hogan, *Response Re Freedom of information Act 2000 (FOIA)* (Benefits and Credits, 7 Jan 2015) FOI 3252/15. Available at: www.whatdotheyknow.com/request/303796/response/752016/attach/2/reply.pdf.

[47] S Kennedy, 'Child Benefit and Child Tax Credit for Children Resident in Other EEA Countries' (House of Commons Library, 18 July 2014) SN06561, 6-7. Available at: researchbriefings.files.parliament.uk/documents/SN06561/SN06561.pdf.

[48] Expert interview 5.

[49] Expert interview 1.

[50] On the different modes of administrative decision making, and how they present competing (and interacting) goals, such as efficiency and legality, and how they create different (but related) models of procedural fairness, see M Adler, 'A Socio-Legal Approach to Administrative Justice' (2003) 25 *Law and Policy* 4, 323.

culture, influenced by derogatory messages from the state, can seem a hostile administrative culture.[51]

## E. Administrative Hostility

This nebulous side-effect is hard to trace, but evidence gathered in focus groups and interviews suggests that some advisers sense some hostility. A national expert interviewed said: 'You do start to believe there is some sort of bias. Migrant worker claims are checked more'.[52] A focus group participant pointed to the prevailing political rhetoric and suggested that unless there was frequent, rigorous training among decision-makers, discrimination was inevitable because 'people don't live in glass jars'.[53] She suggested that meant that those in positions to exercise discretion, or to help clients in other ways, were less inclined to do so: 'the willingness to go the extra mile, to chase up something when it doesn't seem right, just isn't there'. She gave an example of phoning up social services about a client whose family was suffering real hardship and being told 'well, I think they should just go home, they've no real right to be here anyway'.[54] Later, she suggested that EU clients seemed more depersonalised by the process: 'to them [decision-makers] it's a job, it's not a person'.[55] Two other members of the same reflective focus group spoke of concerns that in managing EU nationals' expectations, we as advisers, might be contributing to perpetuating a culture of administrative obstruction:

> C: We've almost come to the point a six-months delay is acceptable. And we're saying to clients, it could be six months it could be longer. I don't want to raise their expectations ...
>
> A: But you're almost making that acceptable ...
>
> C: Yeah ...
>
> B: That's what happened isn't it?

In terms of the cases within the *EU Rights Project*, there did seem to be an institutional acceptance within DWP and HMRC of administrative obstacles, expressed in acknowledging without apology that the internal mail is slow, that departments

---

[51] Collingbourne finds that the environment of administrative decision-making in the context of social care as characterised by 'competing and conflicting logics, which lead to instabilities, frustrations, dilemmas and tensions for practitioners and service users alike', and that in this environment, there are examples of 'continuing oppressive use of discretionary power' (T Collingbourne, 'Administrative Justice? Realising the Right to Independent Living in England: Power, Systems, Identities' (2013) 35 *Journal of Social Welfare and Family Law* 4, 475, 486. On the multiple pressures placed on decision-makers, see T Evans, *Professional Discretion in Welfare Services: Beyond Street-Level Bureaucracy* (Abingdon, Ashgate, 2010).

[52] Expert interview 3.

[53] Reflective focus group.

[54] ibid.

[55] ibid.

cannot speak to each other, that applications go missing, and that it can take a long time to get the information needed to make a competence decision. This bled into hostility at the moments when the burdens created by these failings were unthinkingly placed on claimants, and when claimants were in turn blamed, explicitly or implicitly, for their claims not having progressed:

---

**Case Study: Elena**

Elena's case has been subject to a series of administrative errors on the part of the DWP. She did not however receive an apology, and I faced repeated incredulity on the part of the EU decision-maker, who found it hard to believe that Elena had not received information, or that Elena had submitted evidence as required. Elena's credibility as a witness was however made stronger by my having witnessed most transactions with the DWP:

*Field notes: EU Decision-maker stated there was no record on her file of [Elena] having presented her marriage certificate. She repeatedly said 'the client has not given us any evidence'. When I contradicted her, she said' I am not saying she is lying, but …'.*

*… I pointed out that the original claim was made months ago. EU DM said 'It's not all our fault. We have been waiting for her to provide evidence' and added that claimants are told when they have an appointment at the Job Centre Plus what evidence to bring along. I explained client had made her claim over the phone and was not invited then to submit evidence, and did not receive a written request for evidence. EU DM [said] she could not believe client had not received a letter asking for it, though she did not mention one on the system.*

---

The repeated insistence that Elena had 'not provided evidence', in spite of both Elena's, and my, testimony to the contrary, revealed the little credence the decision-maker gave us both. In contrast, she had rather surprising faith in the machinery of the system, since she had no evidence to support the assertion that the client would have received information much earlier about evidence needed. It seems pertinent to remember that if decision-makers are influenced in their decision-making by how they construct claimants, they have been subject to a barrage of government material warning them about the risk of deceptive EU nationals mounting 'rogue' benefit claims and seeking to 'abuse the system'. They have also been subject to a series of changes that dehumanise the process, by disregarding need, social circumstances, or considerations of proportionality, and supplanting them with the list of right to reside conditions.

## V. SUMMARY

Administrative decision-making is an important filter and modifier of EU rights. The Charter of Fundamental Rights recognises this, and provides for a 'right to good administration'[56] though only as regard the actions of the 'institutions and bodies of the Union'. But national and local decision-makers are administrative gatekeepers to those rights, and ought also to handle claims 'impartially, fairly and within a reasonable time'.[57] The systems put in place, the rules, the guidance, and the overarching government communications, all carry within them embedded messages curbing decision-maker discretion, and steering them towards a style, mode and direction of decision-making. Mechanisms that discourage the gathering of information at first instance, such as narrow guidance, scripted interviews and forms with limited options, interact with the general thrust of government guidance about limiting benefit entitlement, and legal changes establishing a presumption of unequal treatment, to feed a 'refuse first, ask questions later' culture. Low institutional standards when it comes to delay—such as HMRC setting an 'average' target that is over four times as long as that for UK national claimants, even though many cases should not require extra investigation—and strong institutional presumptions against the honesty of EU nationals and the validity of their claims (in the promised enhanced compliance checking specifically for EU nationals), contribute to a lowered sense of institutional responsibility. It encourages a loss of focus upon the welfare of the claimants, and their children, who are expected to bear the disadvantages created by administrative failings (in the form of data not recorded and documents that go missing).

Systems that prioritise form over substance (through requiring specific, separate forms of authority, that must be hard copy originals, and which cannot be sent or received any way other than through the post, regardless of the client's wishes or the client's location), systems that prevent a client from notifying the authorities of his wife's death (but would simultaneously penalise him for not notifying them), systems that preclude the passing of materials between two offices sharing the same address (when they've gone to the wrong one) all encourage the prioritising of bureaucracy over justice. Systems that screen clients out from being able to speak to anyone, through automated helplines that do not recognise words in different accents and then disconnect clients, and systems that withhold, or erase, contact details, or provide numbers that lead you to people who do not know they are answering that line, all encourage the distancing of clients and keeping decision-making remote and opaque. Systems that prevent different links in the decision-making process chain from talking to each other (let alone the claimant

---

[56] Art 41 Charter of Fundamental Rights of the European Union [2000] OJ C-364/01.

[57] Art 41(1). Though note that even if the Charter did apply to national decision-makers, there would still be a dispute over whether the Charter was engaged (In Case C-333/13 *Elisabeta Dano and Florin Dano v Jobcenter Leipzig* EU:C:2014:2358, the Court reached the surprising conclusion that even in a case of cross-border movement, it was not engaged unless the claimant complied with the requirements in secondary law; in such cases the Member State was not implementing Union law and so under Art 51(1) the Charter did not apply. It could be argued during a dispute that the purpose of the dispute is to establish whether a claimant has so complied, and so the Charter should be triggered unless it could be shown that was not the case. Though the bigger question is why the (conditional) primary law right, under Art 21 TFEU, does not in itself trigger the Charter.).

being able to speak with them), and only permitting them to share documents through a slow and unreliable internal mail process, encourage complacency about delay and blame-shifting between different offices and discourage efficient and informed decision-making and the 'ownership' of those decisions.

The process and substance of decisions are inextricably interlinked; as Nick O'Brien put it, we need to recognise 'the inevitable link between administrative justice and social policy, even to the extent that ... administrative justice is in fact an aspect of a broader conception of "social justice".[58] The administrative obstacles to social justice are heavily influenced by political and legal environments. The UK should pose a cautionary tale to the EU, and other EU Member States, about the ramifications of creating a culture of obfuscation of, and disdain for, questions of social justice. Yet we still need to ask ourselves: is European social justice possible?

---

[58] O'Brien (2012), above, n 6, 500.

# 9

# *Is European Social Justice Possible?*

## I. INTRODUCTION

THE EU'S PERPETUAL existential angst has led to commentators analysing legal developments as 'soul-searching'[1] or as attempts to win hearts or minds.[2] In asking whether and how a 'social Europe' can be reconciled with its economic objectives, some point to the constitutional asymmetry of the Union,[3] or critique the neoliberal philosophy vested in its economic constitution[4] which appears to underwrite (at least some of) the ECJ's jurisprudence.[5] The key tension at the heart of EU welfare law is the continued salience of nationality, so that nationals can be full citizens, and EU nationals market citizens only. The clash of nationality-based welfare rules with the principle of equal treatment, and in particular the prohibition on direct discrimination, is philosophically problematic, and so has inspired academic attempts to reconcile the relevance of nationality with a broader theory of European solidarity. This chapter argues that the construct of market citizenship makes any such reconciliation impossible: market citizenship contributes to political, legal and administrative obstacles to social justice. It suggests some practical tools for moving away from a market citizenship framework and building up principles of cross-border, European social justice. These include a reinvented, and codified, duty of proportionality review, and an explicit duty to have regard to key social justice principles—promoting child welfare and gender equality—when implementing/administering free movement law.

Political distaste for EU nationals does not render the case for fundamental shifts in our ways of thinking about each other's citizens impractical and unfeasible. It makes it all the more necessary. Evidence of Euroscepticism has been interpreted as weighing in favour of more 'market' and less 'citizenship'—so rolling back on social Europe—but this chapter argues that this interpretation is deeply

---

[1] C Semmelmann, 'The European Union's Economic Constitution Under the Lisbon Treaty: Soul-Searching Shifts the Focus to Procedure' (2010) 35 *EL Rev* 4, 516.

[2] M Dougan, 'The Treaty of Lisbon 2007: Winning Minds, Not Hearts' (2008) 45 *CML Rev* 3, 617.

[3] F Scharpf, 'The European Social Model: Coping With the Challenges of Diversity' (2002) 40 *Journal of Common Market Studies*, 645.

[4] J Habermas, *The Postnational Constellation* (Cambridge, Polity Press, 2001).

[5] M Everson, 'From Effet Utile to Effet Néolibéral: Why Is the ECJ Hazarding the Integrity of European Law' in C Joerges and T Ralli (eds), *European Constitutionalism Without Private Law* (Oslo, ARENA Report Series, 2011), 41.

flawed: evidence shows that citizens have felt disillusioned, alienated and excluded from an EU that concerns itself with the economic elite. Moreover, it is unwise to adopt discriminatory policies in the hope that they will placate the perceived discriminatory urges. The UK referendum vote to exit the EU was the culmination of a programme of declaratory discrimination by the state. History has already told us that discriminatory policies engender further discrimination and prejudice— they do not defuse them. If the EU and other Member States also adopt an approach of capitulating to Euroscepticism, by dehumanising the process by which EU nationals gain welfare entitlements, they will stoke up, rather than damp down, discrimination. EU citizenship will cease to mean anything. Euroscepticism is not a fixed matter of political reality—in matters of equality, law and policy can and have been used to shift the parameters of the possible. A commitment to see social justice served to each other's nationals is a first, basic step in recapturing the aims of social Europe and reshaping discourse for the better.

## II. NATIONALITY IS STILL DETERMINATIVE

Much of the literature on the welfare dimension of a social Europe seeks to reach some neat theoretical framework that justifies different treatment on the grounds of nationality, while allowing us to retain the grammar of equal treatment. De Witte has argued that an answer lies in 'comparability' and framing differential treatment around citizens, not in comparable situations.[6] Neuvonen suggests emphasising the subjectivity of EU nationals, and their right to establish 'equal relationships' with other citizens, giving more weight to the impact that differential treatment has on those relationships.[7] Both approaches have conceptual appeal and could theoretically require decision-makers to take greater account of non-economic factors that might make claimants more comparable or promote equal relationships. But both are abstract and open to manipulation: either might be invoked now to defend the status quo, through didactic pronouncements that EU nationals are not in comparable situations, unless and until the decision-makers find otherwise. Similarly, it is because of the idea that EU nationals by default do not have equal relationships with home-state nationals that the UK government has played up the language of benefit tourism and contributions.[8] There is an inherent tension—if not a flat contradiction—in the idea of equal treatment on the grounds of nationality in the context of EU market citizenship. Nationality has persisted as a deciding factor for EU nationals' rights. As explored in chapter six,

---

[6] F de Witte, 'The End of EU Citizenship and the Means of Non-Discrimination' (2011) 18 *Maastricht Journal of European and Comparative Law* 1–2, 86.

[7] P Neuvonen, *Equal Citizenship and its Limits in EU Law: We the Burden?* (Oxford, Hart, 2016) 188.

[8] According to the Rt Hon Iain Duncan Smith MP, 'The British public are rightly concerned that migrants should contribute to this country, and not be drawn here by the attractiveness of our benefits system' (DWP, 'New Rules to Stop Migrants Claiming Housing Benefit' *Press Release*, 20 January 2014. Available at: www.gov.uk/government/news/new-rules-to-stop-migrants-claiming-housing-benefit.

conditional equality is an oxymoron, and equality just for workers is equality for no one. The results examined in this book cannot simply be explained by replacing the word 'nationality' for 'comparability'. For many, their situations are in several meaningful senses comparable to those of own state nationals, but for the variable of nationality—think of the 17-year-old born in the UK, who has only ever lived in the UK and has no family connections anywhere else.[9] It is nationality that is the pivot upon which rights hinge.

The possible relevance of nationality does not come down to a binary choice: there are matters of degree possible along the spectrum from irrelevant to totally decisive. At one end, nationality might be disregarded as irrelevant for benefit eligibility, and so EU nationals would need to comply with the same rules and conditions, while enjoying the same entitlements, as own-state nationals. This could be a form of 'full solidarity' with EU nationals.[10] Moving along the spectrum, nationality might be treated as not pertinent in itself, but as a possible indicator of relevant factors (such as integration) which might be considered alongside social justice objectives. This would suggest a degree of social solidarity. Further along the spectrum it may be treated as a relevant but not decisive factor, triggering an investigation of that person's integration and contributions, so suggesting a degree of individualised, or contractual, solidarity. Or, reaching the other end of the spectrum, nationality may in itself be determinative of a person's rights, in which case it might be more honest to drop the language of equal treatment and EU citizenship.

Currently, the last approach applies. Nationality is determinative: it triggers investigations not into social factors, or factors of integration, but into economic status and history. A European commitment to social justice would require, if not severing the tight link between nationality and social protection, then loosening it. A reaffirmation of EU citizenship requires confirmation that the categories of rights to reside in Article 2004/38 are not exhaustive, and that states and decision-makers should have regard to social factors, and look to degrees of integration. To avoid this resulting in another version of a responsibilisation test, or the establishment of a parallel right to reside test featuring alternative, exhaustive, exclusionary criteria, these factors should be interpreted in light of Union objectives to promote social justice. In short, we would need to not only resuscitate, but fortify, and codify, proportionality.

This is not merely a nostalgic lament for the halcyon days of *Sala*,[11] *Trojani*[12] and *Baumbast*.[13] In spite of both the optimism and concern in academic commentary regarding the apparently mounting power of EU citizenship,[14] proportionality

---

[9] *Secretary of State for Work and Pensions v Sequeira-Batalha* [2016] UKUT 511 (AAC).

[10] Though only as fully solidaristic as the system for own nationals happened to be.

[11] Case C-85/96 *María Martínez Sala v Freistaat Bayern* EU:C:1998:217.

[12] Case C-456/02 *Michel Trojani v Centre public d'aide sociale de Bruxelles (CPAS)* EU:C:2004:488.

[13] Case C-413/99 *Baumbast and R v Secretary of State for the Home Department* EU:C:2002:493.

[14] For optimism, see D Kostakopoulou, 'The Evolution of European Union Citizenship' (2008) 7 *European Political Science* 3, 285; and H Verschueren, 'European (Internal) Migration Law as an

as conjured up in those cases never really meant all that much when it came to attempting to assert concrete rights at first instance in national settings.[15] Right to reside tests and their ilk have been applied not just in the UK, but in states such as Germany,[16] Belgium,[17] Austria[18] and the Netherlands,[19] for years. The UK test cleaves to specific categories derived from Directive 2004/38, and first instance decision-makers have had no recourse to alternative routes to such rights. At best, claimants who make it as far as a First-tier Tribunal, and have sympathetic facts, and a judge willing to treat proportionality as a justiciable issue, were able to mount proportionality-based arguments in the alternative to other possible routes. In some cases these were successful.[20] This was certainly better than nothing, and has proved in some cases a crucial 'last resort' plea for those who fall outside of the Directive's categories due to circumstances such as domestic violence.[21] But it was not enough: a concept that could only be invoked when litigating an appeal, and whose success depended entirely on the willingness of the judge involved to consider the concept legally relevant, created a necessarily quite exclusionary avenue of claim. It did not mean much, but it means even less now. Resuscitating proportionality would require stronger codification to make it an accessible route of claim at first instance, or at least, for any EU national appealing a first instance decision. It is an opportunity to revisit and recapture the idea of 'fairness' framed not as a matter of pushing a neoliberal agenda packed with claimant-blame,[22] but as a matter of justice, societal responsibility and some shared collective endeavour.[23]

Instrument for Defining the Boundaries of National Solidarity Systems' (2007) 9 *European Journal of Migration and Law*, 307. For concern, see: K Hailbronner, 'Union Citizenship and Access to Social Benefits' (2005) 42 *CML Rev* 5, 1245; C Tomuschat, 'Annotation of Martínez Sala' (2000) 37 *CML Rev* 2, 449; A Somek, 'Solidarity Decomposed: Being and Time in European Citizenship' (2007) 32 *EL Rev* 6, 787.

[15] And Davies argues that those cases were not nearly so transformative at EU level as many commentators suggested, pointing to the restrictive substance of *Grzelczyk*, for instance (see G Davies, 'Migrant Union Citizens and Social Assistance: Trying to Be Reasonable About Self-Sufficiency' *Research Papers in Law* 2/2016 (Bruges, College of Europe, 2016)).

[16] C O'Brien, E Spaventa and J De Coninck, *Comparative Report: The Concept of Worker Under Article 45 TFEU and Certain Non-Standard Forms of Employment* (Brussels, Free Movement and Social Security Coordination Network, 2016) 83–84. Case C-67/14 *Jobcenter Berlin Neukölln v Nazifa Alimanovic and Others* EU:C:2015:597.

[17] Hence the dispute in Case C-140/12 *Pensionsversicherungsanstalt v Peter Brey* EU:C:2013:565.

[18] See M Blauberger and A Heindlmaier, 'Enter at Your Own Risk: Free Movement of EU Citizens in Practice' (2017) 40 *West European Politics* [online] 13 March 2017.

[19] Hence the dispute in Case C-158/07 *Jacqueline Förster v Hoofddirectie van de Informatie Beheer Groep* EU:C:2008:630.

[20] As for Anita and Paulina.

[21] As was the case for both Anita and Paulina.

[22] As implied by the language of responsibility, as in the universal credit agenda, and the 'commitment to overhaul the benefit system to promote work and personal responsibility' (DWP, 'Universal Credit: Welfare That Works' *White Paper* Cm 7957 (presented to Parliament November 2010), 2).

[23] Somek suggests that while we have 'lost faith in the greatness that comes from common action ... that is exactly the faith that Europe would need' (A Somek, 'Alienation, Despair and Social Freedom' in L Azoulai, S Barbou des Places and E Pataut (eds), *Constructing the Person in EU Law: Rights, Roles, Identities* (Oxford, Hart Publishing, 2016) 54.

## III. PROPORTIONALITY AS A MEANS TO REDEFINE FAIRNESS

There is a whole sub-discipline that has grown around fairness theory. It is not a clear-cut concept with a single, self-evident meaning,[24] and as such we should feel able to challenge its appropriation to serve xenosceptic, welfare-curbing ends. Restrictions on EU citizenship-based rights to welfare have been repeatedly justified through invocations of fairness, though they rely on an ideologically specific construction of fairness.

### A. Fairness as Rights-Restricting Rather than Rights-Giving

The UK government considered that excluding *Zambrano* families from welfare benefits was 'a proportionate means of achieving the legitimate government aim of encouraging migrants who can make a valuable contribution to our economy, whilst delivering fairness for the taxpayer by maintaining the current level of support the benefit system is able to provide to the general population'.[25] It has been brandished as the driving force behind welfare reforms more generally in the UK, all aimed at reducing welfare entitlement.[26] In a report for the EU Commission in 2011, the UK Treasury promised welfare reforms that would promote 'personal responsibility' and create a 'fair, simple and efficient' benefits system.[27] Fairness has been readily elided with responsibility-centred, conditional welfare entitlement. The then Secretary of State for Work and Pensions described the proposed reforms as 'not about punishing people … [but] about establishing a principle that fairness runs through the whole of the benefit system'.[28] The concept that *did* run throughout the whole of the Welfare Reform Act was responsibility with claimant

---

[24] AW Cappelen, E Sørensen and B Tungodden, 'Responsibility for What? Fairness and Individual Responsibility' (2010) 54 *European Economic Review* 3, 429; see also L Corchón and I Iturbe-Ormaetxe, 'A Proposal to Unify Some Concepts in the Theory of Fairness' (2001) 101 *Journal of Economic Theory* 2, 540; H Egger and U Kreickemeier, 'Fairness, Trade and Inequality' (2012) 86 *Journal of International Economics* 2, 184; C Fong, 'Social Preferences, Self-Interest and The Demand for Redistribution' (2001) 82 *Journal of Public Economics* 2, 225; L Kamas and A Preston, 'Distributive and Reciprocal Fairness: What Can We Learn From the Heterogeneity of Social Preferences' (2012) 33 *Journal of Economic Psychology* 3, 538. Dworkin presents a conception of fairness related to distributive justice and equality of welfare and resources (R Dworkin, 'What is Equality? Part 1: Equality of Welfare' (1981) 10 *Philosophy and Public Affairs* 3, 185, and 'What is Equality? Part 2: Equality of Resources' (1981) 10 *Philosophy and Public Affairs* 4, 283). Sen has suggested that the search for justice should be a dynamic and progressive rather than a hunt for a timeless, ossified ideal (A Sen, *The Idea of Justice* (London, Penguin, 2010)).
[25] A formulation used four times in a six-page document (pp 2, 3, 4, and 6 of DWP, 'Access to Benefits For Those Who Will Have a "Zambrano" Right to Reside and Work' *Equality Analysis for the Social Security (Habitual Residence)(Amendment) Regulations 2012*, October 2012.
[26] BBC, 'Welfare Reform Will Restore Fairness, says Duncan Smith' *BBC News*, 5 October 2010. Available at: www.bbc.co.uk/news/uk-politics-11478801; Sky News, 'Cameron: Welfare Reforms "Put Fairness Back"', 7 April 2013. Available at: news.sky.com/story/1074902/cameron-welfare-reforms-put-fairness-back.
[27] HM Treasury, *Convergence Programme for the United Kingdom April 2011*, 4.16 and 4.18. Available at: http://ec.europa.eu/europe2020/pdf/nrp/cp_uk_en.pdf.
[28] Iain Duncan Smith, 3rd Reading of the Bill, HC Deb, 15 Jun 2011; col 881.

commitments mentioned 86 times. Fairness has been equated not with better decision-making but with reduced entitlement. The UK government has conflated reduction of welfare with increased fairness announcing that the 'government is committed to reforming the welfare system to make it fairer [and] more affordable', and that 'universal credit … will create a leaner but fairer system'.[29]

Those pushing a neoliberal agenda, and claiming the concept of fairness for their cause, find some support in the Union's activation policies. Member States are encouraged to target 'the inactive … like disabled, lone mothers, women at home, early retired, or those on sick leave'.[30] The message that 'each Member State should develop its own flexicurity arrangements'[31] comes with a clear ideological thrust: 'more people need to work'[32] and benefits must be withdrawn to decrease 'the burden for the welfare system'.[33] It should not therefore be surprising to see Member States apply the same principles, more forcefully, in the context of EU law and those exercising free movement rights.

The government press releases announcing the raft of changes introduced in 2014 all invoked the concept of fairness. In the release detailing the scrapping of EU jobseeker rights to housing benefit, the government stated: 'Ministers want to make sure the system is fair for hard-working taxpayers'.[34] The release included a quote from then Secretary of State for Work and Pensions, Iain Duncan Smith, saying: 'These reforms will ensure we have a fair system—one which provides support for genuine workers and jobseekers, but does not allow people to come to our country and take advantage of our benefits system.'[35] The same quote was used in the release about the minimum earnings threshold. The press release about the exclusion of EU national jobseekers from universal credit stated 'our new rules for universal credit will ensure we have a fair system where people cannot claim means tested benefits until they have worked',[36] curiously not mentioning that no such condition applies to UK nationals. The legitimacy, or fairness, of imposing 'fairness' conditions in a discriminatory fashion is assumed. The press release continued, stating that the government 'wants a credible, fair and transparent system that helps people move within the EU to work and supports migrants and non-migrants alike'. The then Economic Secretary to the Treasury, Nicky Morgan,

---

[29] DWP, above n 22, 5, 6.

[30] Public Employment Services 2020 Working Group, *PES and EU 2020: Making the Employment Guidelines Work* (2011), 4. Available at: ec.europa.eu/social/BlobServlet?docId=3692&langId=en.

[31] Principle (3) in Annex to the Annex ('The Common Principles of Flexicurity') to Council of Ministers of the European Union, Working Party on Social Questions 'Towards Common Principles of Flexicurity—Draft Council Conclusions' 15497/07 (2007) SOC 476 ECOFIN 483 (Brussels, 23 November 2007).

[32] European Commission, 'Agenda For New Skills and Jobs', *DG Employment, Social Affairs and Inclusion: Europe 2020 Initiatives*. Available at: ec.europa.eu/social/main.jsp?catId=958&langId=en.

[33] Public Employment Services 2020 Working Group, above n 30.

[34] DWP, above n 8.

[35] ibid.

[36] DWP, 'EU Jobseekers Barred from Claiming Universal Credit' *Press Release*, March 2015. Available at: www.gov.uk/government/news/eu-jobseekers-barred-from-claiming-universal-credit.

was quoted saying that the government was 'building a system that is fair and consistent, one that supports those who want to work hard'.[37]

But while fairness is invoked to justify welfare restrictions in general, and welfare exclusions of EU nationals in particular, there is nothing about fairness that makes it an inherent champion of welfare retrenchment and/or discrimination. In an administrative justice context, it carries quite a different meaning, and quite different implications, altogether.

## B. Fairness as a Rights-Giving Principle of Administrative Justice

Before it was disbanded, the Administrative Justice and Tribunals Council (AJTC) published guiding principles for administrative justice that is 'fair, accessible and efficient'.[38] The first principle is that a good administrative justice system should 'make users and their needs central, treating them with fairness and respect at all times'.[39] This emphasises the fair treatment owed to claimants, rather than using the label of fairness as a weapon against them. The second principle is about ability to challenge decisions and the explanation states that procedural fairness is 'vital to administrative justice ... three rules underpin fairness'.[40] Those three rules are: (1) that there must be an opportunity for a 'fair hearing';[41] (2) that those dealing with the case should not be biased; and (3) that reasons for decisions should be given. Understood as relating to procedural justice, fairness implies a moral duty upon the state and upon society, not just upon individuals. The AJTC also published *Right First Time* on the subject of first-instance decision-making, arguing that more should be done to improve decisions, which are 'the foundation of the administrative justice system'.[42] 'Right first time' means, inter alia:

> making a decision or delivering a service to the user fairly, quickly, accurately and effectively, applying the appropriate legislation, procedures and criteria and the rules of natural justice (avoiding conflict of interest or bias) ... taking into account the relevant and sufficient evidence and circumstances of a particular case.[43]

Again, fairness is central. Key to fairness is 'taking relevant evidence and circumstances into account'. A system of EU law that deems key circumstances relating to the 'fairness' of a case irrelevant, because Directive 2004/38 is treated as exhaustive of residence and equal treatment rights, might well reduce its own claims to

---

[37] DWP, 'Further Curbs to Migrant Access to Benefits Announced' *Press Release*, 8 April 2014. Available at: www.gov.uk/government/news/further-curbs-to-migrant-access-to-benefits-announced.
[38] Administrative Justice and Tribunals Council *AJTC Principles for Administrative Justice* (London, Ministry of Justice, June 2011), November 2010, 1.
[39] ibid, 2.
[40] ibid, 7, para 22.
[41] ibid.
[42] Administrative Justice and Tribunals Council, *Right First Time* (London, Ministry of Justice, June 2011) 6.
[43] ibid, 7.

fairness. Rawls puts forward a vision of justice not as utilitarianism or efficiency, but as fairness, suggesting that fairness requires justice to serve the needs of the vulnerable and of the minority. To be just, according to Rawls, practices must be considered acceptable by all of those affected, and would be were there no power differential: 'A practice will strike the parties as fair if none feels that, by participating in it, they or any of the others are taken advantage of, or forced to give in to claims which they do not regard as legitimate'.[44] An approach to administrative justice that prioritises fair and accurate decision-making would require reinvigorating the concept of proportionality and viewing the restrictions in EU equal treatment law through a social justice lens. This would not only have the effect of offering protection to those with strong social integration-based claims who fall outside of the rigidly defined categories in Directive 2004/38, it would potentially protect those who were incorrectly found to fall outside of those categories too. Thus it would reduce the impetus to find claimants outside of the Directive 2004/38 categories, and reduce the effects of adopting narrow interpretations, disregarding evidence, or failing to seek it.

A system that is fraught with arbitrary cliff-edges invites decision-making that is relatively indifferent to inaccurate, negative outcomes: without a moral component, or worse, with only morally punitive components, there is incoherence. It is not clear why it should make such a difference that a claimant is still married, or that their child is in school. By recognising a degree of social solidarity, and some social duties owed to EU nationals, those subjects of the system would be re-humanised. It would reintroduce a positive moral component to the laws currently being applied technically, impersonally and negatively. A hint of duty or social responsibility might encourage decision-makers to more fully recognise their own responsibilities to give effect to legitimate claims, and in protecting the dignity of claimants, rather than to see themselves as gatekeepers against unwanted intruders. Directive 2004/38 has been turned on its head from being an instrument to promote free movement and EU citizens' rights into a mechanism to prevent the more-or-less non-existent phenomenon of benefit tourism, but we might yet set it back on its feet. A 'social justice' lens may include many considerations. I will here note two key themes currently neglected that ought to be considered when applying a principle of proportionality: a duty to protect child welfare and a duty to promote gender equality.

## IV. EUROPEAN PRINCIPLES OF SOCIAL JUSTICE

A renewed and strengthened duty of proportionality review would mean that the ECJ's current approach of finding legislation inherently proportionate was no longer tenable. But a duty of proportionality review on its own would not be

---

[44] J Rawls, *Justice as Fairness* (Cambridge MA, Harvard University Press, 2001) 178.

sufficient to better protect EU nationals' access to social justice: guidance would be needed on how proportionality is to be assessed. The definition adopted in the UK courts is that it is only disproportionate to withhold a right to reside if a claimant narrowly misses out on fulfilling the given economic criteria in the Directive. But this is essentially allowing a margin of error around the fringes of the existing categories. It cannot help deal with the disproportionate, unjust impacts of people who fall through the considerable gaps in the Directive or the free movement framework generally. In order to provide a more human, citizen-based assessment, the question of proportionality should engage with impacts upon key European social justice principles. The two highlighted here are those most frequently jeopardised in *EU Rights Project* cases: protecting child welfare and promoting gender equality. Those goals cannot be siphoned off from the operation of the free movement framework—we cannot detach the economic from the social, and we should not treat the social exclusion and destitution resulting from artificial constructs of the market as inevitable accidents of nature.

## A. Protecting Child Welfare

As discussed above in chapter four, the EU is increasingly claiming to place child welfare on its agenda. The protection of the rights of the child is a Union objective according to Article 3 TEU, and it also features in the Charter of Fundamental Rights. Article 24 is entitled 'The Rights of the Child' and requires all public authorities to treat the child's best interests as a 'primary consideration' in 'all actions relating to children'.[45] This duty stands at odds with the ECJ's treatment of Directive 2004/38 as an exhaustive circumscription of rights to reside, and with the reduction of EU citizenship to entitlements attaching to economic activity. Actions relating to children's entitlement to welfare are actions relating to children, especially in light of the Charter requirement that children get the protection and care necessary for their well-being,[46] and in light of the acknowledgement in the UK Supreme Court that child-related benefits are 'designed to meet the needs of children considered as individuals',[47] to 'reduce child poverty'[48] and so 'attach to the child rather than the parent'.[49] The Charter only applies within the scope of EU law, but children whose claims arise as a result of free movement (or are invoking a *Zambrano*[50] right), fall squarely within that scope.

It is hard to imagine a scenario in which Article 24 would be more relevant and applicable than for that of a child whose family have exercised free movement rights. Their welfare has been imperilled because of free movement, which itself

---

[45] Charter of Fundamental Rights of the European Union [2000] OJ C-364/01, Art 24(2).
[46] ibid, Art 24(1).
[47] *R (SG & Ors) v Secretary of State for Work and Pensions* [2015] UKSC 16, 125.
[48] *Humphreys v Revenue and Customs* [2012] UKSC 18, 25.
[49] ibid.
[50] Case C-34/09 *Gerardo Ruiz Zambrano v Office National de L'Emploi (ONEm)* EU:C:2011:124.

indicates a failing in the EU free movement framework. They apparently have no rights to reside in their own right, having at best parasitic rights that disappear once their parents fall outside of the categories in Directive 2004/38. They signify not only a significant gap in the Directive but also a chasm in EU citizenship if that citizenship cannot mean anything to a child who is not yet an economic actor. Both the traction of EU citizenship, and the commitment to the rights of the child, depend on proper recognition and protection of EU citizen children's rights. Yet the ECJ failed to mention the issue, let alone accord it any weight, when the right to child benefits was at issue in *Commission v UK*.[51] Domestic legislation and case law have adopted an approach of the law-as-lists, rather than law-as-justice (or justice as fairness), with children being found not to fit, or to not have fitted, within the Directive's categories.[52] That is, when they are even considered at all, as many decisions have direct impacts upon children but are viewed purely as decisions relating to their parents' eligibility. In several *EU Rights Project* cases, children at risk of destitution were considered legally irrelevant to the operation of EU free movement law.[53]

Member States are required to respect fundamental rights guaranteed in the Charter when implementing Union law. Legislative amendment may be the clearest and most complete way to address the gaps in the Directive, but that is a long, rocky and uncertain road. The invisibility of children in the ECJ's right to reside jurisprudence can be tackled through reading social justice duties into any proportionality review of the existing rules. Such a reading could be used to challenge domestic law and practices that create disproportionate detriments for EU national children, and which mean that those children, even while they enjoy rights to reside, live continually on the 'precipice' so long as it is possible for their parents' rights to disappear. Such insecurity can place them in harm's way. For example, if a primary carer mother is scared of leaving an abusive relationship, because as an unmarried partner she will have no right to reside unless and until she finds alternative work, or, in lone parent families, where the imposition of the minimum earnings threshold means that the mother is not recognised as being a worker, she may be forced to work leaving children unattended, because she is not entitled to financial help with childcare.

The very rationale of market citizenship excludes children. The mantras of activation lurking behind suspicions of 'benefit tourism' are manifestly inappropriate in the context of children. Market citizenship, investing value in EU nationals only insofar as they provide the requisite amount of the requisite type of economic activity for the requisite period, exemplifies the moral shortcomings of neoliberal activation-driven thinking, not least since a child cannot (or, according

---

[51] Case C-308/14 *Commission v United Kingdom* EU:C:2016:436.
[52] *Mirga and Samin v Secretary of State for Work and Pensions & Anor* [2016] UKSC 1; *Secretary of State for Work and Pensions v Sequeira-Batalha* [2016] UKUT 511 (AAC).
[53] They might at best trigger a domestic residual duty of care, though as we found, it was difficult to activate that duty, and questions have been raised over its adequacy in general (ch 4).

to international norms on child labour, should not) become a 'homo economicus'. In treating children as irrelevant, and having no claim to social entitlements, market citizenship has echoes of the criticism Sim levelled at neoliberalism, in that it allows those in power to 'reproduce a heartless set of social arrangements that appear to have no moral compass or boundaries in terms of the human waste and destruction generated'.[54]

Market citizenship, fuelled by the rhetoric of activation, instructs us to valorise economic activity so that the market does not simply drown out morality, but becomes the new morality, whose tenets are prioritised over humanity and dignity. It disregards key social components of citizenship, which, as Dougan points out, are often the components most valued by citizens themselves.[55] While integration sometimes gets a mention in the case law, it has been in a restrictive or punitive sense. Barbou des Places argued that the Court took a 'moral turn' in *Onuekwere*[56] when it found that time served on a prison sentence could not count towards permanent residence, because being in prison shows 'the non-compliance by the person concerned with the values expressed by the society of the host Member State'.[57] But this reference to values does not indicate a rise in importance of social integration, or of values beyond the main moral imperative to not take oneself out of the labour market. It has not been complemented with findings that positive indicators of social integration other than work should be taken into account in a non-national claimant's favour. Integration plays a larger role in the case of own-state nationals challenging obstacles to movement created by their home state[58] (where it is effectively a byword for nationality). In such cases, the concept of real links allows states to continue to imbue nationality with decisive, even discriminatory, importance.[59] It does not allow non-nationals to prize open nationally bounded welfare regimes.

The damage suffered by EU national children is not questioned and is seen as implicitly tolerated by the EU free movement framework, and a necessary corollary

---

[54] J Sim, 'Review Symposium: Punishing the Poor: The Neoliberal Government of Social Insecurity' (2010) 50 *British Journal of Criminology* 3, 592.

[55] '... creating a revealing disjunction between the union's own understanding of Union citizenship (on the one hand) and the individual's personal expectations and experiences of being a European migrant (on the other)': M Dougan, 'The Bubble That Burst: Exploring the Legitimacy of the Case Law on the Free Movement of Union Citizens' in M Adams, H de Waele, J Meeusen and G Straetmans (eds), *Judging Europe's Judges: The Legitimacy of the Case Law of the European Court of Justice* (Oxford, Hart, 2013) 152.

[56] Case C-378/12 *Nnamdi Onuekwere v Secretary of State for the Home Department* EU:C:2014:13.

[57] S Barbou des Places, 'The Integrated Person in EU Law' in L Azoulai, S Barbou des Places and E Pataut (eds), *Constructing the Person in EU Law: Rights, Roles, Identities* (Oxford, Hart Publishing, 2016) 187.

[58] Eg Joined Cases C-523/11 and C-585/11 *Laurence Prinz v Region Hannover and Philipp Seeberger v Studentenwerk Heidelberg* EU:C:2013:90; Case C-224/02 *Heikki Antero Pusa v Osuuspankkien Keskinäinen Vakuutusyhtiö* EU:C:2004:273; Joined Cases C-11/06 and C-12/06 *Rhiannon Morgan v Bezirksregierung Köln and Iris Bucher v Landrat des Kreises Düren* EU:C:2007:626.

[59] C O'Brien, 'Real Links, Abstract Rights and False Alarms: The Relationship Between the ECJ's "Real Link" Case Law and National Solidarity' (2008) 33 *EL Rev* 5, 643.

of the need to coerce parents to work (or else to punish them for not working). It is an amplified version of the activation system imposed on national families. The EU Commission has explicitly pressured the UK into doing more to coerce the parents of young children into work, in the context of the general welfare system, finding that 'lack of conditionality' for single parents of children aged seven and under was a 'significant issue'.[60] Conditionality has now been imposed for lone parents of five-year-old children.[61] In this context, the subjection of EU national children to an 'activation-plus' regime—where conditionality applies to parents of children below the age of one—is deemed legitimate, because they are not even owed a safety net.

The emphasis on conditionality and activation forms an important context for the UK rules targeting EU migrants. While the UK earnings threshold is, in practice, possibly at odds with EU case law on the definition of work, it draws support from messages elsewhere in ECJ case law about the need to guard against benefit tourism and the widening of the category of benefits subject to access restrictions. EU nationals have become something of a testing ground for 'pure' activation theory, untrammelled by concerns of social justice.[62] EU market citizenship, with its economic conditions for acquiring full personal status within EU law, is a manifestation and extension of activation, negating the validity of EU nationals not in paid work. Sharon Wright suggested that activation makes employment the 'only valid source of well-being',[63] but market citizenship makes employment the only valid source of *being* in the Union.[64]

Market citizenship, drawing upon the principles of activation and of benefit-tourism prevention, is impervious to the rights of the child. In a study of social assistance and poverty thresholds in Europe, Kenneth Nelson has suggested that focusing on the principles of activation 'may have affected the moral foundations of European welfare states in terms of providing just social minimums'.[65] It would seem that market citizenship has excavated the moral foundations of European

---

[60] European Commission, 'Assessment of the 2011 National Reform Programme and Convergence Programme for the United Kingdom, Accompanying The Document Recommendation for a Council Recommendation on the National Reform Programme 2011 of the United Kingdom and Delivering a Council Opinion on the Updated Convergence Programme of the United Kingdom 2011–2014', *Commission Staff Working Paper* (2011) SEC(2011) 827 final.

[61] Social Security (Lone Parents and Miscellaneous Amendments) Regulations 2012, SI 2012/874, reg 2(2).

[62] C O'Brien, 'From Safety Nets and Carrots to Trampolines and Sticks' in D Schiek (ed), *The European Union's Economic and Social Model in the Global Crisis* (Abingdon, Routledge, 2013); and C O'Brien, 'The Pillory, The Precipice and The Slippery Slope: The Profound Effects of the UK's Legal Reform Programme Targeting EU Migrants' (2015) 37 *Journal of Social Welfare and Family Law* 1, 111.

[63] S Wright, 'Relinquishing Rights? The Impact of Activation on Citizenship for Lone Parents in the UK', in S Betzelt and S Bothfeld (eds), *Activation and Labour Market Reforms in Europe: Challenges to Social Citizenship* (Basingstoke, Palgrave Macmillan, 2011), 65.

[64] C O'Brien, '"I Trade, Therefore I Am": Legal Personhood in the European Union' (2013) 50 *CML Rev* 6, 1643, 1674.

[65] K Nelson, 'Social Assistance and EU Poverty Thresholds 1990–2008: Are European Welfare Systems Providing Just and Fair Protection' (2013) 29 *European Sociological Review* 2, 387.

welfare states, failing to offer the least protection to children, and failing to recognise the value of their citizenship, time and integration into a host state. Joseph Weiler's conclusion that the Union's value 'is measured ultimately and exclusively with the coin of national utility and not community solidarity'[66] is transferable. The value of EU citizens themselves is measured in the coin of national economic utility, narrowly defined, a currency in which children will always be found wanting. The disregard for child welfare, especially in the context of policies with detrimental impacts upon single parent families, has gendered effects, impacting upon and limiting the freedom of movement of women, even just as *potential* mothers (we will look at the gender dimension of social justice in decision-making next).

## B. Promoting Gender Equality

A law-as-lists approach to residence rights is gendered. The free movement and social security coordination regime has grown up around a 'typical' male pattern of work (which is arguably now not so typical even for men, in low-status, low-security, sporadic work) and lists of male social security risks. In *St Prix*,[67] the Court acknowledged that there was a gap in Article 7(3) on conditions under which workers could retain worker status, and found that it should also cover women temporarily not working due to the late stages of pregnancy, and to maternity. That gap was however indicative of a systemic gender tilt that remains unaddressed (for example, there is no coverage in Article 7(3) for people who have temporary breaks from work for child care, or care for adults, activities which disproportionately fall to women).[68] The disregard for indicators of social integration when it comes to establishing a right to reside, combined with the disappearance of calls upon proportionality, has had significantly gendered consequences so that long-term female residents with broken work patterns due to caring obligations will find it harder to make a claim to permanent residence, and will be likely to be found not to have a right to reside. A focus solely on economic activities and contributions, and the treatment of Directive 2004/38 as exhaustive (approved by the ECJ in *Alimanovic*),[69] means that national measures (such as the minimum earnings threshold) also hit single parents more harshly. They are simultaneously more likely to have reduced working hours/earning capacity, and more likely to be in need of social protection. If they fall foul of the threshold, they are more likely to be deemed not to be workers, or to never have been workers, and their permanent residence clock will keep getting put back to zero.

---

[66] JHH Weiler, 'After Maastricht: Community Legitimacy in Post-1992 Europe' in WJ Adams (ed), *Singular Europe: Economy and Polity of the European Community After 1992* (Ann Arbor, University of Michigan Press, 1995) 39.

[67] Case C-507/12 *Jessy Saint Prix v Secretary of State for Work and Pensions* EU:C:2014:2007.

[68] Case C-325/09 *Secretary of State for Work and Pensions v Maria Dias* EU:C:2011:498.

[69] Case C-67/14 *Jobcenter Berlin Neukölln v Nazifa Alimanovic and Others* EU:C:2015:597.

The findings of the *EU Rights Project* point in particular to the problems encountered by single parents. The fact that their disentitlement has serious implications for their children creates even more distress, and in all could act as a significant disincentive to movement not only for single parents, but for women who are part of a dual parent family, since the possibility of separation might carry with it too extreme a risk of destitution (and also for women with no children). The simple fact that they might possibly become pregnant before having clocked up at least five years of the right amount of the right kind of work means that they are taking a substantial risk in moving. If they do have a baby during those first five years, they will be expected to re-enter the labour market promptly, but unlike UK nationals, EU nationals in the UK will be expected to meet a high earnings/hours threshold, especially if they are in fixed-term, temporary or casual work, since the decision-maker guidance seems to suggest such work is less likely to pass the 'genuine and effective' test if earnings fall below the threshold.

Another gender gap in the free movement framework, as noted in chapter six, is that of domestic abuse, which can punctuate a woman's working life, and result in a sudden need for housing assistance for herself and her children. The failure to offer adequate protection against this risk was evident in *NA*,[70] in which the ECJ prioritised the technical, literal letter of provisions of Directive 2004/38 over their apparent purpose. In that case, the claimant was the third-country national spouse of an EU national from whom she suffered domestic abuse. Following an assault on *NA* while she was five months pregnant, the husband fled, and later notified the UK authorities that he was resident in Pakistan and asked that they rescind *NA*'s right of residence in the UK, in what itself might have been an act of coercive control. After he had left, *NA* initiated divorce proceedings, which were complete at the time of the hearing. *NA* appeared to fall through the technical gaps in Directive 2004/38, which allowed for a retained right of residence for EU nationals in the event of the *death or departure* of their EU national spouse who had been residing on the basis of the Directive,[71] but only provides for such retention for third-country nationals in the event of the death of the Union citizen.[72] The Directive separately provides for spouses to retain rights to reside in the event of divorce,[73] including for third-country nationals in specific cases, such as when warranted by domestic violence.[74] In *NA*, the claimant sought to rely on this protection as a victim of domestic violence, divorced from an EU national worker, but the Court found that this was only available to those who divorce *before* the EU national spouse departs the Member State. The claimant's departure severed the right to reside, so there was nothing to retain in the event of domestic violence. This is an unusually literal approach on the part of the Court, and is insensitive to context.

---

[70] Case C-115/15 *Secretary of State for the Home Department v NA* EU:C:2016:487.
[71] Art 12(1) Dir 2004/38.
[72] Art 12(2) Dir 2004/38.
[73] Art 13(1) Dir 2004/38.
[74] Art 13(2)(c) Dir 2004/38.

If we construe the purpose of the provisions in question as offering some protection to the victim of domestic violence, we should recognise that their main concern may have been getting away from the perpetrator, and that they will have no control over the perpetrator's whereabouts. During times of crisis, such as escalated abuse, it may be difficult to control the precise chronology of events, and is unreasonable to expect victims to apply for divorce at the strategically 'right' time (not least as some victims may not know the whereabouts, or plans of their abuser).

Making the victim's rights contingent on their abuser's whereabouts at a particular point—so that victims may retain rights when their abusive spouse is still in the territory of the state up until the divorce, while victims whose abusive spouse has left the territory before the divorce lose those rights—makes no sense.[75] The Court defended this position by arguing that the provisions were meant to offer legal safeguards to third-country nationals who might be blackmailed by the threat of divorce. But what of blackmail and threats to leave the territory of the state, when the right of residence would be expunged? In spite of the Court's claim to a 'literal, systematic and teleological' interpretation,[76] this case gives effect to an odd technicality regardless of the coherence, or justice, of the result. It is in keeping with the disregard for the problem of domestic abuse elsewhere in the free movement framework (when it comes to retaining worker status, for example, or in the loss of family member status for unmarried partners who separate following abuse).

As with the rights of the child, the EU has declared a commitment to gender equality; it is one of the Article 3 TEU objectives of the Union, and it makes an appearance in the 'values' provision of Article 2 TEU. Article 23 of the Charter of Fundamental Rights requires equal pay for men and women. Article 8 TFEU declares that in 'all its activities, the Union shall aim to eliminate inequalities, and to promote equality, between men and women', and the EU has legislated in the field of gender equality and social security.[77] Consequently, the EU has the competence to address the gender tilt in Directive 2004/38, and theoretically has the motivation, but had failed to acknowledge the gendered nature of actions taken to denigrate and disentitle benefit claimants. The overwhelming majority of child benefits and tax credits are paid to women. Estimates submitted to the Welfare Reform and Work Bill Committee put the proportion of female recipients at 94 per cent for child benefit and 80 per cent for tax credits.[78] The vast majority

---

[75] For a scathing analysis, see S Peers, 'Domestic Violence and Free Movement of EU Citizens: A Shameful CJEU Ruling', *EU Law Analysis*, 25 July 2016. Available at: eulawanalysis.blogspot. co.uk/2016/07/domestic-violence-and-free-movement-of.html.

[76] *NA* judgment, above n 70, 49.

[77] Council Directive 79/7/EEC of 19 December 1978 on the progressive implementation of the principle of equal treatment for men and women in matters of social security OJ [1979] L6/24.

[78] 'Benefit Freeze' *Welfare Reform and Work Bill Committee* Session 2015–16. Written evidence submitted by Chwarae Teg (WRW 48); (Prepared 14 October 2015) 5.2. Available at: www.publications. parliament.uk/pa/cm201516/cmpublic/welfarereform/memo/wrw48.htm.

of lone parents in the UK are women (ONS statistics for 2016 put the figure at 86 per cent).[79] Yet this aspect of the right to reside restrictions placed on both benefits went unmentioned in *Commission v UK*. The EU's apparent indifference to the gendered effects of restricting the benefit entitlement of EU migrants was made clear during the lead-up to the UK referendum on EU membership, when a new settlement between the EU and UK was proposed which would have included a 'brake' on *in work* benefits of 'up to' four years.[80] Thus even workers would be excluded from entitlements to equal treatment. It was never very clear what the term 'in work benefits' covered, but tax credits were likely high on the list, benefits that are disproportionately awarded to women. Working tax credit includes a crucial childcare component. The proposed brake would have departed quite significantly from the principle of equal treatment for workers, and for women in low-paid work, this would have amounted to a four-year sterility pact. Even when working full-time, life would become unaffordable with children, but without financial support for childcare. The Commission has already noted that lack of affordable childcare is a significant issue in the UK.[81] However, this deal was offered without a single mention of gender equality throughout the published negotiation documents.

A commitment to pursuing or promoting social justice in EU law requires a renewed commitment to the rights of the child, and to gender equality, in matters of free movement, Union citizenship and social security coordination. This presupposes a desire to promote cross-border social justice, and it may be that a Eurosceptic turn in various Member States (expressed in extreme form by the UK's referendum vote to leave the EU) indicates that there is no appetite for even a degree of international social solidarity, and that European populations will more readily tolerate restrictions than expansions of rights of non-nationals. It was not just a UK minister, but also ministers from Germany, the Netherlands and Austria, that wrote a letter to Donald Tusk complaining about supposed pressures on national welfare systems created by free movement.[82]

---

[79] ONS, 'Families and Households in the UK: 2016' *Statistical Bulletin* (Release date 4 November 2016), section 4. Available at: www.ons.gov.uk/peoplepopulationandcommunity/birthsdeathsandmarriages/families/bulletins/familiesandhouseholds/2016.

[80] European Council, 'European Council Meeting (18 and 19 February 2016)—Conclusions', *EUCO 1/16* (Brussels, 19 February 2016); Annex I 'Decision of the Heads of State or Government, Meeting Within the European Council, Concerning a New Settlement for the United Kingdom Within the European Union, section D 2(b).

[81] European Commission, above n 57. Citizens Advice also reported on the hidden costs of childcare (K Hignell, *The Practicalities of Childcare: An Overlooked Part of the Puzzle?* (2014), available at: www.citizensadvice.org.uk/Global/Migrated_Documents/corporate/the-practicalities-of-childcare---an-overlooked-part-of-the-puzzle.pdf.

[82] Joint letter from J Mikl-Leitner (Minister of the Interior, Austria), HP Friedrich (Minister of the Interior, Germany), F Teeven (Minister for Immigration, Netherlands) and T May (Home Secretary, UK) to the President of the European Council for Justice and Home Affairs and to Commissioners Reding, Malmström and Andor, (April 2013). Available at: docs.dpaq.de/3604-130415_letter_to_presidency_final_1_2.pdf.

There are a number of problems with the idea that greater social justice is not politically feasible, and I will focus here on two. First, it presupposes that persisting inequality makes the Union more politically palatable than the alternative. But restrictions imposed to try and make free movement more appealing actually make it more stratified, and so of less use to more and more people, making it less attractive and more a subject of resentment. Secondly, it presupposes a simplistic, and rather offensive, cause-effect mechanism at play: that people are xenophobic and the law must follow, in the belief that the law is only legitimate if it reflects prevailing popular rhetoric. But there is no such single direction of influence; politicians have played a significant role in shaping the Eurosceptic discourse of our time, and have deployed the law as a tool of that discourse.[83] The law has significant normative power. History tells us that we do not ameliorate discrimination and prejudice by sanctioning discriminatory or prejudicial laws. We begin to tackle those ills through equal treatment laws, measures that affirm the humanity of law's subjects, and that indicate the society we want to be.

### V. SOCIAL JUSTICE AND EUROPEAN SOLIDARITY: UNITY NOT DIVISION IN ADVERSITY

If we were to conclude that in the face of apparently rising Euroscepticism,[84] and in situations of recent recession which have left many on a low-income feeling left behind, we should be slowing down the development of EU social rights, we implicitly accept the premise that our only common interests are purely economic ones, and that a pared-down neoliberal market is the most politically palatable version of the Union possible. But this vision sets worker against worker, as Somek argues, it exalts the principle of competition over that of cooperation.[85] A shared set of principles of social justice would rest upon the commitment to a shared endeavour, and a recognition that low-paid workers of different nationalities face similar challenges and risks of exploitation and poverty in a socially adverse labour market. Those risks are exacerbated by market citizenship.

### A. Market Citizenship Instrumentalises and Alienates

The idea that a socially thin, economically driven Union would be more easily accepted by a disenchanted workforce flies in the face of the evidence that suggests that a system according rights only to privileged citizens (or, rather, that can only

---

[83] As in the programme of declaratory discrimination, outlined in ch 6.

[84] B Stokes, *Euroskepticism Beyond Brexit: Significant Opposition in Key European Countries to an Ever Closer EU* (Washington, Pew Research Center, 2016).

[85] A Somek, 'From Workers to Migrants, From Distributive Justice to Inclusion: Exploring the Changing Social Democratic Imagination' (2012) 18 *European Law Journal* 5, 711, 726.

be utilised by the privileged)[86] exacerbates alienation. In *Euroclash*,[87] Neil Fligstein drew upon a wealth of opinion data and Everson interpreted his findings as meaning that 'an economically driven process of integration has been of great benefit to a small elite of Europeans (10–15 per cent)'.[88] Everson concluded—rather presciently, in light of what followed in the UK some years later—that the failure to pay attention to the roots, and role, of citizenship as binding together different classes, would threaten the project of integration. If we accept Fligstein's characterisation of the EU as a social class project,[89] it may be that the appropriate response is not to make the exercise of EU rights even more the prerogative of the privileged, but to provide protection against the dangers posed by an increasingly flexible labour market.

'Flexicurity', as conceived by EU institutions, creates benefits for employers and dangers for employees—it is far more 'flexi' than 'curity'.[90] Similarly the emphasis in 'work-life balance' policies is all on increasing the work done by people with families, rather than increasing the time spent on 'life' for those in work.[91] The failure to adequately protect the right to strike in the '*Laval* quartet'[92] of cases also speaks to a willingness to treat workers as production factor labour, and a lack of interest in guarding market citizens against the vicissitudes of the market. As Everson put it, those cases underlined 'the class-based forgetfulness of European institutions and its law'[93] and 'the bourgeois sentiments of the European judge-kings'.[94]

---

[86]  M Galanter, 'Why the "Haves" Come Out Ahead: Speculations on the Limits of Legal Change' (1974) 9 *Law and Society Review* 1, 95, 126 on how costs persuade people not to exercise 'rights'.

[87]  N Fligstein, *Euroclash: The EU, European Identity and the Future of Europe* (Oxford, OUP, 2010).

[88]  M Everson, 'Class Bites Back: Europe and the Delusion of the Common Man' (2009) 8 *European Political Science* 4, 462, 463.

[89]  Fligstein, above n 87, 251.

[90]  Somek is particularly scathing about the Union's policies in this regard: 'Nothing, indeed, could be further removed from the ideal of human emancipation than the sketch of the ideal individual employee that the Commission seeks to breed through the channels of the open co-ordination process. In a "rapidly changing world", Commission says, people need to avail themselves of opportunities at different stages of their lives' (A Somek, 'Europe: From Emancipation to Empowerment', *LSE Europe in Question Discussion Paper Series* LEQS Paper Number 60/2013 (April, 2013) 70.

[91]  L Wacquant, *Punishing the Poor: The Neoliberal Government of Social Insecurity* (London, Duke University Press, 2009), 86.

[92]  Case C-438/05 *International Transport Workers' Federation and Finnish Seamen's Union v Viking Line ABP and OÜ Viking Line Eesti* EU:C:2007:772; Case C-431/05 *Laval un Partneri Ltd v Svenska Byggnadsarbetareförbundet, Svenska Byggnadsarbetareförbundets avdelning 1, Byggettan and Svenska Elektrikerförbundet* EU:C:2007:809; Case C-346/06 *Dirk Rüffert v Land Niedersachsen* EU:C:2008:189; Case C-319/06 *Commission of the European Communities v Grand Duchy of Luxemburg* EU:C:2008:350; see C Barnard, 'Free Movement and Labour Rights: Squaring the Circle?' *University of Cambridge Faculty of Law Research Paper No 23/2013* (12 August 2013); C Joerges and F Rödl, 'Informal Politics, Formalised Law and the "Social Deficit" of European Integration: Reflections After the Judgments of the ECJ in *Viking* and *Laval*' (2009) 15 *European Law Journal* 1, 1; ACL Davies, 'One Step Forward, Two Steps Back? The *Viking* and *Laval* Cases in the ECJ' (2008) 37 *Industrial Law Journal* 2,126; C Barnard, '*Viking* and *Laval*: An Introduction' (2007–08) 10 *Cambridge Yearbook of European Legal Studies*, 463.

[93]  Everson, (2009) above n 88, 467.

[94]  Everson refers to the 'infamous and shocking historical analogy ... *Lochner v New York* [198 US 45 (1905)] ... in which the democratic right of the State of New York to set its own working conditions (including the rights of workers to strike) was overturned with reference to the US Constitution's

Under such circumstances, doing even more to unfetter market forces to create a highly manipulable, subservient and unprotected sub-class of EU immigrant labour seems unlikely to provide an answer to the EU's loyalty crisis. We should carefully consider the consequences of reducing the ambitions of the EU to offer greater social cohesion or greater social protections against the threats of an integrated market.

Recent retrenchment has seen not only a bifurcation of rights between workers and non-workers, but also an increasing stratification of rights amongst workers: the more privileged a worker is, through secure hours, job permanence, full-time work, and high pay, the more they are likely to benefit from the protections in the free movement regime. An increasing distaste for enabling equal access to benefits provided as a means to protect 'dignity' (that is, that are awarded to poorer people), combined with domestic presumptions of marginality for part-time, variable hours, fixed-term and temporary work, and a narrow approach to the limitations of worker status retention, all serve to disadvantage workers in lower socio-economic strata. This is why I have claimed that class, rather than 'work', is emerging as the new guiding principle for free movement rights.[95] The legislation, and much of academia, assumes a 'bright line' between economic activity and economic inactivity and some suggest that the social credentials of the Union hinge upon how the latter is treated.[96] But this is a misleading distinction as there is a fluidity to the statuses not properly accommodated in the law or its analysis, with people in short-term periods of work having considerably broken work patterns. Measures that supposedly only disadvantage the economically inactive, redound upon the economically active in a number of ways (by creating a precipice, which means that their lives are not lived equally to those with more security or protection) and their choices, and their power, are reduced. Even those who manage to get by without teetering on that precipice will feel the impact of increased administrative burdens, delays, hoops, evidential issues, and administrative hostility all engendered by EU-national targeting rules. The road is still a long

---

absolute guarantee for property (see M Everson, 'A Very Cosmopolitan Citizenship: But Who Pays the Price?' in M Dougan, N Nic Shuibhne and E Spaventa (eds), *Empowerment and Disempowerment of the European Citizen* (Oxford, Hart, 2012) 163.

[95] C O'Brien, 'Civis Capitalist Sum: Class as the New Guiding Principle of EU Free Movement Rights' (2016) 53 *CML Rev* 4, 937. Cf Barbou des Places, above n 57, who argues that the diminishing relevance of work is due to a greater concern with social integration—that work is not valued in itself so much but now is a marker of integration.

[96] D Thym, 'The Elusive Limits of Solidarity: Residence Rights of and Social Benefits for Economically Inactive Union Citizens', (2015) 52 *CML Rev* 1, 17; R Zahn, '"Common Sense" or a Threat to EU Integration? The Court, Economically Inactive EU Citizens and Social Benefits' (2015) 44 *Industrial Law Journal* 573; S De Mars, 'Economically Inactive EU Migrants and the United Kingdom's National Health Service: Unreasonable Burdens Without Real Links?' (2014) 39 *EL Rev* 6, 770; N Nic Shuibhne comments: 'If these Union citizens can engage in or even commit to engaging in economic activity, their status radically transforms' in N Nic Shuibhne, 'Limits Rising, Duties Ascending: The Changing Legal Shape of Union Citizenship' (2015) 52 *CML Rev* 4, 889, 932. H Verschueren notes the sometimes blurred line between economically active and non-active persons in 'Free Movement of Citizens: Including for the Poor?' (2015) 22 *Maastricht Journal of European and Comparative Law* 1.

one, and perhaps a disappearing one, towards the 'Arcadian objective'[97] of full free movement rights. Until equal treatment is better decoupled from economic status, even the economically active are not being treated equally.

Market citizenship does not offer much to alienated sections of the European population, and a belief that offers a less controversial future for the EU than its alternatives cleaves to a mistaken view that the market is somehow ideologically or ethically neutral. It creates, perpetuates and depends upon power imbalances, and market citizenship embodies the objectification of workers as production factor labour. This is not a force of nature, but a force of artifice, serving vested interests and masquerading as the natural order of things.[98] In sum, the moral failings of market citizenship, with its competitive heart, alienating tendencies and dehumanising outputs, contribute to disenchantment, and are not in themselves an argument for more market and less citizenship.

## B. Declaratory Discrimination Amplifies Prejudice

The perceived unpopularity of free movement—and, by extension, of EU migrants—is not a sound basis for adopting socially unjust policies. It is morally shallow, for a start, to suggest that the law on non-discrimination and social justice should be blown about by the political wind. The pragmatism argument, that own state nationals would be less resentful of EU nationals if free movement were more restricted, also fails as a matter of socio-political reality. Delineating 'other' statuses in which people have fewer rights helps to fuel the process of othering, and creates a baseline of discrimination. Continually lowering that baseline normalises the process of discrimination, which makes it harder to challenge.

A core problem with making reference to xenophobic sentiments when making law is that xenoscepticism is not a given phenomenon or an inevitable reaction to recession and globalisation. A lot of perceived sentiment has been cynically manufactured, and not just by explicitly Eurosceptic parties. The UK referendum result is the culmination of a long-term programme of declaratory discrimination, and the creation of declaratory obstacles to movement, by the UK state. A distorting feedback process is at play, whereby politicians have attempted to second-guess public sentiment, and in so doing, perpetuating and amplifying toxic discourse. This echoes Schumpeter's warnings that politicians continually recreate the political landscape, while presenting themselves as being merely responsive:

> The incessant competitive struggle to get into office or to stay in it imparts to every consideration of policies and measures the bias so admirably expressed by the phrase about

---

[97] HUJ d'Oliveira, 'Union Citizenship: Pie in the Sky?' in A Rosas and E Antola (eds), *A Citizen's Europe: In search of a new order* (London, Sage Publications, 1995) 70.

[98] Fred Block suggests that when people imagine the market as an ethics-free zone, we should remind them that 'the same Adam Smith who is endlessly invoked by free market theorists had also published *The Theory of Moral Sentiments* in 1759 with its emphasis on moral norms as the foundation for any market activity (F Block, 'Relational Work and the Law: Recapturing the Legal Realist Critique of Market Fundamentalism' (2013) 40 *Journal of Law and Society* 1, 27, 47.

'dealing in votes' … the government's dependence upon the voting of parliament and of the electorate—is likely to distort all the pro's and con's.[99]

Veblen argued at the end of the nineteenth century that 'all economic change is … always in the last resort a change in habits of thought'.[100] A change in our habits of thought on EU citizenship and social justice is possible, but must be accompanied by a change in the habits of *speech* on the part of national governments. Speech includes public statements, press releases, and also domestic laws which, in some cases in the UK, have been public relations exercises. The raft of measures introduced in 2014, presaged and accompanied by high-profile government announcements about the need to tackle 'abuse'[101] of or the 'taking advantage'[102] of, or the 'rogue claims'[103] made upon the welfare system, were no more nor less than a smear campaign against EU migrants. The measures were poorly justified, with a distinct absence of evidence of claimed problems, and a similar absence of projections as to savings to be made.[104] EU migrants proved a handy foil, and were the subject of manufactured outrage. For instance, politicians across the political spectrum have expostulated on the 'absurdity'[105] of exporting child benefits, even though those workers who do export family benefits represent quite a bargain for the state, since they get the parent's work and tax contributions, while another state is dealing with their children's education, housing and other care needs.[106] In some cases, denouncing the rights of EU nationals was a pretext for instigating wide-ranging reforms. The UK government scrapped an entire benefit—employment and support allowance in youth—supposedly just because it did not like the ECJ's decision that it was an exportable benefit.[107] Free movement is continually presented as a threat and in opposition to the welfare state. In the lead-up to

---

[99] JA Schumpeter, *Capitalism, Socialism and Democracy* (New York, Harper and Row Publishers, 1976) 287.

[100] T Veblen, 'Why Is Economics Not an Evolutionary Science?' (1898) 12 *Quarterly Journal of Economics* 4, 373, 391.

[101] DWP, 'Minimum Earnings Threshold for EEA Migrants Introduced' *Press Release*, 21 February 2014. Available at: www.gov.uk/government/news/minimum-earningsthreshold-for-eea-migrants-introduced.

[102] DWP, 'Tough New Migrant Benefit Rules Come into Force Tomorrow' *Press Release*, 31 December 2013. Available at: www.gov.uk/government/news/tough-new-migrantbenefit-rules-come-into-force-tomorrow.

[103] DWP, 'Accelerating Action to Stop Rogue EU Benefit Claims' *Press Release*, 18 December 2013. Available at: www.gov.uk/government/news/accelerating-action-to-stop-rogueeu-benefit-claims.

[104] Eg DWP, 'Equality Analysis for Removal of Access to Housing Benefit for EEA Jobseekers', 27 February 2014. Available at: www.gov.uk/government/uploads/system/uploads/attachment_data/file/322808/equality-analysis-eea-jobseekers.pdf.

[105] E Mills and J Grimstone quoting the then Secretary of State for Work and Pensions Iain Duncan Smith in 'Ban Migrant Welfare for Two Years—Duncan Smith: Alliance Builds Over Benefit Tourism', *The Sunday Times*, 12 January 2014. It was not just the Conservative Party criticising the practice: the Labour Party's Rachel Reeves, then shadow Work and Pensions secretary, also called for an end to the 'absurdity' of exporting family benefits (in P Wintour, 'Labour will Curb Tax Credits for EU Migrants, says Rachel Reeves', *The Guardian*, 19 November 2014.

[106] And possibly health costs too, if the child is in the household of someone working in that other state.

[107] For more on this strange excuse, see O'Brien, above n 59.

the UK referendum, the government kept reiterating that there were significant problems with free movement, with the then Prime Minister writing an article for *The Telegraph* expressing concern about the 'magnetic pull' of the UK benefit system.[108]

The EU has not only tolerated and humoured this cavalier approach to evidence when it comes to denigrating EU nationals, it has been complicit in it. The Commission attached a declaration to the new settlement, proposed in case the UK voted to stay in the EU, about the proposed in-work benefit brake. The Commission stated that:

> the kind of information provided to it by the United Kingdom … shows the type of exceptional situation that the proposed safeguard mechanism is intended to cover exists in the United Kingdom today. Accordingly, the United Kingdom would be justified in triggering the mechanism in the full expectation of obtaining approval.[109]

The wording is vague, to say the least. What 'kind of information'? It was presumably information that contradicted the DWP's own assertion, reported in a 2013 European Commission study, that there was no available evidence of benefit tourism.[110] It must have been information that overturned the Commission's own findings that EU migration had largely been beneficial to the UK,[111] the OECD's findings that the UK has a higher positive fiscal impact from migration than the OECD average,[112] and the forecasts of the Office for Budget Responsibility that suggest that the fiscal impact of migration 'is likely to be positive'.[113] Whatever information it was, it seems that Daniel Korski, David Cameron's deputy director of policy and aide in the negotiations, was not privy to it.[114]

Even so, the Commission declared itself satisfied with the UK's 'information'. In the area of social welfare, it seems that Member States are becoming subject to a different (low) standard of proof when it comes to a desire to discriminate. In *Bressol*,[115] the Court found that indirect discrimination based on nationality

---

[108] 'We're also making sure people come for the right reasons—which has meant addressing the magnetic pull of Britain's benefits system' (D Cameron, 'We're Building an Immigration System that Puts Britain First', *The Telegraph*, 28 July 2014.

[109] European Commission 'Declaration of the European Commission on the Safeguard Mechanism referred to in paragraph 2(b) of Section D of the Decision of the Heads of State or Government, meeting within the European Council, concerning a new settlement for the United Kingdom within the European Union' Annex VI to the European Council conclusions of 18–19 Feb 2016, above n 77.

[110] GHK ICF for the European Commission, 'A Fact Finding Analysis on the Impact on the Member States' Social Security Systems of the Entitlements of Non-Active Intra-EU Migrants to Special Non-contributory Cash Benefits and Healthcare Granted on the Basis of Residence' *Final Report* (October 2013; revised December 2013) 10.5.2.

[111] ibid.

[112] OECD, *International Migration Outlook 2013* (Paris, OECD, 2013), Table 3.7, 159.

[113] Office for Budget Responsibility, *2013 Fiscal Sustainability Report* (London, Office of Budget Responsibility, 2013), 144.

[114] D Korski, 'Why We Lost the Brexit Vote' (2016) *Politico*, 20 October 2016. Available at: www. politico.eu/article/why-we-lost-the-brexit-vote-former-uk-prime-minister-david-cameron/.

[115] Case C-73/08 *Nicolas Bressol and Others and Céline Chaverot and Others v Gouvernement de la Communauté française* EU:C:2010:181.

may be justified with reference to certain 'risks', but that 'it is for the competent national authorities to show that such risks actually exist'. A Member State seeking to derogate from 'a principle enshrined by European Union law' was obliged to show 'in each individual case that that measure is appropriate for securing the attainment of the objective relied upon and does not go beyond what is necessary to attain it'. Any claimed legitimate objective must be backed up by 'specific evidence substantiating its arguments'.[116] But the Court has not put Member States under much pressure to show the existence of any actual risk to public finances posed by EU migrants when endorsing restrictive welfare rules that exclude the possibility of proportionality assessments.[117]

The UK's programme of measures targeting EU nationals, coupled with discriminatory announcements, problematised something for which there was no evidence of a 'problem'. It was a programme of declaratory discrimination, in which declarations through statements, articles, press releases and laws themselves were discriminatory acts. The programme created deliberate, declaratory obstacles to movement, attacking the tenets of, and promoting a reduction of, free movement. These were acts of considerable normative power and it should, with hindsight, come as little surprise that the government found it difficult to row back in the space of a few months on the strident, emotive, prejudicial narrative it had constructed over several years pillorying EU nationals.[118] How a state chooses to implement and present EU law plays a significant role in shaping how its nationals conceive not only the EU,[119] but also other EU nationals.

The evidence of declaratory obstacles to movement is abundant and, in the public domain, it more than surpasses the rather low evidential threshold applied to finding obstacles in the context of the free movement of goods, wherein 'judicial hunches or intuitions' sometimes suffice.[120] Not much intuition is required to see that a government declaring that it wishes to reduce EU immigration, that it does not want EU nationals to come to the UK, might dissuade EU nationals from coming to the UK.[121] Adopting a *Feryn*-plus-*Buy Irish* formulation, such declarations from a state may dissuade potential migrant workers from exercising their free movement rights, and may act as negative advertising of other states' nationals to

---

[116] ibid, 71.

[117] *Commission v UK*; above n 51.

[118] C O'Brien, above n 59, 111.

[119] Barry Jones suggests that 'the substantial corpus of state-level control of policy … [and the] practical implementation [of EU law] by State authorities' diminishes the 'positive salience of the EU to the majority of its putative "citizens" and weaken[s] the strength of notions of an emergent multiple or dual citizenship' (RJ Barry Jones, 'The Political Economy of European Citizenship' in R Bellamy and A Warleigh (eds), *Citizenship and Governance in the European Union* (London, Continuum, 2001) 159).

[120] D Wilsher, 'Does *Keck* Discrimination Make Any Sense? An Assessment of the Non-Discrimination Principle within the European Single Market' (2008) 33 *EL Rev*, 1, 3, 3.

[121] As it happens, net migration from the EU to the UK rose anyway: ('Immigration to UK hit record levels prior to Brexit vote, data shows', *The Guardian*, 1 December 2016). But this does not preclude the application of *Gourmet* logic that it might have risen higher but for the measures: Case C-405/98 *Konsumentombudsmannen (KO) v Gourmet International Products AB (GIP)* EU:C:2001:135 EU:C:2001:135, 22.

prospective employers or landlords, so creating obstacles to movement. The Union has an interest in combating such discrimination and such obstacles. Indeed, in 2014 it enacted the Enforcement Directive, noting that the effective exercise of free movement was still 'a major challenge', and that Union workers still suffered unjustified discrimination and obstacles to the exercise of free movement rights, that they were in a 'potentially more vulnerable position' than other workers, and that there remained a 'gap between the law and its application in practice that needs to be addressed'.[122] The Enforcement Directive created duties on Member States to ensure the effective implementation of equal treatment rights contained in Directive 492/2011,[123] such as a requirement to designate a body 'for the promotion, analysis, monitoring and support of equal treatment of Union workers and members of their family without discrimination on grounds of nationality, unjustified restrictions or obstacles to their right to free movement',[124] a requirement for Member States to engage in social dialogue with non-governmental organisations fighting discrimination and obstacles to movement,[125] and ensuring Union citizens have access to information about their rights.[126] It would seem that refraining from engaging in acts of declaratory discrimination and declaratory obstruction of movement would be a minimal requirement for furthering the aims of the Directive; it makes little sense to oblige a Member State to clamp down on employer discrimination, when it is deploying its own discriminatory methods that discriminate and potentially obstruct movement at an anterior stage in a more wide-reaching fashion. The UK government's declaration that free movement must be less free in itself runs counter to the very premise of that directive: free movement is a 'a fundamental freedom of Union citizens and one of the pillars of the internal market in the Union' that ensures that 'every citizen of the Union, irrespective of his or her place of residence' has 'the right to move freely to another Member State in order to work there and/or to reside there for work purposes', and so existing obstacles should be removed, not more obstacles created.

A discriminatory attitude on the part of states should not be accepted as inevitable and nor should we assume that discriminatory law making is necessary to give effect to perceived popular sentiments in the hope that such measures will placate the population and make EU migrants seem less of a threat. Discriminatory laws do not destigmatise, they stigmatise. Equal treatment laws are key normative tools in shaping our relationships with each other, and in setting baselines. I would like to draw upon Neuvonen's argument that 'those who are treated equally (will) belong'.[127] Mark Bell has similarly argued that equal treatment laws contribute

---

[122] Directive 2014/54/EU of the European Parliament and of the Council of 16 April 2014 on measures facilitating the exercise of rights conferred on workers in the context of freedom of movement for workers OJ [2014] L 128/8; preamble, recital (5).

[123] Regulation (EU) No 492/2011 of the European Parliament and of the Council of 5 April 2011 on freedom of movement for workers within the Union (codification) OJ [2011] L 141/1.

[124] Directive 2014/54, Art 4(1).

[125] ibid, Art 5.

[126] ibid, Art 6.

[127] Neuvonen, above n 7, 176.

positively to attitudes and behaviours, promoting 'inter-citizen solidarity'.[128] But perhaps one of the clearest statements about the normative role of the law, and the duty of lawmakers to direct its normative powers to good ends, comes from Aristotle: 'Lawgivers make the citizens good by training them in habits of right action—this is the aim of all legislation and if it fails to do this it is a failure; this is what distinguishes a good constitution from a bad one'.[129]

The UK government has failed in this duty, using the law-making process for political posturing, and to spin a discriminatory narrative. But it is not the only Member State dealing in myth and prejudice when it comes to EU migrants. The EU, if it wishes to commit to European social justice, must confront discriminating states and challenge declaratory obstacles to movement. If we are to agree that prejudice is a problem, then we must not fool ourselves that we can make it go away by permitting discrimination, and we should not imagine that increased poverty and destitution among EU migrants and their children will blunt nativist tendencies. The EU must not fall into the trap of treating people as though they are natural xenophobes, but should model the 'habits of right action' (that is, asserting the norm of non-discrimination in our lawmakers' habits of speech, to guide us to better habits of thought). The EU is not a powerless object trapped in a fixed environment and tossed about by irresistible political discourse: it is part of the environment and a shaper of discourse. Neither it nor we should feel helplessly resigned to the inevitability of market citizenship or assume that pernicious rhetoric is irresistible.

## VI. SUMMARY

So long as EU citizenship remains a form of market citizenship, nationality will remain determinative for social rights. Nationality distinguishes between citizens to whom states owe basic social duties and those who can be subjected to an activation-plus regime in which any state support is conditional on economic activity. The persistence of direct discrimination sits uneasily with the theoretical principle of equal treatment. Rather than allowing right to reside tests to be explained away as establishing that EU nationals and own-nationals are not comparable, and so not entitled to equal treatment ex ante, we need to address the tension directly, affirming the relatively primary and secondary legal provisions on equal treatment, and acknowledge that exclusions from benefits on the grounds of nationality are departures from that principle. Those departures should therefore be subject to the normal requirements of justification and, in particular, be subject to a proportionality review. Resuscitating proportionality is not enough. Even in its heyday it was a relatively weak tool, of no use until appealing before a court.

---

[128] M Bell, 'Equality and Diversity: Anti-Discrimination Law After Amsterdam' in J Shaw (ed), *Social Law and Policy in an Evolving European Union* (Oxford, Hart, 2000) 161.

[129] Aristotle, *The Nichomachean Ethics: Ethics II.I* (Ware, Wordsworth, 1996) 33.

To lead to fairer decision-making, it would need to be strengthened, and create an explicit duty on the part of first-tier decision-makers.

This could help us to recapture the concept of fairness, currently bandied about to advocate for the restrictions of rights and the introduction of punitive welfare measures. Fairness in administrative justice carries different connotations—of giving effect to rights. Proportionality is a means to reassert this approach to fair decision-making (if the proportionality assessment is informed by principles of social justice). Regard must be had not just to how closely a claimant conforms to a given category in the Directive, or the claimant's economic identity, but to the EU's duties to see that EU citizens have access to social justice. In particular, the EU has a duty to see that its laws and policies (and the laws and policies of Member States applied to EU nationals) do not endanger child welfare and do not create disadvantage on the grounds of gender. Currently, these objectives seem to be legally segregated and barely considered in cases of free movement and welfare.

In asserting European principles of social justice, and requiring proportionality reviews that prohibit disproportionate infringement of those principles, the EU would shift the centre of gravity of EU citizenship away from the wallet and towards the person. A rejection of market citizenship requires us to challenge ideological fatalism, redolent of the 'there is no alternative' mantra of 1980s neoliberalism. It is possible to disrupt the momentum of market logic, not least since it leaves so many people behind. We should not legislate to appease an (over-estimated) popular appetite for xenophobia, but work to make the EU more meaningful for the less privileged, and use the law as a weapon of equality and empowerment, not of minority suppression. In order to promote solidarity, it is vital that the EU tackles declaratory discrimination by Member States, and confronts them over declaratory obstacles to movement. States should not be able to indulge in discriminatory behaviour forbidden to employers—their actions have far wider ramifications for the exercise of rights and the treatment of EU nationals. Member States wishing to persuade their populations of the merits of Union membership would be well advised to steer away from xenophobic law-making. Reducing the rights of minority groups and engaging in dehumanising policy-making does not make them less of a threat: it accentuates otherness, creates a culture of obstruction and legitimises a whole Pandora's box of prejudices.

# 10

# *Unity in Adversity: Some Conclusions*

E U MARKET CITIZENSHIP entails ideological, legal and administrative obstacles to social justice. Taken together, this book has argued that these strands reveal that equal treatment on the grounds of nationality is an illusion. An economically stratified market citizenship alienates low-paid workers and discriminates against those disadvantaged by existing market forces (namely, women, children and disabled people). Within this framework, the UK embarked on a programme of declaratory discrimination, creating declaratory obstacles to movement, issuing discriminatory statements that would be frowned upon in a private employment context, and expressing a clear intention to reduce free movement in such a way as to amount to negative advertising against the employment of, or offering of accommodation services to, or awarding of benefit to, EU nationals.

Before the EU could credibly tackle Member States' declaratory obstacles to movement, it would need to tackle its own social justice deficit, since the very premise of market citizenship is discriminatory by default. EU welfare law was devised to serve the interests of the single market, and is unconcerned with the content of welfare entitlements, with questions of need, or of social justice. Social security coordination and equal treatment on the grounds of nationality are means of reducing obstacles to economic movement. They have not become any less mechanistic as a result of the introduction of EU citizenship, which remains a resolutely market form of citizenship.

While EU citizenship never offered all that much to those deemed economically inactive, the ECJ did develop a kernel of financial solidarity, in the concept of proportionality. Although primary law-based rights could be conditioned by secondary law-based limitations, those limitations had to be treated as derogations from a primary law right and subject to a proportionality review. But in recent years it has dispensed with this requirement, condoning Member States' treatment of the conditions and limitations as constitutive of residence and equal treatment rights, and entrenching market citizenship as a deeply stratified status, creating economically contingent entitlements. The Court has condoned directly discriminatory right to reside tests that exclude non-nationals from social protection. As a result of the law-as-lists rather than law-as-justice framework, EU nationals can face quite arbitrary cut-off points, with welfare rights, and rights to reside, being withdrawn from families without regard for degrees of social integration, past economic activity or the welfare of children. This makes EU citizenship incoherent: it is not only stratified, but is also fragmented, with little attachment to a coherent sense of social justice.

Market citizenship commodifies EU nationals. It is fuelled with ideological presumptions that link rights to economic activity. An activating market citizenship provides its own internal moral code, justifying the exclusion and punishment of the poor and low-paid workers. Under the guise of 'responsibility', the activation agenda disadvantages women, children and disabled people and, at the same time, redefines non-discrimination rights as little more than the right to engage in market activity, on the market's terms, conforming to labour market norms. The women-targeting reconciliation agenda, and the ECJ's medical approach to disability, both speak to the objective of conformity in the name of formal, rather than substantive, equality.

Children are in some ways the litmus test for EU social citizenship, but they get lost in this framework. They do not fit onto the legal lists in their own right. They have at best a parasitic status, over which they have no control. Even in cases about benefits to protect child welfare—as in *Commission v UK*—the best interests of children are not a consideration, let alone a 'primary' consideration, as the Charter of Fundamental Rights requires. Instead we become desensitised to enforced child poverty and destitution, because that is what the list in Directive 2004/38 says. That directive, now being treated as an all-but exhaustive expression of residence and equal treatment rights, is full of gaps. Children who have been born in the host state, and lived there for over a decade, and never lived anywhere else, fall through. Women who have punctuated work histories and relied upon their partners' right to reside once they had children, then leave due to domestic abuse, fall through. Women who have worked for years (but without technical compliance with the worker registration scheme) then moved to part-time work after having a child, are deemed by the UK no longer to be workers, fall through. Women who have married working British nationals and done unpaid work supporting their spouse's business and taking on familial care, fall through. Men and women who have resided for decades but have insufficient documentary evidence of their work, or whose work history was punctuated and so the clock kept getting restarted, fall through.

The welfare reforms introduced in the UK make it more likely that the lawful residence clock will be started more frequently, since they increase the risks of status gaps by redefining workers as not workers, by making it harder to keep retained worker status for over six months, and by limiting jobseeker status to three months. Constantly re-set clocks make it harder to reach the point of having permanent residence recognised, even if an EU national has been resident and working for far longer than five years. These, and other changes (such as the removal of housing benefit from EU national jobseekers, the three-month wait for benefits, and the exclusion of EU national jobseekers from universal credit in its entirety), set up an activation-plus regime for EU nationals. As market citizens, they are readily subjected to an activation regime taken to its logical conclusion— that is, when you are out of work, you are out of luck.

One of the biggest problems with this approach, explored throughout this book, is that there are no bright lines between those who are economically active and those who are not. The assumption that the former have earned entitlement, and that the latter have not, rests upon a false dichotomy. Measures targeting the 'inactive' actually redound upon the economically active in a number of ways. The UK's redefinition of migrant work, through the introduction of the minimum earnings threshold and the creation of a presumption of marginality, means that economically active people, who would under the broad EU law definition be found to be workers, are being reclassified as economically inactive, and so disentitled from welfare support. EU national workers may have punctuated work patterns, or move through a series of short, fixed-term jobs. If so, they run the risk of having each period of work assessed as being marginal, even if overall they are practically continually employed. For even relatively brief periods between jobs, they may be found to have lost worker status if they have not complied with the requirements for retaining worker status, later preventing a claim to permanent residence.

Those who do have, or are the family members of those with, worker status are still affected by measures targeting those who do not. Those measures make their situations more precarious. Less income security can damage their health and wellbeing, and it also makes them more vulnerable to harm, making them less able to extricate themselves from exploitative work or abusive relationships. The measures also have a significant impact upon all EU nationals in the UK, because they set up more distinctions, more conditions and more exclusions, so they create more tests, more evidential requirements, and more administrative hurdles with which EU national workers must comply. This is not just a matter of inconvenience: each extra test creates another opportunity for administrative error and delay. Moreover, each extra test further differentiates EU from UK claimants, and 'others' them in the eyes of decision-makers.

Market citizenship results in administrative indifference to child poverty and migrant destitution. Decision-makers are not bound by any fundamental duty of social protection when it comes to EU nationals, and are encouraged to apply the law-as-lists, not least by the government's discriminatory declarations, which are expressed in the form of official statements, media appearances, decision-maker guidance, impact and equality analyses, and the laws themselves. The mechanistic origins of EU welfare law are threaded throughout the coordination and free movement framework, so that there is little sense of communal responsibility when an EU national makes a claim that engages the law of two Member States. Shortcomings in the coordination regime—such as inappropriate benefit classification and unclear provisions regarding the distinction between 'competence' and 'applicability of legislation by priority right'—and malleable stipulations on provisional payments, have played into the hands of Member States who wish to avoid responsibility for paying benefits, even if this means claimants get caught between two systems and disentitled from both. Alarm bells do not automatically go off for administrative decision-makers if a decision might result in potentially unfair loss of entitlement or destitution. Such consequences are a feature of the system.

A default of benefit-restriction for EU nationals has not emerged organically from the free application of decision-maker discretion. It has been cultivated through a set of systems and mechanisms that discourage the gathering of information, steer decision-makers' questioning, steer decision-makers' interpretations of EU concepts, and encourage decision-makers to refuse first, ask questions later. Low institutional standards when it comes to delay, or to claimant convenience, or to customer service, make EU nationals bear the brunt of administrative error. Systems that create unnecessary bureaucratic hurdles, prevent communication between government departments when dealing with the same case, and stop claimants from speaking to decision-makers, generate an opaque process remote from claimants and from immediate points of accountability. The opportunities for administrative injustice multiply when dealing with EU nationals and the risks become more acute during a period of legal transition. Good administration requires a commitment to fairness and to proportionality: it requires a measure of social justice. To improve administrative access to rights, Member States need to recognise a degree of duty of social justice towards EU migrants.

While presenting some difficult, sometimes farcical, and sometimes harrowing cases, this book has also put forward some positive, constructive proposals for reconstituting EU citizenship around a core, shared commitment to European social justice and social protection. It is possible. A first step is reaffirming the primacy of primary law and reintroducing (and reinforcing) the duty of reviewing the proportionality of derogations from primary law rights of equal treatment and free movement. Proportionality is not an alien or unworkable concept: it is a basic principle of good administrative decision-making and is necessary in order to make fair decisions, where fairness is a rights-giving principle of administrative justice.

But the idea of proportionality is not enough: that word alone does not tell us about the factors and values to be weighed, as is evident in the confusion surrounding *Brey*. It is here, in informing the process of proportionality review, that we can most readily import principles of social justice into EU law. I have sketched out the basis for identifying a couple of European principles of social justice (the protection of child welfare and the promotion of gender equality). These principles would weigh in favour of taking factors into account that have been hitherto disregarded (requiring a law-as-justice approach), they would require consideration of the disproportionate impact of welfare restrictions and they would raise questions of need and vulnerability.

Such proposals require us to remove the shackles of political fatalism and to rethink the parameters of the possible. We should not assume that in the face of waves of Euroscepticism, and the UK's referendum result, that European social integration has been rejected. Rolling back the social dimension of Europe, and further paring down citizenship to a bare market construct, would not provide the solution to the EU's loyalty problems. Attempts to make free movement and the rights attendant upon EU citizenship even more the preserve of the privileged economic classes would be more alienating. More stratification creates more division, not more unity. The UK's cautionary tale to the EU is one of the perils of ignoring questions of social justice and of manufacturing rights that reward the well-off and instrumentalise the poor. To other Member States the cautionary tale is one of the corrosive effects of declaratory discrimination. Discriminatory law-making does not promote solidarity or tolerance, and it does not make populations feel sufficiently accepting of each others' nationals as to vote to remain in the EU. It promotes discrimination. It segregates EU nationals within the administrative processes and 'others' them, subjecting them to different requirements, different conditions and different exclusions. If other Member States wish to persuade their populations of the merits of EU membership, they would do well to remember that in the past the law has shown itself to be a powerful driver of social progression and a means of asserting values of equal treatment and social justice. The UK has instead used it as a shabby tool of stigma. The law should not be deployed to simply follow, echo, applaud and amplify oppressive and unjust prejudices. The point is to change them.

# Index